A PIECE OF CAKE

A memoir

Cupcake Brown

BANTAM BOOKS

LONDON • TORONTO • SYDNEY • AUCKLAND • JOHANNESBURG

A PIECE OF CAKE
A BANTAM BOOK: 0553818171
9780553818178

First publication in Great Britain

PRINTING HISTORY
Bantam edition published 2006

7 9 10 8

This book is a work of non-fiction based on the life, experiences
and recollections of the author. In some limited cases names of
people, places, dates, sequences or the detail of events have been
changed [solely] to protect the privacy of others. The author has
warranted to the publishers that, except in such minor respects
not affecting the substantial accuracy of the work, the contents
of this book are true. Whilst the publishers have taken care to
explore and check where reasonably possible, they have not
verified all the information in this book and do not warrant
its veracity in all respects.

All names in the text have been changed except the following:
Chaney Allen, Frank Brown, Larry Burns, David Curnow,
Martin Jenkins, Joyce Kennard, Bill Logue, Tim Long, Khoi Nguyen,
Venita Ray, Ken Rose, Robert Rose, Ray Stearns (Jr.), Paul Sutton,
University of San Francisco School of Law, Gail and LeRoy Westwood,
Carol Wilson.

Set in 10/11.5pt Sabon by
Falcon Oast Graphic Art Ltd.

Bantam Books are published by Transworld Publishers,
61–63 Uxbridge Road, London W5 5SA,
a division of The Random House Group Ltd,
in Australia by Random House Australia (Pty) Ltd,
20 Alfred Street, Milsons Point, Sydney, NSW 2061, Australia,
in New Zealand by Random House New Zealand Ltd,
18 Poland Road, Glenfield, Auckland 10, New Zealand
in South Africa by Random House (Pty) Ltd,
Isle of Houghton, Corner of Boundary Road & Carse O'Gowrie,
Houghton 2198, South Africa.
and in India by Random House Publishers India Private Limited,
301 World Trade Tower, Hotel Intercontinental Grand Complex,
Barakhamba Lane, New Delhi 110 001, India.

Printed and bound in Great Britain by
Cox & Wyman Ltd, Reading, Berkshire.

Papers used by Transworld Publishers are natural, recyclable products
made from wood grown in sustainable forests. The manufacturing
processes conform to the environmental regulations of the
country of origin.

For God, who never turned His back on me,
even when I turned my back on Him.

And, for my Momma and my Grandma.
How I miss you so. I love you.
I'll see you both 'after while.'

Where there is Life,
There is Hope;
Where there is Hope,
There is Trust;
Where there is Trust,
There is Love;
Where there is Love
There is Faith;
Where there is Faith,
There is Success;
Where there is Success,
There is God.

—Tim Long, aka 'Pops' aka 'daddy'

A PIECE OF CAKE

1

The booming music coming from Momma's radio alarm clock suddenly woke me. I could hear Elton John singing about Philadelphia freedom.

I wonder why Momma didn't wake me? I thought to myself.

It was January 1976. Wasn't no school that day. But Momma still had to go to work. So, while Momma was at work, I was goin' over to Daddy's house to play with Kelly, the daughter of his lady friend.

I wonder why she didn't wake me? I thought again to myself as I climbed out of bed.

When I passed the dresser I caught a glimpse of myself in the mirror. Boy, was I ugly.

'Skinny, black, and ugly.' That's what the kids at school called me. Or they'd yell out, 'Vette, Vette, looks just like my pet!'

My name was La'Vette, but my first birth name was Cupcake. At least that's what my momma told me. Seems Momma craved cupcakes when she was pregnant with me. She had three cupcakes a day, every day, without fail, for nine and a half months (I was two weeks overdue). Momma said that even if she didn't eat anything else, she'd have her daily dose of cupcakes.

Anyway, seems that while 'we' were in labor, the hospital gave Momma some pain drugs. Once Momma popped me out, the nurse said:

'Pat' – that was my momma's name – 'you have a little girl. Do you know what you want to name her?'

Tired and exhausted from eight hours of hard labor, Momma lifted her head, smiled sheepishly, and said, 'Cupcake,' before she passed out.

So that's what they put down on my birth certificate. I mean, that *is* what she said. (The nurses thought it was due to the excitement of motherhood, Momma said it was the drugs). A few hours later, however, when Daddy came to the hospital he decided he didn't like 'Cupcake.' Momma said Daddy wanted to name me La'Vette. So, just to make Daddy happy, Momma said she had the hospital change my name. I didn't mind, really. I loved my daddy; so as far as I was concerned, he could change my name to whatever he wanted. But, Momma said that to her I would always be Cupcake. She never called me anything else, 'cept sometimes she called me 'Cup' for short.

Anyway, the kids at school always told me that I was ugly. They teased me, saying I looked like 'Aunt Esther,' that old lady from *Sanford and Son,* the one always calling Sanford a 'fish-eyed fool.' She was the ugliest woman I'd ever seen. So if the other kids thought I looked like her, I knew I had to be ugly. Besides, everybody knew a black girl wasn't considered pretty unless she was light-skinned with long straight hair. I was dark-skinned with short kinky hair. I hated my complexion. I hated my hair. I hated my skinny legs and arms.

But, my momma thought I was beautiful. She'd say:

'Cup, you're only eleven years old. You will appreciate your beauty as you grow up.'

Shoot, I couldn't *wait* to grow up!

Momma always said things to make me feel better. I loved my momma. She was my best friend and she *was* beautiful: she had cocoa-colored skin and her long black hair hung way past her shoulders. And, Momma had the biggest, prettiest smile you ever saw. People always told her that she looked like Diana Ross because of her long hair and wide beautiful smile – all teeth.

I passed the black ugly thing in the mirror and continued toward Momma's room. The radio alarm continued to blast. I giggled to myself. Momma was like me. She *hated* getting up in the morning, so she put the clock way across the room and turned it all the way up so it would scare her awake in the morning. That way, she'd have to get out of bed and walk across the room to turn it off.

I wonder why she didn't turn the alarm off? I thought as I made my way through the kitchen toward the large living room that led into Momma's room. The floor was cold because there wasn't no carpet in our house. Still, I loved our old house. It was Victorian style, three bedrooms and one bathroom.

We lived in San Diego in the heart of the ghetto, though I never knew it until I got older. We had our share of dilapidated houses, and run-down apartment buildings, but most of the houses and apartments in the neighborhood were in decent order. I mean, we didn't have any mansions, but most folks made sincere efforts to keep their houses decent-looking: they watered their tired brown lawns, trying to keep them up (as kept up as a lawn could be with kids runnin' over it all the time), and tried to replace windows that had been broken from runaway fly balls that escaped the imaginary fields of street baseball games.

We had a great neighborhood store, Sawaya Brothers, that had everything you could need or want, including the most delicious pickled pig feet. We had a neighborhood park, Memorial Park, a boys' club *and* a girls' club.

I thought my family was rich because I was the only kid in the neighborhood who had her own bedroom, furnished with a white princess-style bedroom set complete with a canopy bed, matching nightstands, and dresser. There was a pink frilly comforter with matching frills for the canopy overhead. And, I had a closet full of clothes. Unlike other kids in my neighborhood, I never had to share clothes or wear hand-me-downs. Momma loved to sew and made most of my clothes.

The other kids thought we were rich too. Little did we know that we weren't rich – it's just that both my mom and dad worked while the other kids only had one parent trying to raise several kids either on one income or, more commonly, on welfare, though being on welfare wasn't nothing to be 'shamed about. Most everybody was. In fact, I envied my friends on welfare because they got government food that you couldn't get from the store, like this great government cheese. You ain't *had* a grilled cheese sandwich till you've had one made with government cheese.

The blasting radio brought me back to my immediate mission: finding out why Momma didn't wake me.

I wished she'da woke me up, I thought as I followed the sound of the blasting radio. I was excited about going to my daddy's.

My momma and daddy didn't live together. Daddy lived around the way with my brother, Larry. I hated Larry. Larry was thin and lanky like me. And he was dark-skinned like me. Although he was two years older than me, he never acted like a big brother. He never protected me. In fact, HE was usually the one I had to be protected FROM. And, usually, it was ME jumping in a fight to protect HIM. I thought he was a wimp.

Larry hated me just as much as I hated him, but for different reasons. He was jealous of me. He'd never admit it, but I knew he was. I was the one who always got good grades and saved my weekly allowance so I could buy something nice and big, while Larry hated school (and was always on the verge of flunking out) and spent his money faster than he got it – and then had the nerve to get mad when he didn't have anything left.

Our hate for each other resulted in fierce fights: cussin' each other out (a skill I'd turned into an art from an early age) and throwing knives and hammers (or anything else lethal we could find) at each other. Our fights were no joke. We were trying to kill each other for real, or at least cause loss of body parts. In our house, before Larry went to live with Daddy, I could never slack up and always had to watch my back because we were always trying to sabotage each other.

Once I woke to Larry trying to smother me with a pillow. Bastard. He just woke up one day and decided he'd try to kill me. I had to fight, kick, scratch, punch, and scream to get him off me. I got him back, though: I tried to poison him.

Larry was always trying to boss me around. One day, after yet another unsuccessful attempt at killing me, he'd ordered me to get him some Kool-Aid. And I did – with a little rat poison in it. But watching my sudden obedience, he got suspicious. Talkin' 'bout he smelled 'somethin' funny.' He ordered me to take a drink first. I took a sip, but I didn't swallow. I just held it in my mouth, hoping he'd now be willing to drink. He was smarter than I thought. He fucked around and fucked around twirling the Kool-Aid in the glass with a sly grin on his face till I couldn't hold what was in my mouth anymore without swallowing.

Oh shit! I thought, *I can't kill myself! That'd be right up his alley!*

I ran for the bathroom, which confirmed Larry's suspicions that something was up. He ran ahead of me and blocked the bathroom door with his body, laughing hysterically at the irony of the situation. My only other option was out the front door – halfway 'cross the house. I'd never make it.

'Swallow it, bitch!' he ordered, his body still blocking the doorway, hands up in the air like a soccer goalie. Damn, I hated him.

But, I would have the last word on this one. It took me a moment to think of a way out, but then it came to me. As I realized my way out, the look of terror on my face from envisioning what seemed to be my impending death slowly changed into a wide-ass grin: I spit the Kool-Aid in *his* face. And with that, it was on – we tumbled, kicked, bit, and scratched, until we tired ourselves out and retreated to opposite ends of the house to await the next battle.

So I was really glad when Momma sent Larry to go live with Daddy. Larry had started talking back to Momma, being smart-mouthed and sassin' her. I remember the day Larry left. Momma told Larry to move a can of paint from off the back porch. Larry angrily stomped toward the paint can, but instead of moving it, he kicked it (as if punting a football), toward Momma. I don't know if he meant for the can to hit her. But it did. The can flew into the air like a football toward a goalpost. It struck Momma on the shoulder as it made its way back down. The impact from the can hitting Momma's shoulder caused the lid to topple off and paint flew everywhere.

Momma stood there for what seemed like forever, although it was really only a moment, paint dripping off her clothes and face like icicles off a tree. I swear I thought I saw smoke coming out of her ears. She balled her fist. I thought she was going to knock the shit out of Larry (actually, I was hoping she would; then maybe I could get in a kick or two), but instead she spun suddenly and quickly on her heels (her long black hair flying out behind her reminded me of Batman's cape), stomped into the house and over to the phone, and called my daddy.

'Come get this lil nigga fo I kill him!' she screamed.

Needless to say, Daddy quickly came and Larry quickly went. Larry had lived with Daddy ever since. Daddy saved Larry's life that day.

* * *

After Larry left, we really didn't see much of each other; which was fine with both of us. Daddy and Momma would switch me and Larry on the weekends so each parent could spend time with the child he or she didn't live with. This meant that Larry and I had to see each other only in passing (and even that was too much for me).

I loved my weekends with my daddy. We'd dress up: Daddy would put on his one suit and I'd put on a nice dress and we'd go out on a date. We'd usually go somewhere for dinner and then to the movies. My daddy was the only person besides my momma who thought I was pretty. He'd hop me up on his knee and ask:

'Who's the prettiest girl in the whole wide world?'

And, in between giggles, I'd say:

'I yam.'

But I never believed it. He HAD to think I was pretty. He was my daddy. When we were out on our dates, he'd ask everyone:

'This is my daughter. Ain't she pretty?'

What were they going to say?

'Actually sir, she looks like shit'?

No, they smiled and lied and told Daddy I sho was pretty. I didn't care that they were lyin'. I loved my daddy and I loved our dates.

Didn't bother me that Momma and Daddy didn't live together either; they still loved each other. Daddy did have a lady friend, Lori – but to me, she was just that: his friend. Lori was a tall, thin white woman. She reminded me of Popeye's girlfriend Olive Oyl, but I still liked her because she made the best chocolate cake (my favorite). I really liked her daughter, Kelly, a pudgy Mexican-looking girl with long black hair, only six months younger than me. Neither of us had a sister, so we decided we'd be each other's sister. We played together and always had fun together. She didn't mind being silly, and she was always willing to play my favorite game: Africans. I'd be 'Unga-Bunga,' and she'd be 'Oooga-Wooga.' We'd jump around with fake spears, acting a fool. I had no idea what it was like to be a real African so I imitated what I'd seen on TV. I didn't know that TV was run by white folks. What do white folks know about being African?

Nothing. But at the time I was too young (and really didn't care) to know.

Anyway, I couldn't wait to get to Daddy's house so Kelly and I could play.

Why didn't Momma wake me? I thought again as I continued walking toward her room, my head down in deep thought while I contemplated which outfit I would wear to Daddy's. I looked up and froze. I'll never forget what I saw.

The radio was still blasting in the background. Momma was lying facedown on her stomach. She was hanging off the side of the bed from her waist up. Her long black hair was hanging down, covering her face. Her arms hung limp to the floor.

'Momma?' I asked, walking slowly toward her.

The radio continued to blare. As I got closer, it seemed to get louder.

'Momma?'

I thought maybe she was kidding. Momma was always playing with me. Just the night before we were playing house and doing each other's hair, dancing around and acting silly. I thought Momma was just playing another game, so I expected her to jump up like a jack-in-the-box and scream, 'Boo!'

But she didn't move.

I touched her arm. She was cool. I didn't know what that meant, but I knew it wasn't good.

'Momma?' I repeated as I tried to lift her up by her shoulders so I could see her face. I didn't know death was so heavy. When I tried to lift her, her body slid off the bed and onto me, and we both hit the floor with a thud. As she landed on top of me I heard a gurgling noise in her throat. She was heavy.

Still I didn't panic.

It took awhile but I managed to squeeze myself from up under her and turn her over. She was so beautiful – even dead.

I don't know how I knew she was dead. I'd never seen death before. I just knew.

I got up and slowly walked over to the nightstand where the phone lay and called Lori.

'Hello,' Lori answered.

'Lori, this is Vette. My momma's dead.'

I said it so casually, Lori thought she'd misunderstood what I'd said.

'What'd you say?' she asked.

'My momma's dead.' I repeated in the same casual voice.

'Are you sure?'

'Yeah.'

'Stay right there! I'm gon' call your father!'

I hung up and almost immediately the phone rang. I nonchalantly picked it up.

'Hello.'

'Punkin, this is Daddy.' My daddy always called me Punkin. Never 'Pumpkin', always 'Punkin.' Once I asked him why, and he said because when I was a baby, I had big chubby cheeks that made my face look like a little roun' pumpkin, and ever since, he's called me Punkin. I never had no problem keeping up with all of my different names. Momma called me Cup. Daddy called me Punkin. Everybody else called me Vette.

'Hi, Daddy!'

'Punkin, what's going on?!'

'Momma's dead!'

'Are you sure?'

'Yeah, I'm sure!'

We were screaming at each other because the radio was still blasting. I'd never turned it off.

'Call the police, I'll be right there!' he yelled before slamming down the phone.

I didn't call the police. Somehow I knew that once they came they'd take Momma away and I'd never see her again. So instead, I went back to her, scooted my little body under hers so I could put her head in my lap, and began singing our favorite song: 'Chain of Fools' by Aretha Franklin. We used to play that song as we sang and danced around the house. In fact, we had just been dancing to it and singing it the night before. I hadn't known then that that would be our good-bye party. It was then I began to cry.

And that's how Daddy found me a half hour later: sitting on the floor with Momma's head in my lap, stroking her hair and, through my tears, singing 'Chain of Fools.'

'Did you call the police?' he screamed as he bent down to feel her neck.

I didn't respond. I just kept stroking and singing and crying. The radio kept blasting.

Daddy ran outside. A police car happened to be passing by and Daddy flagged them down. When the cops entered the room, they seemed a little shocked at the scene: a thin little black girl cradling a dead woman, singing and crying. A radio blasting.

One cop picked me up, gently laying Momma's head on the floor, and took me outside while the other called for an ambulance.

Daddy and I followed the ambulance to the hospital. A little while later, as Daddy and I stood outside in the parking lot, a doctor walked up and told us Momma was dead.

Boy, I thought to myself, *I could've told y'all that – how long'd ya go to school for that one?*

He said Momma had had an epileptic seizure and that she'd swallowed her tongue and choked on it. She'd suffocated on her tongue. The thud of our bodies hitting the floor when she'd fallen on top of me had caused her tongue to dislodge, which was the gurgling sound I'd heard.

She was thirty-four years old.

Daddy began to cry. He was so mad he kicked the brick wall beside us. I was surprised he didn't break his foot. He cried for a long time. Once he got himself together, we got in the car and headed for his house.

As we pulled up to Daddy's house, Lori, Kelly, and Larry were waiting on the porch. Daddy told them what I already knew: Momma was dead. No one said anything for a while; everyone just cried.

As the tears slowly turned to sniffles, we all climbed into Daddy's lil red Nova. (He'd bought red because it was my favorite color.) Although I'd just found my mother dead, that was no reason for a truce between me and Larry. He slapped my head as he climbed into the car and I punched his side. Bastard. I hated him.

Daddy drove us to the library. He said he wanted to get books to explain to us what epilepsy was.

Who cares? I snarled to myself. *Whatever it is, it killed my momma!*

On the way back from the library, a song came on the radio: Neil Sedaka's 'Breaking Up Is Hard to Do.'

I began to cry again and Daddy reached over and turned the

radio off. But it was too late. That was now our song; Momma's and my other song. 'Chain of Fools' would be our live song, and 'Breaking Up Is Hard to Do' would be our death song.

Shit, I thought. *Life sucks.*

Little did I know, my hell hadn't even begun.

2

Why do people act a fool about death? Soon as word got out about Momma's death, folks were at our house trying to get her stuff. Her body wasn't even cold and they were fightin' over who was going to get what.

Momma didn't have any sisters, and she only had one brother: my uncle Jr. His name was Ray, but we always called him Uncle Jr. Uncle Jr. was a stocky man who stood about five foot three. He was cocoa-colored like my mom, and had the same smooth, silky black hair. 'Good hair' is what black folks called it – not woolly and kinky like mine. He was the only uncle I had and I loved him a lot. That was one thing about me. I didn't have many people in my life, but those I had I loved fiercely.

Uncle Jr. was really quiet. Probably because he was a junior high school teacher and was around badass, hollerin' kids all day. He taught at one of the worst junior high schools in San Diego – which is where he was the morning Momma died – teachin' dem badass kids. But as soon as he got the call about Momma, he came to Daddy's.

Although Uncle Jr. was my only uncle, he was my favorite uncle. He and my grandma lived five blocks from us. We lived on Thirtieth and Oceanview, and they lived on Twenty-fifth and Oceanview. We were always down at their house or they were at ours. My momma and her brother were extremely close, so he was like a second father to me. I remember the day I realized he loved me. Uncle Jr. and I had gone to Taco Bell to get some food to go. As Uncle Jr. got out the car to order the food, he warned me not to touch anything. Problem with that was I loved to 'drive.' Jr. and Grandma's car was a 1962 Ford Falcon and the gear shift was a funny-looking stick that protruded from the steering wheel. No sooner than he'd closed the door, I climbed into the driver's seat and began pulling up and down on the gear shift as I voiced make-believe sounds of a car transmission shifting gears: 'mmmmmmmm, mmmmmmmmmmm.' Well, in messin' around with the gears, I must have accidentally shifted the car in neutral and in another playful movement released the emergency brake. The car started moving. The Taco Bell sat on a small hill. When the car started moving, it started *rolling backward down the hill*. I looked out the rear window and saw that I was rapidly headed for a huge tree. My eyes bulged and I started screaming, 'Jr., help! Help!'

I still remember the look of sheer terror on his face as he threw tacos and sodas in the air and bolted toward the car. His eyes were now bulging like mine. He caught up with the car as it kept rolling backward. Somehow, he snatched the driver's door open, tossed me aside as he hopped *half* of his body in – his left leg being dragged along as he used his right to slam on the brakes. When the car came to a sudden stop, we both lurched forward and I almost shot through the windshield. We'd come within an inch of hitting that tree. It was then I knew he loved me – by the fear on his face and the way he ran like hell to save me.

But, after I got over the fact that my uncle loved me, I started crying. Not from any physical pain, but because I knew my momma was gon' whup my ass when she found out what I'd done. She was always getting on me about playing in the car. The more I thought of the spanking I had coming, the louder I cried. Finally, Uncle Jr. was able to calm me down with a taco and soda. When we got home, he told Momma that *he'd* left the emergency brake off. He took all the blame. I never stepped up to say, 'No, it wasn't him. It was all me.' Nope, I let him take the blame, because hell, I knew he wasn't gon' get no ass whupping for it. But, his covering for me sealed our bond that day.

(To this day, if you ask him what happened that day, he'll tell you he must have left the emergency brake off, causing the car to roll backward. Damn, I love that man!)

It was my uncle Jr. who'd also given me my love for learning.

He was a schoolteacher and real smart. He was always telling me interesting facts and stuff. For example, he told me that my great-great-great-grandmother was kidnapped by an Indian tribe and forced to be a concubine. She got pregnant by one of the braves, and the baby was born under Indian captivity. She and the baby were subsequently rescued by a buffalo soldier whom she later married. Of course, I asked Uncle Jr. what a buffalo soldier was and, as a result, got a short history lesson on the historic segregated black cavalry and infantry soldiers who kept order and protected the settlers in the southwestern part of the United States.

The only family I'd ever known were my momma, Larry (who I was constantly trying to get rid of), my grandma, Uncle Jr., and Daddy. My uncle was a very important, customary part of my everyday life, especially after Larry went to live with Daddy. Jr. would check on us periodically, because Momma and I were 'two women living alone.' I used to put my hands on my hips when he said that, and reply, 'I ain't no woman!' and we'd both crack up laughing.

Poor Uncle Jr. He didn't even have time to mourn his only sister's death. Since Momma had left him in charge of everything in the event of her death, he was too busy trying to fight everyone off Momma's stuff while trying to pack it, *and* trying to tend to me and Larry, *and* making funeral arrangements, *and* taking care of his own momma, my grandma, who had Alzheimer's. She was once a schoolteacher too. Now, she just sat. Most times she didn't even know who we were.

I remember when Grandma started 'losin' it.' She had long hair like my momma and she used to love for Momma to wash it. But, one day while Momma was trying to wash Grandma's hair, Grandma started fighting her. I mean, she just started swinging on her! (Now you know where Larry and I got it from.)

Momma struggled and struggled and finally got Grandma under control, but not before taking several powerful blows.

Grandma's condition quickly worsened after that. Soon, Momma and Jr. had to move Grandma to a convalescent home. It was weird no longer having Grandma down the street from me, where she'd lived most of my life. Momma hated that her mother had to be in one of 'those homes,' so she or Jr. visited

Grandma every day. Grandma wasn't there long, though. Momma and Jr. got a frantic phone call one night. It seems an elderly white woman with Tourette's syndrome had been placed there. The woman called Grandma a nigger. Grandma hopped out of her chair and took off after that woman. She was gon' whup that woman's ass! She may have been severely incapacitated and extremely forgetful, to the point where she often didn't recognize her own children, but she remembered the insult behind *that* word. The convalescent home said Grandma was too violent and had to go.

Anyway, all I remember is one minute Jr. was fightin' kinfolk off Momma's stuff, and the next he, Daddy, Larry, and I were sitting in a large, plush office.

I was trying to figure out what the hell was going on because there seemed to be some confusion as to what was supposed to happen to me and Larry. Momma had been dead a couple of days. There was a white man in a black robe sitting behind a big desk. I knew he was a judge because his nameplate said so. Next to the judge was a tall black man I'd never seen before. There were two other white men (who I later learned were lawyers), my daddy, Uncle Jr., me, and Larry. They were discussing what was going to happen to us children. The tall black man said he wanted us to go with him. Daddy said we was going with him. The judge looked like he didn't know where we should go.

'We goin' wit' our daddy,' I said defiantly as I climbed up into my daddy's lap. He wrapped his arms around me protectively.

I'd always been headstrong and straight out. I ain't ever had a problem letting someone know what I thought. Momma once told me I was too straight out. Once, we were in the grocery store and this old white man bent over, gave me a wide grin and said, 'Hey, pretty lady!'

He didn't have no teeth! So, I asked him:

'Where yo' teeth at?'

Before he could answer I continued:

'Ain't you got welfare? My friend Marcia got welfare and they gave her momma a whole new set of teeth after her daddy knocked 'em out. You should go down to the welfare office and see if you can get you some tee—'

Momma rushed over and cupped her hand over my mouth and looked at the man sheepishly. He looked at her, embarrassed. I looked at both of them, confused and pissed because I didn't get to finish my sentence. I was just tryin' to help the man. I mean, hell, he needed teeth and I knew where he could get some.

'Cup, some things don't need to be said,' Momma scolded as she rushed me out the store. 'Girl, we gotta get you some 'couth.'

I didn't know what 'couth' was, but if it meant you couldn't speak your mind, I didn't want it.

All of the grown-ups were arguing. For some strange reason, the tall black man said he wanted us. I didn't want him. I wanted my daddy and my uncle Jr.

The judge said Larry and I could stay with Daddy at least until after Momma's funeral, which was in a couple of days. He said by then he'd have decided where we were going to go.

Daddy took us home. The next couple of days were a really quiet, solemn time. I kept waiting for folks to bring over food. I mean, a few months ago, my friend Rosemarie's dad had died. Actually, he was killed during a robbery. After he died, Rosemarie's family brought all kinds of food over to their house – cakes, pies, chickens, turkeys – all kinds of good stuff. So, when my momma died, I kept waitin' on my folks to bring *me* some food. But no one did.

Didn't matter, because like I said, those were some really fucked-up days. Larry and I didn't even fight. We were sad and missed our momma. But it was more than that. I guess we was too worried about what was going on. Yeah, it was really quiet around there.

I wanted to wear a really pretty red dress to my momma's funeral.

Lori said, 'You s'posed to wear black to a funeral.'

But black wasn't my favorite color. Red was. At the top of my lungs, I started screaming, 'I wanna wear *my* favorite color to *my* mother's funeral!'

'Let her wear what she wants!' Daddy snapped. He had been talking less and less. He now spoke as few words as possible, and always in harsh, abrupt phrases.

'Yeah, bitch!' is what I *wanted* to say. Instead, I said, 'Y-e-a-h,' but in a 'You tell her Daddy' kind of voice.

Jr. said he was bringing Grandma to Momma's funeral. I don't think she realized what was going on. Jr. said that when he told Grandma Momma died, she cried for a moment, and then just went off into a blank stare. Or maybe she felt the way I did about the whole thing – helpless.

It was raining the day we buried my momma. A lot of people came. Great-aunts, great-uncles, cousins. A lot of folks crying. Don't know why. Not only did none of them ever bring any damn food, most of 'em never even called us. Never said, 'You and the kids need some help?' 'You got everything you need?' 'Kiss my ass' or nothing. See, my momma was sort of the 'white sheep' of the family, and she didn't like folks in her business. Family likes to get in yo' business. But Momma, like me, was extremely private. Oh, we'd show up at family functions; we just didn't let 'em get in our business, which pissed them off. They called us uppity. Anyway, now, they're cryin' and carryin' on. Probably out of guilt because it sho wasn't love – you can't show love to someone when she's dead. Even *I* knew that.

The dark gray clouds created a dreary, drab day to match my dreary, drab attitude. The rain made the ground wet, mushy, and difficult to walk on. For the interment, the mortuary had set out two rows of chairs in front of Momma's casket for some of the family members. But no one wanted to fight their way through the mud to sit on them. Seemed to me like we owed it to Momma to make the effort. They were getting ready to put her *in* the mud, but folks didn't want to walk *on* it? Assholes.

I marched right through that mud and sat in the first chair. Solemnly I sat; the tears mixing with the raindrops falling down my face. Soon, Daddy came and sat. Then Uncle Jr., leading Grandma. Then Larry. Kelly and Lori soon followed. No one else did, though. They didn't want to get wet. And they called *us* uppity?

Anyway, the preacher was talking something about 'The Lord giveth . . .' and then he went into something about 'dust to dust.' I just sat there, my skinny black legs dangling. I said good-bye to my momma, and wondered where the fuck was this 'God' that the preacher kept talking about.

I didn't know much about God, 'cept that if you pissed Him

off, He'd getcha one day. My momma knew God – she was raised a Methodist. In fact, her daddy was a Methodist preacher. Still, Momma said she wanted more from God, so for the past couple of years she'd been searching for more. I got to go with her on some of those searches.

First, we tried the Jehovah's Witnesses. They were cool, till I learned they didn't celebrate Christmas. God or no God, I wasn't giving up Christmas! Then we tried the Muslims (or the 'Black Muslims,' as Momma called them). I didn't like them because when we got to their church (which they called a mosque), they made us change our clothes and put on some of their clothes: floor-length dresses and material to wrap our heads in so our hair wouldn't show. And they searched us too, which pissed me off. But Momma seemed to understand; she said it was because white folks thought the Muslims were militant, so white folks was always messing with 'em – you know, harassing them, arresting them, threatening them. Momma said the Muslims had to be careful so that's why they were searching folks.

During Momma's God search, we tried a few other religions. I never really did care one way or the other. I never really seriously thought about God because, no matter what the religion, they all wanted you to be perfect. And I knew I was far from perfect. So I figured God wouldn't wanna mess with me. I don't know which religion Momma finally decided on. Maybe she realized she didn't need a particular religion to know and love God or for God to know and love her. Whatever she decided, she also decided that she wasn't going to choose for me. She wanted to wait until I was old enough and then let me decide my religion.

Sitting there staring at my momma's casket, I wondered why God didn't save my momma. I decided whoever and wherever this God was, He must not like me very much because instead of saving her, He killed her. And, since He didn't like me, I didn't like Him. In fact, I decided I hated Him.

So there I sat, staring straight ahead, eyes blank, wishing the preacher would shut up about God. Soon enough he did, and folks began making their way back to their cars, some doing a light sprint to get out of the rain.

I didn't move.

Soon, Daddy, Uncle Jr., and the others slowly rose and began heading for the limos. I continued to sit. They started to lower my momma's casket into the ground. Still, I sat. Finally Daddy came, scooped me up, and carried me to the car.

A couple of days after Momma's funeral we had to go back to the judge's office. The tall black man was there again. And he was wearing the same suit. The two white lawyers were also there.

The judge finally introduced the tall black man to me and Larry.

'Children, this is Mr Burns, your father.' He said it so nonchalantly. As if he were reacquainting us with an old, familiar friend.

My father? My father? If I didn't know this white man was crazy before, I sure knew it then.

'That ain't my daddy!' I screamed as I ran to my daddy and climbed upon his lap. 'Dis my daddy!'

Daddy scooped me up and gently stroked my hair. There was a tear running down his cheek. This was the second time in my life I'd ever seen my daddy cry. Second time in less than two weeks.

'I'm sorry, Mr Long,' the judge said to Daddy, ignoring my outburst, 'but my hands are tied. California law clearly states that when a parent dies, the surviving biological parent gets first choice as to the custody of the children – absent a showing of unfitness. So, I'm afraid I'm going to have to give the children to Mr Burns.'

'Unfitness?' Daddy yelled as he bolted out of his seat, almost dropping me to the floor.

'Unfitness?! I'll give you unfitness! Where in the hell has he been for the past ten and a half years? Where in the hell was he when *my* kids were sick? When *my* kids needed school clothes? During their recitals and ball games, huh? Where the fuck was he? Why weren't they *his* kids then?'

I'd never seen Daddy so pissed. I decided that if he went for the judge, I'd have his back. We'd kick that white man's ass. Talkin' 'bout that tall black man was my daddy. That wasn't *my* fuckin' daddy!

'Please, Mr Long,' the judge begged. 'Please watch your language.'

The judge was scared. I could tell by the way he was fidgeting with the papers on his desk and erratically moving things around. Sweat was pouring off his face. The tall black man, Mr Burns, he was scared too. He just stood there, not saying a word.

I was confused. How could Mr Burns be my daddy? So what if we had the same last name? I never saw him before in my life. He wasn't there when I had to go to the hospital to get my tonsils out. He wasn't in the front row for my first violin recital. He didn't build my fancy red stove. My *daddy* did.

See, my daddy could build stuff really well. So, he built me this toy stove. It looked just like a real stove and it was almost as big as me. Daddy painted it red (my favorite color). It had burners and knobs and everything. It even had a little oven door with a window. And when you opened it, there were two baking racks inside. All the girls in the neighborhood wanted to play house at my house so we could cook on my stove. Mr Burns never built me a damn stove!

He never sang to me either. My daddy used to sing to me every night before I went to bed. Even after he and Momma didn't live together anymore. On our weekends together, he'd sing to me. He'd tuck me into bed and in my sweetest, 'Daddy's little girl' voice I'd say: 'Daddy, sing 'Everybody.' '

And, he'd sing the old Dean Martin classic.

I loved that song and I loved my daddy. That tall black stranger was *not my daddy.*

The room was chaotic. The white lawyers were arguing. Daddy and Mr Burns were arguing. The judge was scared. Uncle Jr. was trying to keep everyone calm. Wasn't working.

'I love my kids!' Mr Burns abruptly shouted.

Was he was trying to convince us or himself?

'Well, if you love them,' Daddy sneered, 'where's the $18,500 in back child support you owe?'

The room grew suddenly silent.

My daddy paid child support for us. I knew he did because I remembered when he and Momma were in front of the divorce judge. The judge had looked at some papers my daddy had given him and said:

'I see here they've got you down for child support. You don't have to pay for these kids.'

29

'Sure I do,' my daddy replied. 'They're my kids.'

Momma later told a friend that Daddy'd never missed a payment. *And,* he still gave us our allowance (which, personally, was all *I* cared about). Child support and visitation. That's all my daddy wanted out of the divorce. He *wanted* to pay child support and he *wanted* to be able to see his kids. And, my momma was so nice, she gave him both.

But, Mr Burns ain't never paid one dime in child support. *Pay* us? Hell, he never even *called* us! Came to see us. Wrote us. I had no idea who he was.

The judge looked so sad. Seems in California, it didn't matter if you've never paid for your kids. Didn't matter if you never visited 'em, saw 'em, loved 'em, or sang to 'em. None of that mattered at all. All you had to do was *have* 'em.

'What about me?' Uncle Jr. asked. 'Why can't they go with me? It just doesn't make sense to take them from their only family and give them to a complete stranger so soon after losing their mother.'

The judge looked at Uncle Jr. like he really understood his dilemma. He replied that I couldn't live with Jr. because I was a girl and they 'won't let a girl go to a home where there's not a woman in the home.' And since Uncle Jr. wasn't married, there wasn't a woman in his home.

I later learned that my father married Lori just days after my mother's funeral. His lawyer had told him he didn't have a chance in hell to get us because he wasn't a blood relative, let alone the biological parent. But, the lawyer said he *really* didn't have a chance in hell if he wasn't married, because of the requirement that a woman be in the home. So, he married Lori and moved into her apartment, which was larger. The plan completely failed. Meanwhile, I was unaware of Daddy's reasons for marrying Lori – I just took it as a sign that he didn't love my mom, which gave me a resentment against him I would carry for years.

'Besides,' the judge continued, 'the system is designed to keep the children together. So that, together with the fact that Mr Burns is their biological father, gives me no alternative.'

'Well,' Daddy yelled, 'the system's fucked!'

The judge repeated that, under the law, he had no choice but to give us to Mr Burns.

Before anyone could respond, Mr Burns said, 'What about the money?'

The room grew silent again.

'What money?' the judge replied.

'The insurance money their mother left them. I understand there's an insurance policy. Whoever gets the children gets the money, right?'

The judge looked confused. He quickly riffled through the pile of papers on his desk.

'Ah, yes,' the judge said. 'Yes, there is a life-insurance policy that requires two payments. One at age eighteen and another at twenty-one. However, it seems that the children's mother has placed the life-insurance proceeds in a trust fund, and has named her brother Ray as trustee.'

'Just what does that mean?' Mr Burns snapped. Now *he* looked pissed.

'Well,' the judge replied, 'it means that no matter who gets the children, Mr Stearns controls the trust, and therefore, the life-insurance money.'

So, that's it, I said to myself. It didn't take a rocket scientist to figure out that Mr Burns never wanted *us*. He thought he had to have us to get the life-insurance money. And now he was stuck with two kids and no money! Served him right.

Uncle Jr. chuckled quietly. He, too, was enjoying the fact that my momma was yet getting the last word.

The judge, unfazed by Mr Burns's sudden interest in the life-insurance money, was continuing his instructions about 'what the law required him to do.' He told Daddy to hand me and Larry over to Mr Burns immediately. Daddy began crying. Uncle Jr. began crying. Larry, overwhelmed, began laughing hysterically.

I started screaming.

'No! No!'

I wrapped my arms around Daddy's neck and held on for dear life.

Daddy was trying to calm me down, in between shedding his tears. Larry was now wrapped around Uncle Jr.'s legs. It must have been quite a sight: one skinny black girl wrapped around Daddy's neck like a scarf, wailing at the top of her lungs; and one skinny black boy wrapped around Uncle Jr.'s legs like a cobra, wailing at the top of his lungs.

Daddy and Jr. were each trying to hush our cries and gently pry us off. Wasn't working. Finally, Uncle Jr. asked the judge, lawyers, and Mr Burns to give him and Daddy a few moments alone with us. Mr Burns stormed out of the room. I don't think he was pissed because we didn't want to go with him; I think he was pissed because now we *had* to go with him and he wasn't getting any money.

Once they left and Daddy calmed us down, Daddy, Larry, Uncle Jr., and I all sat in a close little circle. Daddy told us he loved us and that he always would. He told us to remember that as long as we remembered our mother and carried her in our heart, she would not die because her spirit would live on in us. Soon, he couldn't talk anymore. He was crying too hard.

Uncle Jr. wrapped one arm around Larry and the other around me. He told us that he, too, loved us and that he would always be there for us – no matter what. And that if we ever needed him, to call him. He couldn't talk anymore either.

(During the next several years, Daddy, Lori, and Kelly would move around and change phone numbers quite a bit. However, Jr. refused to move or change his number – he wanted to be sure that, if we ever needed him, we would always be able to find him or get in touch with him. To this day, he still lives in the same house and has the same phone number.)

The four of us stood there in a group hug for a few moments, crying. I was wishing we could stay like that forever. But, soon the judge came in and said we had to go. I walked out backward, tears rolling down my face. I waved good-bye to the only real family I ever knew. I waved till I rounded the corner and couldn't see them no mo'. Even then I kept on waving. Even after I was in Mr Burns's car and we were driving off. I must have waved for ten minutes. The four of us would never be together again.

3

Mr Burns was *pissed*.

He took off out of that court parking lot like he was rushing to a fire, swerving and weaving in and out of traffic. Larry and I didn't say a word. Besides, what would I say to him? What do you say to a stranger who you just found out is your father? And, he was driving like a maniac. I was too scared to talk. Shit, I just hoped his crazy ass didn't kill us all.

The veins in Mr Burns's forehead were popping out. He was yelling about how his house wasn't ready for us. He never bothered to explain why, if he wasn't ready for us, he had fought my daddy so hard to get us. He said that until he was ready, he was going to send us to live with a lady who ran a foster home. Didn't matter much to me. Momma was gone. Daddy was gone. Uncle Jr. was gone. Everybody I loved was gone (except Larry and they could *have* him). I didn't know what a foster home was, but I hoped they had food. I was hungry.

No one said a word when we pulled into the parking lot of Mr Burns's apartment building. As we parked and got out, a large black woman got out of a car parked beside us. This was the fattest, ugliest, blackest woman I'd ever seen. She stood at least five foot eleven and weighed three hundred pounds. Her arms looked like a couple of gigantic watermelons that had been strung together and hung from her shoulders. Her big arms led down to equally gigantic hands. And she had black moles all over her face. She wore a short black afro and had a deep, husky voice.

Mr Burns called her Diane. He introduced her to us as Mrs Dobson. She bent to shake my hand. She was so huge, as she leaned over, I was sure she was going to topple over onto me. But she didn't. She gripped my hand. Hard. So hard it made me wince. Then she wrapped her huge hands around Larry's to shake his. I could tell she shook his hard, too, because once she let go of his hand, he started trying to shake the pain out of it.

Mr Burns got our bags out of his car and threw them in the trunk of Mrs Dobson's car like he was throwing out yesterday's trash.

'Go with her,' he barked at us. 'I'll come and get y'all later.'

We were too sad to argue and too scared to question what was going on. I suppose we thought it didn't really much matter anymore anyhow. So, we miserably and quietly obeyed. As we climbed into Mrs Dobson's car, a skinny little black girl sitting in the front seat spun around and proudly introduced herself as Connie, Mrs Dobson's daughter. Mrs Dobson stood outside for a moment talking to Mr Burns. I could hear her asking him about 'the money.' Mr Burns, still pissed, didn't want to talk about it. He told her that something had 'come up,' and he needed to do some research on it, but he'd get back to her.

'Okay,' she snapped, 'but make sure you do. I didn't drive all this way for nothing, and I don't keep nobody's bratty kids for nothing.' With that, Mrs Dobson climbed into the car and we drove off.

Larry and I never even saw the inside of Mr Burns's apartment. And I never saw Mr Burns again.

4

We drove for what seemed like forever. Neither Diane nor Connie said one word to us, and we didn't speak to them. I didn't know what to say. As we passed a sign that read 'Santa Ana,' Diane announced she was tired of driving and needed a break. A few moments later, she pulled up to a house, which I later learned was owned by her other daughter. No sooner than we'd stepped into the entryway, Diane ordered me and Larry to go outside. As we headed out the front door, I glanced back and saw her and her daughters head toward what looked like a large living room. Larry and I went outside and sat on the curb, each in our own haze of uncertainty and despair. Suddenly Connie came out of the house, stomped up to us, and announced that she'd come to 'lay down the rules.' She hadn't said a word to us since she'd introduced herself back in San Diego. Now, she was standing over us with her hands on her hips, a snarl on her lips, and swinging her big butt back and forth to emphasize her nastiness.

'Listen, you little shits,' she snapped at me and Larry.

Connie was three months younger than me, black and skinny like me, except her butt was bigger and she had moles on her face like her mother. But her moles had hairs coming out of them. The hairs in the mole on her top lip moved when she breathed. They danced around her mouth whipping here and there with every twitch, so you couldn't help but stare at them as she talked.

'*You* are the foster kids,' she stated with obvious authority. '*I* am the real kid. Don't forget it. If you piss me off, I'll make your lives hell.'

With that, she turned and ran into the house. Bitch. I didn't know what a 'foster' kid was and really didn't care whether I got to be one or not. As for being 'real' kids, we were real, weren't we? Larry must have been thinking the same thing because simultaneously we both started looking at our arms and legs, feeling them as if to check to see whether they were real. Crazy heifer. What was she talking about? One thing I *did* know was that I didn't like her. And she obviously didn't like us. Something told me that Larry and I were in for trouble.

Once we'd hopped back into the car and continued on our way, I was soon fast asleep. When I awoke, a sign informed me that Lancaster was twenty miles away. I wondered to myself why Diane didn't live in L.A. with her other daughter. She must have been reading my mind because she began talking, to no one in particular, about being forced out of L.A. She angrily ranted about how, a couple of years before, L.A. wrongly took her foster license; something about some twins that had died in her care. Something about giving them aspirin when they had the chicken pox or measles. She was talking so fast, and with all of the cussing and fussing, the details were hazy. But, the bottom line is she did *something* to them when they were sick that you *ain't supposed to do*.

Even though what happened was labeled an accident, apparently her foster license was taken away. Diane sat silent for a moment. Then, she gave us a sly grin in the rearview mirror and declared that she didn't care; she'd just moved, changed her name, and got another license. (The foster-care system wasn't computerized in 1974, so I guess Diane didn't have to worry about any cross-checking.) I don't know if Diane was telling the truth or just saying that to scare us. It didn't matter, though. We didn't have to stay with Diane long to realize that if she had done something to those twins, whatever it was probably wasn't an accident. As we pulled up to her house, Diane proudly stated that Lancaster was a 'new' town and 'all white' – like somehow that made it better than any other town. New, old, white, green; I could give a hoot. I was learning not to care too much about anything or anyone anymore.

The house was very nice; I'd never seen one that nice before. There wasn't an apartment building anywhere in sight.

Everywhere you looked there were picture-perfect sprawling green lawns and everything was sparkling clean. It looked like a neighborhood straight out of *Leave It to Beaver*. All the cars were nice and new, neatly parked on the street; no old broken-down hooalties haphazardly thrown against the curb like in the hood. And it was so quiet. Not like where I came from. No loud music from hooalties slowly cruising by. No home stereos blasting the latest soul hits out of open windows. No kids strolling down the block with boom boxes on their shoulders. In this neighborhood, you could actually hear birds chirping. And, there were no children visible or audible. No street football games or little girls on porches playing dolls or jacks. There were no dodge ball games breaking out on the sprawling green lawns. We were definitely *not* in the hood.

It was then I realized I would probably never see my hood again, the kids playing football in the street, separating like oil and water when cars passed through; children playing hide-and-seek using trees, Dumpsters, and cars to hide behind; little girls giggling as they played house or combed their dolls' hair into the latest, hippest styles. One look down *this* street and you knew that kind of love didn't live here. Everything looked so sterile, I wasn't sure that kind of love could move in if it wanted to.

As we walked into Diane's house, my mouth dropped. It was huge. We entered into the dining room. To the right was a huge kitchen, bigger than my bedroom back in the hood. Catty-corner and to the right of the dining room was what Diane called the 'formal' living room. It was really pretty in there. Everything was white and baby blue. The couch was white with gold trimming; it was covered with beautiful plush baby-blue cushions and pillows. Diane said it was 'European' furniture. There were fancy glass tables everywhere, with beautiful crystal lamps on them. There were hundreds of knickknacks and figurines made of glass, brass, china, and crystal, all perfectly displayed around the room. Huge floor-to-ceiling sliding glass doors allowed sunlight to dance and sparkle off its choice of reflective surface.

And the carpet was also baby blue – and when you stepped on it, your feet just melted into its plushness; it was like sinking in quicksand. I was standing on the carpet, marveling at its softness, when I *heard* the punch. I looked up and saw that

Diane had punched Larry in his arm, hard. Before I realized what had happened (and before I could run), Diane punched me in my arm.

Now, I'd been punched before. I'd gotten into fights at school – plenty of times. But those were kid's punches and they never hurt too much. But this one *hurt*. Before I could say, 'Ow,' Diane snarled.

'This room is off-limits to you little bastards. The only time I want to see you in here is when a social worker comes. If there's no social worker in this house yo' lil asses better'd not be in *my* living room. Is that clear?'

I didn't know what a social worker was, but I knew I didn't want to be in this room if it meant I was gonna get hit.

'Yeah,' we replied as the tears rolled down our faces. I don't think we were crying from the punches, though they did hurt like hell. I think we were crying because we knew that life as we knew it was over.

Diane's house had five bedrooms and two baths. She gave us the tour, shoving us from room to room, pointing out the only two 'approved designated spots' for foster children. One was the den, which really wasn't a den at all. It was just a small room where Diane had stuck a TV and an old tattered couch. The other was our bathroom, which was huge. A person could easily lie down in there.

Because Diane was obsessive about cleanliness and us being outside of our 'designated spots,' there weren't many places in her house we could go unless we had a reason to be there – which usually meant cleaning. We weren't allowed in her precious European living room, except to clean it. We weren't allowed in her or Connie's bedroom, except to clean them. We weren't allowed in the kitchen, except to clean it. We weren't allowed in the dining room unless we were cleaning it or eating. We weren't even allowed in our *own* bedrooms unless we were cleaning 'em or sleeping. We weren't allowed in the front yard or anywhere in the front of the house, for that matter (Diane said we'd bring down the neighborhood). So, the den, the bathroom (if you were using it), and the backyard were the only places foster children were allowed. Newcomers quickly learned that to be found outside of a designated spot guaranteed a punch, kick, or worse.

For now, Larry and I would have our own rooms; however, Diane told us not to get used to it. She had six other foster kids coming in a few days, and we would be sleeping four to a room. Except Connie. Connie would continue to have her own bedroom; she was never required to share anything with the foster children. She didn't use our bathroom – she used her mother's. She didn't have any designated places. She could even play in the front yard.

Diane's nephew Pete was also living with her. Pete was a tall, slender black man. His skin was the color of black coffee. He had deep-set brown eyes, which seemed to hide a secret hatred. Pete never smiled or talked much. He pretty much ignored the 'foster kids' but seemed to really enjoy Connie's company. Though slim, he was well built and prided himself on his body. Pete was waiting to go into the army, but lately he'd been getting into 'a lil bit of trouble.' Diane said if he didn't go into the army, he'd end up dead or in jail. But, until he left – which was supposed to be in a few days – he would stay at Diane's and sleep in Larry's room. He stayed at Diane's because his family considered Lancaster safe. Surrounded by a bunch of white folks, what trouble could he possibly get into?

The night after our arrival, Pete and Diane got really happy. They were drinking what I called 'feel-good' liquid. The more they drank, the happier they got. Larry, probably mentally exhausted from the emotional turmoil of the last couple of weeks, had gone to bed early. Shortly after Pete and Diane began drinking, Pete staggered into the den where I was sitting and shoved some of his 'feel-good' at me and said: 'Here, drink dis.' As he staggered away, he slurred out that it was rum and coke.

Whatever it was I liked it – instantly. I didn't like the taste. But I wasn't drinking for the taste. The more I drank, the happier *I* got. The more I drank, the better I felt about myself. After a while, I didn't feel so dark, black, and ugly. After a while, I didn't care that my momma was dead and my daddy and Uncle Jr. were gone. I didn't care that I could get punched simply for being in the wrong room. I was h-a-p-p-e-e!

Yup, I loved that feel-good liquid. I was sitting in the den, humming to myself (I always did that when I was happy), enjoying my newfound pleasure, when Pete staggered back in.

'Meet me 'n the bafroom in five minutes,' he slurred, and staggered away. I thought he was going to have more feel-good liquid. I was there in two minutes.

When Pete came in a few seconds later, I was sitting on the toilet, happily dangling my feet and waiting. Not for him so much, but for the feel-good.

Everything happened so fast it seemed like a blur. Suddenly Pete wasn't so drunk anymore. He wasn't staggering or slurring, looking harmless as he had been just a few minutes before when he was drinking and laughing. Suddenly he was very much in control of himself and very angry. He snatched me off the toilet and slapped me to the ground. I gave a little scream as I landed on my tailbone. It hurt like hell when I hit the floor. But before I could give the scream full force and effect, he slammed a wash-cloth over my mouth. My eyes were bulging and watering. I was scared and didn't understand what was going on.

Pete snatched up my dress, grabbed my panties and ripped them off. It seemed to me they tore like paper. I was astonished at how easily they came off.

Why don't they make these things stronger? I was thinking as Pete began to climb on top of me; forcing my legs open.

Shit, he was heavy. Sort of like my momma was when I found her. But he wasn't dead like she was (although I was starting to wish he was). I wasn't sure what he wanted to do. My butt still hurt, but I couldn't rub it because his heavy body had pinned me down.

I thought I had seen something like this in my sex-ed class, but I couldn't quite remember right then. I knew what sex was. At least I *thought* I knew; although I'd never actually seen it.

That's when I screamed – although the only thing that actually came out was a muffled yelp because Pete was still holding the washcloth over my mouth. In fact, it had started to slip deeper into my mouth. It was wet and soggy from my spit. I started panicking because I thought I would choke on it like my momma did with her tongue. I began trying to cough it back toward the front of my mouth.

Suddenly the feel-good liquid quit working and I didn't feel so good anymore. In fact, I began to feel the most horrific pain I'd ever encountered, like someone was trying to push

40

something through my coochie and up into my stomach.

Pete was getting more and more pissed as he barked something about having a hard time getting 'it' all the way in. But after several thrusts and then one forceful horrific plunge, I felt something inside me give way, ripping like a paper towel being torn from the roll. Pete was pumping his thing in and out of me while trying to keep the towel over my mouth. He was sweating and grunting. I was crying and squirming, and Pete was having trouble keeping control of me and the towel at the same time. But him being twenty-one, and me being eleven, he managed.

As Pete lay on top of me humping for what seemed like forever, my mind begin to wander. I needed something else to think about besides the nightmare on top of me. First, I wondered why they didn't make little girls' panties stronger. Then, I begin to recall my hatred for God. I didn't know Him, but one thing I did know is that people said He could see the future. Well, that told me that God must have known that if He took my mother all of these fucked-up things would happen to me. Besides, not only was it fucked-up for God to take my mother, I felt like it was extremely fucked up for Him to allow me to find her dead body. So, I figured He couldn't like me very much. I resolved again, right there and then on that bathroom floor, that I hated God because He hated me. I decided again, once and for all, that I would not be bothered with Him.

And then, suddenly, it was over. As Pete stood up and began pulling up his pants, he growled:

'If you tell anyone, I'll kill everyone in your family.'

Now, while it was true that I hated Larry, I wanted to be the one to kill him – not someone else. Nor did I want anything to happen to my daddy and Uncle Jr. They were the only family I had. They'd been through enough, and I didn't want to be the reason for their deaths. I already believed that somehow I was to blame for my momma's death (like if I'd've woken up earlier, I could have called for help and saved her). So I wasn't about to be the cause of Daddy's, Uncle Jr.'s, and Larry's deaths too.

Suddenly I got a glimmer of hope. I began to think that maybe Diane could help me. Pete must have read it in my face. Or maybe it was the way I was longingly looking toward the door.

41

'You think she gives a fuck?' Pete snapped. 'Who do you think sent me in here? She's not going to help you. She hates y'all.'

That answered the question of why Diane never came looking for me.

'Y'all just a paycheck to her,' he continued, 'paychecks and maids. Nothing more *and a whole lot less*.'

He stated the last phrase with a calm, sly grin that, by itself, was frightening.

With that, he walked out of the bathroom and left me lying there. I was bleeding. I could feel the blood sliding down my leg like raindrops drifting down a windowpane. I cried as I got up and begin to wash myself with the same washcloth that had muffled my screams. My coochie hurt. My tailbone hurt. And I felt dirty. I didn't know why, but I did. I wanted to wash the dirt away. I *tried* to wash it away. But, no matter how hard I scrubbed, the feeling of filth and shame remained.

Shortly after my momma died, I heard someone say that the dead come back. I had been secretly hoping my momma would come back. Come back and take me from that house of hell. But, that night, while washing the blood that was still dripping down my legs, while stifling my tears and sorrow, I realized that the dead can't come back because if my momma could've come back, surely she would have done so then. She would've come back to rescue me. But she didn't come. No one came.

I didn't say a word to anyone about what happened that night. Who could I tell? Everyone who knew and loved me was hundreds of miles away.

The next day, Pete pretty much ignored me. He acted like I disgusted him; like I made him sick; which was fine with me. I just hoped he'd stay the fuck away. Later that day, Larry noticed I was limping and asked why was I walking funny. Unfortunately, we were within earshot of Pete who turned and glared at me, his lips in a snarl as he awaited my response. I remembered his promise. I didn't want Larry to die. I didn't want anyone else in my family to die. So I told Larry I'd hurt my legs while cleaning the bathroom (we'd only been there two days and already had cleaned the entire house). He seemed satisfied with that excuse.

Up until the moment he ordered me back into the bathroom

two days later, Pete completely ignored me. I started to cry as I slowly shuffled toward the bathroom. I knew what lay ahead and I knew how hopeless it was. I didn't know where Larry was, but I tried to cry quietly because I didn't want him killed. Pete walked behind me shoving me toward the bathroom. As he got ready to close the door, I heard Diane bark, 'She'd better be able to work tomorrow!' That pretty much confirmed where Diane stood on the matter. Who else could I tell? Besides, Pete said that no one would ever believe me because no one cared about foster kids. And, from the unfettered violence Diane was beginning to unleash on us at whim, I believed him.

A couple of days later, just as Diane said, six other foster kids came: three girls (two of whom were sisters), and three boys. An hour before they were scheduled to arrive, Diane shoved me and Larry into the den and told us not to say a word or we'd be sorry.

Several hours later, the six children arrived with a white woman who I later learned was a social worker. As they all sat in the living room, I heard the woman tell Diane how pretty her living room was and how lucky the foster-care system was to be able to call on a wonderful person like her who was always willing to take so many children.

Diane glowed in the praise.

We were to discover that every new foster child who came to Diane's received the same initiation. These six were no exception. As soon as the social worker's car pulled off, they each received the warning punch about her living room and how only the presence of social workers allowed them to sit in there. They also received the grand tour and instructions about designated areas.

None of the new arrivals' mommas were dead. They were there for various reasons: some of their mommas were on drugs, some just couldn't keep them, some just didn't want them. We didn't really spend too much time on why each of us was there. Didn't matter why they were there. Only thing that mattered was they were stuck in hell with us.

That night, packed into the tiny room Diane called the den, Larry and I learned all about 'the system.' We learned what Connie meant when she called us the foster kids. Until my encounter with Diane, I had never even heard of foster children. So I listened in horror as the children talked about the foster homes they had been in and how the white folks who ran the system pretty much stuck kids wherever they could. Some of them had been in four and five homes *before* Diane's. Some of them weren't surprised at her violence – in fact, they expected it and learned to accept it. I learned that social workers were the people who were supposed to come and check on you, but they hardly ever did. And when they did, they always called first, which meant Diane would always have time to prepare.

It was quickly apparent that Pete was telling the truth when he said we were just paychecks to Diane. She was plainly in it for the money: she had us kids stacked in her house like sardines. And, with eight foster children, each drawing a monthly paycheck, she was getting paid quite nicely; yet she did everything as cheaply as possible. Our beds were two sets of raggedy bunk beds with hard tattered mattresses. Breakfast was always generic corn flakes with powdered milk. Lunch and dinner were always the same: beans and rice (which she bought in bulk). The portions weren't very large, and we weren't allowed seconds. She and Connie always ate what she called 'the good stuff': fried chicken, steak, pork chops. And they could eat as much as they wanted.

Nor did it take long to discover that Pete had also been right about us being Diane's maids. You see, Diane was a neat freak. She was obsessive about a clean house. Everything had to be cleaned, and *all the time*. And, if you didn't do it right, you earned a slap, kick, punch, or, as time went on, worse. Diane would literally come behind us with white gloves to check our work. And, no matter how hard we tried, it was never clean enough. She always found something wrong, always found some reason to go off and hit us. Diane had been doing this long enough so she'd made a science out of her abuse. She knew exactly how and when to hit us. She would only slap us in our faces. Other blows, however, could land anywhere: our backs, arms, stomachs, legs, butts. And, she'd beat you with whatever was most convenient: her shoe, her fist, a belt. She enjoyed inflicting pain – in any way possible.

I quickly learned to hate that gorgeous living room of hers. One of my many chores was to clean it – *every day*. To Diane, cleaning meant getting on your hands and knees and cleaning the floorboards with toothbrushes. It meant shining the floor-to-ceiling windows and every single piece of fucking glass on the crystals that hung from the lamps. It meant cleaning each of those damned glass tables as well as the knickknacks she had lying on them: beautiful copper elephants, each with their trunks lifted upward for good luck; spectacular china dolls with pretty silk dresses and matching fancy hats; crystal unicorns of varying colors and sizes; delicate teacups displaying intricate designs, which, according to Diane, were made from the world's finest china. And, if you didn't do the cleaning to Diane's satisfaction, it meant getting beat. And in case we'd forgotten – as if we could – she would often remind us that she'd 'accidentally' killed before and could 'accidentally' do it again.

5

A few days after I arrived, I decided to run away. I didn't even know what 'running away' was. I had never done it before and never knew anyone who had. I just knew I had to go. I didn't know where. But I had to go. Any place was better than where I was. Besides, I had made a promise to myself that Pete would never 'take' me again. I didn't know the new kids well enough to trust them and tell them about Pete, and I didn't want Larry to get killed.

For now, Pete was still ignoring me. I once saw him eyeing one of the new girls. I didn't know if he had gotten any of them. And, to be honest, I didn't care as long as he stayed away from me. But even if he had gotten to one of the others, I didn't know how long she would hold his attention before he came back my way. I swore that the last time he took me was the last time. Ever.

I hated Diane. I hated Connie. I hated cleaning. I hated that house. I hated being a foster kid. I had to get out. I didn't want to leave Larry, but I couldn't worry about him. Shit, it was everybody for themselves now.

That night, after everyone went to sleep, I quietly got up (I had started sleeping in my clothes just in case Pete decided to try to get me in my sleep), and crawled out the bedroom window. Because Diane's house was a single story, it was a short drop to the ground. At first, the still evening air felt good against my face. It felt like freedom. Then, a quick gust of wind made me realize it was chilly. All I had on was a thin T-shirt and jeans. I thought about going back and grabbing something to keep me warm, but was unsure if I could spare the time.

It's now or never, I convinced myself. Deciding to forego the jacket, I began to run. I ran and ran and ran, not knowing where I was, and not paying attention to where I was going. Houses, cars, and street signs passed by in a blur. As I ran I cried; cried because of the pain and shame of what Pete had done to me, cried because I missed my momma, cried because of Diane's abuse, cried because I missed my daddy and Uncle Jr. I cried and ran until I was out of breath.

When I finally stopped, I was in a park. I spotted a bench and sat down. I was hungry and tired. And, now that I was no longer running, I was also cold again. I sat on the bench, shivering, wondering what I was going to do and where I was going to go. I had no idea. I realized I hadn't thought my plan out very well.

It was then I noticed a pretty white girl walking toward me. She looked young – like maybe nineteen or twenty. She was very thin – she reminded me of Lori – and pale, but she had large, full breasts that begged for room as they oozed out from the sides of her halter top. Her long legs jutted out from a miniskirt so short that when she bent over – even slightly – I could see her pink panties. She was pretty but had a face that had seen hard times.

She sat down next to me, saying nothing for a while, just listening to me cry. Finally, she said, 'My name is Candy. What's yours?'

'Vette,' I whimpered. I was too hungry, cold, and tired to be afraid of her.

'What are you doing out here?' she asked.

Her speech was very proper, not punctuated with slang like we used in the hood. She didn't cut off her words or run them together. Instead, she enunciated them fully. For example, she said, 'What are you doing . . . ?' not 'Whatcha doin' . . . ?'

We walked to a nearby coffee shop where Candy bought me a donut and a cup of cocoa, and I started telling her about Momma, my daddy, and Uncle Jr. I hesitated when I got to the part about Pete. I wasn't sure if I should tell her or not, remembering Pete's threats. But, she was a stranger. And maybe I just felt she was trustworthy, or maybe I just needed to get it off my chest – to tell someone.

Whatever the reason, I told her – just blurted it out – that Pete made me do it with him several times on the bathroom floor. I was starting to cry again. I tried to stifle my tears. I continued on about Diane, her obsession with cleanliness and the punches and kicks I got when I didn't clean to her satisfaction. As I talked, I wrapped my hands around the cocoa, warming my small cold hands. I tried to eat the donut as slowly as possible, knowing it would probably be my last meal for a while, but I was too hungry for that. Besides, having eaten only beans and rice day in and day out, the sweet-tasting donut was a welcomed change. So I devoured it in between sentences and gulps of cocoa.

Candy sat across the table from me and listened carefully, though she seemed indifferent to Pete's behavior or Diane's violence. In fact, her facial expression never changed – like maybe she had heard it all before or had even lived it.

'Listen,' she said casually as I finished my story and my donut and clung to the cocoa, 'it's a tough world out here. No one gives a fuck about you, and nothing in this world is free. Now, I bought you that cocoa and donut, but from now on, you're going to have to take care of yourself.'

I didn't know what she meant, but before I could ask, she skipped outside to a car that had pulled over at the corner and honked. I watched intently through the coffee shop's windows as she leaned over into the driver's side window to talk to the driver. I couldn't see the driver very well, except to see he was a baldheaded white man. Whoever he was, I figured he must be important, because as Candy stood there talking to him, she changed her stance. She was now . . . well, sexy. Her butt stuck out in the street, raising her miniskirt just enough to show the lace trimming of her pink panties. She placed a hand on her hip and casually laid the other on the hood of the car. She smiled and laughed a lot.

Whatever they're talking about, I thought as I watched her, *it must be funny.*

After a few minutes, Candy ran around to the passenger side, hopped in, and the car took off. I sat there for a moment wondering what my next move was going to be. I figured the man in the car was a friend of hers and so she was gone for good. But, as I finished my cocoa and stood up to go, Candy came hopping around the corner back into the coffee shop.

'Where'd ya go?' I asked.

'To turn a trick,' she replied as she grabbed a small mirror from her purse and quickly applied bright red lipstick. She'd perked up and actually seemed happy about this 'trick.' And she said it so matter-of-factly, I figured a 'trick' was something like an old friend, though I wasn't sure.

'What's a 'trick'?' I asked.

Candy laughed as she sat me down and schooled me on the world of prostitution. I sat there in horror as she explained that girls – and sometimes boys – took money to let someone to do to them what Pete had done to me.

'Listen, girlie,' Candy snapped, noticeably irritated by my facial expressions, maybe because she thought I was judging her, 'you might as well start charging for what your foster father is taking for free.'

Pete wasn't my foster father. But that wasn't important. What was important is that what Candy said made some sense.

'Listen,' she continued, 'how old did you say you are? Eleven?'

'Well,' I retorted, 'I'll be twelve real soon.'

'Doesn't matter,' she responded. 'It wouldn't matter if you were sixteen! Who's going to give you a job? How are you going to eat? That hot chocolate and donut weren't free!'

She had a point. I remembered that just a little while earlier I was hungry and tired and cold. Candy told me that by turning tricks she'd make a hundred dollars on a good night. I thought about it for a few moments. It didn't take me long to realize she was right – both about me needing money to take care of myself and about no one giving a fuck about me.

I really didn't have any choice.

'Okay,' I whispered, giving in to necessity, 'show me how to do it.'

She laughed.

'You already know how to *do it*,' she said. 'Pete's been making you *do it*. Now, you just need someone to show you the ropes.'

With that, she stood up, smoothed out her miniskirt, and headed out the door toward the corner. I slowly followed her with my head down and heart pounding, wondering what lay ahead.

While we stood on the corner waiting, for what I didn't yet know, Candy reached into her halter and pulled out a joint and a Bic. She lit the joint, took a couple of puffs, and handed it to me.

'What is it?' I asked as I examined it.

'Weed, girl!' she snarled, irritated at my ignorance.

I took the joint and sucked in as I had watched her do. I started coughing so hard that I was sure the cocoa I'd just drunk would come up through my nose. I grabbed my nose to try to keep anything from coming out, but nothing did. My nose and throat burned as I gagged out a cloud of smoke. Candy laughed.

'You've got to hold it in for a while once you inhale,' she said, taking the joint and showing me how to take a hit.

I watched her again, then took the joint and sucked. Although I did choke a little, I was able to hold the smoke in for a few seconds before exhaling. And just as I had reacted to the 'feel-good' liquid Pete had given me, I instantly loved it. In a few moments, I was hitting the joint like an old pro. While we passed it back and forth, Candy reached into her purse and broke out a small bottle of her own feel-good, except she said it was called 'Mad Dog' (the label read 'MD 20/20'). Shit, between the joint and the Mad Dog, within moments I was feeling really, really good.

Not long after finishing the joint, I got my first customer. An older, small-boned white man driving a very nice Caddy pulled over to the curb where Candy and I were standing. With the joint and booze, I wasn't even feeling the cold night air.

'Hey, ladies,' he said with a sly voice. 'Nice night, isn't it?'

I didn't say a word. I didn't know what to say. So, as I had done with the weed and Mad Dog, I just watched Candy and followed her lead.

'Yeah, handsome,' she said. 'Beautiful night. What are you looking for?'

'What are you offering?' he replied.

They both spoke so properly.

'Well,' Candy said, 'are you looking for a single or a double?'

I later learned a single meant one girl, and a double meant two.

He looked from her to me, back to her, and then back to me. His indecisiveness reminded me of how Momma once looked when she was trying to choose between two colors of paint that she wanted to put on the walls.

Don't think about Momma now, I told myself. *It'll make you sad and that will make you cry. In fact, don't ever think about her again. You can't afford to be sad or do no more cryin'. You gotta take care of yourself now. You gotta do what you gotta do!*

'How old is she?' the man was asking Candy, bringing me back to my bleak reality.

'Eleven,' she replied. 'So she'll cost you extra.'

They were discussing me as if I weren't even there.

'I know,' he said.

Obviously this wasn't his first time with little girls.

'She does look very young, though,' he continued, looking at me and licking his lips. 'I like them young.'

Candy, a pro at seizing an opportunity for extra money, added, 'She's a virgin.'

I wasn't really sure what a virgin was. Oh, sure, I had heard the term before. Around Christmastime, folks always talk about the Virgin Mary. But they talk about her only at Christmas, so although I had heard the word, I didn't really know what it meant. Didn't matter, though. The joint and Mad Dog kept things simple for me.

No one gives a fuck about you.

'I'll do a single. Just her,' he said, a huge grin appearing on his face.

With that, Candy opened the door, shoved me in, and said, 'I'll see you in a few minutes.'

She slammed the door and looked down the street behind us, as if she were expecting another car.

When we drove off, I looked out the window at her pretty much the way I'd looked out the window at my daddy and Uncle Jr. when Mr Burns drove off with me and Larry. I was wishing she'd run after us, pull me from the car and say, 'No, don't take her,' then take me home and take care of me herself.

The man didn't talk much, except to say his name was Joe. He looked like he could be around my daddy's age. He drove for a few blocks and parked on a small, residential street. It was immediately apparent that no one would see us because this street was exactly like Diane's: perfect – and empty. There weren't any people hanging out on their porches like we did in the hood. No police cars cruising by as they often did in the hood. Nope. Not a soul in sight. Just me and Joe. He didn't want to talk. Almost mechanically, he got out of the driver's seat and climbed into the backseat. I stayed in the front seat, staring straight ahead, not knowing what to do.

'Come back here,' he said.

He didn't yell it at me like Pete would have. Just a firm request. I nervously and quietly obeyed. I was glad for the joint and Mad Dog and the way they made me not feel. I liked not feeling.

That night in that car with 'Joe,' I turned my first trick. Right there in the backseat. (Luckily for him, we were both short.) Although he was doing to me what Pete had done, it didn't hurt as much. And he didn't hit me. Kinda funny, but just the absence of violence made the experience better.

When he was done, he worriedly asked me if I had started my period because he hadn't used 'protection.' I knew what a period was (I'd learned about that in sex ed), but I didn't know what protection was. I told him I hadn't started my period.

'Good,' he said, ' 'cause I wouldn't want you getting pregnant.'

Like we'll ever see each other again! I thought, but said nothing.

As we got back into the front seat, he slipped me two twenty-dollar bills. Forty dollars! I felt like I was rich!

This ain't so bad, I thought while I held on to the money for dear life.

Joe was blabbering on about something as we drove back to the coffee shop. I wasn't paying any attention to him, though; too busy thinking about all of the soda and candy I was going to buy with the money in my hand.

As Joe let me out at the corner, Candy was waiting.

'You all right?' she asked, handing me another joint and what was left of the Mad Dog.

I didn't answer her right away. I took a hit off the joint and finished off the Mad Dog. As the weed and the booze began to soothe my mind and body I knew that, with them, I could do anything. I tenderly looked at the money still clutched in my little hand. I loved that I'd found a way to take care of myself.

'I am now.'

'Come on, girl,' she said as she wrapped her arm around my shoulders and guided me down the street. 'It's late. That's enough for one night. I'll tell you what. You can crash with me.'

Cool, I thought. We headed off for her place, arm in arm, like two best friends out for an innocent walk and enjoying the evening air.

The joint we were smoking and the forty dollars in my pocket kept my mind and my conscience clear. In fact, I was beginning to think that Candy's life wasn't all that bad. As we walked, I began daydreaming of the great life we could lead – just she and I, sisters against the world. It was a nice dream, and one that I thought just might come true. That is, until I got to her house and met her pimp.

On the way to her house, Candy schooled me about pimps. She said a pimp was someone who protected you and kept you from getting beat up by tricks (or anyone else for that matter). After the experiences of being hit at will by Diane and repeatedly raped by Pete, I decided I could use some protection. She said her pimp's name was 'Money' and that he was good to her.

'Come to think of it,' she said, stopping for a moment to ponder, 'he's better than most pimps.' She didn't say why.

All the streets in Lancaster looked alike to me, so, as far as I was concerned, Candy's street looked like Diane's. Her house was even shaped and laid out like Diane's, except nothing was blue and white. Instead, everything was red and black *velvet.* The living room had a big ugly red velvet couch and matching love seat. Huge black velvet pillows trimmed with shiny gold tassels were strewn everywhere. The pictures on the walls showed all kinds of people and creatures – women, tigers, clowns, etc. – each painted onto a black velvet canvas. These velvet monstrosities covered every wall. There was a black marble coffee table with smoked glass in the middle. Matching end tables bracketed the red velvet couch. In the center of the coffee table and each of the end tables were black ceramic vases, which held silk red roses. Even the carpet was red shag.

Now I love red, but this is ridiculous!

'Make yourself at home,' she said, heading to the back of the house. I'd no sooner sat down on the couch than she returned to say that Money was in the bathroom.

'He likes to take bubble baths,' Candy said as she sat down beside me. She reached under the couch and pulled out a bright orange tray. It reminded me of the kind they had at fast-food restaurants. On the tray was weed, Zig-Zags, and a bent playing card. I wasn't sure what these items were for until she began using them. She pulled two Zig-Zags from the pack licked the edges and then stuck them together. Using the playing card, she scooped up some weed and put it in the papers. Then, with precision and skill, she rolled the weed back and forth between her thumbs, middle, and forefingers until she had a perfectly proportioned joint. After looking it over approvingly, she pulled out her Bic and lit it.

Money finally emerged. He had on a beautiful silk black robe and diamond rings on every finger, which I noticed as he reached out and gently shook my hand. Candy introduced us and informed him that I was a runaway.

So that's what I am, I thought.

Money was pale white like Candy, but very handsome, tall with a slender build. He obviously worked out because he had muscular arms and a *rippled* chest, easily observable through his open silk robe. He had the deepest, bluest eyes – when he looked at you, you felt his eyes on your soul. His wavy black hair hung to his shoulders and matched the fine soft black hair that formed his mustache and goatee. He was soft-spoken and had the most beautiful white teeth when he smiled – which he did often. Shoot, he was fine.

When he asked Candy how much she'd made, I watched her reach into her halter and give him all of the money she had stuffed in there. I got nervous.

I hope he didn't expect mine! I didn't do that shit for him!

But he didn't ask me. In fact, he never even looked my way – it was as if I weren't even there. While he was talking to Candy about his money, his entire focus and complete attention remained on her – as though he were studying her. He counted the money and, obviously happy with the amount, turned to me and asked:

'Are you hungry?'

'Yeah,' I replied.

Hungry? I was starving! I had never been that hungry before in my life. I felt like I could eat an elephant. I hadn't yet realized that my ravenous hunger coincided with the decline of my weed high.

Money whipped us up some of the best tuna I'd ever had. It wasn't until we were sitting around, each of us eating our third tuna sandwich, that they gave me the scoop about the munchies and weed. After we finished eating – three tuna sandwiches each, plus chips, cookies, ice cream, soda, and popcorn – Money 'hipped me to the skip.' That is, he laid down the rules.

'Listen here . . .' he said, leaning forward to talk to me while he lit another joint.

Full and satisfied, we had returned to smoking weed and drinking. It seems that when Candy wasn't turning tricks, all they did was smoke weed, drink, eat (because of the munchies), then smoke more weed, drink, and eat some more – a never ending cycle that seemed cool to me.

'. . . nothing in life is free,' Money continued. 'If you're gonna stay here, you're going to work and earn your keep. Starting with all that damn food you just ate.'

It never occurred to me that Money expected to be paid for feeding me. I had forgotten Candy's warning that 'nothing is free.'

Completely unconcerned about what I might be thinking, he went on. 'Now, to be one of my bitches, requires working every night – except when you're on your period. And all my girls have a daily minimum.'

I looked around when he said 'all my girls,' because I hadn't seen anyone else in the house except me, him, and Candy.

'At first, yours will be lower than the rest,' he continued, ignoring my search for his phantom harem, 'that is, until you've learned the ropes. But, then I'll actually be raising your quota because you're young and can charge more. You'll give me my money each night, and if you don't meet your minimum, I'll kick your ass.'

He wasn't yelling. He never even raised his voice, but the intensity in his eyes and the firmness in his voice told me he was *very, very* serious.

He went on and on about his rules, and how I'd better have his money. I wasn't listening, though. As soon as I realized what he was saying – that I had to give him all of the money I made from turning tricks – I started tuning him out. It was obvious that this arrangement was *not* going to work for me. I couldn't understand the reasoning in allowing someone to do to me what Pete and Joe did and then give *someone else* the money. Hell, I figured if I'm going to go through the misery and degradation of doing it, I should at least get to keep the money, right?

His ending was short and sweet:

'You really don't have a choice. If you don't join my stable, I'll kick your ass. In fact, every time I see you I'll kick your ass. And if I catch your little ass working my turf without giving me my money, I'll kill you.'

Then, as his lips turned up into a nasty snarl, he crooned, 'Welcome to the Money Train, girlie.'

With that he stood up and casually strolled to the back of the house, snapping his fingers at Candy as he went. Before she ran after him, she leaned over to me and whispered:

'It's not as bad as it seems. Besides, what else are you going to do? Money will take good care of you. You'll see. Just give it a chance.'

She seemed to be almost begging me.

'Candy!' he bellowed from the back of the house. Startled, she jumped and went scurrying off in the direction of his roar.

I sat there, trying to figure out what to do. It was cold outside. All I had was forty dollars.

What should I do? Should I stay and join his stable (whatever that was)? Turn tricks and give him all the money? Or should I go back to Diane's? Where else could I go? How would I get there?

I decided to run. Fuck it. What did I have to lose?

I waited until I heard sounds coming from the back – sounds like those Pete and Joe made when they were doing it to me.

As I headed toward the front door, I noticed a jacket lying on the back of the red velvet couch. I grabbed it and quietly slipped out.

I began walking. I didn't even know in which direction I was going. I just walked. It was very early in the morning. It was cold. I was lost. What in the fuck was I supposed to do now?

6

As I walked I came upon a very busy road. A nearby sign said the road led to some highway. I didn't know where the highway went, but it looked like it was heading out. There was a stump sitting a few feet off the road. I sat down on it to rest and contemplate my next move. I realized I couldn't return to Diane's, even if I wanted to, because I didn't know where she lived or how to get there. What a mess I was in! I sat there, tired, cold, and hungry, when a car approached.

The passenger-side window slowly slid down. The driver, a white man, leaned over and asked if I needed a ride. Before I could respond, a police car pulled up behind him. The policeman hadn't stopped for me. He stopped because he thought the motorist was having car trouble or in need of some kind of help. It wasn't until after the cop had gotten out of his car and started approaching the motorist's window that he noticed me sitting on the stump. He paused, looked at me, then at the motorist, then back at me, as if he were trying to decide which needed his attention first. He decided the small black girl sitting on the side of the road would be first.

'What are you doing here?' he asked softly, beginning to move toward me slowly and cautiously, trying not to startle me. I heard him, but didn't respond. I was trying to think of what to say. I mean, I had been taught to trust the police. I never had a reason to distrust them. Until now. I was starting to realize that everyone wanted something.

'Do you live here?' he asked as he continued toward me. He seemed like a nice man. The motorist had also gotten out of his car and was following behind the policeman.

'Do you know her?' the cop asked the motorist.

'No,' he replied. 'I just saw her sitting there, which seemed strange. I was concerned, so I pulled over.'

'What's your name?' the cop asked.

'La'Vette,' I replied.

'La'Vette. That's a pretty name. What's your last name?'

I told him. But since I didn't trust him, I only answered direct questions.

'Are you lost?'

'Yeah,' I replied. It wasn't a lie. I *was* lost. He didn't ask me why I was on the stump so early in the morning. He didn't ask me if I'd run away. He didn't ask me if I'd been raped, beaten, or what. He asked if I was lost, so that's the question I answered.

'Well, where do you live?'

I was uncertain about how to answer this one. *Should I say San Diego?* Although that's where I was from, I didn't live there anymore. *Or should I say Lancaster?* That's where Diane lived and it now looked like that's where I'd be stuck.

'I don't know,' I replied.

He noticed me shivering and asked if I wanted to sit in his car while he made a call to see where I belonged. He gave me a big smile.

'Yeah,' I answered. *Besides,* I thought, *it's gotta be warmer in there than out here.*

The cop told the motorist he'd take over from there. He opened the passenger door of his cruiser for me and told me not to touch anything. He got in and radioed the dispatcher to see if a child with my name had been reported missing. We waited a few moments while she checked, neither of us saying anything to the other. He flipped through some papers on his clipboard. I had never been inside of a police car before, so I marveled at all the intriguing gadgets.

Soon, the dispatcher came on and told him that no one with my name had been reported missing.

'Do you have any relatives?' he asked, turning to face me.

'No,' I said. 'I live in a foster home.' I was tired. There was nowhere else to run, and I didn't know what the alternative to Diane's would be. I had no more fight left in my little body. I had given up.

'Do you know the name of your foster mother?' he asked. I told him. The dispatcher was able to tell him where a 'Diane Dobson' lived, and we headed that way. Within minutes, her house was in sight.

Turns out that road with the stump was less than a half mile from Diane's house. And that road would have led me right out of Lancaster.

Diane's house was dark when we pulled into the driveway. Holding my hand as we approached the door, the cop rang the doorbell. When Diane opened the door, the cop cheerfully said, 'Looks like we found something you lost!'

'Oh, yes,' Diane cried with tears in her eyes. 'Where did you find her?'

She shoulda been an actress, I thought.

Diane continued. 'She must have been sleepwalking again and wandered off. She does that a lot.'

I didn't speak up. I didn't say, 'Liar!' I had admitted defeat.

'Can I speak to you privately for a moment?' he asked Diane. He was looking at me as if I were a little slow and might be harmed by what was about to be said.

'Sure,' she replied as she grabbed his arm and gently led him into the formal living room. When she turned on the light, he seemed immediately impressed with what he saw.

Refusing her invitation to sit down in one of the beautiful plush baby-blue chairs, the cop stood talking to Diane for a few moments. Because they were whispering, I couldn't understand what they were saying. I did notice that, as they talked, the cop was admiring the living room. When they ended their discussion and made their way back to me, he commented on how beautiful the living room was.

'Why, thank you!' Diane exclaimed, obviously proud that someone had admiration for her precious room.

Whatever Diane told the cop, he seemed to accept it.

He bent over so that he could put his face really close to mine, smiled, and asked if I was okay.

'Yes,' I whispered. I wanted to scream, *Don't go! Take me with you! This chick is crazy!* But I didn't. I just stood there with my head hanging down. Something told me that screaming would be useless.

With that, he told me to be more careful, patted my head, bid us a good day, and left. It all happened so fast and matter-of-factly.

As far as I know, there was no discussion as to how I came to land on a stump by the roadside. He never asked Diane if I had run away or why. He never asked her why she hadn't reported me missing. He never asked why, if Diane knew I had a habit of 'sleepwalking,' she hadn't taken better precautions to prevent me from sleepwalking right out of the house.

Diane closed the door and watched through the window as the cop left. I didn't move. Neither of us spoke. But as soon as the cop was out of sight, she spun on me so fast I felt the sting before I saw her hand coming. She slapped me. Hard. I fell to the ground crying. I kept trying to tell myself, *Don't cry; don't cry,* because I knew she got off on making us cry. But it hurt real bad. So I sobbed, all the while trying to hold it in.

The other children were now awake, but afraid to come out of their rooms. Diane hollered, 'Git yo' stupid asses out here so y'all can hear this!' The others grimly marched out of their rooms and gathered around us. Diane liked to do things with an audience.

'Listen, you little bitch,' she snarled as she grabbed me by my hair and forced my face up toward hers, 'I hate a lot of things, but one thing I really hate is cops at my fucking house! Lucky for you, I didn't even know your stupid lil ass was gone. But the next time you call yourself 'running away' you'd better stay gone, because if and when you come back, I'm going to beat the shit outta you. Do you understand?'

'Yes,' I cried, and she allowed me to drop my head.

But then she angrily snatched my head back again, forcing me to look into her hateful eyes. We stared face-to-face for a moment before she slammed my head into the floor and stormed off. At first, I couldn't understand why I felt severe stinging in the back of my head. I looked up after her and realized why: strands of my hair were hanging from her still-clutched fingers as she walked away. The other children stood there, quietly staring at me and listening to me cry. Slowly they turned, one by one, and went back to their rooms. Crying and rubbing my bruised forehead and reddened cheek, I followed.

No sooner than I went to my room and laid down on my bed to try and get some sleep, she was ranting and raving about how dirty her house was and how lazy we were. She stormed in the room, told us to get our 'lazy asses' up and clean. I was exhausted. I hadn't slept in almost twenty-four hours and the booze and weed I'd done at Candy's had long since run out. Diane ordered me to start in the bathroom. I obeyed.

I didn't mean to go to sleep but I was so tired. I sat down to 'rest,' and didn't wake up until one of the kids came banging on the door screaming that they had to go to the bathroom. Luckily for me, Diane was still cautious of the police so she only cussed me out; she didn't hit me. We cleaned the entire house that day, same as always. By the end of it, I was too tired for my nightly reflection on the events of the last couple of weeks. It was the first time, since finding my mother dead, that I got a full night of uninterrupted sleep. One good thing that came out of the cop returning to me to Diane's was that, for some reason, he scared her – at least for a while. She was very calm for the next few days. And, for the first time that I knew of, she warned Pete to behave himself. Diane really hated police. Even though the cop took no report and in no way inquired into the situation at her house, for several days she nervously roamed from room to room, looking out the windows for something – what, I didn't know.

Shortly after the cop returned me to Diane's, I turned twelve. There was no party, no cake, not even a 'Happy Birthday.' Didn't matter, though, because my birthday was the same day Pete left for the military. I figured not having to worry about him anymore was my birthday present.

Diane's fear of the cops returning didn't last long. As time went on, her abusive rampages became worse and more frequent. Severe infractions got you beat with what Diane called her 'bull whip' – a stick wrapped tightly in leather with individual leather strands hanging from the end, small knots tied throughout each strand. Diane told us that the 'wonderful' thing about her whip was that not only did it hurt like hell, but it never left lasting marks. She said this was because the whip was made of 'special child-beating leather.' She regularly warned us that if we ever told anyone about being hit, they wouldn't believe us; and what's more, no one gave a fuck about us anyway.

And she'd fuck with our minds. We'd clean a room, but by

the time she got through with 'inspection' she had us thinking our crazy asses hadn't done shit. She'd be ranting and raving about dust and dirt being everywhere. Or she'd ask you to find something that she had hidden. For example, one day she started screaming and yelling that one of her precious teacups was missing from the living room. She warned that it'd better be found, and fast, or there'd be hell to pay. The foster kids frantically scrambled around trying to find it. Connie remained in her room, comfortably watching TV. The cup wasn't found that day. As punishment, we were restricted to our rooms for the remainder of the evening and weren't given any dinner. Later that night, as I passed Diane's room on my way to the bathroom, I heard her and Connie laughing at their game and the fear on our faces. Diane was holding the supposedly missing teacup and telling Connie she'd hidden it in Connie's room.

That bitch! Of course we'd've never found it. No one even thought to look in Connie's room!

When I returned to my room to tell the other girls what I'd overheard, they didn't believe me. They knew that Diane was crazy, evil, and manipulative. But for some reason, they felt that such a trick, if true, was just too cruel. I gave up trying to persuade them, deciding to leave them to their own beliefs.

We were regularly called 'fuckers,' 'bitches,' 'hos,' 'sluts,' 'whores,' 'lil mothafuckas,' 'black sons of bitches,' 'goddamn sons of bitches,' 'goddamn worthless fucks,' 'worthless pieces of shit,' 'useless fuckups,' 'foster fuckups,' 'good-for-nothings,' 'dumb fucks,' and anything else she could think of.

Diane often neglected to feed us, and since we weren't allowed in the kitchen ourselves (other than to clean), we sometimes went hungry. When we did eat, our meals were almost always beans and rice.

Though we rarely got meat, there was one way to get it. I discovered this trick when I'd failed to clean the hallway baseboards adequately. I'd worked all day and was starving; my stomach had gone from growling to howling. I was actually looking forward to the usual ration; so I was pleasantly surprised when, instead of beans and rice, Diane set a plate of chicken and rice before me. Ignoring the rice, I reached for the drumstick like it was water in the desert. I grabbed it and took a bite. It wasn't very flavorful, but I didn't care. I was eating meat, though very, very greasy meat. Grease was dripping down both sides of my chin like a waterfall. As I wiped it away using the back of my hand, I glanced up to see the other kids staring at me with what looked like horror. I stopped chewing immediately.

'What's wrong with y'all?' I asked. No one replied.

Forget 'em. I told myself. *They just jealous.*

Just then, I looked down at the drumstick. For some odd reason, the grease oozing from inside was red. Nervously, I looked at the back of my hand that I'd used to wipe my chin. It too had a streak of red splattered across it.

Red? Where the hell is all this red coming from? . . . Then it hit me. The bitch had given me half-cooked chicken. It was still bloody inside. I dropped the drumstick, spit out what I had in my mouth, and pushed my chair back from the table so hard it toppled over. As I ran to the bathroom, I heard Diane and Connie laughing. They had been standing behind me, watching me, waiting on me to discover their chicken surprise.

Once in the bathroom, I plopped down on the floor and stuck my head in the toilet. I hadn't eaten all day, so there was nothing to throw up. I sat there dry-heaving trying to free my mind of the image of eating half-cooked chicken. Once I was sure nothing was coming up, I flushed the toilet, washed my mouth and hands, and returned to the kitchen. Diane and Connie were still there, and so was the bloody plate. Diane pointed to it and told me that I had to eat it or go hungry. It was a hell of a predicament to be in. I chose to go hungry. Unfortunately, it wouldn't be the last time.

Diane's emotional abuse was especially painful because we all came to her already burdened with some kind of catastrophe or misfortune. One set of sisters from Oceanside had been removed from their home because they told a teacher that they were being molested by their stepfather. The rest of the story wasn't clear, but they said that the situation came to a point where the social worker assigned to their case told their mother that, if she got rid of the stepfather, the girls would be allowed to return home. The girls got quiet for a moment. One started to cry as the other finished telling the story. Without hesitation, their mother told the worker that she had never been without a man, was getting older and wouldn't be without a man; in fact, couldn't be without one. She looked the worker dead in the eyes and told her, 'keep 'em.' Several days later the girls were at Diane's.

We children had had enough despair and distraction in our lives. I missed my family immensely. I longed for my mom, to see her face, to hear her voice. I desperately needed guidance, support, and love – none of which was ever found at Diane's. Physical touching of any type was forbidden (other than Pete's). We weren't even allowed to hug or touch each other.

Connie, too, had her own forms of cruelty: she would use her status and approval as a means of turning the foster children against each other. There was a pecking order among us foster kids. Whoever was in Connie's good graces got promoted to special treatment. That person would get extra helpings of food (the good food that Connie and Diane ate), could play in the front yard (as long as Connie was with that person), and could even go into Connie's bedroom (where she had a big-screen color TV, a stereo, and every game a child could want). One word from Connie and her favorite could pass his or her chores on to some less-fortunate kid; or could at least escape a punch to the stomach from Diane for some random transgression.

As a result, the foster kids turned on each other and were in constant competition for Connie's friendship and approval. But I refused to kiss her ass. I acted like I didn't care whether she or any of the other kids liked me. Inside, I knew better. I wanted to be liked, longed for someone to love me. But I would not allow them the satisfaction of seeing that they were hurting me or that I needed anything from them. They may have suspected they were getting to me, but I sho as hell wasn't gon' show it.

7

One day, I was sitting on the floor in the den watching TV. I had resigned myself to the fact that I was stuck in this torturous hellhole, so my new strategy was just to pretty much stay out of Diane's way, especially since her latest trick was to tell me that I deserved what Pete had done to me because I was dark, ugly, motherless, and insignificant.

The other children were in the backyard playing – vying for Connie's attention. I never played much anymore. I wouldn't allow myself to chase behind Connie for her approval. Besides, I was usually too tired, too sore, or too sad. Out of the blue Diane came in, plopped her fat ass down on the couch, snapped off the TV, and slapped me on the head.

'You ain't never gon' be shit,' she sneered, ' 'cause you ain't got no mother.'

My mother hadn't been dead three months.

Damn bitch, I thought. *I'm in here minding my own business and here you come fucking wit' me!*

'Now, *Connie,*' she continued, putting emphasis on the name, 'She's gon' be something because she's got a mother!' With that, she popped me on my head again and walked out.

I just sat there thinking about what Diane had said. It got my blood flowing again. It renewed my determination to get the fuck out. Because, hell, if I wasn't going to be shit, I damn sure wasn't going to be it in Lancaster! I decided it was time to try to run again. Only this time, I'd do it right.

Diane enrolled me in school. I was grateful to be in school because it allowed me to get away from Diane during the day.

Connie and I went to the same school – which was 99 percent white – but we didn't hang out together. She referred to me as her cousin because she said that calling me a foster child was too embarrassing – *for her*. I didn't care what she called me as long as she stayed the fuck away from me.

Luckily, I'd found a couple of portals out of my life: booze and weed, thanks to Pete and Candy. I smoked and drank every chance I got. I loved being loaded. Everything looked and felt good when I was high – even me.

It's true what they say about birds of a feather. I quickly found other kids like me – kids who wanted or needed oblivion. One good thing about hanging out with kids who drank and smoked weed is that it didn't matter that I was black and they were white. The only color we all cared about was green – be it money or weed. Green was keen.

Buying booze was easy, even for a twelve-year-old. I just stood outside the liquor store and asked an adult who was going in to buy me some beer or whatever type of alcohol I wanted. If they agreed, and most times they did, I just gave them the money and waited for them to come out with the goodies. If they refused, I waited and asked the next person.

After watching my friends do it, I began shoplifting small things – purses, wallets, and cigarettes – which I would then trade for money or weed. I was really good at stealing cigarettes – which I'd also begun smoking. However, I never really had to worry about the money for my habits – at least not yet – because all of my friends got allowances and were more than willing to share what they had.

I started using my friends to unknowingly assist me in my plan of escape. From talking to them, I began learning about Lancaster and the nearby towns. Walking to and from school, I also started to figure out how to navigate my way around town. And my friends taught me that, by sticking out my thumb, I could go anywhere for free. One of my friends told me she'd heard that I had to be gone for twenty-four hours before Diane could report me missing (*if* she reported me missing), but she wasn't sure if that was true or not. I hoped it was, because it would give me at least a day's head start.

Although my friends knew my home life was fucked up, they never asked for particulars and I never told them (besides, we were usually so high, anything I told them would've probably been forgotten). I figured the less they knew, the better, because if anyone asked them anything, when they replied that they didn't know, they wouldn't be lying.

My friends gave good information about how to get out of Lancaster, but no one knew how to get to San Diego. They had heard of San Diego, but no one knew how to get there. It never dawned on us to look at a map. I figured I'd just wing it.

One night, while cleaning Diane's bathroom, I failed to polish the sink faucet to her satisfaction, so I got the whip. That damn whip was becoming my regular form of punishment. As I got ready for bed, my body stinging from the beating, tears streaming down my face, I knew it was time to go – again.

Just as before, I went to bed in my clothes. Around four in the morning, when I was sure everyone was asleep, I slipped out the window. Learning from previous mistakes, this time I grabbed a jacket on my way out. I felt more in control because I had a plan and I knew where I was going. I walked swiftly, but I didn't run. No need to. Diane wouldn't even know I was gone; and even if she did, she couldn't report me for twenty-four hours. I made my way down to the familiar stump – a welcome sight, because this time I knew that once I left that stump, I'd be leaving Lancaster.

I was glad I had grabbed the jacket, which provided adequate protection from the crisp morning air. I stood with my thumb out for an hour or so before a van finally pulled over. I ran to it and hopped in.

The van was empty inside except for a few tools strewn around the back. The driver was a thin black man, dressed in a cool tie-dyed T-shirt and jeans.

'Where ya going?' he asked.

I wasn't prepared for *that* question. I thought you just hopped in the car and went.

'As far as you can take me,' I replied. It wasn't a lie. I hadn't thought this part out. I figured I'd first get out of Lancaster and then worry about getting to San Diego.

'I'm going to Thousand Oaks,' he said. 'I'll take you that far.'

'Cool,' I replied as we pulled off. I didn't realize I was going in the opposite direction of San Diego.

We rode in silence for a few moments. He didn't ask any questions and I didn't talk.

'You smoke?' he asked as he pulled a joint from his breast pocket and lit it.

'Hell, yeah!' I replied. *Wow, what luck!*

'Good,' he said. 'I got some Grand-ma-yang too.'

I'd never heard of Grandma Yang, but if it made me feel good, I was down. The bottle he handed to me read 'Grand Marnier' but I guessed that it was pronounced 'Grandma Yang.' And, like everything else alcoholic I'd drunk before, I loved it.

Oh y-e-a-h! I said to myself as we continued to cruise away from Lancaster. *This running away and hitchhiking is all right!* I took another swig of the 'Yang' and another puff off the joint and congratulated myself on a well-executed plan.

A little while into the ride, the driver, who said his name was Bob, asked me if I was looking to make a little money.

'Sure,' I replied. 'What's up?' I thought he was talking about stealing something.

He looked at me, his mouth forming into a sly grin. He slowly took his right hand off the steering wheel and began rubbing his crotch area. As I glanced back up at his face, he was looking at me and licking his lips. It was then I realized what he wanted. He wanted what Pete had wanted, what Joe had wanted.

I sat there for a moment thinking about it. I hadn't done that since the night with Candy. In fact, I had pretty much put it out of my mind. Whenever it did come up, I'd get high or drunk enough so that I'd either forget it ever happened or didn't give a fuck. I'd surely never planned on doing it again. But now that it had come up, I remembered that it could be a way to make money. I had nowhere to stay and nothing to eat; I would need food and shelter. And I remembered Candy saying that nothing in life is free; no one was going to give me a job; and that no one gave a fuck about me, which Diane had proven. Still, I remained unsure – until Bob gave me another swig of the 'Yang.'

Fuck it, I thought as the liquid warmed my insides. *Whadaya got to lose? Besides, you gettin' the munchies!*

So I turned my second trick – with Bob. He wasn't violent or mean in any way. In fact, he was kind and gentle. He promptly paid me my money and dropped me off in Thousand Oaks, just like he said he would.

The lessons were clear: men want you only for sex; sex makes you money; money bought necessities like food, shelter, booze, and drugs; drugs and booze make life – and the sex – not so bad. Most important, doing *anything anywhere* was better – and safer – than just sitting at Diane's waiting for the next beating.

8

I'd never been in Thousand Oaks, so when Bob dropped me off, I plopped down on a curb, enjoyed my high, and checked out my surroundings. A gas station sat catty-corner across from me. What looked like a flower shop sat on one corner, a small market on the other. I looked behind me to see what was on my corner. It looked like a two-story office building. Since there were no apartments or houses in sight, I figured I was in some sort of business district. A couple of blocks away, I thought I saw a hotel sign.

Enough looking around, I scolded myself. *You gotta figure out what you're going to do now.*

I didn't know where I was or where I was going. I hadn't thought much about what to do, now that I'd successfully made it out of Lancaster. I pondered the question for another half hour or so. Finally, a little voice told me to call Jr.

I walked across the street to the gas station to use the pay phone. I picked up the receiver, dialed 0, and told the operator I wanted to make a phone call. She told me to put in a dime. All I had were the two twenty-dollar bills that Bob had given me.

'Do you want to call collect?' she asked. I didn't know what collect was, but so long as it didn't require coins I was for it.

'Sure,' I replied. She asked for my name and Uncle Jr.'s number and then put me on hold. A few minutes later when I heard Uncle Jr. say, 'Hello,' I started crying. I couldn't talk. I was so happy. All I could do was cry. We hadn't spoken since Mr Burns took us away because Jr. had no idea where we'd been taken, and Diane never allowed us to use the phone. I was so busy trying to survive, it never dawned on me to try to sneak and call anyone. But now, hearing my uncle's voice, I could let out all of the sadness and hurt I'd been holding in. He let me cry for a while.

Once I got myself together, he asked me where I was. I told him I was in a city called Thousand Oaks. I gave him the run-down of how Mr Burns had given us to Diane who had taken us to Lancaster. I briefly told him about Diane's violence, but didn't go into great detail. I didn't tell him about Pete because I still remembered Pete's threat.

Jr. listened intently. He was angry and wanted to call the police, but I told him not to, because they would only return me to Diane's, just as they had done the last time I'd run away. He asked about Larry. I told him I didn't know about Larry – it was everybody for themselves. He moaned when I said that.

'Cup, he's your brother.'

'Fuck him!' I screamed. 'I'm having enough trouble trying to take care of myself!' I began to cry again.

'Okay. Okay. Calm down.' He sounded distressed.

We decided he would send me some money through Western Union and I would catch a bus to San Diego. We'd worry about what to do with me once I got there. I gave him the name of the gas station I was at and the surrounding streets. He took down the number to the pay phone and said he'd call me back in a few minutes. As I waited for him to call me back, I again checked out my surroundings. I was sure that that was a hotel I saw several blocks away.

Maybe I could stay there.

There was also a park nearby.

The sound of the phone ringing startled me. I answered it. It was Jr. He said there was a Western Union about ten blocks from where I was. However, it would take two to three days for the money to get there. Jr. asked if I could wait that long and what I would do in the meantime. I lied and told him I had a friend who lived nearby but that the friend didn't have a phone. I also told him I had some money. He didn't ask about the friend or where I'd gotten the money. Thank goodness. My money was for drugs and booze. His was for the bus ticket. We agreed I would call him every day until the money arrived.

I didn't want to stay on the phone too long. I was concerned someone would notice me and call the police. But I didn't want to hang up either. Just his voice was comforting.

'I love you,' I blurted. I just felt like I had to get it out.

'I love you too,' he replied softly. 'And, don't worry. It will be okay.'

We hung up. Now all I had to do was lay low for a couple of days and I'd be home, sweet home.

I made my way to the hotel. It was a dump; but they still wanted twenty-five dollars a night! I had at least two nights to go until Jr.'s money arrived and all I had was forty dollars.

I decided to skip the hotel and headed toward the park. On my way, I bought some booze. Enjoying the midday sunshine, I was sitting on a park bench drinking when I spotted some white girls sitting in a car nearby smoking what I was sure was a joint. Without hesitation or shame, I approached them and asked where I could cop some weed. They gladly drove me to their connection's house around the corner where I bought a dime bag. We returned to the park, where I smoked a joint with them. (That's one thing about druggies, they'll gladly take you anywhere you need to go, if there's a high in it for them.)

I spent the next couple of days partying in the park, and the nights sleeping under park benches or the freeway underpass. As promised, I called Jr. collect every day. He didn't know that I was drinking and doing drugs. Still, he was concerned about my being out there all alone. But what could he do? We both knew if he called the police they would take me back to Diane's. And I swore to him that I'd just run away again.

Finally the money came. I walked the ten blocks to Western Union, but the little old white lady behind the glass counter said she couldn't give me the money because I didn't have I.D. I.D.!

'Fuck!' I yelled, 'I'm twelve years old! I ain't got no fucking I.D.!' I was pissed. I don't know when it happened, but at some point I'd lost the ability to control my anger. I was stomping around cussing and crying. The little old lady was scared, concerned, and confused. She said she wanted to help me, but the rules required I have I.D. After enduring a little more of my temper tantrum, she decided to call Jr. who vouched for me. Still, it took awhile for Jr. and me to convince her that we wouldn't sue her before she finally agreed to give me the money.

Jr. sent me one hundred dollars. I was rich! I asked the

Western Union lady to call me a cab. She said it wasn't something she would normally do, but seeing as that I was so young and obviously out of place, she agreed.

I stood outside waiting for the cab. It took only fifteen minutes to get there, but it seemed like forever. I was excited about going home, and ready to go. Finally, an old Mexican guy pulled up in a bright yellow cab. I hopped in, told him I was heading to the Greyhound station but we would be making a stop along the way. In broken English, he said he'd stop anywhere I wanted as long as I paid the waiting fee.

We stopped at a nearby liquor store. I paid the cabbie five dollars to go in and buy me some Mad Dog. I also had to pay the meter fee during the time he was in the store. I didn't care, so long as I got my drink. He dropped me off at the Greyhound station, where I drank the booze while waiting for the bus. Four hours later, I boarded a bus headed for San Diego. I had a long bus ride ahead of me, but I didn't care. For one, I was quite tipsy from the Mad Dog and would sleep most of the way. Second, I was out of Lancaster and away from Satan herself. And, most important, I was finally going home.

9

Jr. met me at the Greyhound station in downtown San Diego. I could tell from his bulging eyes and dropped jaw that he was shocked when he saw me. First of all, I was dirty (it never occurred to me that one should bring a change of clothes when running away). On top of that, my hair was a mess (nor did I think of bringing a comb). And, worst of all, I stank (I hadn't bathed in days because I'd been living in a park). He was happy to see me nevertheless.

'The first thing we're going to do is get you a bath!' he chimed as he gave me a big hug. He said he couldn't get ahold of my daddy, so my aunt Pam was going to keep me until they could figure out what to do. Aunt Pam was one of my maternal grand-mother's nine siblings. Finally someone from my sorry-ass family was steppin' up to the plate.

When we got to Aunt Pam's, she immediately stuck me in the tub. When she came into the bathroom to bring me a towel, she noticed the weltlike marks on my back. Although they were now fading, they were still visible.

'What are those?' she asked.

I couldn't see what she was referring to, but I didn't need to – I knew what she was talking about: I remembered the painful pounding of Diane's whip just a few days before.

'Those are from the whip,' I replied nonchalantly.

'The whip!' she screamed. 'What whip?'

I told her about Diane and her abuse. Aunt Pam scurried out of the room saying she was going to call 'the authorities.' After a while, she returned saying she had also called Jr. who was coming over to see the welts for himself.

'Why'd you call the authorities?' I asked.

'Because this looks like child abuse!' she screamed.

So that's what it's called, I thought.

When Jr. got there, Aunt Pam told him she had already informed the child welfare agency who'd said they were sending someone over. Jr. looked at my back and winced.

He tried to wait for the agency folks, but had to go to a mandatory meeting at work. Aunt Pam convinced him that she could handle the authorities by herself. It's a good thing Jr. didn't wait. It took them forever to send someone. The little white lady they finally did send wanted to know who had legal custody of me. Aunt Pam tried to explain what she knew – that I'd been given to my biological father who, in turn, had given me to a foster mother whom I had run away from. The lady interrupted Pam and told her that the first thing they had to do was determine where I legally belonged. However, in the meantime, because neither Jr. nor Aunt Pam had the legal right to have me, they would have to take me to Hillcrest Receiving Home. Hillcrest was a large facility in San Diego that housed children who had been abused, neglected, or abandoned.

Aunt Pam walked with me to the lady's car while telling her about the welts on my back. The lady never lifted my shirt to see them. She said that the folks at Hillcrest would 'look into it' as part of their investigation.

I hugged Aunt Pam before hopping into the car headed for Hillcrest Receiving Home.

I loved Hillcrest. It was like a big party. Tons and tons of kids.

Several days after I got there, Larry came in. It seems he, too, had run away from Diane's, though he refused to tell anyone why. Just as he'd done for me, Jr. sent him some money to return to San Diego. None of the other kids at Hillcrest knew Larry and I were siblings. We didn't feel or act like brother and sister, so we never told anyone we were.

Shortly after Larry's arrival, Jr. heard that the elementary school I'd been attending when Momma died was having its sixth-grade graduation ceremony. Believing that allowing me to see friends I'd grown up with would lift my spirits, someone (I don't know who) decided I should attend the ceremony. I was ecstatic – I'd get to see my old friends and my sixth-grade teacher, Mr Johnson, on whom I had a secret crush. I told Jr. I wanted to wear one of my mother's outfits to the graduation. I knew exactly which one too; one of her favorites: a red-and-white suit. Yup, that's what I would wear.

'Cup, you can't fit in her clothes,' he gently responded.

'I don't care! I want to wear something of my mother's!'

'Okay, okay,' he agreed.

After Momma's death, Jr. had moved all of our belongings (or at least what wasn't taken by scavengers) into his garage. Because everything was done in such a hurry, it wasn't organized in any way. So he spent hours going through box after box to find that red-and-white outfit. He brought it to Hillcrest, along with the red shoes and matching purse I'd told him about.

I thought I looked cute in my momma's outfit. The clothes were way too big, the shoes a lil high, and the large white vinyl purse way over the top for a twelve-year-old. Still, in my eyes, I looked like my momma, so I looked good. But when I got to the graduation, I was crushed. My friends didn't react the way I thought they would. In my mind, I had imagined a tearjerking reunion with everyone saying how much they'd missed me and how great I looked. Instead, they laughed at me. Even my two closest friends, Mona and Rosemarie (who we called 'Rose' for short) fought back giggles as they asked, 'What *are* you wearing?' They did at least say they'd missed me and were sorry to hear about my momma's death.

The other kids, though, were nowhere near as polite. They said I looked like an old woman. They laughed and pointed and whispered. Even some of the parents looked shocked at my attire. I heard one of them murmur in the most piteous voice, 'Poor thing, she looks so pathetic because she lost her mother, you know. There's no woman to dress her.'

I wanted to run and hide. Soon, my hurt turned to anger as the people I *thought* were my friends, the people who hadn't seen me in months, said nothing about my momma's death or my unexplained absence, and instead teased me about my clothes and how grown I looked. Life at Diane's had taught me how to put on a mask to make hurt and pain imperceptible. I'd learned that no matter how much someone hurt you, you never let that person know or see it. So, amongst the giggles and snickers, I squared back my shoulders, stuck out my chest, proudly walked across that stage (actually I wasn't used to the three-inch heels, so I more likely stumbled across it), and received my sixth-grade diploma.

A couple of days later, the court scheduled an 'emergency' hearing. Jr. had called Daddy to tell him what was going on, but neither of them, nor Aunt Pam, were allowed to go to the hearing. Larry and I weren't either, so I don't know what happened. What I do know is that one of the counselors in Hillcrest said the court needed time to 'investigate' things and check out my story. Since Hillcrest wasn't really a long-term facility, and because they were unsure as to how long the investigation would take, they decided to place us in foster homes in the San Diego area.

Another hearing would take place in a couple of months, at which time they would have decided what to do with us. But they couldn't find a home willing to take me and Larry together, so we would be put in separate homes (which was cool with both of us). What pissed me off, though, is that the court said that until it was decided where we would go, there would be no 'nonparental' visits, which meant that neither Jr. nor anyone else would be allowed to visit us.

Momma still hadn't been dead six months.

I was sent to live in a foster home in a small town east of San Diego. The foster mother who came to get me said her name was Mrs Bassinet. She was a short, plump black woman who wore a wig. It wasn't a very good one, because even I – a child – could tell it was a wig. She had piercing gray eyes and large, thick lips that opened into a wide smile. Mrs Bassinet lived in a nice big house, just like Diane's, except the Bassinets' was twice as big. It was two stories, and they had a pool in their backyard. I never knew any people who had their own pool.

Mrs Bassinet's husband was a tall, burly light-skinned black man with green eyes, who pretty much kept to himself. He didn't speak much, just grumbled a lot. As we entered the house, he grumbled a barely audible 'Hi.' The Bassinets had two boys of their own who were nine and fifteen. They also had two temporary-foster boys who were brothers.

Diane and Mrs Bassinet shared similarities other than their big, beautiful homes. One was their obsession with cleanliness. But the major difference between them was that at the Bassinets, *everybody* cleaned – at least all the children did. The only person who never cleaned was Mr Bassinet.

The Bassinets drank a lot. Every day, actually. Which meant there was always booze around for me to steal. And, because they stayed drunk, they were oblivious to what I was doing.

Mrs Bassinet wasn't as physically abusive as Diane, but she cussed us out daily something terrible. She'd talk about you so bad, you'd wish she *would* hit you and get it over with, because when she'd been drinking (which was all the time), she just wouldn't shut up. She'd talk about yo' momma, yo' momma's momma, and even *her* momma! She really did have a talent for making you feel like shit. 'Ugly lil black bitch,' she called me. I didn't need any help with feeling ugly.

Still, I felt like I could handle being at the Bassinets. I still had to clean like a slave, and I got cussed up one side and down the other all the time, but at least I wasn't getting raped and beaten, and I was eating okay. But I still hadn't yet seen the real Mr Bassinet.

Because I'd missed quite a bit of the sixth grade, the nearest junior high, La Pressa, thought I'd be more 'caught up' if I took some summer-school classes. I actually enjoyed summer school because I had great classes: English and choir. English was my favorite subject, probably because I was good at it without really having to try. And although I couldn't sing a lick (I couldn't carry a note if you put it in a bag), I still loved to sing. I also liked the mixture of kids at La Pressa – they weren't all white or all black.

Shortly after starting summer school, I decided to sign up to be a cheerleader for a children's football league. I'd heard they were accepting cheerleaders, and I'd always wanted to be one, so I thought, *What the hell.*

When I asked Mrs Bassinet, she screamed, 'Hell, no! You don't have time to be doin' no fuckin' cheerleading!'

Damn, she was mean.

'Let the girl cheer,' Mr Bassinet grumbled from behind his newspaper. He was sitting at the table. At first I wasn't sure it was he who spoke. He normally just walked around like a drunken mummy, grumbling under his breath. He never responded when Mrs Bassinet cussed him out (which was daily), and he never reacted when she cussed us out (which was also daily). All he did was drink and watch TV and, periodically, grumble.

I was shocked. I didn't know what to say or do. Mr Bassinet had never spoken up for me before. Not even the time when Mrs Bassinet had slapped me for failing to clean to her satisfaction. That day, as I lay on the floor sniffling from the blow, he walked right by me.

'Let her cheer, woman. It's not like she doesn't do enough around here. The least you could do is let her have some fun after school.'

He spoke very softly and very slowly, as if he were trying to convince her cautiously.

I just stood there. I didn't know what to say.

Obviously, neither did Mrs Bassinet. She just stood there, fuming.

'Fine,' she retorted. 'The lil bitch can cheer – if she can *get* there!'

What little hope I had was beginning to fade. Cheerleading practice was held at a football field a few miles away from the Bassinets' house. There was no way I could get there if no one would drive me.

'I'll take her,' Mr Bassinet replied. He was still speaking quietly and cautiously.

'Humph,' Mrs Bassinet snorted as she angrily hurled a dust rag at me. It smacked me in the face. Happy that she'd hit her mark, she turned and stomped upstairs.

I took the rag and began dusting the living-room furniture. When I realized that I was actually going to be a cheerleader, a smile actually started to crack my face for the first time since I couldn't remember. It looked like my luck was finally starting to turn around.

A couple of days later, Mr Bassinet and I were on our way to cheerleading practice. We were in Mr Bassinet's big yellow van. Vans were in back then and his was wildly fixed up. It had a small TV that sat in a specially made cabinet in the back. It had a jammin' stereo system with twelve speakers strategically placed around the inside of the entire van. It even had a lil refrigerator that housed all of Mr Bassinet's beer. Everything was covered in bright yellow fur – the seats, the carpet, the dashboard, even the steering wheel. I was so excited about cheerleading that I didn't even mind being in his gaudy old van. I was finally going to do something creative, something positive.

There was a Kmart half a mile or so from the Bassinets' house. I'd seen it a dozen times because you couldn't get to or from the Bassinets without passing it. Mr Bassinet pulled into the parking lot.

Maybe he's got to get something, I said to myself. *Maybe he'll get something for* me.'

But once parked, Mr Bassinet didn't get out of the van and go into Kmart. Instead, he climbed into the back and sat down on the couch that made up the rear seat. I stayed in the front, not moving. *Shit.* I knew what climbing into the back meant. I felt all of the enthusiasm drain from my little body.

'Com'ere,' he slurred. It was then I realized he was slightly drunk. Unfortunately I wasn't.

Obediently, I made my way to the back. He reached into his shirt pocket and pulled out a little pink pill. As he handed it to me with a beer he said it was 'acid or LSD.'

Which is it? I asked myself. *Acid or LSD?*

I'd never heard of either one, but Mr Bassinet didn't look like he was *asking* me if I wanted to take the pill. The frown on his face and the wrinkles in his huge forehead told me he was *ordering* me to take it. So I did.

As I swallowed the pill and chugged the beer behind it, Mr Bassinet stood up, unhooked his belt and pulled his pants and underwear down to his ankles. By now, I knew what that meant, so I started to lie down. But he stopped me. He grabbed me by my hair and forced me to kneel in front of him. He pointed his thing at me.

'Suck it.'

Was he kidding? No one had ever asked me to do that before. This was something new. I was pondering this odd command when he punched me in the jaw. The blow knocked my head into the refrigerator next to me. A tear trickled down my face as

I straightened myself back up. He grabbed my head and forced it down.

'If you bite me, I'll kick your ass!' he hissed.

It became obvious to me that my dream of being a cheerleader was just that. But soon it no longer mattered because the little pink pill began to kick in. All of a sudden my jaw stopped hurting and the horrible reality in front of me transformed into a lovely fairy tale. Suddenly, it seemed I was sucking a lollipop in a sunny, daisy-covered field! And the van wasn't a van after all. It was a beautiful giant yellow butterfly that was gonna fly me away from this wretched place.

Yup, I'd started trippin'.

We never made it to cheerleading practice. In fact, I never, ever went to a single cheerleading session. Instead, three times a week, when we were *supposed* to be at practice, we were in the parking lot of Kmart. Mr Bassinet said that our 'cheerleading practices' were okay because we weren't having sex. Since I didn't know any better, I believed him.

Besides LSD, Mr Bassinet also introduced me to cocaine, what I came to think of as white heaven. Indeed, in my encounters with Mr Bassinet, he always had plenty of weed, LSD, and cocaine, as well as a never-ending supply of booze – all for me and all at my disposal.

During our 'practices,' I would often marvel at how inattentive people can be. I asked myself if anyone else wondered about the yellow van that was frequently parked in the Kmart lot; if anyone noticed that no one ever got out of it and no one ever got into it. But the people continued milling around and about the parked van, going about their shopping tasks. No one ever wondered about the big yellow van.

It was during one of our practices that it occurred to me who actually gave me the name La'Vette. See, when Momma told me that 'Daddy' changed my name because he didn't like Cupcake, I thought she had meant *my* daddy – *not* Mr Burns – hell, I had never even heard of Mr Burns. But it was not my daddy; it was Mr Burns who'd changed my name from Cupcake to La'Vette. The same Mr Burns who caused me to be up in that van having 'cheerleading practice' with my forty-five-year-old foster father. That man was no father – he was an asshole, plain and simple.

Nor did he deserve the right to change my name. I made up

my mind right then and there that I would never refer to him as anything except *asshole* (although years later I also allowed myself to call him *sperm donor*). And I would take back my birth name – the name my mother gave me. From now on, I would use my real name – Cupcake. And, since La'Vette was the name chosen by the fucked-up asshole – who was directly responsible for my fucked-up life – I would use *that* name when I did fucked-up stuff. La'Vette would be my bad name, and Cupcake would be my good one. That realization was one good thing that came out of those cheerleading practices.

But there was another. Mr Bassinet began to stand up for me. He would no longer let Mrs Bassinet hit me or even cuss me. 'Leave her alone!' he would bark in my defense. I mistook his protection for love. In my mind, what I was doing *to* him was okay because, in return, he was doing something *for* me – protecting me. After attending a few practices, he cut down my chores so I wouldn't have to clean as much. And whenever Mrs Bassinet left the house, he'd let me ditch my chores and watch TV with him (though he never touched me in any way unless we were at practice). And when Mrs Bassinet returned and started fussing, he'd step up and tell her to 'get off it!'

Our 'practices' also afforded me a continuous supply of drugs and alcohol, which I had come to depend on – for sanity, tranquility, and confidence. Mr Bassinet also made sure I always had plenty of cigarettes. In other words, once we started cheerleading practice, Mr Bassinet took care of me.

I learn quickly. Mr Bassinet never had to punch me again during practice. I learned to do what he liked and how he liked it. But don't get me wrong – although I acted like I liked it, I was very much aware of how fucked the whole setup was. I was a twelve-year-old druggie and boozer that sometimes turned tricks, and whose only claim to fame was being good at cheerleading practice.

A short time later, I started my period. Although I knew what it was, I wasn't expecting it. I was at school one day when one of the girls told me I had something on my pants. I went to the bathroom to discover them soaked. The school nurse called Mrs Bassinet to come and pick me up. All the way home, she cussed me out because I'd 'messed up' my clothes.

A couple of days later at practice, Mr Bassinet told me not to worry about getting my period or about what we were doing. He said that since it wasn't sex, I couldn't get pregnant.

'Cool,' I said. 'But could you keep that bitch wife of yours off my ass?' I asked as I bent to snort a line of coke. He poured me another rum and coke and laughed. 'I'll do what I can.'

Our practices became parties of a sort. We'd get high and drunk and have bitching sessions about Mrs Bassinet – I actually began to look forward to them because it seemed Mr Bassinet hated her just as much as I did.

One night I was awakened by a policeman. He was gently shaking me and telling me to get up. At first I was disoriented.

What's a cop doing in my bedroom?

As my mind begin to clear, I could hear Mrs Bassinet downstairs yelling and cussing at the top of her lungs. Something about 'bitch, ho, slut,' etc. Nothing unusual had happened that day, so I had no idea what all of the fussin' was about.

The cop, a stocky white man, looked at me and said, 'Get up, sweetie, you have to go.'

'Why?' I asked.

'Your mother wants you to leave.'

'She's *not* my mother!' I retorted.

'Get up, get your clothes on, and get your things together,' he replied, oblivious to my outrage. 'I'll wait outside.'

It didn't take me long to get my things. I had left Diane's with no clothes, so all I had were the few outfits I'd been given while I was at Hillcrest. Mrs Bassinet had not spent one dime of the money she'd been paid for me *on* me. So my things fit easily into a paper bag.

I gathered my little bag and stepped outside my room. The bright hall lights hurt my eyes. The cop waited a moment, and then we made our way down the hall to the stairs. As we reached the end of the hallway, I froze. Glaring up at me from the bottom of the stairs was Mrs Bassinet. Her eyes were blazing red, and she was really drunk, really pissed, and screaming at the top of her lungs.

'Git that bitch out of my house! Git her out!'

Mr Bassinet sat on the couch, drink in hand, head down, not saying a word.

I didn't understand what was going on. She was so enraged. *Had she found out about cheerleading practice? But who told her?* Not me. I hadn't told a soul.

The cop's partner was at the bottom of the stairs, trying to pacify Mrs Bassinet.

'Now, ma'am,' he was saying, 'we *are* taking her. But, we need you to calm down.'

Mrs Bassinet wasn't payin' him any attention. 'Get that ho, slut, black bitch out of my fucking house! Git her out!'

I was scared that if they made me pass her, she'd punch me. I didn't mind being cussed out, but I didn't want to get punched. The cop must have sensed my apprehension. He took my hand, and we slowly began to descend the stairs. Mr Bassinet never looked up and Mrs Bassinet never quit cussin'. When we were four or five steps from the bottom, I stopped. The cop's partner took Mrs Bassinet's arm and moved her aside so we could pass.

As we approached the police car, I asked the cop if I could sit in the front. 'No,' he said, 'you have to sit in the back.' Although it wasn't my first time in a cop car, it was my first time in the back. The metal grate separating me from the cops made me feel like I was in a cage. We sat there; neither of us saying anything. A few moments later, his partner came out and we took off – back to Hillcrest.

I never found out why Mrs Bassinet was cussin' or why I had to leave. All I knew was that obviously *I* must have done something wrong to be caged and returned to the place for unwanted kids. I never saw the Bassinets again. Didn't matter. They'd left me with memories I'd never forget.

10

Back at Hillcrest, no one ever asked me what happened at the Bassinets' or why I had been put out. It was just like everything else that had happened in my life: shit happened and no one gave a fuck. I was getting angrier and angrier.

Someone decided it might be beneficial to have a psychiatrist talk to me and determine if there was any truth to my allegations of child abuse. The shrink was a short, fat white man. As I entered his office, he welcomed me as if I were an old friend.

Don't jive me! I wanted to shout. *We both know you ain't my friend and that you don't really give a fuck about me!* Instead, I shut my mouth and plopped down in a large brown leather chair. He gave me a wide, warm caring smile. The gentle and kindhearted way he looked at me gave me a glimmer of hope.

Despite my suspicions, I decided to give him a chance. I figured I'd tell the truth – one last time – to see if someone, anyone, could help me out of the hellhole my life had become.

I began to talk. I didn't mention the cheerleading practices. I figured, hell, if they were having trouble believing my stories about life at Diane's, they sure weren't going to believe what was going on at the Bassinets.' Neither did I tell the shrink about Pete, Candy, or turning tricks.

But I did tell the shrink about Diane's abuse and about my running away and sleeping under park benches and the freeway underpass. He listened with what looked like great interest and periodically jotted down notes. I began to get excited, like maybe he would do something to keep me from going back to Diane's.

Too quickly my time was up. As I got ready to leave, I asked to see what it was he had written. He said I didn't get to see what was in his report, but that he'd give it to the judge. I left feeling good about my decision to be half-assed honest. The good feeling didn't last long.

That bastard shrink went back and told the court that he doubted any abuse had occurred, and that, in respect for my 'father's' wishes, I should be returned to Diane's. He had an explanation for everything: that any marks I'd had were probably caused by sticks and shrubbery when I'd slept on the ground or under bushes. And that with Diane's impeccable record, it was doubtful that she had done the things I'd claimed. Besides, none of the other foster children in her home would confirm my story.

Based on the psychiatrist's report, Mr Burns's lies, and Diane's 'impeccable' Lancaster reputation, the decision was made that I would be immediately returned to Diane.

Although Mr Burns did show up at court (to lie), he didn't have the balls to come to Hillcrest to get me and take me to Lancaster. Diane herself came to pick me up. So accommodating. Heifer.

The ride to Lancaster was just like the first one. No one said a word. Diane drove the entire way without stopping. By the way she was driving, I could tell she was pissed. Connie was with her, sitting silently in the front seat in her new Nordstrom clothes. Spoiled little bitch. I was already thinking about how, and when, I'd run away again.

There were still four boys and four girls at Diane's. But, of the original eight foster children, six were new.

Because I was a repeat I didn't need the 'Don't be in my living room' speech, the tour of designated places, or the initiation punch (though that ain't saying much because sooner or later at Diane's you got punched). When we got to Lancaster, Diane took a nap. I went and sat in the den to get the 411 on what'd been hap'nin since I'd left: who'd run away, who'd got sent back to their families, who'd been beaten, tortured, or starved, and so on.

'Speaking of beatin's,' I snapped when the conversation had turned to that subject, 'why didn't y'all speak up when they asked you if she beat y'all?'

'Come on, Vette,' a girl who had been one of the original eight replied. 'You know how "the system" works. If we woulda told, they wouldn't have believed us. Hell, this is my fifth foster home and I've been hit in every one! But what does my social worker say when I tell her dey beatin' my ass?' She paused to make a snooty face as she imitated her social worker's voice: ' "Stop exaggerating!" or "You should be grateful someone's willing to take you!" '

'Besides,' she continued, in her own voice, 'Momma woulda beat us and you know it!'

I slumped to the floor because I knew she was telling the truth. Then what she said hit me.

'Momma?' I gasped. 'Why'd you call that bitch Momma?'

Seems Diane had instituted a new rule since my departure. Everyone had to call her 'Momma' – not 'Mrs Dobson' or 'Diane,' as it had been when I left. I didn't have to ask why. I knew why. It made her look friendlier and more charming, caring, and loving when the system came calling. But more important, it probably gave her a demented sense of pleasure because she knew how much we hated doing it. (She even got to the point where she made the children sign their school pictures to 'Momma,' *thanking her* for everything she'd done.)

'And, by the way, don't call me La'Vette anymore,' I announced. I figured now was a good time to reveal my original true name. 'My real name is Cupcake, and that's what you'll call me from now on.' I'd stood up and put my hands on my hips. My demeanor told them I was not playing.

'Cupcake?' they all chimed in unison. I steadied my legs, ready to pounce. If any of them said anything smart or shitty about the name my momma gave me, I was gonna pop 'em good.

'That's cute!' they replied, again in unison. I relaxed my stance, since it was clear they weren't going to try to talk shit about my real name.

'But don't tell Diane,' I warned.

'Momma!' they quickly corrected me while looking around, afraid she'd heard. 'Call her Momma. If you don't, she'll hit you!'

I'd forgotten the new rule just that fast. Didn't matter too much, though. Like I said before, no matter how hard you tried to be good, sooner or later, you'd get hit.

While I was away, some of the children had begun stealing food.

Since no one would own up to being the culprit (indeed, each child blamed the others), Diane put a lock and chain around the refrigerator. This wasn't difficult because the fridge and freezer stood side by side. So she just slipped a metal chain around the entire thing, brought it through both door handles, and locked it with a padlock. Only she and Connie had keys.

Diane's lock and chain around the fridge also provided Connie with another form of sick amusement. Connie's key hung on a gold chain around her neck. To taunt us, she'd walk around swinging the chain in a small circular motion. This was especially torturous on extremely hot days when we'd pass by staring at the fridge and freezer, knowing there was ice-cold water, sodas, and multiflavored Popsicles inside. This caused even more rivalry and dissension among the foster children because if you were in Connie's corner, you got to get stuff from the fridge whenever she did.

Connie had instituted a heinous and hateful trick of her own: 'hot foots.' One night she turned it on me. While I was asleep, Connie and two or three of the foster children (the ones who, at the time, were in her good graces) crept up to the foot of my bed and slowly, cautiously, and quietly lifted the covers. Taking a book of matches and tearing them off one by one, they carefully placed two to three matches in between each of my toes. Then, they lit 'em. I was slammed into consciousness by the pain of fire on my feet. I bolted straight up in the bed, screaming, crying, and waving my hands, shaking them in an attempt to put out the blaze. Connie and her crew howled with delight. Realizing that blowing at my feet with all my might wasn't working, I jumped up, ran to the bathroom and literally jumped into the toilet. By the time I limped back to bed, the culprits were rolling around on the floor, holding their stomachs, crackin' up laughing.

As the 'hot foots' became more regular and frequent, Connie's cronies learned to block the bathroom door to deny the burning kid access to the toilet where they (learning from my lead), would jump in with their flaming feet. On several occasions, bedding began to burn from the flames. To prevent this, Connie and her crew would stand by with a bucket of water to throw on the bed. This added to their fun because even if the bedding didn't catch on fire, they threw the water on you. Since we each had only one set of bedding, the victim would have to sleep on wet bed linen until it dried.

Now, more than ever, it was important to win Connie's approval. Since I refused to play her game, I got more than my share of 'hot foots.'

I fought back as best I could: I began sleeping with socks on, or with my covers 'double-tucked' at the bottom of the bed, or both. Problem with this strategy was that Connie and her crew would chill out on the hot foots for a couple of weeks, making you think the danger was over. Soon as you slipped up and forgot to wear your socks or double-tuck your sheets, they'd getcha.

Diane was aware of this behavior, and seemed to love it. She called it a game.

No one got hit for the first few weeks after my return. It seems Diane was worried about being watched. Whoever had questioned her about my accusations of abuse had obviously scared her – for a little while anyway. It wouldn't last long; didn't need to since she had several things working for her benefit: she was such a good actress and she lived in a nice big house. What's more, she was always willing to take children that were 'difficult to place.' Social workers loved her.

But about four months after my being returned to Lancaster, the system unequivocally confirmed it really didn't give a shit about me.

Diane had been ranting and raving about my failure to scrub the bathroom baseboards to her satisfaction. When I insisted that I had scrubbed them, she said I was talking back. She chased me through the house swinging that damn bull whip. I was fast, but not fast enough. She caught me and delivered a few good whacks.

A couple of days later, I happened to go to school. I was *enrolled* in the nearby junior-high school, but I hated school, so I usually ditched. However, for some reason, this particular day I decided to go. Unbeknownst to me, the school had been giving kids random medical checkups. It seems they'd kept trying to give me one, but I was never there. Somehow, word got to the nurse that I was present that day, so she called me to her office.

I took off my clothes, put on the little blue paper dress she'd given me, hopped up on the table and waited. Some friends had scored some killer coke and were just dying to share it with me, so I was hoping the nurse would hurry up and get the damn thing over with.

The nurse entered the room and began her exam. She checked my blood pressure, humming softly to herself. She used her little stethoscope to listen to my chest, periodically moving it here and there while instructing me to inhale, and exhale. When she removed the paper dress to listen to my back, she gasped.

'Where did you get these marks?' she asked.

Diane's recent whipping was fresh in my mind.

'My foster mother,' I replied matter-of-factly.

'Oh, my God!' she exclaimed.

Her outburst startled me. I hadn't expected her to care.

The nurse said she was going to call the police and instructed me to put my clothes back on.

When the police arrived, they spoke with the nurse while I waited in another room. I couldn't hear, but I could see them. The policemen were studying the nurse very seriously as if trying to decide if she were lying. I wondered what might happen – and whether my life would be any different from before.

Then, one of the policemen approached me and said that they were going to take me to Diane's to 'get my stuff.'

'Cool,' I replied, still unsure of what was going on, but a little pissed to be missing the coke party.

As we pulled into Diane's driveway, I could just imagine what was going on inside. I was nervous because I remembered how she'd reacted the last time a cop brought me home. Oblivious to my uneasiness, the cops walked me to the door and rang the bell. Diane opened the door and laid on her best 'mother of the year' charm, but I could tell she was nervous. She *looked* scared. One of the cops escorted me to my room to get some clothes while the other stayed up front, talking to Diane. The other children stayed in the den – scared to move. Connie was standing next to her mother, hands on her hips, visibly annoyed and glaring at me.

I don't think the cops ever noticed the lock and chain that hung around the refrigerator.

It wasn't until we left Diane's that I was informed of the plan. It seemed that the nurse suspected some type of abuse. The cops said policy required me to be removed while they investigated. So they were taking me to a shelter home.

The shelter home was in Simi Valley and was headed by a pleasant little Mexican lady named Maria who spoke broken English. Maria had four small children who also spoke broken English.

I didn't care about being at the shelter home. I had become desensitized to different homes, different cities, and different people. I had learned to make the best of where I was. Maria gave me half-cooked eggs for breakfast. At the time, I didn't know they were called over easy. All I knew was that they reminded me of Diane's half-cooked meat, and I just couldn't bring myself to eat 'em. Maria was nice about it and never forced me to. She was a great cook, though – she made the best chicken enchiladas I'd ever had.

Maria never hit me, and since she couldn't speak English very well, if she ever did curse me out, I didn't know it. I left the house every day telling her I was going to school, and then I'd hang out and get high.

One day a social worker came to see me. She told me her name was Cindy, and she was quick to inform me that she wasn't my assigned worker; she was just helping out with the overload. Maria had agreed to allow her house to be used only on an emergency basis, meaning she wanted to keep children only for a few days – a week at most. As I'd been there more than a month, she couldn't keep me any longer. Unfortunately, there was nowhere else to take me, or no one who was willing to take me. So Cindy said they had decided to return me to Diane's.

I literally gasped.

'What? Y'all just took me from her! Remember the marks on my back? Remember?'

Why was I the only one that could remember stuff? And I was the druggie! I couldn't believe what I was hearing.

91

Cindy had the saddest look on her face as she explained that their hands were tied: I had to be returned to Diane's because the nearest other available home was in another county, and for some unexplained reason, I couldn't be placed there. She said Diane had admitted to hitting me and supposed she might have been 'a little rough' when doing so, but strongly denied any abuse. With that half-assed admission, together with her foster-mother-of-the-year persona and her 'impeccable' record, they believed her. As far as I know, no one mentioned Hillcrest and the previous investigation or accusations of abuse.

'But,' Cindy said sternly, as if to make me feel better, 'we've told her that we'll be watching her.'

Y'all ain't been watching her! I wanted to scream. But I said nothing. I just hung my head in despair.

The next day, Cindy and a cop drove me to Diane's. I felt like I was going to the electric chair. I knew how much Diane hated the police, and thanks to that dumb-ass school nurse they'd now been there, again, because of me. Now, she'd get to make me pay for it; I'd get beat good for sure.

As Cindy and the cop sat with Diane in the formal living room, informing her that they would be watching her, and as the other children sat scared to death in the den, I slipped out the bedroom window.

I never saw Cindy again.

11

I ran with all my might. A house located at the bottom of the hill had hedges all around its backyard. I hopped the fence and hid under the hedges. I'd have to lay low for a while because it was early afternoon and still light outside. I couldn't hitchhike out of town till dark.

After a while, I could hear Diane in her new car with some of the the kids as they drove back and forth *pretending* to look for me. They were laughing and joking too much to be doing any serious searching. I stayed under the hedge till it was completely dark and I was sure that neither Diane nor any cops were still looking for me. Then, I quietly slipped out from under the hedges, hopped back over the fence, and made my way to the familiar stump.

I had no fear and no hesitation. I was angry.

'Return me to that bitch?' I shouted to the sky. 'Fuck you! I can take care of myself!'

I stuck out my thumb and quickly hitchhiked out of town.

Since running away the first time, I'd heard rumors about hitchhikers getting raped and beaten. I knew I needed to protect myself, so before leaving Maria's I had stolen a butter knife and put it in my sock. That was my 'protection.' Not a steak knife – a *butter knife*. What the fuck was I going to do with a butter knife? Still, you couldn't tell me I wasn't tough shit.

I caught a ride with a Mexican guy who took me to Ventura. I turned a trick with him.

I decided to hang out in Ventura. 'Hanging out' meant doing whatever came my way: hanging out in front of a store with newfound friends; getting high with whomever, whenever;

getting down with petty crime for more get-high money; *whatever.* I'd been hanging out in Ventura for a few days when my money got low, my doper friends had no moneymaking schemes to hatch, and no one was picking up hitchhikers. So I decided to steal something. My plan was to steal some cigarettes and beer from a small liquor store and just hang out. But the clerk was smarter (and quicker) than I thought. She caught me putting beer cans down my pants. She had her son hold me while she called the cops.

The cops arrived to find me sobbing uncontrollably (like Diane, I had become an excellent actress). I usually lied to cops and told them I was three to four years older than I really was, but this time I revealed my real age. I sang my sad story about finding my mother dead and having no family and no place to go. The cops felt sorry for me.

I thought they would let me go. But my plan backfired. Instead of releasing me, they called in my name to find out where I belonged and then personally returned me to Diane's.

I didn't bother begging and pleading with them not to. I knew it was pointless. So after two weeks of absolute freedom, I was returned to hell. And, true to form, Diane beat the shit out of me. Didn't matter. Almost immediately, I was gone again.

I never again mentioned Diane's abuse to anyone.

This became the pattern: every few weeks I'd run away. When I was caught, I'd be placed in a home in whatever city I was caught in. If no home was available, I was returned to Diane's. The first couple of times, I'd called Daddy collect. He would cry as he told me his hands were tied and that no matter what he or Jr. tried, everyone said there was nothing they could do. After a while, I quit calling Daddy. It was useless and I didn't want to bring my pain and trouble down on him.

Running away, turning tricks, and hitchhiking seemed to go hand in hand. Since my experience with Candy and Money, I would never again stand on a corner to get tricks because it was too risky. Money's threat to kill me if he caught me on one of his corners, and info I'd heard here and there on the street, convinced me that pimps would kick my ass if I worked their corner without being in their stable. Also, being young and of school age, I knew I was more likely to be noticed by the cops if I stood in one place for an extended period.

Besides, it was easy enough getting my tricks hitchhiking because most folks who picked up hitchhikers wanted to turn a trick. For me, hitchhiking ended up being a double bonus: I got to make some money, and I got a free ride, although I was never going anywhere in particular; I just wanted a ride that was going away from whatever home I'd been placed in. Most of the time, I also got a free high or drink. I was no longer ashamed or bothered in any way by turning tricks. I was surviving and doing what I had to do. If it did start to bother me, I would just get high. By now, I got high on *something* every day.

Running away so often made me learn the laws of the street very fast. For example, I learned it was best to sleep somewhere covered and not too out in the open because other homeless people would fuck with you or try to steal your shoes. I learned to eat cheaply – when I did eat – which most times meant half-eaten hamburgers out of the trashcan of McDonald's. I'd watched some homeless people do it. At first, I said, 'Ugh!' and turned up my nose at the thought. But, being hungry and with limited funds, I soon followed their lead.

Besides, I'd tell myself, *after the never-ending beans and half-cooked meat you've had to endure, these trash-can burgers are like steak!*

After that, I never felt much shame or disgust about it. I simply remembered that I was trying to survive. Anyway, eating was never my number-one priority – getting high was.

During these escapades, I learned about free clinics that gave free birth-control pills. Problem was, I stayed high so much that I had a hard time keeping up with them. I often forgot where I'd put them. Other times, I'd forget to take them, so I'd take two or three pills in an effort to make up for the missed ones. I figured it really didn't matter, though. I didn't think I could get pregnant. During my periods, I suffered horrific cramps and bled profusely – for days. I suspected that Pete had seriously damaged something inside me.

Diane never really seemed to mind my running away. It just gave her extra pleasure in mistreating me upon my return. And, I was always returned because I was a problem child. No one wanted problem children; they all wanted the cute children. I had long ceased being cute.

Nor did Diane fear any more accusations of abuse. The

system wasn't asking, and the children weren't telling. Nor was she concerned about my health or safety during my running episodes. Diane got paid very well for me and Larry. So as long as the system continued paying her for keeping me, even during my absences (and they did), she could care less about where I was or what I was doing. (I later learned that she got paid twice for me and Larry. Larry and I were entitled to social security payments as orphans. Somehow Diane figured out how to get those checks *and* the foster care checks.)

So, she didn't really mind my running away as long as she still got her checks. In fact, she stopped calling me by my name (when she used my name and not 'bitch,' 'slut,' 'ho,' 'darky,' etc.) and began calling me 'Runaway, Child Runnin' Wild,' after the title of a song by the Temptations.

Although Larry was also following this run away–return pattern, we always ran away and returned at alternating times. So once I left Hillcrest in San Diego, Larry and I never saw each other again.

12

You grow up fast living on the streets. Very fast. I walked differently and talked differently than the little girl who'd found her mother dead.

I didn't think of turning tricks as prostitution. I saw it as a job: it afforded me food and shelter. If I turned enough tricks, I could get a halfway decent hotel room; if not, I slept where I could. If I turned enough tricks, I could eat. If not, I resorted to 'trash can' burgers. Most importantly, turning tricks allowed me to buy drugs and booze that helped me forget my past, ignore the present, and be absolutely oblivious to the future.

I ran away so much that I got quite comfortable with hitch-hiking. I'd stick out my thumb like it wasn't shit. And I'd get into *anybody's* car. No fear whatsoever – I had my butter knife!

One day after a night of heavy drinking, I woke up in a strange place. I was very groggy, so it took me a moment to realize I was in a bed.

But, whose bed? I didn't know. I tried to remember the events of the night before. I couldn't.

I lay there trying to remember whom I'd been with and what we'd done, when I suddenly realized that everything around me was white: the walls, the floor, even the ceiling! I kind of thought I knew where I was; however, the thought became a certainty when a short white woman walked in wearing a white dress, white stockings, and white shoes.

A nurse! I thought, excited that maybe I'd at least figured out where I was. *I bet she's a nurse!*

I waited until she leaned in close to check my IV before speaking.

'Are you a nurse?' I asked meekly. My voice was low and squeaky, probably because I still felt very weak.

'Why, yes!' she said, obviously happy that I'd recognized what she was.

'Where am I?'

She responded that I was in a hospital. When I asked why, she explained that I was found passed out on the street in the wee hours of the morning. I never thought to ask *which* morning.

'What's wrong with me?'

She paused for a moment as if trying to decide what, or how, to tell me. Then, she softly responded that I'd gotten alcohol poisoning.

Alcohol poisoning! Crazy white woman. Wasn't no such thing. At least, I'd never heard of such a thing. Rat poisoning, yes. I'd even tried it on an enemy or two. But, alcohol poisoning? No way could alcohol be poison. Only a few sips and any fool could tell it was happy juice!

She was fussing and carrying on about how I was too young to be drinking.

'How old are you, by the way?'

I lied and said I was sixteen.

'Where did you get it?'

'Get what?'

'The alcohol.' She stared at me with a stern look on her face.

I said I didn't remember. It wasn't a lie. Then, she wanted to know my name. I told her it was 'Suzie Sally Smith.'

'Suzie Sally Smith?' she repeated. 'Your mom liked *s*'s didn't she?' She laughed at her joke. I didn't. As she began fussing with the IV bottle, she said that now that they knew my name, she could contact my parents and tell them where I was and explain what happened.

'I'm sure they're terribly worried,' she said with enthusiasm. I remained silent. She fussed with the IV bottle a little longer and then headed for the door. Just before she stepped through the doorway, she turned around and gave me a big smile. She instructed me not to worry, to get some rest, and that the doctor would see me in the morning.

Like hell he will, I snapped to myself.

I waited for her to leave and then yanked the IV out of my arm. I was too frantic to pay attention to the pain. I had to get the hell out of there before they figured out who I really was. I jumped out of bed and fell straight to the floor.

'Shit!' I screamed. Aware that I didn't have time to wait to get my bearings back, I crawled to the closet, hoping my clothes were on the floor or at least within arm's reach. Luckily, there they were piled in a heap on the floor like a pile of trash. I slowly got dressed, unaware that my shirt was on backward and inside out. By the time I'd got my pants on, my mind had cleared a little more. Slowly, I stood up, using the wall for support. Once I was sure I could stand, I staggered to the elevator. Amazingly, no one saw me. The nurses were too busy rushing to something the overhead speaker was announcing as a code blue. Once I hit the front door, I knew I was clear.

I trudged down the road a bit and stuck out my thumb. It wasn't long before a ride picked me up.

'Where you going?' the young white man behind the wheel asked as I hopped in.

'Wherever you are,' I replied.

After we'd ridden for a few miles, he pulled out a joint and asked if I smoked.

'Of course!' I exclaimed as I took the joint and lit it. I must have been out of it for a while because the first hit made me cough like crazy.

'You okay?' he asked, alarmed at my intense hacking. I nodded that I was.

'You need something to rinse it down,' he said as he reached under his seat and pulled out a beer. 'You do drink, don't you?'

I didn't even respond. I just grabbed the can and popped it open.

And they said I had alcohol poisoning! I thought as I took a long swig of the beer. *Bullshit! This stuff ain't poison. It's paradise!*

I didn't know what city I was in when I left the hospital. I didn't know to what city the driver I'd hitched a ride with was going. I didn't care about either. So long as I was *going*.

He drove for about a half hour or so. Unfortunately, he didn't want to conduct any 'business.' No problem. The next ride did.

I partied, hitched, and conducted business for the next few days. The last ride dropped me off in Hollywood – a place I came to love. At night, the streets were filled with people, young and old, hanging out and partying. There seemed to be a night-club on every corner, each with long lines of anxious partiers wanting to get in and get their groove on. But luckily for people like me, who either didn't have proper I.D., or didn't want to spend what lil money we had on a cover charge, there was always a free house party going on somewhere nearby. Nor were the parties limited to houses. Get a group of kids together and we'd party in the park, in the street, or behind a liquor store.

The greatest thing about the place was that runaways were everywhere. White kids, Mexican kids, and black kids, boys and girls, gay and straight. Some turning tricks to survive, others boosting for a living, some doing both. Some hoping to make it big in movies or music; others planning to get rich quick, though they weren't sure how; some chasing dreams, though they hadn't yet figured out what their dreams were. Regardless of their star-studded dreams or get-rich-quick schemes, they all seemed to get high, drink, or both. The police didn't seem to mind that so many unexplained kids were out at night. I mean, if they caught a kid doing a crime, they'd take him or her in, or if someone called the cops, they would come. But other than that, they didn't mess with us. We walked the streets at night without fear of being pulled over and questioned about why we weren't at 'home.' Maybe it was because they realized that trying to run us off was useless, or maybe they were off chasing real criminals. Most likely, it was because there were just too many of us.

Hollywood was a place where I felt completely free and totally uninhibited to be whoever I wanted, do what I wanted, whenever I wanted, for as long as I wanted. Still a 'bird,' I found those with like 'feathers' no matter where I was. So Hollywood and I partied hard. So hard, in fact, that the specifics are just a blur. I remember faces, but not names; party scenes, but not exact locations. One night I was smoking weed and guzzling tequila shots in an apartment with a bunch of long-haired hippy-looking white kids; another night I partied in a park with a group of gay Mexican and black boys. What I do remember is that I was having a ball. I was like a kid in a candy store.

One day a druggie friend invited me to a party that night that he promised would be jammin'. When I got there, I grabbed a drink, stood in the corner, and checked out the crowd. It was a nice mix – blacks, whites, a couple of Mexicans, an equal amount of men and women. There was coke in the kitchen and booze in the dining room. Once the dope kicked in and the booze told me I was feeling good, I decided I wanted to dance. But no one was dancing; everyone was standing around talking. I didn't want to talk. I wanted to dance.

Fuck 'em, I told myself. I began dancing by myself. It wasn't long before others followed my lead. The dance floor was soon crowded.

A man was standing up against the wall, chillin' and checking out the center of the living room where the crowd danced. Although I was in the center of the crowd, I was still dancing by myself. Jeffrey Osborne and L.T.D. were informing us that when they party, they partied hearty. I wasn't aware that the man against the wall had begun checking me out.

Once the record was over, it was time for another drink. I left the dance floor and headed for the bar – a long table covered with booze. As I passed the man against the wall, he grabbed my arm and said he liked the way I danced. I thanked him and continued on my mission to the bar. He followed me and we began to talk. His name was Tim. He was twenty-five. I actually told him my real age – thirteen. (I had become partial to older men.) He was a tall, thin light-skinned black man with light brown eyes and round thick lips. He wore his hair in a huge afro.

We hit it off immediately. We talked about all sorts of stuff: where we came from (he was from Texas, me from San Diego); our favorite drugs (he liked weed, I liked anything that was free); and favorite foods (his was hamburgers, mine was anything that was free). He said he liked my sense of humor and carefree personality.

I felt comfortable around Tim because he didn't ask too many personal questions, like where was my mom and dad, though he did comment that I looked and acted older than thirteen. He never asked me why a girl so young was at a party of obviously much older people. In fact, he only asked questions about superficial, immaterial stuff.

Another thing I liked about Tim was that he didn't try to have sex with me right away, probably because we were so busy getting high. Still, it intrigued me because that's the first thing men usually did. We spent the evening getting drunk and high, laughing and talking. I fell in love instantly, or what I thought was love (in my mind, if I was willing to have sex with a guy without expecting to be paid, it had to be love). I loved him for several reasons. First, he saw me as more than just a piece of ass. He asked about my hopes, dreams, and fears. Though I'd never actually thought about that kind of stuff, I thought up quick answers to give him. I told him I hoped to stay in Hollywood forever, dreamed of becoming an actress, and feared running out of dope. But mostly, I think I loved Tim because he said he loved me.

Tim lived with his elderly mother and hung out all day running his business, which was selling pills – uppers and downers – known on the street as black beauties, yellow jackets, and red devils. As his girlfriend, I got as many pills as I wanted – for free. I also loved Tim because what money he didn't use to 're-up' and buy more pills, he used to refill my arsenal of other favorites – booze, weed, LSD, and cocaine. Another great thing about Tim was that he didn't like the idea of me turning tricks, so he fed me and let me live with him so I wouldn't have to sleep on the streets. He'd just sneak me into his mother's house at night after she went to bed.

We lived this way – selling dope, hanging out, and getting high – for a little over a month. I loved my life in Hollywood and was beginning to think that maybe this was something I could do for a while.

One day, Tim and I were hanging out at a nearby liquor store. Because the store was so close to his house, he went there regularly to buy booze, so the clerks knew him and didn't complain about his hanging out in front. Most of his clients knew he hung out there too. It wasn't unusual for a client and Tim to take a walk around to the back of the building to handle business. We were hanging at the store, drinking beer, and talking shit with acquaintances who intermittently passed by when Tim told me that he had to go home to get something he'd forgotten. He didn't say what it was or why it was so important that he get it right then. I was sitting on a milk carton enjoying my buzz and the warm Southern California sun. I wasn't in the mood to move, so I told him I'd sit tight and wait for him to return. He never did.

A few hours later one of his clients came running up to me shouting that he'd just seen Tim get busted with some pills. Seems he sold some yellow jackets to an undercover. He was swiftly carted off to jail. Those sales and possession charges, along with a couple of outstanding warrants, meant that he would be locked up for a while. I had nowhere to go.

I was hanging out at a park a few days later, trying to figure out what to do, when some cops noticed me. It was a school day and I wasn't in school. They scooped me up, and before I knew what had happened, I was returned to Diane's. But this return was like no other before it. Before long, I was even happy about it.

13

I found nothing odd about the fact that I couldn't stand the smell of chicken being fried. Nor did I find it weird that I'd begun throwing up in the mornings and couldn't hold food down. At first, I thought it was a bug or maybe just a natural reaction to the nasty-ass food Diane shoved at us.

It was Diane who told me I was pregnant.

'Ya lil fast bitch!' she shouted at me. 'You done fucked around and now society's gonna be stuck with another worthless nigga chile!'

Pregnant? Me? I didn't believe her. I'd never thought of having children. I'd been having so much fun hitchhiking, hanging out, and getting high, I'd never seriously thought about getting pregnant. I figured it was my innate flyness that had allowed me to roam the state, forget to take my birth-control pills, and behave promiscuously with no repercussions.

Diane sent me to the doctor, who confirmed that I was indeed pregnant – almost three months. Although Diane lied and told the doctor I was seventeen (instead of thirteen), he was still shocked that I was pregnant so young. I was delighted at the idea that finally I was going to have someone who loved me and someone I could love. I decided it was time to start living right, because now I had someone to take care of, someone to look after.

Diane hated the fact that I was pregnant. She said I made her 'look bad' because we were one of the few black families in town, and, just as white society expected, one of us had ended up barefoot and pregnant. Diane wanted me to have an abortion. At first she tried to force me to have one. In fact, it wasn't until the abortion clinic told her that I couldn't be forced to do it that she finally gave up on the idea.

She took me to the thrift shop and bought me two maternity tops, but she refused to buy me any maternity pants. So I had to wear my regular pants, unzipped and hanging open below my quickly growing belly. She also immediately took me out of the regular junior high and put me in a school for pregnant girls. I didn't care. All I cared about was having and loving my baby.

I tried to call Tim, but his mom wouldn't accept my collect calls. One of my fellow pregnant school friends took me to her house and let me use her phone to call the county jail to see if Tim was still there. He was. I wrote a letter telling him he was going to be a father. I didn't hear back from him. But I told myself that I didn't care. The only thing that was important was my baby, and we'd be just fine without him.

Life at Diane's didn't change because I was pregnant. I didn't get more food, nor were my chores reduced. In fact, they were increased. She said I should do more because I had brought inexcusable shame on the black race. I didn't care.

I don't know what pissed Diane off more: the fact that I was pregnant or the fact that I was happy about it. She absolutely abhorred seeing me exhibiting any kind of joy. And, in a perverse sort of way, her displeasure added to my happiness. I loved being pregnant. I started going to school every day, and for the first time since I was eleven years old, I didn't drink and only smoked weed.

Around my sixth month I finally heard from Tim. He was out of jail and ecstatic about our baby. He promised to get himself together and help me and the child. He said his mom was sending him to Texas because L.A. was nothing but trouble for him. He said that once he got a job and a place to stay, he'd send for us. Diane said he was 'full of shit.' But I believed him. I had to. His interest in the baby gave me renewed hope of finally leaving Lancaster forever. More important, his declared love for us invalidated Diane's put-downs of black men as worthless men and irresponsible fathers. He promised to call again. I would sit by the phone, staring at it, waiting for it to ring, and, when it did, hoping it was Tim. But it never was.

* * *

I was six months pregnant when Diane unleashed her worst abuse on me to date, though physically *she* never did a thing.

Diane, Connie, and the other three foster girls were standing around in the garage talking, when Diane called me out there. I thought nothing of it. I figured she probably wanted me to clean something (when she got in a cleaning frenzy, no area was off-limits – not even the garage). As I waddled toward them, Diane stepped back, leaving Connie and the three foster girls facing me in a semicircle.

'What's up?' I asked as I waddled closer.

'This, bitch!' One of the girls screamed as she drew back her arm with all her might and slammed it forward into my stomach. The surprise coincided with the intense pain I felt. The blow knocked me to my knees.

'You think you all that, bitch?' another shouted as she socked me in my back. Stinging rays of pain rushed up my back.

Partly from pain and partly to protect myself, I doubled over as all three began throwing punches. It took a moment for me to realize that I was actually being jumped. Once I realized this was an all-out fight, I tried to fight back, but with four on one, and me with a bulging belly, I didn't have a chance. My swinging was awkward, and none of my punches were reaching anyone.

Conceding that fighting back was useless, I focused instead on trying to protect my baby. The blows were too fast and too hard. As my knees gave way, I fell to the ground, still trying to guard my stomach by wrapping my arms around it as far as I could. The blows came faster and harder, pounding my forehead, my cheeks, my neck. *Protect your head!* I screamed to myself. *Protect your head!*

I decided to try to curl myself into a ball, to help protect both my stomach and my head. Before squeezing my head into the fold of my now agonizingly throbbing body, I caught a glimpse of Diane standing back, hands on her hips, watching, a contemptuous grin stretched across her face. Bitch. That peek cost me a punch to the ear.

I quickly tucked my head into the fold of my fetal position and cried as they continued to beat me: kicking my body, clawing at my face and hair, punching at will, until Diane finally announced, 'That's enough.' And then, as suddenly as they began, they stopped. They stood around me, panting and out of breath from the energy they'd exerted beating my ass. Then, as if nothing had happened, they casually strolled out of the garage, laughing and talking as if chatting about a good movie they'd just seen. They left me lying there, still on the ground, doubled over in agony, every part of my body pulsing with pain. But I wasn't so concerned about that; I was worried about my baby. I lay there for a while crying. I felt beaten in every way – physically, mentally, emotionally.

As I lay there, my pain slowly turned into anger. I was pissed because I knew that Diane had the girls jump me at a time when I couldn't fight back. I'd've kicked some ass if I hadn't been pregnant, but they knew that. Running away, hooking, doing drugs and alcohol had given me a badass attitude: get me drunk or loaded and I'd fight any kid. And I was always talking shit. I talked shit so good, folks figured I had to be able to back it up. So Diane and her crew had waited till I was vulnerable, till I couldn't defend myself, and that's when they struck. Scary-asses.

I lay there for what seemed like forever, though it was only a couple of hours. I slowly got up, expecting to feel pain in my stomach. But there was none. Although every other part of my body hurt like hell, my stomach didn't. I began to think maybe the beating I had taken had missed my baby. I got up and began walking (or rather waddling) very slowly and bent over like a hunchback – unable to stand up straight because of the pain racing up my back. Each step felt like knives were shooting up and down my body. I had to pass Diane and the girls as I walked through the kitchen. They were eating the 'good food' – a reward for their performance.

I was in too much pain to care. I just wanted to get off the cold garage floor and lie down. I could still hear them laughing as I waddled down the hall and into my room.

'Did you see that punch to her stomach?' Connie bragged as I closed the bedroom door and began to slowly inch my way toward my bed.

A few seconds later the door swung open, the sound of it slamming against the wall startling me.

'Don't you close no doors in my fucking house!' Diane screamed, stepping into the doorway. She stood there for a

107

moment sporting an evil grin and savoring my pain. Then she turned and rejoined the party in the kitchen. I watched her leave before lying down – unsure if she'd gotten in the mood to continue the beating herself. As I lay down oohing and aahing from the pain of each movement, I looked after her and wondered how so much evil could be in one person.

I had been asleep a few hours when I was suddenly awakened by a sharp pain in my stomach. I was used to the extreme cramps I suffered during my period. But this pain was *ten* times as bad. I awoke with a scream.

'Shhh,' one of the girls said.

Sometime during the night, they had crawled into their beds. Since the beating, none of the girls had spoken a word to me, except periodic snickering. They'd spent the evening enjoying Diane's approval.

'Yeah, bitch, shut it up,' another snapped as she turned over to go back to sleep.

I couldn't keep quiet. The pain was horrific. I got up and waddled to the bathroom. I was starting to panic because I knew something was wrong. Once I got to the bathroom, I felt like I had to pee. I sat on the toilet hoping to be able to hurry up and pee so the pain would let up. But instead of pee, a large clot of blood plopped out and landed in the toilet. 'Oh, no!' I screamed. Something was terribly wrong.

Without thinking (or out of habit), I flushed the toilet.

I didn't care about waking everybody up. I didn't even care about Diane being pissed. I was more concerned about my baby – about the only thing I had that was going to love me. I waddled into Diane's room as quick as I could and flicked on the lights (something I would have never done before, but like I said, I didn't care anymore).

'Something's wrong with my baby!' I screamed. 'I've got to get to the hospital!'

'Stop your fucking whining!' she shouted as she slowly sat up. 'Ain't nothing wrong with you!'

'Yes it is!' I shouted. 'I'm bleeding!'

I was hysterical. I was crying. I was angry. I was hurting.

Connie was now awake. 'What's goin' on?' she asked, as she

came walking down the hallway into her mother's room, rubbing sleep from her eyes.

'The lil whore is sick,' Diane chimed in a whiny voice.

For the first time, I stood up to her. 'If you don't take me to the hospital, I'll tell them what happened!' I shouted. 'I'll tell them that you let me lay here, knowing I was pregnant and hurt! I swear I will!' I was screaming and spitting a mixture of tears and snot. I was panicked and scared out of my wits.

Maybe it was the hate in my eyes that convinced her I meant it. Maybe it was the thought of police at her house that made her decide to move. I don't know what it was, but suddenly she told Connie, 'Get your clothes on; we're gonna take her to the hospital.'

'Shit,' Connie mumbled as she slowly returned to her room to get dressed.

The pain was so great, I could no longer stand, and I was still bleeding profusely. Diane didn't want blood on her carpet, so she made the other girls help me onto the porch where they had laid sheets. Meanwhile, Diane and Connie took their time getting ready. Even after the girls half-carried, half-dragged me to Diane's car, we still couldn't leave. Diane didn't want blood all over her new car, so the other girls had to lay several sheets on the floor of it before I was allowed to crawl in. I had to lie on the floor because we couldn't risk getting blood on the seats.

Finally, we headed for the hospital. But at the speed Diane drove, you would have never known there was a pregnant, beaten, bleeding child in the back. You would have thought we were early for Sunday school.

When we finally arrived, in between screams of pain, I told a nurse about the lump of blood that had come out in the toilet. That was the last time I spoke to anyone on the hospital staff. Diane angrily informed them that I was a minor, so all communication needed to be with her, my legal guardian. I didn't know if that was true or not, but the doctors and nurses obviously believed it because all the information I got from then on was relayed by Diane.

In between my outbursts, Diane told me that the hospital said they couldn't take me because they didn't have the proper equipment (she never explained what equipment), and that the only hospital with the necessary equipment was thirty to forty-five minutes away. Diane said we'd never make it.

'Besides,' Diane continued, 'they said you're already through most of it. So, the best thing to do is wait and let you do the rest naturally, because really there's nothing left to do.' She added that the doctor had said the mass lump that had come out into the toilet back at the house was probably part of the baby, so there was nothing to be done.

They put me on a gurney and let me lie there to finish what nature had begun.

Nature didn't do this to me! I wanted to scream in between blasts of pain. *That sick, demented black bitch and her little shits did this to me!*

But I didn't. I was in too much pain. And what good would it do? Diane was right: I 'wasn't gon' never be shit' because I didn't have a mother. Candy was right: nobody gave a fuck about me. And I was right: God sucked. All of this was His fault. I hated Him now more than ever.

As I lay there, bleeding and writhing in pain, I sobbed – partly from the physical pain and partly from knowing that I had lost the only thing that might have loved me. Then, my pain turned to anger. I got angrier and angrier. Whatever 'straightening out' I had previously resolved to do for the sake of my baby vanished. Because now, I had nothing left to live for.

14

I don't think I was ever formally admitted to the hospital. I was never put in a hospital room. As far as I know, no one questioned Diane about the black eyes, bloody lips, and bruises that were clearly visible from my recent beating. I lay on the gurney until the pain stopped. Then, I got up and went home. Just like that. The whole ordeal – from the pain that first woke me to the time I walked out of the hospital – took less than twenty-four hours.

Neither Diane nor Connie said a word to me as they drove me home. Their looks of guilt and shame spoke for them. Diane and the others had to know that beating up a pregnant girl would seriously harm or kill the baby. Yet, for some reason, now they wanted to feel bad about it. Diane tried to ease their part in the ordeal by commenting that, if at six months pieces of my baby plopped into the toilet, it must have been abnormal anyway. She said the doctor surmised that, if I had carried the baby to full term, it would have probably been deformed or even stillborn. She spoke very quietly and slowly, like this piece of information would make me feel better.

Any guilt they had did *me* no good. My baby was dead. I was angry and plotting revenge. Actually, I was plotting murder. They had murdered my baby, so they all deserved to die. But to kill them, I'd have to get them to let their guards down. So although I was livid, I acted like everything was okay; like I held no grudge. I decided to kill Diane first.

Everyone was nice to me the first couple of days after my miscarriage. No one said much; I wasn't even cussed out. And for the first time since I had come to Diane's, I was excused from cleaning. Everyone walked around on tiptoe and spoke to me quietly and cautiously, as though I were a little dense. They treated me like a fragile doll capable of breaking at any moment. They didn't realize how accurate they were.

I had been trying to figure out how I could kill Diane without anyone suspecting me. After a few days, it came to me. I'd kill her as I'd once tried to kill Larry – I'd use poison.

The next day, I was lying in my bed crying on the inside about the murder of my baby. I could never again cry on the outside because to do so would have given Diane great pleasure in knowing the ordeal had truly gotten to me. So I mourned on the inside, and wore the 'fuck-you' mask on the outside.

I got up to use the bathroom. As I shuffled past Diane's room, I looked in and saw her sitting comfortably in her large plush bed, watching her large color TV. I decided it was a good day for her to die.

Fortunately for me, Diane was still pretending to be full of pity. So she suspected nothing when, on my way back from the bathroom, I offered to get her a glass of Kool-Aid. It was a hot day, and Diane was clearly burning up from thirst, so she readily gave me permission to enter the kitchen. She gave me her key to the fridge and told me I had five minutes to get her Kool-Aid.

I had to act fast.

The other children were in the den, suffering through the heat. I didn't know where Connie was, but so long as she stayed the fuck away from me, I could care less. My momma had always kept the rat poison under the kitchen sink. I hoped that was where Diane kept hers because I wouldn't have time to search for it.

It was my lucky day. The box was sitting right there under the kitchen sink. I grabbed it and quickly filled a glass half full with the yellowish powder. I added some hot water to dissolve the granules and quickly stirred it. Then I unlocked the padlock, removed the chain, got the Kool-Aid, and filled the rest of the glass with it. I dropped in a few ice cubes, wrapped the chain back around the fridge, closed the lock, and walked back to Diane's room, with revenge in one hand and the refrigerator key in the other.

112

Diane thanked me for the Kool-Aid, but instead of drinking it, she set it on the nightstand next to her. *Shit,* I thought. *Drink it!* I stood there staring at the glass, wishing she'd drink it, when she noticed I was still there.

'Can I help you?' she snapped.

'No,' I replied as I slowly backed out, watching her until she was out of sight. I don't know if she ever drank it. Maybe my behavior was too suspicious. Maybe, as Larry had done, she'd gotten a clue from my uncharacteristic desire to help. What I *do* know is that she never got sick, and she never said a word to me about it. And, worse, she didn't die. But I wouldn't wait for another chance. I promised myself that the latest ass-whuppin' I'd taken would be the last one.

A few weeks after my miscarriage, Tim finally called. He was in Texas and said he was having a 'good ol' time.' When I thought no one could hear me, I whispered to him that I'd lost the baby. He sounded sad, but when I told him that Diane made Connie and the other girls jump me, he didn't believe me.

'Who would do such a thing?' he asked.

Why would I lie about a thing like that? When I first met Tim, I'd told him about Diane and her violence. At the time he believed me; he'd suffered abuse from his own father. But now he thought siccing a group of girls on a pregnant girl was just too unbelievable.

'Maybe they were just playing,' he continued. 'Maybe they didn't really mean to hurt you, but somehow during y'all's wrestling it got out of hand. Nobody could be that mean. That's just downright evil.'

I was sick and tired of telling folks about this crazy woman and no one believing me.

This bitch is evil! Get your head out of your ass! Wake the fuck up! This is real! This shit is real!

But, I couldn't respond. Diane had come and stood in the doorway, staring at me intently as she listened to my conversation.

Tim was still making empty promises about coming to get me, but I no longer cared. I didn't care about anyone or anything – not even myself. Still, I didn't want Diane to know she'd been right about Tim. She had always said that black men

113

'weren't shit,' and that since Tim was a black man, he would never come through for me because he was doing only what all black men did: talk shit. So although I wanted to cuss him out and tell him to kiss my ass for not believing me, I didn't. Instead, I looked Diane dead in the face, smiled, and said, 'Okay, baby, I'll see you when you get here,' and hung up. I never saw or spoke to Tim again.

The conversation with Tim made me abandon any hopes of killing Diane, because I realized that if I got caught, no one would believe me about the things she'd done. Hell, Tim was my man and he didn't believe me. The judge in San Diego didn't believe me. Social workers didn't believe me. With my luck, if I did kill her, I'd just end up in jail; so she'd still win. I decided I wasn't going out like that.

It didn't take long for Diane to return to her old self. Not long after my conversation with Tim, Diane decided she needed to do something about me because she said I 'wasn't gon' bring no more black ghetto bastards' into the world. So she took me to a free clinic and forced me to get an IUD. At first, I didn't know what an IUD was. I sat there as she completed all the paperwork and answered all the doctor's questions. It wasn't until I was screaming from the pain of having the IUD inserted inside me that the doctor told me what it was. 'It's a form of birth control,' he said. 'But unlike the pill, now that it's inserted, there's nothing more for you to do – ever.'

At first I was pissed at Diane. But I soon got over it, because it meant that now I could really run the streets and not worry about remembering to take my birth-control pills, *finding* the damn things, or getting pregnant. And since it was time for me to run again, that would be a plus.

The next night, I slipped out the window and hitchhiked out of Lancaster. I was standing on the side of the highway where my previous ride had dropped me off. I had no idea where I was, nor did it really matter. I stuck out my thumb and waited for the next ride to pick me up. A white car pulled over and a white man told me to hop in. I did.

'Where ya goin'?' he asked as we pulled into traffic (the usual question).

'As far as you can take me' (my usual reply).

We rode for a while in silence. Then, out the blue, he told me he was a cop. He just announced it – just like that. At first I didn't believe him. He wasn't in a police car, he wasn't wearing a uniform, and I couldn't see a gun.

'You don't look like no cop.'

He said his car was unmarked, and that his gun was in a holster under his jacket.

Shit, I thought when I realized he really was what he said he was. It crossed my mind to jump out, but the car was moving too fast.

I asked him if he was going to take me to jail or, worse, to a foster home. He said he wasn't interested in taking me to jail *or* any foster home. Turns out, he was interested in having 'cheerleading practice.'

It no longer shocked or bothered me that men – young and old alike – wanted young girls. I had been turning tricks since I was eleven – always with older men who willingly paid extra *because* of my age. Nor did it shock me that this one was a cop. In fact, I never really thought twice about it because, hell, I figured a cop's money would spend just like anyone else's.

We pulled over on a small, quiet street and, after he removed his holster, we had cheerleading practice in his car. Afterward, he paid me twenty dollars and took me to the county line. I got out, stuck out my thumb, and waited for the next ride.

I continued to hitchhike and turn tricks for a few months. I also added a new drug to my arsenal – methamphetamine, more commonly known as crystal. A white boy had picked me up somewhere near Oxnard and said he was headed for Beverly Hills. Since I rode with the ride and went where the ride went, I went with him to Beverly Hills.

At some point in the ride, he pulled over at a liquor store to get some beer. When he returned, I lied and said that it was my birthday. 'Well, that calls for a *special* celebration,' he said as he reached into his shirt pocket and pulled out a small folded piece of white paper. As I watched with interest, he carefully unfolded the paper, used his pinkie fingernail to scoop up some of the white powder inside, and sniffed. I'd done coke before, so I figured that's what it was. It was white like coke and powdery like coke. But when I sniffed the powder from his pinkie nail, my eyes watered and my nose burned. Coke never burned like that – and I'd had the best of the best. I grabbed my ears and pushed them tight against my head in an attempt to suppress the burning.

'Fuck!' I yelled. He quickly snatched the paper away so the powder wouldn't spill or my breath blow it away. 'What is that shit?' (I'd *do* the drug and *then* ask what is was.)

He started laughing. 'It's crystal, girl. You ain't never had no crystal?'

Nope. That was my first time. But as the burning sensation in my nose began to disappear, and as my heartbeat started to speed up, I knew this would not be the last time.

The ride ended on Rodeo Drive. I had no idea about Rodeo Drive or where it was. I vaguely remembered folks talking about it when I was with Tim, hanging out in Hollywood. But I was loaded and couldn't quite remember what the hype about it had been. I didn't have to stand there long before another car pulled up. A nice Mercedes.

That's my claim to fame in Beverly Hills: I turned a trick on Rodeo Drive.

I finished my fame on Rodeo Drive, copped some vodka and orange juice, and stuck out my thumb to catch the next ride. To where? Didn't matter. Long as I was heading south, I was heading away from Lancaster. I was standing in the middle of the street with my thumb stuck out when a cop pulled over. Normally I would've run, but I was drunk, so it took a moment for my brain to register that he was a cop.

He asked my name. Although I had made a vow to use 'La'Vette' as my bad name and 'Cupcake' as my good one, lately I had begun to confuse the two. Right now, I was so drunk that I'd forgotten which one I was supposed to be.

Don't matter, the booze said.

(You know that alcohol talks to you, don't you? Sure it does. Who do you think convinces the drunk man that he drives better drunk? Who do you think convinces the drunk husband that he should beat the shit out of his wife because she's fucking around on him, or plotting to leave him or kill him? Alcohol! It talks to you. It says, *Go ahead, drive the car! You can see better now than you ever did!* Problem, though, is that it turns on you. Yup, sure does. Once it convinces you to do something idiotic, reckless, dangerous, or stupid, that same voice snickers, *Ooooooh, YOU done fucked up now!*)

The vodka was telling me: *Fuck him. Give him any name – just be sure to end with* asshole.

'Cupcake, asshole!' I bellowed. I tried to get up in his face, but the booze caused me to lose my balance and almost fall on him. Luckily, he caught me.

He was not amused.

'Oh, my God, girl. You're drunk!' He was utterly disgusted. 'All right, young lady, let's go,' he said as he grabbed my arm and half led, half dragged me to his car.

I was cussing him out the whole way. The booze was telling me, *Fuck him! He can't do this to you. Talk about his momma!*

So I did. I talked about his momma, calling her every bad name I could think of.

That's right, the booze egged me on. *Now call him a short white bastard!*

I don't think the cop was really bothered by my talking about his momma, he just ignored me. But I think the reference to his height pissed him off, because he roughly snapped on cuffs and harshly tossed me into the back of his car. As he angrily drove off, the same booze voice that convinced me to curse the cop now, unpredictably, turned on *me*.

Ooooh, you done fucked up now!

I slumped into the seat as I realized the mess I had gotten myself into. My high quickly vanished.

While he drove, the cop kept glancing at me in his rearview mirror. His anger seemed to gradually dissipate as he realized what he was looking at – a drunken *child*. He must have had a change of heart. He pulled over and softly said, 'I'm going to ask you one more time, 'what's your name?' '

Now that I'd sobered up a little I'd remembered which name I was supposed to be – the bad one.

'La'Vette,' I replied, 'La'Vette Burns.'

While he radioed my bad name in, I fell asleep. He awakened me and told me he was going to do me a favor. Instead of taking me to juvie where we were initially heading, he was going to take me to a shelter home that kept children on an emergency basis. He said that a Mrs Dobson had reported me missing. He and whoever he'd talked to decided that instead of taking me to jail I should be returned to Lancaster, apparently with no questions asked.

As we drove to the shelter home, he gave me a long, boring talk about how I didn't belong in the streets, how I shouldn't be drinking, and how dangerous hitchhiking was. His sermon put me back to sleep. It's easy to talk that shit when you have a nice, comfortable, loving home to go to that's filled with a warm, caring family. Asshole. He had no idea what he was talking about. He had no idea what I'd been through. He had no idea how stupid he sounded. I couldn't wait to get to the shelter home so I could escape his nonsense.

Finally, we arrived. I was taken in and introduced to the caretakers, an older, nice white couple. The lady showed me to my bed. I climbed in and immediately passed out. The incessant partying of the past few days had finally taken its toll. The next day, before the authorities came for me, I'd slipped out a window and was gone. I never saw that cop again. Didn't matter. There would be others.

15

I was eventually returned to Lancaster where I was slowly getting my own little pleasure: something was wrong with Diane; she was getting physically ill. Not only was she grossly overweight, but she couldn't hold her urine. She was getting dizzy. Her sickness made her weaker than usual, so the beatings were drastically reduced, but her mouth worked just fine and was meaner than ever.

I wasn't at Diane's long. Within days of being returned, I was gone again.

I hitchhiked south along the California coast, in no particular hurry, with no particular destination. I ended up in Hollywood again. After hanging out for a couple of days, I called Jr. He had good news.

He'd been discussing me with one of my great-aunts, my grandmother's sister. Everybody called her 'Aunt Becky.' Although I had heard the name before, I never remembered meeting her. She lived somewhere in the Los Angeles area and told Jr. she was willing to take me for a while. They weren't sure how long I could stay with Becky once the authorities found out, but it was better than what I was doing. Stories of hitchhikers getting killed were becoming more frequent. Hitchhikers were turning up missing left and right. Jr. was really scared for me.

I wasn't scared. I'd graduated from carrying a butter knife to packing a pocketknife with a two-inch blade. On top of that, I gave men (and women) a mean look when I first got into their cars, and I talked bad and acted bad. Wasn't anybody gon' mess with me.

Jr. was still scared. So we decided I'd go to Aunt Becky's and stay there until the system made me leave. Since Becky couldn't pick me up (she didn't drive), we decided I'd catch a cab to her house. That way, there was no risk of my getting lost. I hung out for a couple of days while Jr. sent me some money by Western Union. During the couple of days I had to wait for Jr.'s money to arrive, I partied hearty! I hung out with my friends (anyone who lived on the streets and drank and used like me was a friend); and did what street folks do.

A couple of days later, the money arrived. I.D. was no longer a problem – the system made me get one after my first couple of running-away escapades. They said they needed me to carry one so that authorities would be able to identify me. A smart-ass social worker said it would help them 'identify my body' once some psycho I'd hitchhiked with had raped and murdered me.

Anyway, I got the money, bought some coke, some booze, and some weed. I figured Aunt Becky could wait. Hell, I had to celebrate. I wasn't going back to Diane's!

It took me a day or two to get to Becky's. I don't remember how I got there – whether a friend took me, whether I took a cab, or what, because I was in a blackout.

(I later learned that a blackout is frequently experienced by alcoholics. They get so drunk, so high that although they're *physically* present – walking, talking, doing things – their minds are so gone that they have no memory of what went on. This blackout was one of many I'd already experienced, and only one of thousands to come.)

All I knew was that one day I was snorting coke and drinking gin (straight), and the next thing I knew, I was standing in front of a house I *thought* was Becky's.

I was standing on the sidewalk, looking up at the house, trying to figure out if it was the one I was looking for. It was a nice-looking house, not a mansion, but far from a shack. In fact, the whole block was lined with nice houses. I was staring up at the house, trying to get the nerve to approach the door. If it was the house, I didn't know the people who lived there. I mean, here was a woman that, although she was family, I didn't know and had never seen before.

What was she like? Was she violent? Mean?

All these thoughts were rushing through my mind when the

front door opened and out stepped a god. No, really. He was gorgeous. A tall, well-built, light-skinned teenage boy slowly approached me. He wasn't wearing a shirt, so you could see the muscles in his chest and arms. And he had the coolest stroll I'd ever seen on a kid. He sort of *glided* toward me.

'What's up, cuzzz?' he asked as he walked up, stopping just in front of me. I had never seen anyone so handsome. I was blushing.

Be cool, I told myself. *Don't make a fool of yourself.*

'Nothing.' I looked at my feet. I couldn't meet his eyes because, when I did, all I could do was grin – a wide-ass, all-teeth grin.

'My name is Ka'son, but my friends call me "Fly," ' he said quietly. His voice was low and sexy. It didn't take long to figure out why they called him Fly – everything about him was fly. Before I could say anything back to him, the screen door flew open and another boy came scurrying out of the house. He sprinted up to me, happy, playful, and very cheerful.

'What's up?' he chimed, never losing his smile. 'I'm Keith.'

'Hi,' I replied. I was getting nervous now. Whenever I crashed or was put in a home with men or boys in the house, it meant I'd have to have some type of sexual activity with them. I didn't like the fact that there were two boys in this house.

My nervousness increased when a third boy came out of the house. He casually strolled up and introduced himself as Kevin.

How many of y'all is there? I asked myself. Just then, the door opened again, and *another* boy came out. He said his name was Kenny.

Was I that high, or did all four of these boys' names start with K s. More important, are there any women here? I thought nervously. *And where the fuck is this Aunt Becky?*

Just then the door opened and onto the porch stepped an older woman, about fifty-five or sixty years old. She was tall, at least six feet, and very slim. She had brown skin and a wide, friendly smile. Her salt-and-pepper hair hung straight past her shoulders. She was strikingly beautiful – even for an older woman. I'd heard we had American Indians in my family. I remembered the story Jr. told me about my great-great-grandmother being half Indian. I never really paid him any attention 'cause every black person I knew claimed to have Indian in them. Every once in a while, though, I thought I could see Native American features in my mother's and grandmother's long straight black hair and high cheekbones. Poised there in the doorway, with the sun dancing off her soft, smooth skin, her long hair blowing out from behind her, Aunt Becky looked like an Indian goddess. Actually, she looked just like my grandma. The resemblance was uncanny. I hadn't seen my grandma since my mother's funeral. Now, staring up at this woman was like staring at my mother's mother. I don't know if it was the beauty of the moment or the booze, but suddenly I wanted to cry.

'Hi, Vette,' she said in a sweet high-pitched voice. She wasn't violent – I could tell by her voice. No one with a voice that sweet could possibly be mean.

'Y'all come on into the house,' she said, 'so we can all get better acquainted.'

Ka'son, Kevin, Keith, and Kenny gathered around me and escorted me into the house. The boys were Becky's grandsons. Ka'son was the oldest. He was sixteen, and it was true that everybody (except Aunt Becky) called him Fly. Kevin was almost fourteen. Keith was twelve, and Kenny was nine. Their mother, Jenny, had been Becky's only child. The boys were my third cousins.

Becky was raising the boys because Jenny had died in a car accident. As Becky told the story of the accident, I slowly began to remember Jenny. I remembered my mom periodically talking about a 'Cousin Jenny.' And I remembered a thin, dark-skinned woman screaming and crying at my mother's funeral. She was hanging over the casket and hollerin' so, they had to carry her out. I think she fainted 'cause she never showed up at the interment. I'd never seen her before, so I figured she was just some nut (of which there were plenty in my family). But I liked and admired her for how she shamelessly showed grief for the loss of my mother. Looking at Aunt Becky, it came to me that she looked exactly like an older version of her daughter. I was now sure that that hysterical woman at Momma's funeral had been Cousin Jenny.

The house Becky and the boys lived in had three bedrooms and one bathroom. I was to sleep in the living room on the sofa, which let out into a bed. I'd never had any brothers (y'all know Larry didn't count!), and the boys had never had a sister, so we took to each other immediately. But there was more to our bond than that. I think we connected because we'd shared similar devastations: we'd all lost our mothers suddenly, unexpectedly, and tragically.

'Vette, you hungry?' Aunt Becky asked me as we sat around the living room getting acquainted.

It was then that I told them of my decision to take back my birth name (though I didn't tell them I'd been having 'cheerleading practice' with Mr Bassinet when I'd made the decision). Because the boys had never met me before, in fact had never even heard of me before, my name change didn't make any difference to them. They said they liked Cupcake better anyway.

Aunt Becky said that she had met me when my mother was alive and that she knew about the 'Cupcake at birth' story.

I must have been too young to remember, I thought, *'cause I've never seen this woman before in my life!*

'I always did like Cupcake,' she said softly as she rose to go into the kitchen and make something to eat. 'I love the story about how you got it. Your mom really liked it too.'

'Why they say your name is La'Vette?' Kenny asked.

I told the boys the story about Momma craving cupcakes and her mistaken request for one that resulted in my name; and how Mr Burns had changed it because he 'didn't like it.' I told them about how Mr Burns took me from Daddy and Uncle Jr. and made me go live with Diane in Lancaster. I left out the sexual and physical abuse.

Still, reciting the story even *without* the abuse slowly built a fire in me. I shouted that I *hated* that name and that I would use *only* the name *my mother,* not some stupid sperm donor, had given me! With that, I stood up, feet spread apart, fists on my hips. I was so angry by now that I was near tears. Everyone was silent; obviously shocked by my sudden outburst and unyielding defiance.

'Okay, okay,' Kevin said lightly. 'Don't get your panties in a wad. Cupcake it is.'

They never questioned the name again. They seemed to be willing to accept me just as I was. I would learn to love those four boys – each in his own way.

Although they sort of looked alike, they each had distinctive personalities. Ka'son, 'Fly,' was the cool one. He said he was a

'Gangsta,' and while I didn't know what that meant, I was soon to find out. Kevin was the smart one, a straight-A student and very good at Korean Hapkido (he'd been studying it since he was five). Keith was the silly one, always joking around, making me laugh. Kenny . . . well he was the baby. He always wanted to play a game – any game, with anyone.

The next day, Becky took me shopping. She bought me new clothes – not hand-me downs. And she bought me pretty undies, some smell-good toiletries, and other dainty shit that girls used. I didn't know what to do with that stuff, but she said I'd learn. She spent quite a bit of money on me, which shocked me because she hadn't yet gotten any money *for* me. She and Jr. were still trying to figure out how to change the social-security payments from going to Diane without my being returned to Diane's. But I didn't care if I had to turn tricks to get the money to stay there. I'd do anything so I wouldn't have to leave.

That night I discovered that Fly smoked weed and drank – though not to the extent I did. (In fact, I was quickly learning that not too many people smoked and drank like I did.) We were sitting in his room watching TV, when out of the blue he said, ''Ey, cuzzz, you smoke?' I didn't know if he meant cigarettes or weed, but it didn't matter: I smoked both.

'Yeah,' I said as he reached under his bed to pull out a little brown tray containing some weed buds and rolling papers. As he started rolling a joint, I gasped.

'You gon' smoke that in here?' I asked, glancing nervously toward the door, aware that Becky could come in at any time.

'Naw, cuzzz. We just gon' roll 'em in here. We'll take 'em outside to smoke.'

'Oh.' Just then, it occurred to me that I had no idea of where in the world I was. So I asked Fly.

'Where are we?'

'What do you mean?'

'I mean, where are we?'

'Los Angeles, dumb shit.'

'Yeah, but *where* in L.A.?'

'On Brighton Avenue.'

Oh, that *clears it up,* I thought.

'But where is *that*? What is this hood called?'

'South Central.'

124

'South Central? South Central what?'

'South Central, Los Angeles,' he said in his low, sexy drawl.

It seemed like a nice town. From what I'd seen, all of the homes were well kept, the lawns nicely trimmed. There were no broken windows or dilapidated houses. Then again, I hadn't been there long. I wanted to ask more questions, but noticed that Fly was becoming irritated with my ignorance, so I decided to drop the subject and just trust that South Central was where I was.

A week or so after arriving at Becky's, Keith hipped me to the party line – a phone line on which you can call and talk to several people at once. Aunt Becky had gone to sleep (she always went to bed early). I got on the party line and started talking to this dude who said his name was Ricky and he was twenty-four years old. After talking awhile, I discovered that Ricky lived nearby, so he suggested we hook up. 'Sure,' I replied, never thinking twice about meeting a complete stranger (hell, I did it all the time hitchhiking). Keith, who was just as naive as me, gave Ricky our address. A short while later, a red Mustang pulled up in front of the house.

I ran to the window to see what he looked like. As Ricky stepped out I was disappointed. He was ugly! At the time, I liked light-skinned, tall men, but he was dark, dark black. Almost blue-black. And short. But I thought, *What the hell?* He had a car; he *said* he had a job and a place to stay. All the things a girl who often found herself 'on the go' would need. So Ricky's having all the required necessities made up for his ugliness.

I grabbed the new coat Becky had just bought me and headed for the door.

'You really gon' go?' Keith asked unbelievingly as I stepped onto the porch.

'Hell, yeah!' I replied. I needed some excitement. And, more important, I needed a drink. I ran outside and skipped toward the car. As I approached the car, Fly came strolling out of the house.

'Where you going, cuzzz?' he asked in that smooth, quiet voice. His question shocked me. I wasn't used to being questioned or having to report my whereabouts to anyone. I was so shocked, I paused for a moment. Fly didn't wait for me to reply. He strolled up to Ricky and asked for his driver's license. Then he walked to the front of the car and noted his license plate. As he walked back to the driver's door where Ricky and I were standing, he asked Ricky where he lived and worked.

As Fly stood there drilling Ricky with questions, I started getting pissed. I felt like he was meddlin' in my business. Fly, oblivious (or indifferent) to my irritation, asked Ricky if he was hip to the 'Gangstas.' Ricky said he was. Then very calmly and coldly, Fly informed Ricky that *he* was a Gangsta. He told Ricky that if anything happened to me – anything at all – Ricky would have to deal with *them*. This bit of information made Ricky visibly nervous. He started sweating and stuttering as he told Fly that we were just going for a short ride and that he'd have me back within a hour or so. 'Make damn sho you do,' Fly softly replied with a look of anger that made me uncomfortable.

Then he turned to me, flashed me his playboy smile, gave me a hug, and told me to be careful. It was then that I realized he'd asked those questions because he was concerned for me. I was so touched. I fell in love with him right there at that moment – the moment I realized he gave a damn. I smiled to myself as I hopped in the car.

Just as Ricky promised, we went for a short ride. All we did was stop and buy some Night Train and park around the corner from the house. Ricky told me he was really scared of the Gangstas. He didn't want to go far because he wanted to be sure and have me back within an hour as Fly had instructed. His fear intrigued me: I made a mental note to find out more about these Gangstas, and what it was about them that would make the mere mention of their name scare the shit out of a grown-ass man.

We drank the 'Train,' smoked a couple of joints that Ricky had brought with him, and talked. At first he seemed a little shocked that I looked so young, but he eased up when I told him I was almost fifteen. That seemed to make him feel a little better – like somehow, being with a fifteen-year-old girl was not as bad as being with a fourteen-year-old one. We talked about sex, though I didn't have sex with him – at least not that night. I would have; it's just that he was too ugly *and* I wasn't getting

126

paid. So I figured I'd wait until his ugliness grew on me – or until I was too high to care.

He took me home after about thirty-five minutes. As we pulled up, Fly was standing on the porch with two other tough-looking dudes. Ricky turned off the car and looked up at them. He was scared. Shit, I was too. He walked me up to Fly and the two dudes, bid everyone good night, and began a brisk walk back to his car. Before he could reach it, Fly shouted, 'Hey, cuzzz, you got any more smoke?' I don't know how he knew we'd been smoking weed. He must have smelled it on us, or maybe it was the cloud of smoke that escaped from the car when we got out that gave us away. Ricky replied that we'd smoked his last joint, but he knew where to get some more.

'Y'all watch out for my lil cuzzzin while I make this run,' Fly shouted to the two guys on the porch as he ran and hopped into Ricky's car.

'Tray dat, cuzzz!' one of them shouted back.

I wondered what language they were speaking and why they kept sayin' 'cuz.' I mean, *I* was Fly's cousin, but who were these dudes? While Fly and Ricky went to cop some more dope, I got to find out.

One said his name was Huck. I'd never heard a name like that before. He was a tall, thin dark brother. He said he lived on Brighton Avenue too – down the street from us. He had a blue bandana hanging out of his back pocket. He said that Fly was his 'homie.' The other guy said his name was 'Dob' (though when he said his name, it sounded like he was saying 'Dōv'). I thought that was also a funny name. But, hell, with a name like Cupcake who was I to judge? Dob also lived on our street and also had a blue bandana. But instead of hanging out his back pocket like Huck's, his was wrapped around his hand like a bandage. At first I thought he'd hurt his hand. But as he talked he wrapped and unwrapped it, and I never saw any blood or scars. So I figured the bandana was some kind of a toy to him.

When Fly and Ricky pulled back up, Dob and Huck and I were standing in the middle of the street. They were pointing down it, trying to show me where they each lived.

''Ey, cuzzz,' Fly said as he and Ricky got out of the car, 'let's go roun' the corner. I don't want Momma to wake up and start hoo-bangin'.'

I didn't know what 'hoo-bangin'' was, but I was down for goin' anywhere where there was dope.

We all hopped into Ricky's car and went around the corner to the same spot Ricky and I had just left. We still had some Night Train left, so we rolled up some fat blunts and got bent. No one talked much, we just smoked and drank. I noticed the higher we got, the more Dob would wrap and unwrap the bandana around his hand. It was then I realized that he wasn't really playing with that little blue rag; rather he was studying it with admiration and adulation. I wondered why.

After we finished the blunts, Ricky dropped us off back in front of Aunt Becky's. Before pulling away, he took down my number and said he'd call me the next day (though it was already two in the morning). I mumbled a 'whatever' and stumbled onto the porch. Dob and Huck slurred 'Later, cuzzz' at us and staggered down the street toward their homes.

I was so high, I'd forgotten the questions I'd intended to ask Fly about the Gangstas and the strange language I heard them speaking. Fly and I went in the house, munched out, and collapsed.

The following day, as Fly and I kicked it on the front porch nursing our hangovers, he gave me my first lesson on gang-bangin'. I'd never heard of gangs before and never knew any gang members, so I sat listening in fascination as he taught me about 'the game.' Fly belonged to a gang called the Eight-Tray Gangster Crips. He explained that many of the gangs in L.A. were named after the streets on which their territory begins. The Eight-Tray Gangsters' 'set' (territory) started on Eighty-third Street – thus the name 'Eight-Tray.' And, because the Gangstas' set name ended with the number three, their gang sign consisted of the middle three fingers being held straight up. Most gangs have several ways to 'sign' their names. The Eight-Trays were no different. One of those alternative signs was to curve the forefinger and thumb into a C, causing the remaining three fingers to stand alone. The C stood for 'Crip,' and of course the three fingers symbolized 'Eight-Tray.' Also known simply as Gangstas, Fly said the gang was one of the most notorious and violent ones in Los Angeles. And, unbeknownst to me, I was in training to become one.

I learned that Crips wore blue and Bloods wore red. Crips loved everything and anything blue and hated everything and anything red. The opposite was true for Bloods. They never, ever wore or acknowledged each other's colors. Why these colors? Why the hatred? The reasons were lost in time.

The Crips' essential word was *cuz* – which they used a lot. *Cuz* was a term of endearment (like *homie*), but it was also substituted for everyday words whenever possible – for example, instead of 'because' they said 'cuz'; instead of 'cousin' they said 'cuz.' (And, whenever Gangstas wrote the word, they used three *z*s signifying the Eight-Trays.) The Bloods' essential word was *blood*. Bloods never said 'cuz' and Crips never said 'blood.' In fact, Crips hated the word *blood* so much that they would say that they had 'cuz-juice' running through their veins.

Crips dissed Bloods by calling them 'slobs' and other derogatory names, while Bloods called the Crips 'crabs.' Their hatred for each other was so severe, wearing the wrong color or using the wrong word in the wrong hood could cause a person serious harm or even cost him his life. Kids living in a particular neighborhood knew which colors to wear and not to wear and which words to say and not to say in order to stay alive.

However, just because another gang shared the same colors didn't mean they were allies. Most gangs have few allies or none at all – whether they share the same colors or not. In fact, the Gangstas' number one enemy, besides Bloods, were the Rollin' 60's – another Crip gang who also wore blue.

Fly also schooled me on the strange vocabulary he'd been using. The word *hoo-bangin'* had several meanings, depending upon the context that was being used. It could mean someone was fussin' or talking shit, which is what Fly meant when, the night before, he'd said we should go around the corner to get high so Aunt Becky wouldn't start hoo-bangin'. However, when bangers hoo-bang one another, it means they're letting you know what set they claim – usually by throwin' up their signs and yellin' out their set's name. And *Tray dat* meant something like 'right on.' Use of *tray* was as desirable as the use of the number three whenever possible.

Fly said the first thing we had to do was to give me a gang name because everyone had one. Most gang members earned their name, while some were just given one. Fly had two. He told me how he got them. He said that one night he and Huck (short for 'Huck-A-Buck') got drunk and decided to get a 'G-ride.' He paused to proudly state that as many cars as he had stolen, he'd never been arrested for a GTA (grand theft auto – the legal term for a stolen-vehicle offense). Anyway, Fly and Huck were testing the ride's power when they noticed the red lights of the LAPD in the rearview mirror. Refusing to pull over (Fly said the gin he'd been drinking told him he could beat them), a chase began. They sped through the streets of L.A., pushing the G-ride for all it was worth, but the LAPD cruiser was built for this kind of chase and closed ground quickly. Fly slammed the car to a sudden, screeching halt, hopped out, and ran. It was this run that earned him his name.

As Fly was running from the police, he booked down a narrow street that was blocked by a parked car. Noticing (or hoping) that both front windows were down, and not having time to run *around* the car, Fly dove *through* the car – entered the passenger window with his arms straight out in front of him like Superman and flew straight through to the driver's window. He almost cleared it, but he was too tall and losing speed. The rim of the driver's window caught his shoe, slowing down his flight. But it didn't stop him. He stumbled onto the sidewalk, jumped to his feet, and continued running. As he hopped a fence, losing the cops behind him, he heard of one them exclaim 'Did you see that nigga fly?' Fly said he'd been called 'Fly' ever since.

But the name also fit because of his stunning good looks and debonair personality. He was so smooth it was sickening. His gorgeousness allowed him to keep three to four fine-ass women chasing him at all times. He walked cool – long, slow strides that made you just want to watch him move. He talked cool – in a soft, sexy drawl that made you just want to drop whatever you were doing and listen to him. He dressed cool – his clothes made you want to undress him to see the sexy body you just knew was waiting underneath. Even his mannerisms were cool. You ever met anyone like that? Someone who was irresistibly charismatic? Who just exuded cool, smooth style? That was Fly – the flyest muthafucka you've ever seen.

But like I said, some folks, including Fly, had more than one gang name. The unofficial leader of the Gangstas was an OG named Sidewinder. (OG means 'original gangster'; it's someone who's been in the gang a long time, has earned his 'stripes,' and is well respected, even revered, by the younger members.) So Fly was also called 'Baby Sidewinder'; it was an honor to be named after an OG. But everybody called him Fly.

Fly told me that Huck-A-Buck got his name the same day Fly had earned 'Fly.' As Fly decided to abandon the police chase and slammed the car to a halt, Huck-A-Buck was thrown head first into the dashboard, causing the loss of several front teeth. Huck had to make the tough decision of whether to try ditching the police by jumping out and running with all his might, or pausing to grab his teeth.

Huck left his teeth sticking in the dashboard and ran. Fly said he'd been Huck-A-Buck ever since.

I didn't bother asking what 'Dob' meant. I just assumed it was short for 'Doberman.'

Hearing the stories about being 'dubbed' – christened with a street name – fascinated me. I wanted one. Fly said I needed a cool name; something that sounded *hard* and *down*. Although Fly liked 'Cupcake,' he said it was too wimpy. We tossed around several choices, but were unable to come up with anything that fit the bill. Finally it was decided that we'd wait awhile till I could earn one like everybody else.

I was starting to have second thoughts. I wasn't sure if I wanted to be in a gang and wasn't sure what it meant or required. And it would mean getting a new favorite color. My favorite color had been red for as long as I could remember. I loved red.

Could I learn to hate it?

Seeing the uncertainty on my face, Fly said, 'Let's go on the set and introduce you to some of the homies.' So we made our way to Eighty-third Street. There I met my new family.

There were a bunch of people sitting on a brick wall that stood in front of a house near the corner of Eighty-third and Normandie. As we approached the crowd, I hesitated a little. These kids looked tough and like they didn't like *anybody*. I'd seen some tough kids during my running-away escapades. But no one nearly as tough-looking as these folks. Fly, sensing my hesitation, grabbed my arm and pulled me up to the bunch who were passing several blunts and 40s of 'Old 8' – forty-ounce bottles of Olde English '800' Malt Liquor (also sometimes called '8-ball').

As we got closer, Fly threw up his three middle fingers and shouted, 'G-a-n-g-s-t-a-s!' This greeting seemed to rile up the others who replied with various greetings. Some said, 'What's up, cuzzz?' Others replied, 'Tray that.' Still others hollered back, 'G-a-n-g-s-t-a-s!' Those who didn't verbally respond either threw up three fingers or a C.

As one of the Eight-Trays handed Fly a joint, he introduced me as his cuzzzin Cupcake.

'Cupcake, huh?' a tall, very thin light-skinned kid asked (whom I later learned was called 'Bones').

'What's up, cuzzz?' the group replied in unison.

A young man who said his name was 'Monster' hopped off the wall and handed me a 40. I'd later learn that Monster was an OG and known for his unusual taste for violence.

Another girl handed me a joint and introduced herself as China. China was Monster's girlfriend and one of the downest homegirls on the set. She was also known as Mooney.

I took a hit off the joint and a sip off the 8-Ball. Instantly I knew that I was with the right crowd.

'Nooney' and 'Spooney' were other female gang members I met that night. Nooney, Mooney, and Spooney were very close – as you might've guessed.

Another girl member was called 'Big Lynn.' She stood six foot two and weighed at least 260 pounds. I *knew* she had to be one of the downest female Gangstas. She was too big not to be.

There were entire families in the gang. 'Crazy D' was another OG, also known for his ability to fight and his love of violence. Crazy D's little brother, 'Lil Crazy D,' was also a Gangsta, as was his sister Peanut.

There were tons of other homies with odd or unique gang names like 'Red,' 'Gangsta C,' 'Diamond,' 'Tray-Bone,' 'Bootsey,' and 'Tray-Ball.' I was trying to figure out the origin of each name but folks were being introduced too fast.

All of a sudden Crazy D hopped off the wall and began walking toward me with his chest stuck out, anger in his face, a blue rag in hand, and snarled, 'What set you from?'

132

I'd never been asked that question before. I was scared and unsure of what to say.

'She don't bang, cuzzz,' Fly interjected as he stepped in between us, 'but she gon' be down wit' us.' ('Being down' means doing whatever the gang says: fighting, shooting, stealing – whatever is best for the gang.)

'Right, right,' Crazy D said. '*Is* she down?' he asked.

'Nigga, you sayin' my cuzzzin ain't down?' Fly snapped as he angrily stepped closer to Crazy D.

I got nervous at Fly's sudden anger. I hadn't yet realized he was using his reputation to help me get started with mine.

'Naw, cuzzz,' D replied as he began to back down. 'A nigga's just asking.'

'Come on, y'all, stop trippin',' Mooney said, irritated by the men's testosterone display.

'What's up, cuzzz?' she asked as she took the joint from me and hit it.

I still hadn't learned the lingo. I shyly responded, 'Nothing.'

I wasn't shy for long. As the 8-Ball and weed began to kick in, I began to feel more and more confident. But not until Monster saw me shivering and offered me his jacket did I realize I was with a different kind of people. During my travels running away and living on the streets, nobody ever *gave* you anything. If someone saw you shivering, she'd grab hold of her own jacket for fear you'd try to steal it. And if you put yours down, you'd better not let it leave your sight or it'd be gone. It was dog-eat-dog out there. So Monster's display of kindness and thoughtfulness was unusual to me. I liked it.

They were so polite and caring. So it threw me off when, the next night, they kicked my ass.

133

16

Following Mooney's instructions, I met her and the other female homies at Peanut's house. I still hadn't learned my way around the hood, so Fly walked me over there. I didn't suspect anything when he refused to go in with me. I figured it was gonna be a girls' night so he would have been out of place anyway.

Waiting for me were Mooney, Nooney, Spooney, Yokey, Pokey, Crip Karen, and Big Lynn. The fellas were out hoo-ridin' on the 60's. (To 'hoo-ride' on another gang meant to drive through their set looking for people to shoot or beat up or both.) I didn't notice that they were all completely dressed in blue. We sat around for a while smoking joints and drinking 8-Ball when suddenly Peanut stepped up to me.

'So you wanna be a Gangsta, bitch?' she snarled.

Before I could respond, Spooney was at her side. 'You down or what?'

While I was trying to think of an answer, I felt a stinging on the right side of my face. Crip Karen had punched me.

I was still stunned from the shock (and pain) when Yokey stepped up and punched me in the arm. Immediately, all the other homies started punching me.

They're jumping me! I realized. *Shit, I thought these heifers were my friends!*

As the punches started coming, Mooney shouted to me, 'Fight, cuzzz, fight! Show us you down! Fight!'

Down? Was I down? Is this what being 'down' meant – getting yo' ass whupped?

As they pounded me, I began to flash back on the last couple

134

of years of my life: finding my mother dead, that asshole Mr Burns, losing my daddy and Uncle Jr.

They kept pounding. The strength of their blows was now knocking me to the ground.

Still, I wouldn't fight.

Still, the punches kept coming.

I continued remembering: Diane, the rapes, the abuse, the cheerleading practices.

The girls now added kicks to the punches.

My past continued flashing: getting pregnant, getting jumped, losing my baby.

All of a sudden the anger began to rise up in me. The rage I had been holding in for years began to quickly swell at the possibility of finally being released.

And released it was, in a flurry of fists as I began to fight – and cry.

I struggled to get to my feet, which was difficult with the blows constantly hitting their marks: my eyes, my head, my ribs, my shoulders, my legs.

I continued to struggle until I wobbled up onto my feet. Once up, I begun wildly swinging at everything and anything. My rage made me forget the intense pain that just a moment before had been shooting through my body.

I swung with everything I had – and for everything I'd lost. I fought and cried and fought and cried.

The homegirls soon realized that I had taken getting jumped in too seriously. They were concerned that if they didn't stop me, they'd have to kill me – to keep me from killing them.

'Damn, homie! Chill!' Spooney shouted as she stepped back to get out of my line of fire.

I kept fighting. And crying.

'Okay, cuzzz!' Nooney shouted as she too tried to ease up on her blows.

One by one, they were trying to pull back while simultaneously protecting themselves from my punches.

I kept fighting. I didn't stop till Big Lynn grabbed me by my neck, her huge right hand blocking my air flow. 'Chill out, lil bitch,' she ordered as I began to slow my swings and weaken from the lack of air.

She effortlessly tossed me onto a beanbag chair on the floor a few feet away, as if tossing a rag doll. We were all huffing and puffing – tired and out of air.

'Lil bitch got heart,' Big Lynn said as she lit up another joint.

'Yeah, that's the kind of swinging we like to see,' Yokey said, taking a swig of 8-Ball.

They all sat looking at me with pride and admiration.

By fighting back, I'd proven I wasn't a mark or a wimp. I'd been jumped in. I'd earned my place in the Eight-Tray Gangstas.

Finally, I belonged to *some*thing.

That night, we got fucked up and celebrated my initiation.

Later, when Fly, Monster, Lep, and some of the other homies came by to see how things had gone, I proudly displayed my black eye, busted lip, and bruised body parts as proof that I was down. I'd made it in.

'I hear you got heart, lil nigga!' Lep said as he gulped down some Night Train.

'What'd you think, cuzzz?' Fly responded before I could answer. 'That's MY lil cuzzzin!'

'Aw, nigga!' they all chimed as they took turns bear-hugging and congratulating me. Their hugs made me wince because my body was still very sore from the fresh beating. But I didn't care. They loved me.

It was then that I knew that as long as they loved me and accepted me, I could learn to hate red. *Fuck it,* I told myself. *I'll find a new favorite color.*

17

There was no difference between male and female Gangstas: they hung together on the set; the girls earned their street names; they were expected to do whatever it took to earn stripes; and they were expected to give their lives for the set – just like the boys.

Gangstas shared everything. No one ever went hungry or cold. If you fucked with one of us, you fucked with all of us. I loved the camaraderie and the fact that I finally belonged somewhere, with people who truly gave a fuck about me. My 'jumping in' ceremony caused the homies to dub me 'Lady Lightning' because when I hit, I hit hard and fast. Except no one ever called me Lightning; everyone still called me Cupcake. I don't know if they did that because that was how I was first introduced to them and so it stuck, or if they did it because they thought that Cupcake was more original and cute. Which it was. Whatever the reason, Cupcake was the name I used and I always 'tagged' (spray-painted) 'Lady Cupcake.'

The Gangstas added a new drug to my already sizable narcotic arsenal: PCP, also known as 'sherm.' It was called sherm after a brand of filterless cigarettes called Shermans, which were dipped into a concoction of several ingredients, one of which was formaldehyde – embalming fluid. The combination was called 'sherm stick.' But sherm is just one of PCP's street names. It is also called 'angel dust' or 'lovely.'

Me, myself, I didn't give a fuck what it was made of – embalming fluid, lighter fluid, or balls of shit. I loved my new drug, but I was loyal; I still loved my old ones too.

Sherm, like acid, is a strong hallucinogenic. It could give you a good trip or a bad one. That never scared me because, hell, finding out what kind of trip you'd have was part of the fun. Besides, most of my trips were good ones, even though that wasn't true for a lot of other people. I had several homies who were killed or seriously hurt because of a bad sherm trip.

One night me and some of the homies were hanging out getting shermed, when my homie Thug started on a bad trip. He was just sitting there smoking when suddenly he started shouting that he was Superman. At first it was funny. He started running around jumping off cars and shit. We thought he was just clownin', until he started strippin'. All of a sudden, he was tearing off his clothes – talking about they were 'on fire' and 'weighing him down.' He really looked funny runnin' around stark naked.

'Nigga, put yo' clothes on,' Bootsey yelled after him as Thug scurried here and there, butt naked, balls dangling with each step.

We were crackin' up. Everyone started yelling at Thug while we all tripped and watched him trip.

'That nigga crazy!' someone hollered.

'Straight that, cuzzz!' someone else yelled. We thought it was all one big joke – that is, until Thug started climbing a tree next to his house.

'Cuzzz, get down from there!' Tray-Ball shouted.

We'd been having so much fun laughing at him, we didn't realize how bad his trip had turned. And, because we were also shermed, we were all pretty fucked up. Some of the homies were so high, they still didn't realize Thug was in danger. Even after he'd jumped from the tree onto the roof, they were still laughing and shouting shit. Some had started on their own trips: staring at their newly discovered skin, or tripping off the street-lights that seemed to suddenly glow green.

Thug continued ignoring our whooping and hollering and just kept climbing. It looked to me like he was moving in slow motion. When he finally reached the top of the roof, he looked down at us with a wild, dazed look in his eyes. Then he stood there for a moment with his eyes closed, as if he were relaxing in the cool evening breeze. He looked so serene. Slowly, he stretched his arms out in front of him like Superman, opening his eyes to stare at me wildly for an instant, then turned up his lips into a shit-eatin' grin, and jumped hollering, 'Superman!' all the way.

It was then I was able to snap out of it and realize what was happening – just in time to see his body plummet to the ground.

Crazy mothafucka! That dive broke both of Thug's arms and legs, his hip, jaw, and a bunch of other shit. It really fucked him up. He was in the hospital for months. Thug was never the same after that. He moved very slowly, like an old man; he was also blind in one eye, almost completely confined to a wheelchair, and slurred his words. But none of that stopped his drug use. Didn't stop none of us. In fact, it made me want more sherm because to make Thug act so crazy, you know that batch was all-the-way live.

That's another name we started calling sherm – 'live.' Niggas sellin' it would holler, 'Got that live!' to potential buyers to let them know they had the good stuff: the sherm that would take you on a trip like none other. So, without hesitation, I quickly became a 'shermhead.' I figured what happened to Thug wouldn't happen to me – I was too slick to let a trip take me that far.

My bad trips never caused me serious physical harm like Thug's had to him, though I did have some I'd have rather done without – like the ones in which I was unable to move. I'd be high, sitting on the couch or floor, and, try as I might, I wouldn't be able to move *any* part of my body. I'd be sitting there commanding my legs and arms to move. Upon realizing that that wasn't working, I'd start *begging* my body to obey. I'd strain and strain trying to just lift a finger. But it was useless. Then I'd try to open my mouth and scream for the homies to come help me. But the mind controls the body, and the sherm was controlling my mind – and it told my mind that my body *could not* move. And it didn't. So, I'd sit there for hours, wanting to get up, but unable to; wanting to ask for help, but couldn't. But that wasn't the worst part of those trips. The worst part was if I needed to go to the bathroom. If the sherm decided the piss could come out, it had to come out where I sat. The sherm was unyielding, uncompromising, and merciless. Even having to piss wasn't excuse enough to break the paralysis. I remained physically frozen till the high came down.

Although I hated those bad trips, they didn't happen often – so even with episodes when I was unable to move, and even with the periodic humiliation of pissing on myself, nothing deterred me from getting shermed.

Learning how to be a Gangsta was a fascinating and raucous education. For instance, I had to learn how to shoot. It was important to be able to handle a gun because everyone was expected to be down for the set, to the point of shooting rival bangers if it came to that. A couple of weeks after getting jumped in, Fly, Huck, and Dob taught me how to shoot, which wasn't difficult. Because gunfire was so common in South Central, it was a constant nightmare for the children, 'squares,' and old folks that lived there. But its regularity also meant that no one paid much attention to it, allowing for shooting practice to happen right in the middle of the hood without fear of the cops being immediately called, which was beneficial to bangers-in-training.

The first type of gun the homies let me shoot was a .38 Special. I'd never seen a gun before, except in old western movies where they had long, thin barrels and seemed larger than life. The .38 had a barrel that was shorter, and it was a lot smaller than the the guns the movie cowboys had, though the .38 was much heavier than I'd thought it would be. Fly taught me how to aim and fire. My practice shots were aimed at a variety of targets: birds flying by, beer cans and bottles lined up along a concrete wall. After my first shot, I felt the gun's kick run all through my arm, and I didn't want to shoot anymore. At the same time, I didn't want to be labeled a 'mark' (a mark is a sucker, a sellout, a wimp, a pussy – one of the worst things a supposed-to-be-down Gangsta could be called). So, I drank more Thunderbird and smoked more lovely to make the pain in my arm go away.

Next, while Crazy D practiced shooting a sawed-off 12-gauge shotgun, Fly and Huck taught me how to shoot a .410 shotgun. Fly said the shotgun was his favorite weapon, but I didn't like it. It was long, heavy, and awkward to handle. I immediately decided that I preferred handguns.

'You sure you got it, cuzzz?' Fly asked me when we'd finished practicing and were making our way to Eighty-third Street to catch up with some of the other homies.

'Tray dat,' I replied, to let him know I'd gotten 'the shooting thang down.'

'Good,' Huck said, 'cuzzz you up Friday night.'

I got quiet when he said that because I wasn't sure what being 'up' meant. I wanted to ask, but one of the first lessons a Gangsta is taught is: 'Don't ask questions.' Simply imitate and obey. So I knew better than to ask. Didn't matter though. I was soon to find out.

Gangsta meetings were periodically called, usually by one of the OGs. The next Friday night, Sidewinder called one at St. Andrew's Park, a spot in our territory we'd rechristened as 'Gangsta Park.'

Because we were such a large gang, day-to-day info had to travel by word of mouth. The meetings were for social and business purposes. First, they provided an opportunity for all of us to get together at the same place and time, hang out, and get fucked up on weed, booze, dust, or whatever. And second, it allowed for discussion about important issues, like welcoming new homies who'd recently been jumped in, getting the 411 on what was hap'nin' with our enemies, who'd died, who'd gotten locked up, jumped, shot, etc.

That night, all of the homies, except those locked up, of course, showed up for the meeting. Everyone was dressed 'to the G' in Gangsta attire: blue or black khaki pants or jeans with tons of starch that formed creases so stiff, the pants could have stood up by themselves; blue khaki shirts with three creases ironed down the front and back; and blue 'rags' (bandanas) that were either wrapped around the leg, arm, hand, neck, forehead, or hanging out of back pockets. Some of the female Gangstas even wore blue curlers in their hair or blue nail polish.

Fly and Dob guided me throughout the crowd, introducing me to homies I hadn't met before. I met Smokey, Lurch, Hunchie, and many others. Each one greeted me with a 'What's up, cuzzz?,' the Tray sign, Crip sign, or some other warm welcome. In the middle of all those flying hand signs, the crazy slang, and the sea of blue, I felt incredibly loved, extremely powerful, and totally safe.

And there was always plenty of 8-Ball, Night Train, Thunderbird, weed, and sherm being passed around.

141

Sidewinder began by welcoming the newest homies. Although my Crip name was Lady Lightning, I was introduced as Cupcake. At first I was pissed that they refused to call me Lightning. I'd got my ass kicked for that name and wanted it used. Besides, Cupcake was so wimpy. Nobody wants to get struck by lightning, so everyone's afraid of it. Who the fuck's afraid of a cupcake?

After Sidewinder acknowledged me, the homies began hugging me or giving me the Gangsta sign or whoopin' and hollerin' our famous hoo-bang: 'Gang-sta Ca-rips!' It was then I realized that I didn't care what they called me – as long as they considered me one of them.

After the welcoming, Sidewinder began the business portion of the meeting. He warned that Fly, Monster, Crazy D, and Tray-Ball had recently beat down some 60's. For payback, the 60's had threatened to hoo-ride. And, several nights previously, some Pirus (Bloods) had blasted on the set, badly wounding one homie and killing another. At this announcement, everyone performed the usual ritual for displaying respect for the dead: pouring a few drops of whatever liquor you were drinking onto the ground. I hated this ritual because I felt that any booze I poured out wasn't gonna do the dead any good; it would do much better in my stomach. Hell, every little bit counts.

I didn't personally know the two homies who'd gotten blasted, though Fly said I'd met them my first night on the set. But he reminded me that that didn't matter. They were *homies*. And any homie killed was like a brother or sister being killed. So like everyone else, I poured out a little of my Thunderbird for the fallen homeboy. These rituals helped instill a profound sense of loyalty and dedication in all the members. It trained us to love the gang more than our family, friends, even ourselves.

Sidewinder announced the location and time of the funeral, and everyone started to discuss who was going to stand watch. I turned and asked Fly what that meant. He explained that the ultimate sign of disrespect to a fallen gang member, his family, and his surviving homies is for his killers to storm the funeral and turn over his casket. The rival gang would rush the church – either 'blued' down or 'red' down (dressed entirely in red or blue), shouting their set and tossing their signs. They'd make a mad dash to the casket – creating terror and complete chaos as the dead boy's or girl's family and friends ran for cover – snatch the casket, and ferociously toss it on its side, the dead banger and flowers flying every which way. Then, they'd casually stroll out of the church, throwing up signs and hoo-banging all the way.

'Casket-turning' was the final fuck-you to the entire set of the dead gang member. So whenever a Gangsta was killed, homies stood watch in front of the church, packed with firepower, waiting – and hoping – for enemies to show up and *try* to turn over the casket. Fly said that although Gangstas had been known to turn a few caskets, we'd never had one turned on us. We refused to be dissed like that. And, if anyone would have, there would've been additional bodies for the mortuary to bury that day.

After discussing the funeral, there was the issue of who was going to avenge the set. Whenever a rival gang hoo-rides, retaliation is required – and fast – which usually means we hoo-ride the same night. But since our homie had been shot, the 'po-pos' (police) had been riding on the slobs pretty hard because the same night they rode on us, they'd shot a cop. We sure couldn't ride while the police were riding, so we had to wait a few days. Those few days were now up and it was time to ride. We were gonna bust on some slobs.

Sidewinder proudly announced that I, with Fly, Dob, and Bones, would be doing my first hoo-ride. I tried not to look surprised (or scared) about Sidewinder's announcement. I glanced toward Fly, thinking maybe he could do or say something to get me out of having to shoot someone. But the wide-ass grin on Fly's face, showing nothing but teeth, removed any ideas I might have had of him offering help. He was clearly looking forward to my first hoo-ride.

So that's what Huck meant by my 'being up.' Shit, could I really shoot someone? Hell, I was a druggie and a boozer, not a killer. Besides, I hadn't been banging a month yet. I'd thought they'd give me time to work into it.

I was busy thinking of how to get out of the situation, when Fly sneaked up from behind me and gave me a long, hearty, bear hug.

'Don't worry, lil cuzzz,' he said in his legendary sexy voice, 'I'll be wit' ya and I got yo' back.'

The love and pride that beamed on his face quickly removed my doubts. I was surrounded by all the homies, everyone drinking, smoking, cussing, and Crip-walkin' to the funky sounds of Cameo, Bootsy, and Parliament. As I looked around me, I was reminded that Fly and the homies loved and accepted me – just as I was. All I had to be was down.

It was then that I decided I'd do anything for them. Anything. I tossed up my three middle fingers to show our beloved Gangstas sign, snatched the Thunderbird from Fly's hand, and gulped till the warm liquid traveling down my stomach turned my fear into courage, and then into anger, and then into rage.

We were in Dob's blue Impala. Every window was tinted pitch-black, which made us invisible to the outside world when the windows were rolled up. But we generally kept the windows down because when you're hoo-ridin' you don't want to conceal your identity. You *want* your enemy to see you. It's imperative that they know who blasted on their set. It was this type of unfettered violence, the straight-out, in-yo'-face blood-shed, murder, and mayhem carried out without the slightest thought of the lives that would be forever touched, that earned a gang its rep for ruthlessness. And Gangstas were notorious for ruthlessness.

Dob was driving. Fly was in the front with a .410 gauge. I was in the back holding a .38. Bones sat next to me. He didn't have a 'gat.' His job was to coach me along and, if necessary, take over in case I punked out. But I wasn't worrying about punking out. I'd drunk quite a bit of Thunderbird and Old 8, and smoked half a sherm stick. In fact, the sherm was telling me that it was those fucking slobs that had paid Pete to rape me and they deserved to die. I was ready to kill!

We rode around the Pirus' hood for a while. The word must have gotten out that we were riding that night because there wasn't a soul in sight. Just as we were getting ready to call it a night and return to the set, Fly spotted some niggas sitting on a porch.

We were about a block away. We quickly rolled up the windows, turned off our lights, silently pulled over, and checked them out. We wanted to make sure they were bangers.

Back then, when hoo-ridin' on a rival gang, you were

considered a pussy if you shot nongang members. It wasn't like it is today: total chaos. Back then, there were certain unwritten rules: babies, kids, parents, and squares were off-limits. Of course, accidents did happen and were even expected. So to shoot into a crowd that included some bangers was acceptable. But to *intentionally* shoot into a crowd where you knew no one present was in 'the game' was seen as weak, the action of a punk or a mark, and it would lose you respect.

Fly and Dob recognized two of the niggas from the N-Hood set. They weren't Pirus but they were slobs, which was close enough. Hell, we were high, pissed, and revved up. We had to blast.

'You ready, cuzzz?' Fly asked me as we turned on the lights and slowly headed toward the house.

'Yeah, cuzzz, I'm straight,' I replied.

There were four of them on the porch. I saw the red ember from what looked like a joint and the familiar shape of a 40-ounce. It didn't occur to me that they were just like us, living mirror images of our own lives. Dob's car was so quiet as it cruised up, and they were so busy smoking and drinking that they never saw us coming – till it was too late.

As we got closer, Fly and I rolled down our windows just in time for the slobs to see the barrels.

'Duck, Blood!' one of them screamed.

Everything happened in a flash.

'Gangstas!' Fly yelled as he let off the .410.

'Ca-r-i-ps!' I shouted as I shot my .38.

The kick was stronger than I remembered. Besides, I wasn't that big. The kick threw me back into Bones who was sitting up behind me, not wanting to miss any of the fun.

'Blast, cuzzz! Blast!' he ordered, grabbing my shoulders and shoving me back up to the window.

And I did. I blasted two more shots as the car sped off. One of the bullets struck the porch light, turning everything black so that I could no longer see who was still standing or what was happening on the porch. *Just shoot in their direction,* I told myself. I didn't want to stop shooting till Fly did. I tried to get off a third shot but the jerk from Dob's speeding off threw me back into Bones again.

As we pulled off laughing and hoo-banging, I didn't have a

care about what I'd just done. I didn't have a worry as to who might have been hurt. If anyone had any doubt before, it was gone now. I was more than down. I was *down*.

We went to Crazy D's house to get the hooptie off the streets and chill. D's would become one of my favorite hangouts because not only was his house close to ours, but he was one of Fly's closest homies, and his sister Peanut was one of mine.

Crip Karen, Peanut, Hunchie, and several other homies were already there.

I walked in expecting everyone to bombard us with questions. No one did. I was goin' crazy with excitement. I wanted to tell them all about my first ride. But I had to be cool and wait till the appropriate moment. No one said anything for a while. We all just sat around drinking 8-ball and Night Train and smoking sherm and Gunji (Jamaican weed).

Out of the blue, someone asked about the night's activities.

'What's up, cuzzz?' Hunchie asked as he passed me the sherm stick he'd just hit.

Finally!

Everyone got quiet, waiting for a report on my first hoo-ride.

'I got at least two of them!' I proudly declared.

'Damn, cuzzz,' he slurred, the sherm already taking affect. 'This shit is live!'

I hit the sherm and passed it. Everyone was so into the sherm, no one was paying much attention to me.

'I said I got two of them!' I stated again, irritated at being ignored.

'Cuzzz, yo' ass ain't hit shit!' Fly teased. 'Wit' yo' nonshootin' ass!'

'Yeah,' Bones chimed in, 'that thirty-eight kick was so tough, if I hadn't been holdin' her up she'da spent all her time layin' down in the backseat!'

Everyone broke out laughing – even me. But I knew that, although they were teasing me with love, they were giving me a subtle message: I needed to bone up on my shooting, or rather my aiming. Missing wasn't allowed.

We later learned that no one was killed from our hoo-ride, though we did hit three of them: two seriously. One was paralyzed from the waist down and would be in a wheelchair for life. Everyone wanted to take credit for his injury. I swore it

146

was one of my bullets. I was hungry to have been the trigger person and didn't think twice about the consequences. But Fly swore it was the pellets from his gauge.

Even though no one was killed, I still earned respect for doing the drive-by. It was the start of developing a reputation. But there would be more lessons to learn before sealing my rep. One of my favorites was learning to Crip-walk. Crip-walking was a popular dance among bangers, done only by bangers. The dance itself is hard to describe, and it has changed over the years, though the basic steps remain the same; a combination of skiplike steps and other fancy footwork. The OGs Crip-walked so sexy, cool, and smooth, it was a real delight just watching them. *True* Crip-walkin' was an art. Real Gangstas could Crip-walk while simultaneously hoo-bangin' and throwin' up various forms of their set's signs, positioning the fingers and thumb to form a gun, tossing the middle finger up to 'the man,' etc., all to the funkiest, hippest beats of favorite songs. One of the Gangstas' favorite songs was 'Freak of the Week' by Parliament. We always took songs and replaced the words with Gangsta phrases. So instead of 'freak of the week,' we said 'Crip of the week.' Another phrase in the song, 'never learned to swim,' was replaced with 'never learned to Brim' (the Brims were a rival Blood gang).

I also learned how to Crip-write and, in perfect Crip style, tagged my name anywhere and everywhere: on bus seats, on the walls of houses, apartments, and businesses. I kept a blue Magic Marker with me at all times. My favorite tags were 'Lady Cupcake, Slob Killer'; 'Lady Cupcake, 60's Killer' (to denote '60's Killer,' I'd write '60's' and then mark a giant X over the *60's*); or 'Lady Cupcake – Gangsta Ca-rip Cuzzz.'

Gangstas also taught me how to make money by 'working a store.' A whole group of us would go into a store, and since the shopkeeper couldn't watch ten to fifteen people at once, several homies kept the sales clerks occupied (or uncomfortably nervous), while others quickly stuffed shit down their pants, under their shirts, in their jackets, or wherever it would fit. All we were usually interested in, though, were things we could quickly sell: clothes, cigarettes, and booze.

I also learned how to rob people. We called it 'jackin'.' Sometimes we used weapons, but a lot of times we didn't. It's not that we were above using guns to make people give up what we demanded; it's just that it often wasn't necessary. Most times our sheer numbers, blended with the Gangstas' violent reputation and the ferocity on our faces, were the only weapons we needed. I didn't have a problem with jackin' folks face-to-face when I was drunk or loaded. But when sober, I still had *sort* of a conscience, which sometimes slowed me down.

But don't get me wrong, I loved the look of fear on the victims' faces. It gave me a sense of power and supremacy. But the problem was that while I knew that *I* wasn't going to seriously hurt anyone (I mean, I'd beat your ass or try to shoot or stab you in a nonfatal part of your body, but that's as far as I'd go), I couldn't say the same for my homies. They were *really* ruthless and would kill yo' ass in a heartbeat – drunk *or* sober. So when I was rolling with the kind of Gangsta whose *extreme* violence was unscheduled and unexpected, I'd stick to my favorite type of jackin': robbin' folks on the bus.

We'd find some unsuspecting sucker draped in gold, sitting near the rear door of a bus. Back then, flaunting gold was the thing and even a lot of squares did it. Anyway, after spotting our victim, we'd ring the bell to be let off at the next stop. As the bus pulled over to let us off, one homie would hold the door open while the others snatched the gold – all of it – necklaces and earrings (leaving big holes and blood where the earrings used to be) and whatever else we could snatch off the person – and run off the bus, laughing and hollering, 'Gangstas!' all the way.

The poor stoolie – if he had the balls to try to chase us, he usually got stopped by the bus door slamming in his face. The homie whose job it was to hold the door would let it go just after we'd slipped through it – and just as the victim reached for it. Or the bus driver, unaware of what was happening, would pull off heading toward his next stop.

In fact, it was best if the victim didn't catch us, because if he did, he'd soon regret it. For us, it would be a free-for-all beatdown – *we'd beat dey ass like* dey *stole something!*

These jacks were my favorite 'cause they always paid well. Unlike face-to-face robberies where you didn't know what you were going to get (sometimes the victim wouldn't have more than five dollars on them), with gold jackin's you almost always got a good payoff. Pawnshops and dope dealers always took gold. Always.

I celebrated my fifteenth birthday with the Gangstas. The homies gave me a jammin' party with plenty of booze, dope, and Crip-walking.

There was a school in the hood – Washington High. I had missed so much school, no one was sure whether I should be placed in ninth or tenth grade. No one could make any real sense out of my muddled, incomplete records, so the school decided the tenth was close enough.

Aunt Becky didn't know Fly and I were bangers, even though a variety of homies were always at our house – especially Dob, Lep, and Huck, who lived down the street. Nor could their personalities have tipped her off. Around her, they didn't act like the violent, vicious thugs that they actually were. They were always extremely courteous and well mannered. In fact, all of the homies were respectful and courteous to, and around, one another's parents and family. You'd get yo' ass kicked for dissin' somebody's momma. Because of Fly's (and now my) member- ship in the Gangstas, Aunt Becky was safe all over the hood. So although she walked everywhere she went (she couldn't drive), she was never jumped or attacked – even when she was coming from the bank.

Fly and I got extremely close during those years. Once I was no longer 'in training,' we did a lot of our crimes together. We spent so much time together that we decided I shouldn't sleep in the living room anymore. He had two twin beds in his room, so I moved into his room with him and slept on one of them. We were so close, a lot of the homies, and all his girlfriends, swore we were screwin'. But we weren't. We were just extremely close. We shared a special bond and it showed. He was like the big brother I'd never had, the father I'd tragically and suddenly lost, and the protective, caring boyfriend I secretly desired. Fly never made an inappropriate move toward me. Never. Still, no matter how strongly we denied the rumors and inquiries about being intimate, no one ever really believed us.

I loved being in South Central. Aunt Becky, really too elderly to be raising young, robust, active kids, pretty much let us do what we wanted. I loved having four brothers and, for once, not getting my ass beat regularly. (During my years as a Gangsta, I'd been jumped on by rivals and beaten up during gang fights, but in my mind, that was different.)

Although I didn't have to, I continued turning tricks – but that's not what I called it. I was now calling it a 'business arrangement.' I never really went looking for my 'business partners'; they always seemed to find me. One night the po-pos had swooped on Gangsta Park, gathered up a few of us homies, threatening to take us in. I was given to a young rookie who was supposed to call in and run a check on me. Licking my lips and giving the sexiest smile I could muster, I propositioned him about a little cheerleading practice. Thinking with the wrong head, he found the offer hard to pass up. He became a regular. Soon, he hipped me to one of his friends who was also a cop and who also became a regular. Whenever one of them heard my name come across the radio, he'd show up and say, 'I'll take care of this one.' It didn't happen often, just enough to prevent a couple of trips to juvie with the others. They took care of me and I took care of them. And, as I did with Mr Bassinet, I viewed their 'taking care of me' as a form of affection, protection, and security. So I saw nothing wrong with what *either* of us was doing.

My homies thought I kept just missing going to jail because I was a fast talker and a good bullshitter. They thought I had 'game.' Boy were they wrong.

My other regular 'business partner' also came by happenstance. Early in my banging, one of my closest home-girls, Peaches, lived in the 107 Hoover territory. (How she was able to claim Gangsta while living in a Hoover's set, I never knew – and never asked.)

Peaches and I were really tight, so I spent a lot of time over her house. Her boyfriend was a Hoover named Devil. Devil also spent a lot of time at Peaches', and often brought along Looney, one of his homeboys. Soon, Looney and I were going together. We didn't go together very long, but it was long enough for me to meet and get to know his dad.

One night, I'd dropped by Loon's house for a surprise visit, but he wasn't home. His father invited me to wait. While waiting, we had a couple of drinks, got tipsy, and well . . . he propositioned me with a monetary offer. I didn't have to think long about whether to accept. And I figured what Looney didn't know wouldn't hurt him. Our business arrangement provided me with a quick way to make money when jackin', robbin', and thievin' were slow. Looney seemed to like the fact that his father and I were so close. He never knew how close.

Unfortunately, my friendship with Peaches didn't last long – that silly girl started going out with Fly. I told her he was a dog, but she didn't believe me. She couldn't get past his fine looks, tight body, streetwise attitude, and irresistible charisma. She fell in love, caught him with another woman (he was always getting caught with other women), and was devastated. She said that her broken heart wouldn't allow her to be around Fly. And, because he and I were so tight, she said I was 'guilty' by association. So, just like that, my 'ace-boon-coon' was gone. Fly didn't care that he'd come in between me and one of my best friends. He just shrugged and moved on to the next victim.

But losing the friendship with Peaches was rough on me. I still had my other homegirls whom I loved dearly, especially Peanut and Yokey. In fact, it was Yokey who'd, unknowingly, assisted me in finding a new favorite color. I'd been trained, taught, and brainwashed to hate, despise, and abhor anything and everything red. (Back then, I wouldn't even admit it had once been my favorite color.) Then one day while hanging out, Yokey gave me a book.

Bangers were some of the most intelligent people I'd ever met. Some of them read regularly; others had a natural talent with numbers and thus were exceptional at math; still others liked art, were good with their hands, etc. Because Yokey liked to read, as I did, we often exchanged books and had deep discussions about those we'd read.

It was during a discussion about that book that I decided purple would be my new favorite color. There was a line in the book that said the color purple just wanted to be loved like everything else, like me. It would take over eighteen years before I would be able to uncorrupt my brain to allow red to return as a favorite color.

Our mutual love for reading was one reason Yokey and I became so close. Still, I missed the extra-special bond I'd shared with Peaches. She'd been my downest, tightest 'homegurl.' Her sudden and seemingly effortless dismissal of our friendship increased my lack of trust. I didn't think I would ever get that close to another girl again – till I met Rabbit and Trish.

Rabbit and Trish were sisters who claimed 74 Hoover. We'd met at a Gangsta party that'd been given to celebrate my homie Bam's release from jail. At the time, the 74's were allies, so many of them came and partied with us. The party was in the backyard of one of the homies' pads. Gangstas and Hoovers were smoking, drinking, and Crip-walking all over the place. I was standing at the side of the house, smoking a joint with Crip Karen and Lady B.B., when Rabbit, Trish, Yokey, and Pokey came walking by. They had to walk single file to be able to pass through the narrow walkway that led from the back of the house out to the street.

'We making a run for more forties,' Yokey said to me as she passed. 'You down, cuzzz?'

'Straight that, cuzzz,' I replied.

As we headed for the store, Yokey introduced me to Rabbit and Trish. Although they were sisters they didn't look alike (probably because they had different fathers). Rabbit was a tall, thin dark-skinned girl, with thick, full lips that opened into a friendly smile. She said 'Rabbit' was short for 'Jack Rabbit,' because she was fast with her hands. Trish was much shorter, with cocoa-colored skin. Though she was thin, she had a full face with chubby chipmunk cheeks. Trish said that 'Trish' *was* her Crip name.

'So you Lady Cupcake?' Rabbit asked me. We'd returned from the store and were sitting around downing the 8-ball we'd just copped. 'I heard you pretty down.'

'Down enough,' I replied. 'What about you?'

'S-h-i-t, dis all Hoover here,' she said in a slow drawl, while throwin' up four fingers – the sign for 74 Hoover.

Trish quickly joined her. They were hoo-bangin' 'H-o-o-v-e-r C-a-rip!' I couldn't just let 'em hoo-bang on me, so I started hoo-bangin' back: 'G-a-n-g-s-t-a Ca-rip!' We hoo-banged and Crip-walked till we ran out of breath and fell to the ground, panting and laughing. That was the start of our friendship. We quickly became best friends. Rabbit and Trish were already tight – they just let me into the circle.

Rabbit and Trish lived within walking distance of my house. So almost every day I was over at their house or they were at mine. Unless you saw us from the back (my shirt had three creases, theirs had four), or unless you saw us hoo-bangin' (I threw up three fingers and they threw up four), you couldn't tell we were from different sets. We were always 'blued' down – even to the blue curlers in our hair and blue polish on our nails. We ditched together, fought against rivals together, hoo-rode together, and jacked together. Rabbit loved bus jackin' just as much as I did – which really sealed our alliance to each other. You had to have each other's back while jackin', because you never knew when you would have to beat down a mothafucka.

I still have a scar on my right finger given to me when Rabbit accidentally cut me instead of the sucker we were jackin'. But that was only one of many jacks that had gone wrong. We never considered stopping, though; we just tossed it up to an occupational hazard.

Rabbit, Trish, and I became inseparable. But then Fly had started 'goin' wit' ' Rabbit. He'd already ruined one special friendship, and I didn't want it to happen again. Luckily, I quickly found a love of my own to take my mind off them. Five fine-ass brothers – Egg, Beat-Down, Hoover Rick, B. Killer (Blood Killer), and Insane – lived in a big house directly across the street from Rabbit and Trish. They all claimed 74 Hoover. Trish was going with Egg. I liked Hoover Rick the moment I saw him. He was thin and brown-skinned, with the cutest smile. He must have dug me too because we started goin' together.

Rick had a nephew named Timmy. Timmy was only five years old, but they called him a 'lil Hoover-in-training.' His mother was Rick's only sister. And she, like a lot of parents, was ignorant of the signs of banging: the clothing (she thought khaki pants and shirts with four creases down the back were the current style), the colors, the lingo. She thought it was cute that Timmy was always donned in blue like his uncles. She had no clue that when little Timmy would announce that four was his favorite number, he was talking about 74 Hoover. Because her brothers used 'cuzzz' all the time, she thought nothing of it when Timmy used it regularly. In fact, most of the homies's little brothers and sisters were always thought of as lil homies-in-training. It wasn't hard. Little kids, like big ones, wanted to be accepted and loved. So they loved hanging with the big homies. They felt the same unconditional love, safety, and power we did and quickly wanted to become a permanent part of it.

Trish, Rabbit, and I were becoming tighter and tighter, though I didn't realize how tight till Fly and Rabbit broke up. I was afraid she'd pull the plug on our friendship like Peaches had done. But Rabbit was a player too. Shit, she shook him off just like he did her. Our friendship never missed a beat. In fact, we got closer.

I also experienced the dark side of the love we shared as a set: I got to bury many homies who'd been killed. One was Bam. Bam was an OG who, when he wasn't in jail, stayed shermed out. He smoked so much sherm that a lot of times he didn't know where he was or who he was. But, when he wasn't shermed, he was a down mothafucka!

Anyway, one night Fly and I were comin' from a party. We saw Bam lying on a bus-stop bench across the street from a donut shop that had a giant donut as its sign. We tried to wake him up and get him to go home because we knew lying around like that would only bring trouble. But try as we might, we couldn't get Bam to move. In fact, he started fightin' us, yellin' at us to leave him 'the fuck alone!' We tried for a while longer, pleading with Bam to come with us. He refused to budge.

'Fuck it,' Fly finally said. 'He ain't movin'. Come on, cuzzz, let's go.'

So we left Bam lying there, singing to a tune only he could hear.

Several days later they found Bam. He'd been beaten, shot, *and* run over. Rumor was the LAPD did it. I wasn't surprised. The LAPD was known for gathering a few homies, taking them off somewhere, beatin' the shit out of them only to bring 'em back and toss 'em from the car as a warning to the rest of us. We never bothered filing any complaints. Shit, we knew that complaining would never do any good. They were cops (the good guys) and we were thugs (the bad ones). Who would believe us?

Anyway, the LAPD hated Bam, because he was always talkin' shit to them.

'Take off that badge,' he'd tell them, 'and I'll whup yo' ass!'

Rumor was that they'd had enough of his talking shit and decided to teach him a lesson.

But, another homie said it was the Rollin' 60's not the LAPD who'd done it. Still another said it was the N-Hoods. Whoever Bam's killer was, the cops certainly never found them. Killers of Gangstas, hooligans, and thugs weren't very high on society's 'most wanted' list.

Fly's best friend, Lucky, was also killed. He'd been set up by his brother's girlfriend who, for a payoff, told the 60's where he lived. They beat him, shot him, and left his body lying at the side of his house for his mother to find. That was the first time I'd ever seen Fly cry. Two weeks later, the brother's girlfriend mysteriously ended up dead.

These were just a few of several funerals I got to attend as a Gangsta. Funerals and death were a part of Gangsta life. I chalked it up to just part of 'the game.' I was never really concerned about dying because I never thought it could happen to me – I seriously believed I couldn't die. I figured the homies who had gotten killed ended up that way because they weren't down enough, fast enough, cool enough, tough enough.

And the brainwashing helped. Gangstas convinced me that dying wasn't a bad thing. They used to say, 'Gangstas don't die, they multiply.' They convinced me that there was a special heaven just for Gangstas – Gangsta heaven – and no matter how many people you killed, robbed, or beat, if you were a Gangsta, you'd go to Gangsta heaven where all the other fallen homies were, and we'd all party forever.

So I had no fear of dying and continued working on earning a rep for being a down Gangsta bitch: robbing, thieving, shooting, stabbing, fighting. I put in work to earn the respect and admiration of my homies. During this time, I'd been in many gang fights and hoo-rides. I got my ass whupped, and whupped some ass. I got hurt and hurt others. *All* of my bangin' activities were done while loaded; most were done while in a blackout. I enjoyed, even welcomed, the blackouts because they allowed me to have no clue as to what atrocities I'd committed. However, the next day my homies would always be more than happy to inform me about everything I'd said or done. Every now and then my conscience would rise up and I'd begin to feel bad about the way I was living and the things we were doing. But then I'd get around the homies. Between their love, the booze, the drugs, and the blackouts, my conscience was shut down.

Besides, there was no time for guilt – I was becoming a ghetto star.

A ghetto star is someone who's well respected in the gang. They can fight, shoot, rob, steal, and have a rep for being ruthless, callous, and down. Several of the homies were already considered ghetto stars: Fly, Sidewinder, Monster, Huck-A-Buck, Crazy D, and numerous others. Several of the Gangsta-lettes had also earned that coveted title: Peanut, Big Lynn, Mooney, Crip Karen, Yokey, and others. I was on my way.

I decided I wanted to die a ghetto star – that is, till those bullets hit my ass.

18

I had been in South Central for over a year when Jr. called to say that Mr Burns had surfaced yet again. He'd called Jr., threatening to remove me from Becky's unless Jr. gave him the life-insurance money my mother had left us. (How he'd discovered where I was is still a mystery.)

Jr. explained to Mr Burns that even if he wanted to give Mr Burns the money, he couldn't. The way my momma had the trust set up, no one could touch it but the children – and not till we turned eighteen. But Jr. said he also made it clear to Mr Burns that even if he *could* give him the money, he wouldn't. My momma had left that money for me and Larry, and Jr. knew that if Mr Burns ever got his hands on it there'd be nothing left for us.

'Well then, I'm comin' to get my daughter.' Mr Burns snapped. He said he'd bring legal action to have 'his child' returned to him.

'And you know I'll win,' he gloated. 'I'm the 'biological parent,' remember?'

He told Jr. to be expecting a legal representative to come and get me in a few days. Before Jr. could respond, he slammed down the phone.

Now why he want to fuck wit' me now? I asked myself. I personally hadn't seen or spoken to Mr Burns since the day he gave us to Diane. And even after Aunt Becky had the mailing address for my Social Security checks changed so that they were sent to her address, neither Mr Burns or Diane contested or even made a peep. (Though later I learned that during my entire time in South Central, Diane continued to collect foster-care payments for me.)

I wasn't physically afraid of Diane anymore. I knew how to fight. And bangin', beatin' up others, and gettin' beat had given me heart. So I knew that if she *acted* like she was gonna put her hands on me, I'd kick *her* ass. But still, I didn't want to be bothered with her, her crazy-ass daughter, and the insanity that was constantly present in their house. So we told Aunt Becky I was returning to Lancaster, but in truth, I ran away. I didn't run far. I kept my clothes in Crip Karen's backyard, and at night I slept at different homies' houses, though I spent most of the time at Trish and Rabbit's or at Hoover Rick's, who'd sneak me into his room after his mom went to sleep. I actually preferred this lifestyle – living from pillar to post – complete freedom. I loved being free.

Fly would keep up with where I was and check on me from time to time. But the good thing about being in a gang was that it was like having lots of brothers and sisters. So if Fly wasn't checkin' on me, Dob, Huck, or one of my other homies was.

My sixteenth birthday was coming up, so I decided to celebrate. Trish, Egg, Hoover Rick, Rabbit, Goofey Grape, Crip Jr., B. Killer, Insane, and I were all hanging out in front of Rick's house. We had a couple of 40s, and fifths of gin, rum, and vodka. Hoover Rick had copped some bo (weed) that was the bomb. It was a very informal party – the girls were sitting on a car that was parked at the curb, while the fellas stood around us. We were all just drinking, smoking, laughing, talking shit, and having a good ol' time. Rick's nephew, Timmy, was running around play-boxing with the homies, screaming 'H-o-o-v-e-r!' and tossing up three fingers. He was only seven and had trouble holding up four fingers. So, although he'd hold up three (the sign for Gangsta), he'd hoo-bang Hoover. He was so little and cute.

Later that evening, Fly and Huck came by to check on me. They said they were on their way to ride on some slobs. Fly told me he didn't like me 'living in the streets like this.' I responded that I had no other choice. He shrugged, as if he understood. Then he did something he'd never done before. He reached into his pocket and took out a twenty-dollar bill. 'Happy early birthday, cuzzz,' he said as he slipped the money into my hand. He bent over, kissed me on my cheek, and told me to be careful.

Then he quickly turned around and started walking away. (I don't know if it was because he was in a hurry or because he didn't want me to see him getting mushy.) Then, Huck stepped up and gave me a big ol' bear hug. He finally let me go, rubbed the top of my head (I hated when he did that), told me to 'stay down,' and took off running behind Fly.

Man, I loved being loved!

Timmy's mom came outside and made him go in. He didn't want to. He screamed and cried and begged her to let him stay with the big homies five more minutes. But it was after seven P.M. and she wanted to give him a bath, so she insisted he go in. The girls all took turns kissing him, while the boys slapped him five and told him to 'stay down.' He tried to push us away murmuring 'yuck,' as if he didn't like to be kissed, but we knew he loved it. And he'd try to look menacingly at the fellas to show he was down. Then, he hoo-banged one last time before turning and running into the house. I loved the feeling of family.

Rabbit and I took the twenty dollars I'd gotten from Fly, copped some lovely, and returned to Rick's where we continued hanging out, smoking lovely, listening to music, and talking shit. We partied as the night went on, just enjoying life and each other when a car slowly rolled up on us. We watched closely as the front and rear passenger windows slid down. A nigga stuck his head out each window and started hoo-bangin': 'Sixties! Rollin' Sixties!' while throwin' up their set. Of course we *had* to hoo-bang back. I hollered, 'G-a-n-g-s-t-a!' while the others shouted, 'H-o-o-v-e-r! Seven-fo'!'

The 60's started crackin' up laughing as they peeled off.

Although they'd identified themselves as Rollin' 60's, I didn't recognize any of them. 'Who was that, cuzzz?' I asked, to no one in particular.

'Dat was No Neck and the Twins,' Egg said. 'Dem niggas' a be back.' He was looking down the street in the direction the car had gone. 'And we'll be ready for 'em when they do!' he hollered as he turned and ran into the house. A moment later, he returned with a 12-gauge shotgun and a .45 Magnum. He gave the .45 to Insane, while he began examining the gauge – making sure it was loaded and ready.

We stood there for a while, ready and waiting, but they didn't come back. This put us in an awkward situation. In South

Central, a bunch of black kids couldn't be standing out in the open – especially with guns – because the po-pos, who get suspicious just by seeing more than two of us in one spot together, would surely stop and search everybody. We had to make a judgment call whether or not to put the guns away. After about twenty minutes with still no sign of the 60's, we figured they weren't comin' back. So Egg took the guns back into the house.

The rest of us went on with my party.

I was sitting on a car parked in front of Rick's house. My back was to the street. Rick was standing in front of me beside a large tree. We had begun discussing whether I should turn myself in and be returned to Lancaster or whether I should continue living from homie to homie. Problem with the latter option was that I was running out of places to stay. Our discussion was turning into an argument as I tried to explain to Rick why Lancaster was not, and would never be, an option.

A few minutes later, as Egg was coming back outside from taking in the guns, the 60's car rounded the corner.

By now, Rick and I were yelling and cussing at each other. All of my attention and energy was focused on trying to make Rick realize my hatred for Lancaster. So I was unprepared and completely taken off guard when I heard a rustling all around me. All of a sudden someone hollered 'Duck, cuzzz! Duck!'

The sherm was better than I'd realized because everything appeared to be happening in slow motion.

I turned my head over my right shoulder to see what all the commotion was about.

It was then I realized we were being revisited by the 60's.

I saw the car slowly moving, seemingly *inching* by. Then, I saw a barrel ever so slowly poke out of the front passenger window.

Then I saw a flash. Actually, it looked more like a bunch of sparks. A sparkly firecracker. The array of sparks started off narrow and seemed to widen as they flew toward me.

I felt a burning in my back on the right side. The force of the blast knocked me past Rick and into the tree beside him. No sooner had I screamed from the pain of my face smashing into the tree, I felt two more ferocious blows SLAM my back. It felt like someone with a huge heated hammer was whacking the shit

160

out of my back – with the force of a lumberjack. One hard whack – bam! And then another. Both blows caused my body to bend awkwardly as both of my arms flung helplessly in the air.

I bounced off the tree and fell to the ground. At first, I didn't know what had happened. I thought I was on fire because my back was burning so badly. Then it hit me. *I think I've been shot!*

So I started screamin', 'I'm shot, cuzzz! I'm shot!'

The group exploded in pandemonium.

Trish started runnin' up and down the middle of the street, screaming, 'Cup's been shot! Goddammit, mothafuckas, Cup's been shot!'

Rabbit wasn't runnin'. She was standing over me and shouting from the top of her lungs 'Oh, Lord, no! Oh, Lord, no!' over and over and over.

The fellas were trying to get me to keep still. I was rolling from side to side, but never able to completely roll over. All I could think of was an elementary-school safety tip: *When on fire, stop, drop and roll.* (I felt like I was on fire. I had already dropped – so hell, I was rolling!)

The burning was unbearable. My body was writhing in pain.

As Rick was bending over me, trying to help the homies keep me still, drops of blood began to drip onto my face.

Shocked, the homies suddenly stopped wrestling with me, and stared at Rick – wondering where the blood was coming from.

Egg was the first to realize what was happening. ''Ey, cuzzz, you bleeding,' he said.

Rick looked down at himself. His entire shirt was soaked red. His pants were beginning to cling to his body from the release of blood. He'd been shot and didn't even know it. But looking at the blood that now soaked the entire left side of his body, he knew it then – and fainted.

We lay there for what seemed like forever. I suddenly realized that I couldn't move my legs. But I wasn't sure if it was because of getting shot or because of the sherm. Finally, one-time (another name for the cops) came. At first, they didn't want to take us to the hospital.

'Why should we waste time trying to save these guys?' the tall

161

white cop asked the crowd of bangers who'd gathered around their fallen.

My pain was intensifying.

'All y'all do is kill each other,' the cop said. 'So what's the use, since they'll probably be dead niggas in a year.' He stated it so matter-of-factly. Not like he was trying to be mean. Just like he was stating reality.

The pain increased. It was excruciating. I began to feel like I was going to pass out. Before going out, I heard Egg snap, 'What the fuck you say?'

I wanted to lift my head and say, 'He said we're worthless,' but the pain was too great. So, like Rick, I passed out.

I awoke in the ambulance. Rick was still out. 'Where we goin'?' I asked the white guy who was bending over me taking my blood pressure.

'To the hospital,' he snapped, as if I were bothering him. Although my back was still on fire, I noticed that I didn't hear any sirens. So I asked the ambulance guy why there was no siren on.

'Isn't this an emergency?' I asked.

'Yeah,' he snarled, seemingly angrier than before. 'It's just that it's soundproof in here.'

'Oh,' I said, accepting his explanation. Years later, a medic told me that those things aren't really soundproof. They didn't have the siren on.

We were taken to Morningside Hospital – the only hospital in the hood. Morningside wasn't like a nice, upper-class hospital where the doctor comes out to talk to the family and calmly and quietly informs them of the patient's condition and possible forms of treatment. My interaction with the doctor went like this: he came into my room, looked at me with disgust, and said, 'You've been shot with what looks like two guns. X-rays show bullets lodged in between your vertebrae.'

He paused and looked at me as if it was time for a question – which was a good thing, because I had one.

'So what's that mean?'

'You may not walk again.' He turned and walked out the room, making it clear that there'd be no more questions.

'I might not walk again?' I screamed after him. 'I might not walk again? What the fuck do you mean I might not walk again?' But my screaming was in vain. He'd spoken his piece and gone.

I tried to move my legs, but couldn't. *Was he right? Or was it just another one of those bad sherm trips?*

I lay there sobbing alone. It was then I realized my homies weren't anywhere around. There was no one to help, no one to call out to.

What about God? This came from inside me, from something I called 'the Voice.'

I'd heard this Voice periodically. During my running-away escapades, it would direct me with things like: *Don't get in that car,* or *Don't go that way, go this way,* or *Don't go to that party.* I never really questioned who the speaker was or why it spoke. I tossed it up to intuition. One thing was apparent though, whenever I *didn't* listen to it, I regretted it.

Would He listen to me? I asked myself in response to the Voice's suggestion. Hell, I'd hated Him since Momma died and had pretty much ignored Him till now. It wasn't like we were friends or anything. Maybe I could try to talk to Him, ask for a favor or two.

I had a slight memory that there was a special way you had to talk to Him. But what was it? I didn't know. Shit, I didn't know a single Bible verse. How was I going to get through to Him if I didn't know the proper way to do it?

Fuck it, I told myself. *Just ask Him, hell.*

So I did. I looked up at the ceiling. I don't know why. I'd heard He lived in heaven and that heaven was 'up there,' so I looked up and began to speak.

'Look here, I know you don't know me. It's not like we be kickin' it or anything. But if you can hear me I could really use some help down here.'

Now the tears began to fall.

'I ain't been the best person, but I s'pose I ain't been the worst neither. Besides, most of the shit I been in you could've stopped. But that's neither here nor there. I didn't come to lay blame. Like I said befo', I need some help. So here goes. Doctors say I may not walk again. And if I can't walk, I can't run. And if I can't run, I'll be stuck in Lancaster, and if you can see down here like they say you can, you know what life is like in Lancaster.'

163

Now I was sobbing. But through the snot runnin' out my nose and the tears streaming down my face, I continued.

'If I'm ever *stuck* in Lancaster, I'll kill myself.'

I paused for a moment to cry and think about how to continue. Then I realized that nobody does something for nothing. Why would God be any different? I had to think of something to offer him. I thought for a moment longer, and then it came to me. I continued my conversation:

'Now, don't get me wrong, I ain't the type to expect somethin' for nothin'. So I'll make you a deal. If you let me walk out of here, I'll quit bangin'. I swear I will. I swear it.'

A nurse walked in, startling me. 'Who were you talking to?' she asked.

'None of your fuckin' business!' is what I *wanted* to say. But as I got ready to open my mouth, I remembered that seconds ago, I'd made a deal with God – a deal He might renege on if I cussed someone out so quickly. So I kept quiet.

The nurse seemed unaffected by my silence. 'I'm going to give you something for pain,' she said.

I wasn't in any pain. But that wasn't important. I asked her what it was she was giving me.

'Morphine,' she replied.

I'd never heard of it before going into the hospital, but since I'd been there, they'd been giving it to me intermittently. And I loved it.

A few moments later, as I drifted off to sleep, I hoped that God would keep His end of the bargain – and wondered how the fuck I was going to keep mine.

19

Rick and I were the only ones shot that night. We each got hit by two guns: a sawed-off 12 gauge and a .22. I got nine pellets from the gauge and two bullets from the .22 – all of which hit me in the back. Rick got one bullet from the .22 and thirty pellets from the gauge sprayed up and down the left side of his body. The doctor said it didn't make sense to operate on either of us. He never explained why. He did say that if Rick 'stayed stable' he could leave in a few days. Me? Well, we'd have to 'wait and see.'

During the next few days, the hospital was inundated with Gangstas and Hoovers visiting. To keep them from having to roam from room to room, we decided we should all hang in one room. I wasn't supposed to get out of bed (I was never told why). So the homies would roll my bed, IV bottle and pole, and all the accompanying gadgets into Rick's room or, when the nurses began complaining about their moving me, they hung out in mine. But no matter whose room we were in, we got high. I couldn't feel my legs; but I didn't know if my paralysis was due to the gunshots, the numerous never-ending shots of painkillers the hospital kept giving me, or all of the dope the homies kept bringing me. The homies brought plenty of liquor and lots of bo. They refused to bring me any sherm, though – said they were 'watchin' out for my health.' The good thing was that between the hospital's pain drugs and the homies' street drugs, I stayed high and happy.

Every day was like a party. But the party didn't last long. The other patients and nurses started complaining about the many visitors, the noise, and the continual smell of 'marijuana and alcohol' coming from my room. So they limited my visitors to six a day.

The night after getting shot, Egg, Insane, and several 74 Hoovers rode on the 60's in retaliation for Rick. A few nights later, Fly, Sodici (pronounced 'soda-kī'), Hunchie, and Huck rode for me. Rumor had it that folks were killed during both rides. But none of those hit were the ones who'd shot us. That didn't matter, though. As long as we got *some* of those mothafuckas I was happy.

A week or so after being in the hospital, I began to have feeling in my legs. The doctor called it 'a miracle.' I couldn't tell if he was being facetious or not. But there was no physical therapy, no exercising. Nothing. The doctor said I didn't need any of that kind of stuff and that I should just be glad that my legs worked. I took his word for it. I was just happy that God seemed to be keeping His part of the bargain.

Several days later, I turned sixteen. My homies helped me celebrate it by bringing in weed, booze, and cupcakes. Egg sneaked lil Timmy in who gave me a big hug and a cupcake.

'I'm so glad you didn't die, Cup,' he said in his soft, small voice as he reached over the bed and gave me his hug. I could tell he was trying not to cry, trying to be 'hard' like the older homies. Only seven years old and already he was learning how to hide fear and sadness.

'Me too, lil cuzzz,' I replied, trying just as hard to not let a tear fall.

Our party was cut short when a social worker showed up to see me. I'd learned to distrust and dislike the people in her profession, so when she gave me her name, I didn't even bother remembering it. She didn't seem to care that she was crashing my birthday party. She casually told me that they were having trouble finding some place to put me – like that was supposed to be a big surprise. What was a surprise is that someone (she didn't say who) thought it best that I not remain in Los Angeles County. Diane was willing to take me and had room, so that's where I would go.

At first I started to protest, but then I remembered my part of the bargain with God. *Could this be my way out?* I knew I wouldn't be able to just walk away from the Gangstas. I knew things. I'd seen things. I'd *done* things. But if I was taken away against my will, well then it wouldn't be runnin' out on the set, now would it?

When Fly came to see me the next day, I told him of the decision to return me to Lancaster. He said that, though he knew how much I hated going back, he preferred that I do that rather than living from homie to homie, or out in the streets.

'You think the homies will come after me?' I asked. 'Or get me for runnin' out on the set?'

'Gurl, ain't no body gon' fuck wit' you,' he snapped. 'Not unless they come through me first. Besides, they know it ain't your choice. And it ain't like you gon' snitch or anything like that, right? RIGHT?'

'Naw, cuzzz. I don't know shit, I ain't seen shit, so I can't tell shit!'

We both started crackin' up laughing. He stood there for a long time in silence. We both knew that our special relationship had come to an end. 'Damn, lil cuzzz,' he stated sadly, 'seems like yesterday you was just arrivin', and soon, you'll be leavin'.' He sat down as we began to reminiscence about our time together.

'Remember that time I almost got hit by that car?' he asked with a chuckle.

I did. We'd been coming home from a party. On our way, we ran into Diamond who told us that some of the homies had blasted on some Pirus who were now ridin' through the hood in payback. We'd stopped at a phone booth, called the boys at home, and told them to take the customary action when a rival gang was riding: turn off all the lights and get down on the floor.

After making sure the boys knew what to do, Fly and I began to make our way home – dodging behind trees and parked cars, staying away from streetlights and running through red lights, not wasting time waiting for the green ones. We were one block from the house. We'd started to dash across the middle of the street, when a car came roaring around the corner. It was dark and we were dressed in all blue, so the driver didn't see us. When he did, it was almost too late. He had to slam on his brakes to avoid hitting us. Seeing the car and hearing the screech, Fly, who was in front of me by a few feet, stuck out his arm as if to stop the car. Actually, he used his arm to help himself hop onto the hood as the car came at him. I stopped and screamed – just knowing they'd killed him. But Fly rolled over the hood and onto the ground, got up, and shouted, 'Come on, cuzzz!' as he began running again. Damn, he was fast.

I stopped to look at the car, wondering if the occupants would emerge with shotguns to finish us off. But all I saw was a lil old black man and woman. They were scared shitless. The man rolled down his window and nervously asked, 'Is he all right?' Before I could respond, another car came speeding around the corner.

Now that might *be Bloods!* I told myself.

I couldn't take time to answer the old man. I had to get going. I took off after Fly, leaving the old man sitting there still shaking.

We'd never discussed that night till now.

'That lil old man was scared shitless,' I said as we both cracked up laughing.

We sat there for a while and continued reminiscing about how we'd fought together, hoo-rode together, stolen together, and gotten high together. About how we'd sit up for hours during the night talking about our moms and how much we missed them. Soon, we both got sorrowfully quiet. Our silence was broken when Rick came into my room to smoke a joint Egg had left with him. I told him that I'd be leaving soon. He looked sad, but said he understood.

As we sat and smoked the joint, Rabbit and Trish came to see me. I again repeated the news that I was being forced to leave the county. We sat and cried for a while. Then we all reminisced about some of our greatest jacks, gang fights, and shootings. We remembered fallen homies and discussed which of the new lil homies coming on the sets would be able to stay down enough to maintain the gangs' reps.

We tried to fool each other and say that it really wasn't good-bye, it was 'so long,' and we'd keep in touch. But I knew those were just words. Every time I was taken from people I loved, they'd never kept in touch. How could they? They didn't know how to get ahold of me. Hell, half the time *I* didn't even know where I'd be. I'd long since learned that *good-bye* meant just that.

We laughed and joked until the nurse walked in and gave

them nasty looks as she gave me a shot of pain medicine. She then told everyone they'd have to leave because visiting hours were over. Each of them gave me a long hug and said good-bye. As they walked out, I tossed up 'Tray' with my right hand and 'Crip' with my left.

With tears in my eyes I looked up at the ceiling, 'I hope you're happy!' I screamed.

A deal's a deal, the quiet voice said.

Yeah, it is, I replied in my mind. I rolled over and went to sleep. I'd need my rest. I'd soon be headin' for Lancaster.

20

Life in Lancaster hadn't changed much, except beatings had stopped for good. Diane's diabetes had slowed her down quite a bit. The doctor told her she had to lose weight, but she said her 'power' was in her weight so she 'wasn't goin' on no fuckin' diet!' As a result, she was still extremely overweight and had to take insulin shots. But even in this state, she was just as mean as ever.

Diane had stopped requiring the children to call her 'Momma' – said it got on her 'last good nerve.' One of the other children told me Diane had screamed at them, 'Who'd want to be *your* fucked-up-ass momma? Don't call me that shit no more!'

Of course, now that I had no physical fear of Diane, I loved messing with her in any way, and as often as, I could. So as soon as I discovered she *hated* us calling her 'Momma,' that's all I called her. And knowing how she hated whining, I'd be sure to say it in the whiniest voice I could muster. I *loved* watching her cringe when I said it. Yup, the tables had turned in Lancaster.

Connie's hot foots intermittently continued, except I never got them anymore. I told them bastards that I'd kill the first one that *looked* like they was fittin' to put a match anywhere near my feet. The other kids knew about my gang activities, and getting shot, and weren't looking to try me. That's all it took to stop Connie's attacks – she was a wimp without her cronies. I still had to watch my back around her, though; she was the type to punch you from behind and run.

I wasn't immediately returned to school. The doctors had told

Diane that I should stay off my legs for a couple of weeks. Once leaving the hospital, I was never taken to another doctor for a checkup, to see if the bullets and pellets had moved or anything. Life went on like the shooting had never happened.

When I first got back to Lancaster, I'd periodically call Fly, Rabbit, and other homies, but Diane started hoo-bangin' about the phone bill, so I began to call less and less. It was quickly apparent that if I didn't call my homies, we didn't talk. No one called to see if I was okay in Lancaster – even though they knew how much I hated it there.

Talk about out of sight, out of mind.

Before long, I got an itchin' to go. It wasn't even my hatred for Diane or Connie. I simply felt, foster home or no foster home, I didn't belong in Lancaster. Although I knew it was time to run, I didn't want to repeat the pattern of run, return, run, return. And for some reason, that lil Voice kept telling me not to hitchhike – not this time.

I didn't trust many people, so I didn't hang with too many – unless there were drugs or alcohol involved. I began talking to the few friends I did have to see if anyone would help me ditch Lancaster one last time. One of these friends, Sylvia, was a white girl who also attended my school. She lived with her twenty-year-old sister, Anne, and Anne's boyfriend, Roger.

Sylvia agreed to help me. She let me use her phone to call Uncle Jr. collect, and he helped me make plans for my return home. We both agreed that the sooner I could get out of town, the better. It was decided that Jr. would go to Western Union the next day and send me some money. But, as usual, it would take a couple of days for Jr.'s money to arrive, and once I left Diane's I couldn't go back. So I'd need some place to stay till the money came. We talked to Sylvia's sister and Roger, telling them as little as possible – that I was running from an abusive foster parent and needed a place to stay for a few days. They agreed to let me stay with them. I returned to Diane's that night, packed a small bag, which I hid in the closet. After everyone went to bed, I took off.

Sylvia's sister and boyfriend did meth. So during the day, I'd lie around and watch TV. But at night, when everybody got home, we'd 'toot' crystal, smoke weed, and drink. When Jr.'s money came, Sylvia and her family took me to Thousand Oaks, gave me a few lines of meth and a joint 'for the road,' and put me on a bus headed for San Diego.

Little did I know, I really was leaving Lancaster for good.

21

When I arrived in San Diego, Jr. had great news: I was going to be temporarily living with my daddy. My *real* daddy.

Immediately after Larry and I had been given to Mr Burns, Daddy and Jr. spent an additional four thousand dollars in legal fees, trying to win us back. The additional money was spent in vain. Daddy and Jr. showed up with their newly hired lawyer who'd filed numerous documents on their behalf. Mr Burns didn't show up, but his lawyer did. The hearing didn't last long. The judge reminded everyone that Mr Burns had been given sole and complete custody and pretty much told Daddy and Jr. to quit wasting the court's time.

My daddy and uncle hadn't really spoken since. But Jr. wanted to make sure that this time I stayed out of Lancaster for good. He was also concerned about my hitchhiking all over California and the possibility of my ending up dead as a result. He'd called Daddy to tell him that I was on my way to San Diego, that he had a plan to get me out of the system but it would take awhile, and he wasn't sure what to do with me in the interim.

'Bring her here!' Daddy had said without hesitation.

I'd long since forgotten the pain of being taken from Daddy and Jr. Actually, I'd pretty much decided to forget that part of my life. I never allowed myself to think about Momma, Daddy, Jr., or Grandma – at least not without being loaded.

Jr. said that Daddy and Lori were separated and Daddy was now living with some chick named Samantha who everyone called 'Sam.' I was excited about seeing Daddy, but I was also troubled. I still carried the resentment about his marrying Lori so soon after Momma's death. And it'd been almost six years since I'd seen my daddy. A lot had happened in between then and now. On top of all of that, I was now grown – at least I thought I was.

Daddy and Sam lived in a little house in a section of San Diego called Normal Heights. As Jr. and I pulled up, I was a nervous wreck.

What if he doesn't remember me?

Don't be silly, I answered myself. *He's still the same daddy.* Problem was, though, that I was no longer the same daughter.

As Daddy came out of the house, he had a huge grin on his face. He still looked the same: smooth cocoa-brown skin; slim, but well built; his curly black hair now had wisps of gray waving through it, and his face had a few more wrinkles. But he was still a handsome man, and he still had those beautiful brown eyes and big warm smile.

He approached Jr. first. They shook hands, gave each other a long, warm hug, and then patted each other on the back before letting go. Then Daddy turned toward me.

I wish these damn butterflies in my stomach would stay still!

He just stood there for a long time looking at me. I looked back at him nervously, unsure of what to say or do.

Oh, hell. Now the butterflies are disco dancing!

Very slowly, he walked up to me and gave me a big bear hug and kissed me on the cheek. We didn't cry. We just stood there staring each other up and down for a while, no one saying anything. Then he introduced me to the white woman standing behind him.

'Punkin, this is Sam. Sam, this is my daughter, Cup.'

Aside from her unusual height (she was five ten), she was a plain-looking woman. She wore no makeup and her dirty-blond hair hung scraggly around her shoulders. Sam and I exchanged hellos. I tried not to stare at her, but it's like they say: 'game recognizes game.' I had been on the streets long enough to recognize a prostitute when I saw one. And Sam was a pro, although the plainest one I'd ever seen. I started to say something, but Daddy spoke, interrupting my train of thought.

'Come on y'all, let's go in and get something to eat.'

I'd forgotten what a good cook Daddy was. We ate, and then

174

sat around laughing and catching each other up on what had been happening since I'd been gone. Jr. told us about the school he was teaching at. He also informed us about Grandma, who'd gotten worse. He said that most times, she didn't even know who he was. I made a mental note to ask him to take me to see her.

Daddy told us all about how he'd tried to make it work with Lori, and about Kelly – who now had a two-year-old son. At the mention of Kelly's son, I felt a small tug at my heart. The baby who had been beaten out of me would have also been around two. Then I remembered the IUD that was still inside me. It must have been working because I hadn't been pregnant since my miscarriage.

I wonder how long they're supposed to stay in? I usually forgot it was even there.

I brought my mind back to the present conversation. Daddy was telling us about Kelly's baby's daddy – a Mexican kid who was in a gang. Daddy said he didn't think that Kelly herself was in the gang, but I knew better. Most kids who hung out with gang members were themselves gang members. Even if that person didn't think they were a banger, everyone else would, so it didn't matter. The night I got shot, those Rollin' 60's didn't step out of the car and announce: 'Okay, everyone NOT a gang-banger please step aside so we can shoot only those who are.'

I made another mental note to talk to Kelly to find out whether I was right.

When it came time for me to talk, I wasn't sure which parts of my past to tell, which to keep secret, and which to pretend never happened. Jr. had already seen the welts on my back, so he wasn't too surprised when I told them about some of the physical abuse I endured at Diane's. But everyone gasped when I told them about the half-cooked meat – that's when I impressed upon them the extreme importance of ensuring that all of my meat was cooked extra, extra, extra well. When I told them about the lock and chain around the fridge, they all hit the roof except Daddy. He got really quiet and started balling and unballing his fists. Jr. gave a heavy sigh.

No one said a word for a while. Someone had to break the silence. I decided I'd do it by continuing my update. Experience had taught me that people – especially adults – have trouble accepting and believing the idea of children having sex. I decided that from then on, the parts of my life involving Pete, Mr Bassinet, and my 'business partners' never happened. So I picked up the story by telling them about Fly, the Gangstas, and getting shot.

I was dying for a cigarette. So it seemed like a good time to announce that I smoked cigarettes – and weed.

At first no one said anything. After a moment, Sam looked at me, smiled, and handed me one of her Marlboros. I preferred menthols, but beggars can't be choosers. I kicked back, took a long drag off the cigarette, and closed my eyes as I enjoyed the soothing feeling of my nicotine jones finally getting satisfied.

Daddy and Jr. were silent. They looked a bit shocked and unsure about how to respond.

'Well, Cup,' Jr. said, 'it's a little too late to be trying to raise you now. But be aware that those cigarettes will kill you. And weed will only lead you to stronger drugs.'

He didn't know how right he was. But for me, it was too late to be worrying about stronger drugs – the only worrying I did concerned where I could find a connection in San Diego to get some. So I just smiled, nodded, and took another hit off my cigarette.

The eerie quiet returned.

Jr. finally broke the silence. He brought us up to date about what he knew about Larry. Since Momma's death, Larry and I had been treading the same road – continuously in and out of foster homes. Several months after I had gotten out of the hospital from my gunshot wounds, Larry turned eighteen and was eligible for his trust-fund money. But six months before his eighteenth birthday, Larry showed up on Jr.'s doorstep, demanding he be given his money early. Jr. explained to Larry that he couldn't get the money till he turned eighteen. Larry became enraged and stormed off. When Jr. asked where he was going, Larry told him not to worry about where he was going but to just make sure to have his money in six months.

When Jr. told us that, it pissed me off.

Of all the people who had treated us like shit since Momma died, why did Larry have to be so mean to Jr.? Jr. was one of the only people who gave a fuck about us, and yet Larry was treating him like he was the bad guy!

176

I forced myself to tune my mind back into the conversation. Jr. had moved on and was now telling us about what happened six months later. Right on Larry's eighteenth birthday, my brother and Jr. did all the necessary legal stuff and signed the appropriate papers enabling Larry to get his twenty-five thousand dollars. What happened next is still not clear. But this is the story Larry relayed to Jr.

After putting twenty thousand in the bank, Larry and some chick he'd met in a park took the rest and caught a cab from San Diego to Disneyland. Why Larry caught a cab to Los Angeles instead of going the much cheaper route of renting a car, no one knows.

Anyway, they went to Disneyland, stayed in the Disneyland hotel for a few nights, partied their asses off, and then caught a cab back to San Diego. Once they returned to San Diego, Larry was out of money and went to the bank to retrieve more. Well, guess who was waiting for him when he got there? Mr Burns.

(Mr Burns knew that we would each get a portion of my mom's life-insurance money when we turned eighteen. However, we never learned how Mr Burns knew Larry had actually gotten the money. Nor did we ever learn how Mr Burns knew that Larry would be at the bank that day, or how long he stood there waiting for Larry to show up. Hell, to us it really didn't matter, since one thing had proven certain: whenever money was involved, Mr Burns had an uncanny custom of showing up.)

As soon as he saw Mr Burns, Larry was getting ready to start cursing him out. But before Larry could really lay into him, Mr Burns dropped to his knees and apologized. He started crying, talking about how he'd made a mistake; how he'd gotten scared to be suddenly stuck with two kids; how he'd done the best he could. He told Larry that he had no clue about how bad it had been for us at Diane's. In between snot and tears, he went on and on about how he'd figured that, as a foster mother, Diane was the best caretaker for us till he could get himself together. He ended his speech by screaming out that he loved Larry and would never intentionally do anything to hurt him – that all he ever wanted was a relationship with his son.

Larry was hard up for love, attention, and acceptance. We both were. I temporarily found some in drugs, booze, and bangin'. And although Larry had also found drugs and booze, their solace and comfort were only temporary for him too.

Larry had been longing to hear those words for years. Now here was his biological father telling him that he loved him. Telling him that he *wanted* to be a part of Larry's life, that he wanted the father-and-son relationship they'd never had. He was almost *begging* Larry to give him the chance to love him.

Larry fell for it – hook, line, and sinker.

They walked into the bank together, with Mr Burns hugging Larry so tight they looked like Siamese twins. Mr Burns kindly and caringly assisted Larry with his withdrawal. Then, because Mr Burns said they could bond better if they lived together, he took Larry to live with him in his house. Actually, Mr Burns didn't have a house. He owned a car stereo–installation shop in National City (a small town south of San Diego) and lived in the back of it. The two of them lived there happily for a couple of months, during which time Mr Burns convinced Larry to invest in his shop. The deal was that Larry would give Mr Burns eighteen thousand dollars, and in return, Mr Burns would make periodic dividend payments to Larry.

Of course, the payments never materialized. And it didn't take long for Larry to run through the little amount of money he had left. Once that was gone, he complained to Mr Burns about not receiving any return on his investment. Mr Burns always had some excuse as to why he wasn't paying, but assured, promised, and swore to Larry that the money was forthcoming.

After a couple of months, Larry finally caught on that Mr Burns had scammed him out of his money. Realizing that he had nothing left to lose, Larry finally stood up to Mr Burns and demanded the return of *all* of his money. For a moment, Mr Burns didn't move or say a word. He just stood there staring at Larry intensely. Then he calmly and slowly walked to the phone, called the police, and had Larry escorted out.

As the police escorted Larry out the door, Burns screamed that if he ever returned he'd have him arrested for trespassing. Once outside, Larry started crying so hard that he was literally blinded by his tears. The police had to take his arms and guide him out to the street. The cops must have felt sorry for him when he told them he had no money and nowhere to go, because they gave him a ride to Jr.'s. Larry showed up on

Jr.'s doorstep, angry, devastated, crying, and completely broke.

Jr. put him up for a while, but Larry refused to work, even when Jr. demanded it. All Larry did was lie around, watch TV, eat, sleep, and run up the phone and electric bills – while not bringing in a cent. And on top of that, Jr.'s house was robbed while Larry was supposedly sleeping on the couch.

Jr. stopped talking. He bowed his head and told us that he'd been forced to put Larry out.

'You should have never taken his sorry ass in!' I snapped.

'Cup,' Jr. said in a voice clotted with sorrow, 'he's my nephew and I love him. There's just nothing else I can do for him.'

No one said anything. Wasn't really anything that could be said. Jr. took a moment to get himself together before continuing his story.

He said that shortly after putting Larry out, he began to get phone calls from people demanding Larry's money. It seems that instead of getting a job, Larry had created his own lil hustle: he'd befriend a family with a sad-sob tale about how *he'd* found our mother dead and how he was placed in brutal foster homes. Once he had them feeling sorry for him, he'd tell them that if they let him live with them, he'd give them some of his trust fund. Problem was, Larry neglected to tell them that the first part of his trust fund was gone, and he wouldn't be getting the rest of it till he turned twenty-one. So, they'd take him in, expecting a big payoff. After a few weeks of his eating them out of house and home and still seeing no dough, they'd demand some money, at which time Larry would direct them to Jr., who had the unfortunate task of informing them that Larry was broke.

At that point, they'd put Larry out. He didn't care; he'd just go on to the next sucker and start the game all over again. But I guess his supply of suckers soon ran out, because Jr. said he hadn't gotten one of those phone calls in a while, and hadn't heard from Larry since putting him out. Jr. had no idea of his whereabouts now.

I was indifferent to the news about Larry. Of course I hoped Larry was okay, but I'd long since stopped allowing myself to get attached to anyone. I really didn't care if we never saw each other again.

Besides, I was too self-centered to think about anyone else. So now that all the catching up was over, it was time to get back to *my* problems. Jr. told us the plan to keep me out of the system permanently. He'd been talking to a lawyer friend of his who told him about something called emancipation, which means the law makes a child legally grown before they're biologically grown. Because emancipated minors are considered legal adults, they're able to legally enter contracts and don't require guardians as other minors do. To get me emancipated, Jr. said the lawyer would have to file some papers with the court. The court would then assign someone to investigate me to ensure that I met all the requirements and was truly capable of taking care of myself.

'What are the requirements for this 'emanciation'?' I asked.

'Emancipation,' Jr. corrected me. He relayed what the lawyer had told him. First, I'd have to have no living relatives willing to take me. (That one was easy, seeing as no one in my family had ever even offered to take me in, except Aunt Becky. But since L.A. didn't even want me in their *county,* Aunt Becky wasn't an option.) Second, I'd have to be living as an adult, meaning completely on my own and in my own apartment.

This thing is starting to sound better and better, I thought.

Finally, I'd have to be regularly attending school and be financially capable of taking care of myself, which meant I'd have to get a job.

Damn, there's always a catch!

'It's the only way,' Jr. said, ignoring my reaction. 'And we need to get the process started as soon as possible, because if we don't, your father is sure to return and take you back to Lancaster.'

'He's not my father!' I screamed. I hated when people referred to Mr Burns as my father. 'His name is *sperm donor, asshole* from now on!' I snapped. 'That's all he's ever done, that's all he's ever been, that's all he'll ever be!'

'Okay, okay,' Jr. replied. ' 'Asshole,' 'jerk,' *whatever* you want to call him, we've got to beat him to the punch. Like it or not, we all know we haven't seen the last of him.'

'Okay, let's do what we gotta do,' I sighed.

It was agreed I would stay with Daddy till we could find me an apartment of my own. Meanwhile, we'd look into having my Social Security checks redirected to me so that I'd have some type of income till I got a job. Jr. was going to have his lawyer immediately start the paperwork to petition the court for the emancipation. We'd have to act fast. From day one, Diane and Mr Burns split all monies – the Social Security and foster care checks – she got for me. So there was no doubt that as soon as Diane stopped receiving money, and as a result stopped forwarding Mr Burns his share, he was sure to come calling. Whenever money was involved, Mr Burns always got a sudden urge to see his children.

With the legal business out of the way, we all sat around laughing and talking – mostly Daddy, Jr., and I talked about Momma and our memories of her. 'Cept we never talked about the day she died. That was still too painful. So, we kept it to the good times. It was the first time since Momma's death that I allowed myself to bring her back to the forefront of my memory. Being there with Daddy and Uncle Jr., I felt kind of safe – just like old times.

After Jr. left and Sam went to bed, Daddy and I had a chance to have a down-to-earth talk. One thing Daddy and I agreed on was that although we were still father and daughter, a lot of time had passed since we'd seen each other, and a lot had happened during that time. He said he didn't need to know the details, he could look at me and tell I'd grown up faster than I was supposed to – or needed to. We decided not to try to start from where we'd left off – I, an innocent eleven-year-old girl, and he, a father desperately trying to get his kids. We agreed to just start from where we were now: I, a young woman, already brutally and involuntarily thrown into maturity and self-reliance; and Daddy, a different man who'd rapidly aged as a consequence of being bitter and resentful about losing the only woman he'd ever loved, and the only children he'd ever had. He said he had vowed to never love again – at least not like he'd loved Momma. We were both totally different people from the man and girl who had stood crying in the judge's office years before.

Since we were gettin' real, I thought it would be a good time to ask Daddy about Sam. As I suspected, she was a ho. But daddy said he wasn't her pimp. He said it was more of a 'business arrangement.' (*This* I understood! But I kept quiet about *my* business partners.) It didn't shock me that Daddy was dating a ho. Sam was cool and I liked her. Besides, I felt I was the last person to be passing judgment.

Daddy, Sam, and I hit it off immediately because they knew it was too late to start trying to be parents or for me to try to be a kid. Sam smoked weed, too, so there was always plenty of it around, and Sam and I regularly got high together. Nor did I have to hide my drinking, since Daddy and Sam drank too. Yup, the three of us were like roommates, and I loved it.

Soon after my return to San Diego, Daddy took me to see Kelly and Lori. They lived in an apartment in the eastern portion of San Diego County called Lemon Grove. Lori looked exactly the same: still skinny, still pale, and still cookin' her butt off! She gave me a big hug and disappeared into the kitchen to make my favorites: macaroni and cheese, and chocolate cake.

Daddy went to help Lori, leaving me and Kelly alone to get caught up. Kelly looked much older than she was and, although she'd never been thin, she was much larger than when I'd last seen her. She told me it was because she'd never lost the fifty-five-plus pounds she'd gained from pregnancy, but the weight gain had been well worth it because she adored her little boy, Jason. I was impressed with her motherly devotion until I realized that Kelly wasn't really taking care of Jason. Her mother did most of the hard work. Lori fed Jason, bathed him, and changed his shitty diapers; she cleaned up his vomit and sat up all night rocking him when he was crying, fussy, and refused to go to sleep. Kelly dropped out of school and spent most of her days lying around the house, watching TV, or hanging out with her homies. She came and went as she pleased and only played with Jason when he was clean, fed, smelling good, and happy. The part I loved, though, was when I found out that although Lori did all the hard work, Kelly still got to keep the welfare check she received every month for Jason.

What a life!

For a moment, I thought about getting pregnant again, because, shoot, Kelly looked like she had it going on – the joys of motherhood without the work, *plus* she got a monthly check. I was starting to seriously contemplate this plan when I remembered that it was only Kelly's mother who allowed Kelly to escape the responsibilities and demanding tasks of motherhood.

I didn't have a mother. So I abandoned what I realized had been a stupid idea.

Besides, what good is having children if they ain't gon' have no grandma to love and spoil them?

Up until that point, I wouldn't allow myself to think about my own grandma. But I suddenly found myself missing her. I got teary-eyed as I thought about her and reminded myself to have Jr. take me to see her. I made another mental note to remember to never have children – since I truly believed you had to have a mother for that.

Kelly handed me a drink, snapping me out of my thoughts. At first, I didn't think to ask what it was – I'd never done that in the past. I always drank and then asked. But as I lifted the glass to my lips, I noticed the peculiar two-layered liquid it contained: dark brown on the bottom and bright white on top. I thought it best that I inquire about this one *before* drinking it.

'What is this?'

'A white Russian,' she said, explaining what the two layers were: Kahlúa liqueur on the bottom and milk on top. She said it could also be made without the milk, which was called a black Russian.

I knew what milk was, but had never heard of Kahlúa.

'Kahlúa,' I asked, 'is that booze?'

'Damn straight!' she responded as she began to stir hers.

That's all I needed to know, because black, white, Russian, Chinese, I didn't care what it was called or who it was named after. It was alcohol, which meant it would get me loaded, which meant I'd love it.

As we drank, Kelly proudly announced that she also smoked weed.

Amateur.

She told me that Jason's father belonged to a gang called the Lemon Grove Mafia. I asked her if she banged too. She threw up an *L* with her thumb and forefinger – obviously the sign for Lemon Grove.

Just as I suspected – birds of a feather.

We drank while I told her all about the Gangstas and she schooled me on the LG Mafia.

I talked and listened to Kelly with some bewilderment. I mean, I thought I knew why *I* drank, used drugs, and banged.

183

But I didn't understand why she did. I mean, she had everything I *used* to have before my mom died: her own room, more clothes than a child could ever need, a loving mother and daddy, and a loving, caring home. She'd never been raped or beaten, had never gone hungry, was constantly given emotional, physical, and psychological support and encouragement. Hell, she didn't even know what a trick was!

But I'd long since learned to mind my own business. So I quit pondering the peculiarity of how two completely differently raised children ended up sinking into the same destructive conduct. Since Kelly liked to drink and smoke just as much as me, I instead focused on enjoying our friendly descent into alcohol-induced oblivion.

Daddy, Jr., and I wasted no time in preparing me to be an acceptable candidate for emancipation. Daddy enrolled me in nearby Hoover High School, which I liked because it reminded me of my Hoover homies. Every afternoon after he got off work, Jr. would come get me and take me to look for an apartment, but no one wanted to rent to me since I was only sixteen with no credit and no income.

One day before going to see a prospective apartment, I asked Jr. to take me to see my grandma. She was in an old folks' home. Jr. said that for the last couple of years, he'd had to place her in several different homes because they kept failing to take care of her properly. They were neglecting to feed her, failing to change her diapers or bathe her, and a bunch of other mean stuff.

Grandma's room was at the back of the home, so we had to just about walk through the entire place before getting to it. We passed old folks just sittin' around, playin' cards or watchin' TV. Some were just sittin' – no one visiting them, no phones ringing – like they'd been forgotten.

When we got to Grandma's door I hesitated. I hadn't seen or spoken to her in over five years.

I stepped into her room. She was sitting up in the bed, staring at her fingers, seemingly in awe of them. Her long black hair fell around her shoulders. She was so beautiful. At the sound of us walking in, she looked up and smiled.

'Hi, Pat!' She exclaimed, obviously thinking I was my mother. 'I wondered when you was comin' to see me.'

I sat down next to her and grabbed her hand.

'Hi, Grandma,' I replied. I tried not to cry.

'Hi, Mom,' Jr. said as he sat down on the other side of the bed and began stroking her hair.

'Um-hmm,' she said, and then went back to the fascination with her fingers.

'How ya doin', Grandma?' I asked. She never spoke again that day. Every now and then, though, she'd look up at me and smile.

I felt my anger at God returning. Why *my* grandma? She'd been a devoted Methodist all her life. She was always prayin' and singin' church songs. She'd even been a Sunday-school teacher. And for what? To end up losing her daughter, getting Alzheimer's, and being constantly abused? Hell, I didn't need God for *that*!

Besides, I'd kept my part of the bargain, hadn't I? He'd let me walk out of the hospital and I'd gotten out of the gang. That meant we were even – I didn't owe Him and He didn't owe me. Good. I'd go back to hating Him.

22

We finally found a landlord willing to rent an apartment to me, a one-bedroom in Chula Vista, a city south of San Diego, close to the Tijuana border. The apartment complex was huge, with over one hundred furnished and unfurnished apartments. Mine was furnished, which was good, since I didn't have any furniture. Jr. paid the first month's rent and deposit out of his own money.

I loved having my own apartment. No more runnin' away. I could go into the kitchen and get whatever I wanted when I wanted. I could go into ANY room and all the rooms were *mine*! I spent the first night dancing from room to room. I didn't have music, because I didn't yet have a stereo. But I didn't need any music. My joy (and the Brass Monkey I'd drunk) was my music. I danced till I passed out tired and drunk.

Jr. gave me some money so that I could buy food and a bus pass to get to and from school and get around to look for a job. I took some of the money, went to the thrift shop, and bought a TV and a small stereo.

Meanwhile the court had begun the process of 'investigating' me to ensure I was appropriate and ready for emancipation.

I began my job search. I swore I wasn't going to any fast-food restaurants. They worked too fucking hard, as far as I could tell. My search was immediately disappointing. I was sixteen with no education, no work experience, and no job skills. On top of that, I didn't have any interviewing skills or a work ethic to speak of. I showed up for interviews late, improperly dressed (usually in a miniskirt or bright, tight disco Spandex pants and five-inch heels), chewing like a cow, and popping my chewing gum. I hadn't particularly mastered standard English, to say the least, so my interviews were studded with 'ain'ts,' 'you'ses,' and all kinds of slang, picked up from my stops up and down the California coastline. Needless to say, no one would hire me.

One day, though, I saw an ad for an 'alarm monitor.' I didn't know what the position required, but when I read 'no experience necessary' I knew I qualified. When I showed up for the interview – late as usual – I was met by a small white woman name Mrs Conocia who, along with her husband, owned and started an alarm company, which operated like this: the buyer purchased an alarm system that was rigged throughout her house. If and when the alarm was triggered, a silent alert was sent to the main office. When this signal was received, it was the on-duty monitor's job to call to determine whether it was a false alarm. If a registered occupant didn't answer or say the correct, prechosen password, the monitor was supposed to immediately send the police. Mrs Conocia was hiring for the graveyard shift: midnight to eight in the morning. Those hours were perfect for me. I attended school from 9:00 A.M. to 3:00 P.M, so getting off work at 8:00 gave me plenty of time to take the half-hour bus ride to school.

Because all I had to do was monitor a screen in a small secluded room, I didn't have to be around anyone. As a result, Mrs Conocia didn't care that I dressed inappropriately. And, because the only talking I'd ever have to do was with a customer or the police, and then only to dispatch the cops to a particular address, she didn't care about my improper English. It was the perfect job for me.

Mrs Conocia must not have had many people apply for that job, because she hired me on the spot – miniskirt, gum-popping, slang-talking, and all.

The job paid minimum wage, which wasn't much. But with my Social Security checks, I would have a nice little income. So now I was set. I had a cute place to live and a real job. And for the first time in a long time, I was attending school every day. I had my daddy and my uncle, and wasn't lookin' for Larry.

23

It was very difficult learning to be responsible. For example, Jr. had my gas and lights turned on, but I never thought about who was going to pay the bill. I figured it out when I came home one day and found the lights cut off. But I also learned how to work with the system. I knew I'd get three or four 'final notice' slips before they actually cut me off. And in between each slip, I could get at least a week's extension.

Although I knew how to clean and could do it correctly and meticulously (I'd learned well from Diane and Mrs Bassinet) I had an intense hatred for it. I refused to do it. As a result, my house stayed filthy. I didn't care. It was mine. And I promised myself that since I'd left the system for good, no one would ever make me clean again.

Although my job was easy, I wasn't very good at it. I never 'monitored' anything. I thought of my job as my time to sleep. After my last class of the day, I'd party right up till it was time to go to work. By the time I got to work, I'd be extremely loaded and completely exhausted. So as soon as the monitor who had the shift before me left, I'd stretch out on the floor and pass out – where I stayed till the next morning. Somehow, I always slept right up until about 7:45 – just in time to wake up, get up, and sit at the monitoring station where my relief monitor would find me – believing I'd been there all night.

'How'd it go?' she'd ask.

'All's been quiet here,' I'd respond as I flew out the door.

Thank goodness no one's alarm ever went off on my shift, because if it had and if there had been a real burglary, they'd have been screwed because my passed-out ass wasn't callin'

188

anybody. If an alarm ever did go off to which I failed to respond, to my knowledge no one ever complained about it.

The emancipation went through without a hitch. The court assigned someone to inspect my apartment, and confirmed that I was indeed working and taking care of myself as an adult. They checked my school records and saw my perfect attendance and halfway decent grades. They called to see how I was doing at my job and spoke to Mrs Conocia who raved about me. No one contested the emancipation – not even Mr Burns or Diane – not even once the Social Security checks were changed to be made out to my name. The court was satisfied with their investigation and granted the emancipation.

The day after I was legally emancipated, I quit school for good. I'd never even finished the first semester of the eleventh grade.

But I kept my job, which still began at midnight. San Diego County had instituted a curfew prohibiting minors under eighteen to be out after 10:00 P.M. without an adult, which meant I had to carry my emancipation papers with me in case I was stopped by the cops on my way to work. I couldn't *wait* to get stopped so I could flash my papers in their faces and say, 'Ha! I'm grown, *s-u-c-k-a-s*!' To my dismay, no one ever bothered to stop me. I'd leave early to go to work so I could be downtown by myself at eleven, eleven-thirty at night – mentally pleading for a cop to stop me and ask why I was out after curfew. Didn't happen though. I never got to flash my papers – not one time.

My next-door neighbor, Rich, was a tall, white twenty-five-year-old guy who was in the navy. He sold 'dime' (ten-dollar) bags of weed. We became good friends, probably because we were both dedicated weed heads. He was impressed that I was living on my own and sort of became an older brother. He used to call me 'Baby Weedy' because I was his youngest customer.

One morning, I was awakened by a sharp pain in my lower abdomen. It felt like someone was stabbing my crotch with a razor-sharp knife. I grabbed my stomach and began screaming from the pain. I could barely move. I tried to reach for the phone, but a pain stabbed me just as I grabbed for it, and I knocked it over onto the floor. The handset rolled away out of

189

my reach. As I tried to stretch my hand out to grab it, I lost my balance and fell to the floor. The thud of my body hitting the floor caused the knives to stab deeper and harder. By now I was screaming at the top of my lungs.

Rich, awakened by my screams, thought I was being attacked. He ran to my door, banging on it.

'Cup! Cup! What's going on in there! Are you okay?'

'No!' I screamed back. 'Call an ambulance! Something's wrong with my stomach!'

I lay there for what seemed like forever in horrific pain. When the paramedics arrived, I couldn't get up to let them in, so they had to force the door open. They found me on the floor, curled in a fetal position, screaming and crying. I was rushed to the hospital.

That fuckin' IUD! The doctor said the X-rays showed it had 'moved into my uterus.'

'It ain't my ut'rus that's hurtin'!' I screamed, wondering, *What the fuck is a 'ut'rus'?* 'It's my stomach! My stomach!'

I was rushed into surgery to have the IUD removed. As I lay in the operating room while the nurses and other folks ran around preparing things, the doctor explained that my uterus was located in my lower abdomen. He said the IUD had originally been inserted into my cervix (like I knew what the fuck that was), but had 'moved' into my uterus.

'WHO moved it?' I screamed through clinched teeth. The pain seemed to be getting worse. He didn't respond, so I thought maybe I needed to scream a little louder. 'How the fuck did it get in there?' I screamed.

He said that it was a side effect that occurred when an IUD was left in for too long. He said it was supposed to be in for only one year, and then it should have been removed, my uterus checked, and another inserted.

A year! No one ever told ME about the year limit. I'd had it in for more than three.

The doctor then blurted that he thought I also had gonorrhea. Before I could ask what that was, a white man sitting next to me inserted a needle into my IV tube and said:

'Now I want you to count backward from ten.'

By the time I got to seven, I was out.

The next day when the doctor came into my room to check

up on me, he scolded me about keeping it in so long. Most of the time I'd forgotten it was even in there! The doctor said I couldn't get another IUD. That one had done severe damage, and my body would need time to heal. He said I'd have to try another form of contraceptive. He suggested the pill. I'd tried those things before – and they failed horribly. But now it looked like I had no other choice. He mentioned something about foam and a diaphragm, but I wasn't down for using anything that required your having to STOP and use it. So the pill it would have to be.

I didn't really have a steady boyfriend. I went through men like water. I'd meet them and fall instantly in love. But for some reason, after a couple of months, we wouldn't be able to stand each other. I didn't know that love and healthy relationships take time. All I knew was what I'd been taught. So I'd meet a guy one day, fuck him the same day, move him in the next, and put him out the following week. I just went through one sick, unhealthy relationship after another, all the while thinking I was a 'playa.'

The doctor started lecturing about my having caught a sexually transmitted disease so young. Thank goodness Rich came into the room, interrupting the doctor's speech. He'd come to visit and make sure I was okay. The doctor quickly left, but not before giving us both disapproving looks.

'Look what I brought you,' Rich said with a wide grin as he pulled out some Brass Monkey, a joint, and some cigarettes. Man, I loved friends.

I was so glad Rich was home that morning to call for help. I don't know what I'd have done if no one had been there to hear my screams. He said I'd scared him to death, though. He'd come to my door wearing nothing but his underwear – and carrying a lamp.

'A lamp?' I asked as we sat in my hospital room. 'What the fuck were you going to do with a lamp?'

He said he thought I was being attacked, but didn't have a weapon, so he'd grabbed the first thing he saw. We both cracked up laughing.

Shortly after that, Rich found out he was being transferred to another base in another state. He asked me if I wanted to take over his business and customers. He said he'd only be comfortable leaving his business to a serious smoker like me. And he said it'd be a great second income for me. I'd never really thought about selling drugs. Sure, I'd been around drug dealers quite a bit, but I never thought of myself as one – a drug *user*, yes; but a *dealer*? However, once I'd given it some serious thought, I realized Rich was right. Who better to sell weed than a weed head?

I loved selling weed. It had several benefits. First, my house became the hap'nin' place to be. I no longer desired to be part of the in crowd; shit, I *was* the in crowd! Folks were always coming and going. And I had lots of friends! I was popular! Well liked! People always wanted to be around me!

Another great thing about dealing was that I always had cash around. And I rarely had to smoke my own stash. Customers were always happy to smoke a couple of their joints with me.

The only downside about dealing was that my customers were military folks and other young adults with day jobs. Since leaving Lancaster, I really didn't hang with folks my own age. I'd discovered that kids my age were too immature for me. All they talked about was who was going to the dance with who, and what outfit they were going to have their parents buy for them. That was kid stuff to me. I had more important things to worry about, like paying rent and bills and going to work, and of course partying. I'd never been to a dance or prom. Hell, I'd never really been on a date.

Since my customers and friends were much older than me and since they loved to party at night after getting off work, these factors made it difficult for me to maintain both my business and my night job. Finally I realized something had to go: partying or work. I figured that with my Social Security checks and dope money, I could make it. So I called the monitor on duty and informed her that I quit.

'Who's going to relieve me?' she asked, concerned she'd be stuck pulling a double shift.

'That's not my problem,' I snapped, and hung up the phone.

Several minutes later the phone rang. It was Mrs Conocia. She was very upset.

'You can't just walk out on me!' she screamed. 'You're supposed to give me two weeks' notice!'

'Okay,' I snapped. I'd become cocky now that I'd been

declared legally grown and had my own business enterprise. (I'd forgotten that just a few months before, I was *begging* for that job.)

'Figure that in two weeks I quit. Till then, I'll be on sick leave.'

'You don't have two weeks' worth of sick – '

I didn't hear the rest. I'd slammed down the phone. I never even went and picked up my last check. And I never spoke to Mrs Conocia again.

At first my plan worked extremely well. I made enough money from selling weed to enable me to regularly add my other favorites – meth, cocaine, LSD, and sherm – to my daily weed and booze consumption. I'd heard that you could get into more trouble for selling the stronger drugs than for using them. So for the moment, I limited my business enterprise to weed.

I had a huge party for my seventeenth birthday. Friends came over and brought tons of dope and booze. We partied till the neighbors called the cops, who shut the party down and threatened to take me to jail for cussing them out. I was known for getting drunk and cussing you out. Alcohol gave me false courage. So I told the cops to 'quit fuckin' with us and go solve some fuckin' crimes!' Of course, it sounded more like 'Quit fwukin' wit' us in go sulve sum fwukin' crime!'

When the cops realized I was drunk, but not of drinking age, they threatened to take everyone to jail. My friends covered my mouth and shoved me in the back room as others groveled and apologized about the noise and my behavior. They kindly explained it was just supposed to be a little party that got out of hand, but that they would immediately shut it down. It worked. I'd gotten reckless and had forgotten that I was still vulnerable. All I knew was it sho was a jamming party!

Shortly after the party, I was enjoying my usual houseful of folks when someone said they had a craving for fried chicken. Drunk, loaded, and trippin', a bunch of people went to the store, got the chicken (actually they stole the chicken), came back, and started frying it up. As soon as I smelled the scent of frying chicken I began to get nauseous. The last time that had happened, I was pregnant. I was still half-assed about taking my birth-control pills.

Could I be pregnant? And if so, whose was it? In the last four months I'd had three boyfriends.

I went to the free clinic, and sure enough, I was pregnant. Fuck! They said I was about two months in, which meant this dude named Calvin was probably the father. I knew the lifestyle I led was not one for children, and I'd be damned if I was going to let the same system that had fucked me over raise my kids. That baby I lost in Lancaster was the first and last I ever intended to keep. So an abortion was the only way out. The nurse told me about a few clinics that offered cheap abortions. Although I hadn't spoken to Calvin in a couple of months, I'd be damned if I was going to pay for the abortion myself.

When I called Calvin to demand half the money, the first thing he asked was, 'Is it mine?' This pissed me off. Yes, I fucked around. And, yes, I slept with a lot of different men. But *he* didn't know that.

'Of course it's yours!' I screamed, though in my heart I really wasn't sure.

He gave me half the money for the abortion, but refused my request to go with me to get it done. I didn't care. I'd long since been used to doing shit *for* myself *by* myself. I caught the bus to the clinic, had the abortion, and was home partying within the hour as if nothing had just happened. I never looked back.

Kids ain't for everyone, I'd convinced myself.

I kept the abortion a secret from everyone. But I made a vow to try to do a better job of taking my birth-control pills.

Every once in a while Jr. would come by and check on me. Although he didn't know I was 'slanging' (selling dope), he was suspicious of all of the people who were always at my house. But I was grown and paying my own rent in my own house, so he never said much, outside of regularly voicing his displeasure with the fact that I'd quit school.

They can't teach me nothing in school I can't learn on the streets. I truly believed that school was for suckers, and I had NEVER considered myself a sucker. So returning to school was never an option.

Jr. was pleased at the thought that I was still working – I didn't bother to tell him I'd quit. Still, he would always fuss at me about my unhealthy lifestyle and how I needed an education to be successful in life.

Shit, I *was* successful. I had a lucrative business and tons of friends. I *stayed* loaded. And I was the most popular chick in the whole complex – if that ain't success, what is?

24

It didn't take long before the plan for my life began to fall apart. Although I initially did make money from selling weed, my required daily minimum was quickly escalating – the more I used, the more I wanted, the more I *needed*. As a result, I was constantly digging into my 'merchandise' for my own personal use. It wasn't long before I was smoking more than I was selling. My first bright idea to fix this problem was to increase my use of the stronger drugs – especially crystal meth and coke. But that backfired because not only were those drugs stronger, they also cost more, which really cut into my available funds. I needed another plan.

Then it came to me. I could try and get my trust-fund money early; though to do so, I needed Jr.'s and the court's approval.

I figured I'd start with Jr., because if he agreed, the court might be more likely to agree too. In my most innocent, saddest, most helpless voice – using the acting training I'd gotten from Diane and Connie – I cried to him about how I'd gotten fired from my job for failing to respond fast enough to a fire alarm and the occupants had almost died. And, because of that serious blunder, I was having trouble getting another job, which meant I wouldn't be able to pay my rent. Besides, I *had been* declared an adult.

'That means I should be able to get my money, don't you think?' I stated emphatically.

He paused for a moment, not saying anything. When he did speak, he said that if the court wouldn't object, he wouldn't either.

The court objected.

Everything was going to hell. I had no job. Money was dwindling. I mean, business was great. But my daily use was steadily increasing and the amount of product available for selling was quickly diminishing.

Fuck that shit, I told myself. I'd need another plan. But, I'd played everyone I knew – except Daddy. Time for plan B.

I approached Daddy about the possibility of us being roommates again. I didn't go into a bunch of explanations. I just said I wanted to save some money. He said he liked the idea, as long as I didn't mind that it'd be just he and I. Sam wouldn't be joining us – at least not at first. He'd decided he needed some time alone. We agreed to move in together and be roommates.

We moved into a large apartment complex in southeast San Diego that everyone called 'the Complex.' It was in the heart of the ghetto, and although it wasn't officially the 'projects,' everyone thought of it as such, probably because of the ever-present dealers, thugs, drugs, and violence. It was the perfect place for illegal activities because it had a graveyard on one side (which meant *those* neighbors wouldn't be complaining), there were only a couple of houses on the other side (whose occupants were loyal customers of dealers *in* the Complex), a big empty lot sat across the street, and behind it stood a row of dilapidated bungalows that housed tons of illegal Mexicans – most of whom didn't speak English. But the best part was that the apartment complex itself sat on a cul-de-sac – so there was only one way in, and one way out. A perfect place for an aspiring businesswoman like myself.

Soon after moving into the apartment, Social Security stopped sending me checks. When I went down to the Social Security office to find out why, the little elderly white woman behind the counter explained that, although I was eligible for the money because of my mother's death, I had to be enrolled in school to receive it.

'School!' My scream startled her so much she toppled her glasses. 'Y'all want me to go to school?'

'Well, yes, dear. To be eligible you have to be in school.'

She didn't know who she was talking to. I cussed her out, told her to kiss my black ass, and walked out.

Fuck the government and their Social Security checks, I told myself. I decided to just resume my business. But, *this time,* I'd do it better.

Later that night, I approached Daddy about my business. We were sitting around happy and full from the wonderful spaghetti he'd just cooked. First, I told him Social Security would no longer be sending me checks (I didn't tell him why). Then, I broke the other news to him.

'Daddy,' I said, 'I sold weed when I lived in Chula Vista. It's a lucrative business, and I plan to continue. Now I can do it from here, or I can stand on the corner. But, one way or another, I'm slangin'.'

I never raised my voice and I wasn't rude, but I meant every word.

He looked at me intently and waited several moments before speaking. He knew I smoked weed, but he had no idea I'd sold it. I sat waiting and wondering how he'd respond.

'Punkin,' he said, 'I sell pills. It's a lucrative business, and *I* plan to continue it.'

He never raised his voice and he wasn't rude, and I could tell he meant every word. He gave me a sly grin.

I was shocked. *Daddy, a pusher? My Daddy a pusher? Me and Daddy slanging together? Cool!*

Ignoring my astonishment, he continued. 'Besides, I know you well enough to know that if you don't sell from here, you'll be out on the corners. That's the last place a young girl should be. That, I don't want. At least if you're here, I'll know where you are and who you're dealing with. So to keep you home and safe, you can continue your business from here.'

He stood up to go into his room. Just before disappearing around the corner, he turned, and said, 'And I'll continue mine.'

I sat there, shocked and surprised. It didn't take long for the shock to wear off, though. I got up, went to my room, and got high.

Later, as we discussed how I'd run my business, Daddy laid down some new rules. Instead of dime bags, I'd sell 'quarter' (twenty-five-dollar) bags. Doing this had several benefits. First, it meant more money per sale. Second, it reduced the amount of traffic because fewer people could afford the larger bags. Third, less traffic drew less attention. Finally, I adopted Daddy's rules and only sold to current customers or people I knew, which cut down on the chances of selling to a narc and getting busted. (Little did we know that most narcs snitch on the people they know *first*!)

Once getting the rules regarding my business straight, Daddy hipped me to his. I wasn't new to pills. I'd known about them from the time I'd lived with Tim, and I took a variety of them myself. But Daddy introduced me to a whole new world. He sold codeines (they were called 'tabloid 4's' and had more codeine than Tylenol with codeine), quaaludes and preludes (both called 'ludes'), T's and blues, Ritalin (which was, and still is, often prescribed for hyperactive kids), and valium. He never sold on the street, and never to anyone he didn't know. Actually he sold only to hos – who loved the pills. Daddy told me that this was actually how he'd started fuckin' with hos – there's always a certain status that goes with being the dopeman's woman.

All the pills Daddy sold could be 'slammed' (shot up) or swallowed. The tabloid 4's were the most popular because four of them slammed with two sleeping pills were almost like heroin – they made a person nod out. 'Nodding' is the physical effect that all heroin users aim for. It's called 'nodding' because users look like most people who fall asleep while sitting up – their heads nod up and down. All the pills Daddy sold were downers, so even if you didn't nod, they calmed you down and put you in an extremely tranquil and euphoric mood.

Although Daddy sold these pills, his connection always gave me plenty of other pills for free: reds, black beauties, and Christmas trees (called that because they were green, yellow, and white). The black beauties were an old favorite. Similar to crystal and coke, they were uppers, so they kept me physically hyper, energetic, and jubilant – giving me an enormous surge of 'happy' energy. Now, don't get me wrong. I'd do downers if there was nothing else around, but I preferred uppers, since I was always trying to maintain a constant state of elation. I got them for free simply because I was Daddy's daughter. However, I was always looking for a way to make money. So although I wasn't really supposed to sell these pills, if a customer happened to mention they were looking for a little 'up,' I'd sell him one or two of my beauties. Since I didn't pay for them, any sale was

100 percent profit. I'd have been a fool *not* to have taken advantage of that.

Our business was 'one-stop shopping.' Whether customers were looking to score a mellow high (weed), or something to make them zoom, zoom (uppers), or something for just chilling (downers), we were equipped to supply *all* of their needs.

Soon after we got to the Complex, Sam came back to live with us. I found out she'd left because she was pregnant. Daddy wanted the baby, but she didn't. She said her lifestyle wasn't appropriate for babies. Once she returned, though, she never mentioned a baby. And I never asked what happened to it, because personally, I couldn't have cared less.

Shortly after Sam's arrival, we were joined by another ho named Slim. Slim was also white, with dirty-blond hair that hung around her shoulders. I immediately recognized why she was called Slim. She stood about five foot seven, but weighed only about 110 pounds – *if* that.

They should call you Bones, I thought as I stared her up and down. I mean, I was skinny, but not THAT skinny. She was a pretty girl, but so thin she looked sickly. Shortly after her arrival, I learned why.

Slim liked to slam heroin. I caught her nodding one day. She was sitting at the dining-room table, her head hanging down as though she were asleep, but I saw the needle sticking out of her arm. I wasn't surprised. I had heard of slamming, but had never actually seen anyone do it – till then. As I stood there staring at her, Daddy came up behind me.

'Damn bitches. I told her about doin' that shit in here. Punkin, I hate for you to see this, but you're old enough to know.'

'Shit, Daddy, don't trip. I've seen worse.'

'Yeah, but I don't ever want to see you doing this shit.'

'I won't,' I promised. I'd long ago told myself that as long as I didn't *shoot* heroin, I couldn't be a dope fiend.

After a while, we even began to tease Slim about shooting up, saying she was going to the 'hotseat,' because soon after slamming, she'd start complaining that the dope made her skin hot and itchy, so much so that she'd start frantically scratching her arms, neck, and legs. Soon, she'd be clawing crazily at her entire body. Sometimes we'd use stiff-bristled brushes to scratch her body, but we were never fast enough for her. 'Do my legs!' she'd scream, and Daddy would kneel to brush her legs. 'Get my back!' she'd holler, and I would run behind her to brush her back. 'Oh, my God, my stomach, my stomach!' No matter where or how hard we scratched, it was never enough. But Slim never quit slammin'.

Whenever Slim was high, she didn't eat. And Slim was always high. All of a sudden, her extreme skinniness made sense to me.

Not long after Slim came Wanda. Wanda looked Mexican, but she was white. She was much bigger than Slim, but not as tall as Sam. She was a pretty girl, with long brown hair, brown eyes, and pouty lips.

Now there were three hos in the house. They all slept with Daddy in his room, and I had my own room. But Daddy wasn't their pimp. It was a 'business arrangement.' They never turned tricks in our house and never gave Daddy money from it. They paid their share of the rent and utilities, and contributed for food – when they ate it. Slim and Wanda both slammed, so really most all their money went to 'horse.' Although Sam didn't slam, she used a variety of other drugs, which ate up all her earnings. So it really was like a business arrangement – Daddy provided them with a safe place to live and get high; in return they worked their jobs and kept all the money they earned, except what they paid in rent, utilities, etc. They always said that the real bonus for them was that they were never beaten, mistreated, or abused like other hos who had pimps. The real bonus for Daddy, was, of course, that the pussy was free.

During the day while Daddy was at work, the hos slept. In the evening, they went to the 'ho stroll' – the street hookers walked to gather their tricks. Their favorite stroll was near the naval training center in San Diego. Since the girls weren't allowed to turn tricks in our house, the tricks would either pay for a hotel room (there were always spots near a ho stroll that rented by the hour) or they'd conduct business in the tricks' cars.

Because I usually partied all night, I also spent most of the day sleeping. But as soon as evening hit, I'd be prepared to hit the streets, generally borrowing Daddy's car. Often, as I made my way out the door, the girls would ask me to give them a ride to the stroll. They were always broke when they arrived at the stroll. So just before letting them out of the car, I'd give them each five dollars and say, 'Now don't y'all spend it all in one place!' They'd take the money, give me a grin – and the middle finger. By the time they got home early the next morning, they'd give me back the five dollars, plus twenty more. Because of this great return on my investment, I was always more than willing to take the girls to work.

The pill business was booming. Even though I didn't shoot up, I learned how to do it because sometimes a customer would be so loaded or unable to find her vein she'd ask me to do it for her. And I gladly did – for a small fee.

To shoot someone up, I'd first crush the pill, then put it in a spoon with hot water. Then I'd gently but quickly wave a lighter beneath the spoon till the pill was completely melted. This procedure is called 'cooking.' Then, I placed a tiny piece of cotton (usually a tiny piece torn off of a cigarette filter) on the spoon, and drew up the solution with a needle. The filter's purpose was to clear out the various additives the pills contained so that the only thing that entered the needle was pure codeine – or whatever dope it was a customer was shooting. This is the same method used when slamming heroin or coke to filter out the numerous impurities they're cut with. (To 'cut' dope means to add additional ingredients to it to bulk up the quantity. For example cocaine is usually cut with baking soda, laxatives, and numerous other household ingredients.)

Although Jr. came over often for dinner, he didn't know we were dealing dope. We knew he wouldn't understand, so we kept that from him. He knew about the hos, though (it didn't take a rocket scientist to figure that out). Although he didn't approve, everyone *was* grown, so Jr. kept quiet.

Everyone in the house, except Daddy, got high off of *something*, so it was one big never-ending party. Daddy did try weed once. One night Daddy, Slim, and I were sitting at the dining-room table, arguing about the effects of weed. Daddy was trying to convince us that weed negatively affected the brain – causing you to forget, slowing your motor skills, blah, blah, blah. We vehemently denied it, telling him that weed *enhanced* your brain – made music sound better, made you think better, made your food taste better; in fact, it made *everything* better. To prove his point, Daddy agreed to smoke a joint. It was red-hair sinsemilla – some of the strongest and best weed I'd ever sold. We warned him not to puff too hard or take in too much. He didn't listen. He took a couple of long, intense puffs. His eyes immediately watered, and he started to spew out a few harsh coughs. Then he was still. He sat there for a while, his eyes slowly getting smaller and smaller, his body beginning to slump as the high began to kick in. But he did not move.

All of a sudden, he announced he was hungry. Slim and I smiled at each other as we realized Daddy was getting the munchies. Slim hopped up and made Daddy the only thing she knew how to cook – scrambled eggs. As she sat the plate of eggs down in front of Daddy, she and I resumed smoking our joint. Daddy didn't touch the eggs. Instead, he just stared at them for a long time. Then, his head began to slowly lower toward the plate. I sat across from him, watching. I thought he would surely stop his head before it hit the plate. I stared in awe as I watched him slowly descend downward until his face smashed into the eggs.

'Daddy's fucked up!' I shrieked, and cracked up laughing.

'Yeah, he is!' Slim replied, laughing even harder.

What we didn't know was that Daddy was so high, he couldn't lift his face out of the eggs. The weed had relaxed him so much, he'd lost the ability to control his muscles. He later told us he was sitting there thinking, *Y'all stop laughing at me and help me. I'm drowning in these fuckin' eggs!*

It took a few seconds for us to pull ourselves together enough to stop laughing. Finally Slim went over, grabbed a clump of Daddy's hair and lifted his head out of the eggs. As she did so, some of the eggs fell from his face, while the rest clung to his cheeks, forehead, eyelids, and chin. Still laughing, she took one arm, I took the other, and we half-walked, half-dragged Daddy to the couch. We dumped him onto it and returned to the kitchen to smoke another joint. No sooner than we'd sat back down at the dining-room table, we heard a thud in the living room. We ran in there to find Daddy had fallen onto the floor.

'Fuck it. Let him sleep it off down there,' I told Slim as I stood over him looking at the crazy way he was sprawled out. 'There's no way I'm gon' try and lift his ass off that floor.'

So we left Daddy sprawled on the floor, pieces of eggs

still clinging to his face. Daddy never tried another drug again.

I actually was glad Daddy didn't use drugs. Counting me, the three hos, my friends, and the customers, there was enough using going on in that apartment.

I celebrated my eighteenth birthday in the Complex. We had a huge party. Friends bought booze and brought dope. Customers bought dope and brought booze. The next day, I didn't have much memory of the party, but I was told it was the bomb.

A couple of days later, Jr. and the court did their thing to give me my trust-fund money. Twenty-five thousand dollars. I thought I was rich. Three days after receiving the check, the phone rang. No sooner than I'd said hello, a voice said, 'La'Vette?' I hadn't been called that name in so long, the mention of it stopped me in my tracks. In fact, no one was *allowed* to call me that name. My hand began to tighten around the phone handle as I began to remember how much I hated that name *and* the man who'd given it to me. The voice continued, snapping me out of the daze. 'This is your father.' It was Mr Burns. 'How are you?'

I know this punk-ass nigga ain't callin' me! I thought as I stared at the phone in disbelief. I couldn't believe he had the audacity to call me – I hadn't seen or spoken to him since the day he'd given us to Diane.

He continued talking about how he missed me and how much trouble he'd had trying to find me. But I wasn't listening. I had too many unanswered questions racing through my mind.

How did he get my number? How did he know where I was? How did he know I'd gotten my money?

Then I remembered that he always showed up when money was involved. I came back to the present. The why and how he'd found me weren't important. What was important was that, after years of pure hell, I'd finally get the chance to give him a piece of my mind.

He'd been talking for about two minutes, going on and on about how he could 'use a little help,' and about how he 'loved his daughter.'

'Love? Love?' I screamed. 'You don't know shit about love, you black sorry bastard of a man. I never even knew you existed. And how did I find out? When your sorry ass took us from the only family we loved and sent us to stay with that sadistic bitch! And for what? So you two could split the foster care and Social Security money! You sold out your kids for money! You are a punk *bitch*!'

I was so angry, tears were falling from my eyes. But I couldn't stop. I *had* to release the rage and hatred I'd been holding in for so long. Mr Burns was shocked into silence by my anger and my language. But I continued.

'Yeah, *I* said it. A sorry-ass punk bitch. That's all you are! You might have pulled that 'I need my kids' shit on Larry, but that shit ain't gon' work with me. I don't want yo' fake-ass love, ya fake-ass nigga. I got a daddy and it ain't *you,* mothafucka! I'd rather lay on a bed of scalding-hot piercing nails *naked* before I'd acknowledge your sorry ass to be my father. Just the *thought* of you leaves a shitty taste in my mouth. You know why? 'Cause you ain't shit! You ain't never been a part of my life and, mothafucka, we ain't fittin' to start now. Now you listen and you listen good, ass-wipe. Don't you ever, and I mean *ever,* call my house again. You hear me, asshole? And, if you EVER come anywhere near me, I'll do what my momma shoulda done years ago, and what Larry shoulda done when you stole his money. I'll kill yo' black ass! You hear me? I'll fuckin' kill you DEAD!'

I slammed down the phone so hard I felt the cradle crack in my hand.

Daddy came running into my room.

'What's all the hollerin' about?' he asked as he threw open my bedroom door, his body crouched as if ready to attack.

With tears still falling and my body still shaking from the intense anger, I told him what had just happened and how glad I was that I'd finally gotten a chance to give Mr Burns a piece of my mind.

'Sounds like you gave him more than a piece!' Daddy joked, grabbing me and giving me a big hug. 'That's my girl!' he said with a big smile.

Mr Burns never called back. And I never heard from him again.

And, hell, I didn't need Mr Burns to spend my trust-fund money – I could do that by myself just fine. And spend it I did. I wanted my own car. I didn't have a driver's license. But that didn't matter. The Gangstas had taught me to drive years before. So I headed to the first Buick dealer I saw and bought a car: a beautiful new Regal. It was a two-tone light-and-dark blue, with a sunroof and spoke wire rims. It was worth only about eight thousand dollars, but I paid twelve thousand for it. Why? Because it was pretty and I wanted it. Jr. tried to tell me it was a bad move, but hey, it was my money and I really wanted that car. So I bought it. Then, to prove I could be responsible, I got car insurance. I also bought clothes, jewelry, and of course, dope. I put the rest in a savings account with the intent to touch it only when I needed to.

The period in the Complex was one of the happiest times in my life. All I did was hang out, get high, and sell dope – which I loved, especially since I had such a variety of drugs to choose from. I'd be down-in-the-dumps depressed one moment, and happy and ecstatic the next. I didn't yet realize the horrific physical and mental toll the constant drug use was taking on my mind and body. Actually, I didn't care. Business was booming. I was legally and physically grown, so foster homes were a thing of the past. I had my own room and phone. I had a little money in the bank. And I had my daddy and Jr. back.

Shit, life was good.

25

I wasn't turning tricks during this time at the Complex, though I should've been because at least I'd have been getting paid. I never really had a steady boyfriend – unless you considered my standard 'relationship' span of two months as steady.

I met most of the men I dated in nightclubs. My favorite club, called the Oasis, was only half a mile from the Complex. It had a reputation for being one of the raunchiest, most violent and hap'nin' nightclubs in San Diego. I quickly began to make my rounds there as well as other clubs in the greater San Diego area. Getting in was never a problem because I had a fake I.D. Actually, it wasn't fake, it was my legitimate I.D., but with an incorrect birth date – a benefit of dealing dope. When I lived in my apartment in Chula Vista, one of my customers worked for the DMV. One day, she needed some dope, but was short on money. I told her I needed to change the date on my I.D., but didn't know how to go about it. We agreed to a little business trade (Hey, fair exchange ain't no robbery!). Thanks to that deal, I had an official California I.D. that listed my age as twenty-one.

Even though my purpose for going to clubs was to party, I always *started* the party way before I got there. I mean, I *had* to drink and smoke reefer and toot while getting dressed. Then, I *had* to stop and get something to drink on the way to the club (even though the farthest club wasn't ten minutes away). And, of course, I couldn't go *into* the club without smoking another joint or tooting another line. By the time I actually got inside the club, I'd be fucked up. Still, I would drink another four to six drinks.

I was a mean drunk. I liked to pick fights, talk about folks' mommas, and just talk shit. For example, one night I went up to this big, muscular guy standing up against the wall. I had to jump up to get in his face. Because I was drunk, each jump up landed in a stumble. That didn't deter me. I continued to talk about him and his ugly-ass momma. At first, he tried to ignore me. But with each insult – not to mention my drunk's bad breath – he was quickly losing patience. He balled up his fist.

That enraged me more. 'You think you gon' hit me, mothafucka?' I yelled.

The anger in his eyes told me he was. Lucky for me, a lot of my customers and friends (which were really one and the same) partied in the same clubs. Realizing I was getting ready to get my ass whupped, they ran over, stepped in between me and the guy, remorsefully apologizing for my behavior and making up a story about me being distraught from a recent tragedy. Seeing as he was falling for their excuse, they grabbed me by the arm and dragged me away – while trying to cover my mouth, which continued to curse him out at the top of my lungs.

My friends comically began to call these the 'save Cup's ass' incidents, since they'd prevented me from getting seriously hurt on many occasions. Each time they saved me, I'd reward them with free dope.

I'd laugh with them as they would relay the story to me the next day, though I usually had no memory of it. I was experiencing blackouts more and more. I would sit in total astonishment as my friends would tell me about the stupid things I'd done or said the night before. However, I soon realized a benefit from, and even began to welcome, the memory loss because it allowed me to remain oblivious to the extremely ignorant and hostile person I became when drunk.

My blackouts also had a negative effect. My friends began to realize that, since I had no idea of what really had happened the night before, they could tell me they'd helped me when they really hadn't. Pretty soon, I was frequently and regularly rewarding people with free dope, believing they'd protected me or saved me from a serious ass-whupping, when a lot of times they hadn't even been in the club!

Of course, I partied so much that there were times when there wasn't a customer around to come to my rescue. I remember one guy was so pissed and tired of my relentless babbling, he shoved my head into the wall with such force that I was actually knocked out for a few moments. I came to with a small bloody knot on my head, and my head imprint in the wall. Then of course, there were times when I just got my ass whupped because my mouth had written a check my ass couldn't cash.

One day, Daddy was in the kitchen frying some chicken. The smell woke me up and made me so nauseous I had to run to the bathroom to throw up. I knew what that meant. Problem was, I had no clue as to whose baby it was. Nor did I try to figure out which of my last three boyfriends it belonged to. Didn't matter. I knew I wasn't going to keep it. I looked through the phone book, located an abortion clinic, and scheduled an appointment for that afternoon.

After tooting a couple of lines of meth, popping a yellow jacket, and drinking some bourbon, I drove to the clinic. Once I had given the receptionist my name and been instructed to sit down, I looked around the room, which was filled with young girls. Some were crying. Some disinterestedly flipped through magazines. Others just sat and stared off at objects only they seemed to be able to see.

I was examined by a doctor, and after making me piss into a small clear plastic cup, was told what I already knew: I was three months pregnant. I was so pissed at myself. How could I have let this happen *again*? I didn't bother answering that question. The 'how' was unimportant. What *was* important is that I get rid of the pregnancy. So I made the necessary arrangements to do so.

Three days later, I popped two ludes, three black beauties, smoked a joint, drank four beers, and then drove to the clinic and had the abortion. An hour and a half later, I was home tooting coke, popping pills, and drinking Seagram's 7 and 7-Up. Soon, I didn't have to think. I didn't have to feel. I didn't have to remember.

As usual, the money I made from my dope business became insufficient because I was using it up faster than I could sell it. I needed a scam, but wanted something where I wouldn't have to risk going to jail. Being able to stay out of jail helped me convince myself that my using and slanging were relatively harmless and recreational. One day while watching the news, I got an idea. The story was about some study that had proven that salesclerks and store-security personnel were more likely to watch minorities – specifically blacks and Mexicans – in their stores than they were white people. I'd finally found an advantage to being not only black, but dark black! But first, I'd need a white girl. I knew that Slim and the other hos wouldn't do; they were too old. I needed a white girl around my age.

I jumped up, ran into the living room, and told Slim what kind of girl I was looking for. A few days later she introduced me to a young white ho named Dot. Slim and Dot knew each other because they sometimes worked the same corner. Dot was eighteen years old, thin but pretty. She was dirty and scraggly, but once showered, shampooed, and cleaned up, I figured she'd do for my purposes just fine.

This is how the scam worked: first, I and five or six black girl-friends would dress as ghetto as possible: dirty jeans or khaki pants, and dirty shirts hanging out over the pants. Though none of my doper friends banged – and I'd long since quit – I had everyone wear blue rags to give us a more suspicious and sinister effect. Then, cursing and loud-talking in a mob, we'd enter a store. As soon as we came in the door, we could see the fear and suspicion in the clerks' eyes. We could *feel* the security guards' entire bodies jump to attention and tense up as we passed by.

Once we were sure we had everyone's attention, we'd slowly begin to walk around the store, lifting items to view and show them to each other, loudly shout the prices to each other, or hold up pieces of clothing to our bodies as if trying to size them up.

Moments after we entered the store, Dot would come in: cleaned, showered, neatly dressed, and looking like the perfect little white citizen. By the time Dot walked in, the clerks and security were so focused on me and my crew, they never even noticed her.

We'd continue to walk around, touch, and compare items we liked. The clerks and security guards were intensely watching us and following us around. They didn't bother trying to be in-conspicuous about the fact that they had us under heavy surveillance, and they knew that we knew they were watching us. What they didn't know was that while they were watching us – so convinced that we were up to something – Dot was robbing them blind. She'd be stuffing clothes into her pants, her shirt, under her hat, in her underwear, anywhere they would fit. Hell, one time she stuck gloves, earrings, and a change purse into her shoes. And she wasn't even trying to be sly about it – she didn't have to. Everyone was so afraid of what my menacing little black crew were doing that no one was paying attention to her.

Once Dot couldn't get anything else into her hiding places, she'd calmly and slowly walk out of the store. We'd wait a moment to allow her to get far enough away, and then we'd stroll out, just as loud and as ghetto as when we'd come in. The security and salesclerks were always thrilled to see us go, patting themselves on the back and giving each other high fives for having 'foiled' another shoplifting scheme.

We'd all meet around the corner. Then, together (we didn't trust each other to do it separately), we'd sell the loot to the coke man, the pawnshop, neighbors, people on the corner, or whoever would buy it, and split the money. We always got a good payoff because Dot stole only nice stuff that was always easy to sell: designer jeans and tops, cute little earrings, bracelets and necklaces, lovely picture frames, scarves, gloves, small purses, etc.

Dot never thought about trying to ditch us once leaving the store with the loot. She knew we'd track her down and whup her ass. Actually, I soon came to realize that Dot was excellent for this part of my scam because the person playing the 'white girl' couldn't be afraid. She had to *exude* confidence and superiority. She had to be convinced of the fact that, as the white person, *she* was the good one, the safe one, the *trust-worthy* one. If this attitude was not sufficiently projected, the store personnel would pick up on her anxiety and nervousness. But not with Dot; she was smooth. Although she was always around a bunch of black folks, she wasn't bothered by her white skin, which she used to her advantage and, in this case, ours.

We never worked the same store within the same month and of the twenty-five or thirty times we did it, we were never caught (of course *we* weren't doing anything but being ourselves). Nor was Dot ever caught when she worked with us. This scam worked *every time*. In fact, we would probably have continued it much longer than the few months we did except Dot got greedy – and cocky. She didn't believe us when we told her that the only reason she was able to get away with stealing like she did was because *we* were the diversion. Dot actually thought she was good at stealing and figured that, without us, she could keep all of the loot money herself. So one day she tried to run the scam solo. She went to a leather store and *thought* she was leaving with several pairs of leather pants, a leather jacket, purse, and gloves. She was busted before she even hit the door.

I never found a white girl smooth enough to replace Dot. So because of her greed, one of the greatest scams I'd ever created came to a crashing, sudden halt. That was all right. Being the hustler I was, sooner or later I'd find another way.

26

After less than a year at the Complex, Daddy said he wanted out. He said he was tired of the business, the hos, the constant traffic, and the lifestyle. When Daddy told me about his plans, I wasn't really shocked. I knew he had been unhappy for quite a while. The Complex's atmosphere was completely out of his element – it was too hard to constantly be around drunks, hos, and drug users when you weren't a drunk, ho, or druggie. He said Lori had been calling and inviting him to give her the opportunity to try to make a relationship with him again, and he'd finally decided to take her up on it. So Daddy would be moving to a new house with Lori and Kelly. He quickly added that I was welcome to come. He pointed out the fact that I didn't make enough from my business to live on my own, which meant I couldn't afford to stay in the apartment by myself without quickly going through what was left of my trust-fund money. He added that, more important, I needed a change in scenery.

I didn't really have any other choice. Daddy was right: I couldn't afford to stay there by myself, especially since I'd long been using more dope than I was selling. And maybe a change of scenery would help me get myself together. I told Daddy I'd go with him.

Our customers were sad to see us go. We always had good dope. Our neighbors were also sad to see us go. We always looked out for them and gladly shared our 'party favors.' Our landlord was sad to see us go, particularly since we were among the few tenants who consistently paid rent on time. The hos were sort of sorry to see us go, especially since Daddy was the only 'business partner' they'd ever had that didn't take their money. On the other hand, they were used to moving around – it came with the territory.

Daddy and I packed up and left the Complex. We left the events and memories of the Complex *at* the Complex. No one, outside of customers, ever knew what went on there – until now.

Lori took Daddy back without question. She really loved him and was so glad to have him back, she said she didn't care *what* he'd done when he was gone. He and Lori rented a three-bedroom house in Skyline, an area east of San Diego. It was a nice house, with lots of large windows and a big front yard. Even though we no longer *sold* drugs, that didn't mean I couldn't *use* them. Hell, quitting drugs was never even considered. Wherever I went, the party came with me. I always found the party animals. Skyline was no different.

Since I'd returned to the San Diego area, Kelly and I would talk periodically, but we never really got close like we had been before my mother died. But that changed when we started living together in Skyline. Kelly also smoked weed and drank, so we quickly became inseparable party buddies. And as usual, Lori took care of Kelly's baby, Jason, so Kelly's motherhood never got in the way of our partying. We'd hear about a party that was happening at someone's house, and we'd just show up – not knowing a soul there and not having been invited. We didn't care. We'd walk in smiling and blowing kisses at people, waving to the crowd as if we were grand marshals on top of a beautifully decorated parade float, stopping to chitchat with everyone. Besides crashing parties, another of our favorite things to do was have midnight toga parties at the beach. We'd invite fifteen to twenty of our friends, bring along plenty of dope and booze, and build a huge bonfire. The rules were simple. You had to drink, smoke, snort, and wear a sheet draped around your body like a toga. At first, most of the men balked at the last requirement. But once they were completely smashed and wobbly from following the first three rules, they'd sloppily and drunkenly throw on a sheet – most times with nothing on underneath. Then we'd spend hours dancing around the bonfire while, at the top of our lungs, screaming, 'Toga! Toga! Toga!' It was a stupid thing to do – and I loved it.

It was at one of these toga parties that Victor, a good friend and regular partier, talked to me about my drug use. He insinuated that I might have a problem with drugs.

Me? A problem with drugs? Shit, only problem I got is when I ain't got any!

I chuckled at my own joke. Damn, I was funny. Victor was looking at me oddly. Like he was trying to figure out whether I was chuckling or choking. I figured I should at least *try* to be serious.

'What makes you think I have a drug problem?' I asked. Now that I realized he was serious, I was insulted he'd suggest such a thing.

'Well, you don't go to school or work. In fact, you don't do shit. All you do is drink, drug, and party.' He looked at me disgustedly, took a swig of Schlitz Malt Liquor, and staggered over to the bonfire to join the toga chanting.

I sat there and thought about what he said.

So that's it? All I got to do to be able to drink and use and not worry about folks thinking I got a 'problem' is get a job or go to school? I could do that. I'd already tried working. It sucked. But I hadn't really tried school.

The following Monday, I set out to find a school. As I was flipping through the yellow pages looking for one, Kelly approached and asked me what I was doing. I proudly informed her I was going to school. At first she didn't say anything. She just stared at me, obviously perplexed. I ignored her and went back to looking. She stood there staring a few moments more. Finally, she turned and walked away.

I found a vocational school that offered a certificate in six months. That sounded good to me because six months was about all of the education I could stomach. At first Kelly had no interest in attending. Then she found out we would get five thousand dollars in student loans. Suddenly, she got a yearnin' to do some learnin'.

Kelly signed up for the legal-secretary program. I signed up for medical assistant. I figured they'd need someone like me to watch over the medicines. But I soon found out that before they'd let me handle meds, they wanted me to learn some medical terminology and biology. Problem was, I *hated* biology and couldn't *remember* any of the medical terms. There were way too many names of body parts, bones, and shit. Hell, to me a finger was a finger. But they wanted you to know all the different bones and veins in the damned thing! After miserably failing my first vocabulary test (I didn't get *one* answer correct), I approached the counselor about changing programs. He took one look at my exam and agreed. He suggested I join Kelly in the legal-secretary program. It was an excellent suggestion.

For some reason, the legal terms just came naturally to me. I could study the words the night before an exam (while smoking a joint and having a drink), and still do well enough to pass with a C- or D+. Kelly, on the other hand, hated it all. She hated the legal terminology and just couldn't get the shorthand. The only thing she did like about school was that Daddy and Lori kept Jason so she could attend classes. So she hung in there, at least till she got her student-loan check. Once the check cleared, Kelly's schedule changed, though she never told Daddy and Lori because she knew once they found out she'd quit, she'd have to stay at home with Jason. So she got up every morning, as though she were going to school, and rode to school with me. But once we got there, she never went in: she'd sit in the car, smoke weed, and sleep while I went to class.

I, on the other hand, actually enjoyed school, especially since there was no math or biology required. In fact, the hardest class I had to take was shorthand, which I loved. It too came naturally to me. And it soon became the perfect 'tweak' for a speed freak like me. 'Tweaking' is what speed freaks do to keep their hands and bodies moving while high on speed. Speed is an upper that charges you with such an incredible amount of energy that you have to do something with it or you'll go crazy. As a result, everyone on speed tweaks in one way or another.

There are numerous ways of tweaking, so long as the person is keeping her hands busy and moving quickly. Some people go on cleaning frenzies. They'll clean everything in the house – twice. Since I hated cleaning, this was never an option for me. Some people play card games, musical instruments, or anything else that can keep their hands occupied. I soon discovered that shorthand was an excellent way to tweak, even when I wasn't in class. I would sit in front of the TV and take down the news. Sometimes, I'd just sit with Kelly and other partiers and take down their conversations. They thought I was nuts. What none of us knew was that by practicing shorthand that often and that much, I was quickly improving my skills and speed. Within three months I was taking shorthand at seventy words per minute.

My regular snorting of meth and coke also provided plenty of energy to stay up for days at a time, and really gave me the extra oomph I needed to study the night before an exam. I was soon impressed with the fact that I was able to go to school, take shorthand faster than anyone else in my class, maintain a D+ average, *and* still party. No drug problems, here.

Three months after I started, I felt like I'd proved my point and was getting a little sick of getting up every morning to go out and gather up a bunch of useless skills. So I decided I needed to quit, but without looking as though I was quitting. It was a tricky problem, but I was up for it.

The following week, I ditched class with Kelly. We were sitting in my car at the corner liquor store, smoking a joint. I was bitching about my dilemma when I noticed Sara walk into the store. Sara was a young black girl who worked in my school's records department. She was a pretty girl who prided herself on the fact that she was able to work *and* maintain her 'get high.' I understood this pride. A few minutes later, she walked out carrying a brown paper bag, which held the easily recognizable shape of a 40-ounce. She looked up and saw us. She immediately skipped over to the car and bent down to peer through my open window.

'Uuummmm, smells *good* in here,' she hinted with a big smile.

I wasn't troubled about Sara knowing that I got high. I knew she was cool because we'd partied together before.

'Girl, get in,' I said, giving her a big grin while opening the door and leaning my seat forward so she could crawl into the back.

Kelly handed her the joint. She handed Kelly the 40 she'd just bought. Kelly opened it and took a long swig. Sara took a long hit off the joint.

'Is somebody gonna give *me* something?' I snapped. Hell, it was my car and I wasn't smoking or drinking anything. They laughed as they simultaneously shoved the bottle and joint at me.

After taking a swig and a hit, I continued my bitching about how sick and tired I was of the whole school thing. Sara listened for a moment. Then she leaned forward,

'How sick of it are you?'

'*Very* sick!' I snapped. *Hasn't she been listening to a fucking word I've been saying?*

'Well, if it's worth your *money,* I can make it worth your *while,*' she stated quietly. She had my attention.

She said that for one hundred dollars cash she could 'update' my records to reflect I'd completed all of the required courses, making me eligible for my certificate and graduation.

'No shit?' I asked, unsure if she was joking or not.

'No shit,' she replied.

Later that night, as I lay in bed smoking a joint and drinking gin and orange juice, I thought about Sara's offer. Should I take the easy way out or, for once in my life, try to actually *learn* something, *earn* something, *finish* something?

Two weeks later I graduated. To me, that meant I'd finished something. (Didn't matter that I'd paid a hundred dollars for it – fair exchange ain't no robbery, right?) I didn't remember one legal term, but my last shorthand exam had been timed at seventy words per minute. To me, that meant I had learned something. I still hadn't earned anything, but hell, I figured two out of three wasn't bad.

Daddy was so proud of me. He bragged to all of his friends that not only did I graduate, but I'd done it in three and a half months instead of the normal six. The downside is that when I graduated and Kelly didn't, Kelly was forced to come clean about dropping out of school. Daddy was furious that she'd lied and taken advantage of them. He swore he and Lori would never watch Jason again.

I didn't show up for the graduation ceremony. I never even went and got my certificate. I didn't do it for the certificate. I did it to prove to myself, and others, that I didn't have a problem with drugs. Because drug addicts don't go to school, right?

27

My nineteenth birthday was coming up, and I wanted to have a party. I was a college graduate, and I'd proven I didn't have a drug problem. Who wouldn't want to celebrate?

I made a list of things to do. First, I needed a party place. The house next door was being rented by two single black guys, Gregory and Brent. We'd become friends because they had a nice huge den that we often partied in. I approached Greg about using his house to throw myself a party. I told him I'd provide the booze, the dope, and the DJ. Always down for a party, he agreed.

Now that I had a party place, I needed party people. The problem was, I really didn't have any friends, not real ones. And although I had people who were always willing to drink and drug with me, they were only a few. I wanted a *huge* party. I wanted to surround myself with lots and lots of people – I wanted a throng to come celebrate me. I decided to make flyers publicizing my party. I printed three hundred flyers announcing the date, time, and location, and in extra-large letters I put that there'd be plenty of free booze. I placed the flyers everywhere – stuck them under windshield wipers of cars in grocery-store parking lots, nailed them to trees in parks, and taped them on the front counters of liquor stores.

I continued with my checklist. I'd taken care of the party place and party people. Next, I needed party favors – booze – and lots of it. I knew just where to go. Kelly, a couple of other friends, and I took a trip across the border to Tijuana, Mexico, where booze was very cheap. In fact, the only time I ever went to TJ was to buy booze because, there, I got a fifth of booze for what a half-pint would cost in San Diego.

Legally, you were only allowed to bring two bottles of booze per person back across the Tijuana border. But being the hustler I was, I had a plan. When the border patrolman approached the car and asked if we were bringing anything back into America, I made sure each of the other five people in the car held up two bottles. Seeing that we had twelve bottles in the car, he seemed satisfied that that would be enough booze for anyone to bring back. He waved us through with no idea that we had another 20 bottles hidden in the trunk: rum, vodka, gin, brandy, scotch, tequila, bourbon, whiskey, and cognac. I didn't stop buying liquor until I ran out of money.

I now had all the necessities for a great party. I just hoped someone would show up for it. In street life, you knew the reliability of your friends was directly proportionate to your supply of alcohol or drugs. Hopefully, the partiers of the city wouldn't let me down.

The big night finally arrived. I wanted to wear my favorite color, so I bought a sexy little, little purple dress to wear. Paired with my signature five-inch heels, I was just too cute for the occasion.

As usual, I started drinking way before the party officially started. I had a rum and coke while getting dressed. Then I had a vodka and orange juice as I helped Greg and Brent set up chairs. I enjoyed a gin and tonic with the DJ as he set up his equipment. I had another rum and coke as I sat around nervously waiting for people to arrive. The flyer said the party started at 9:00. But I knew people wouldn't start coming till 9:30 or 10:00. Finally, they started filtering in.

It didn't bother me that I had to go around and inform people that *I* was the reason for the party. I wasn't insulted that I had to constantly announce to people that *I* was the birthday girl. Nor did their blasé, uninterested responses bother me. Some mumbled a half-assed 'Happy birthday.' Others carelessly looked at me and said, 'That's nice. Where's the bar?' I didn't care. Whether they knew it or not, they were there for me.

I partied hard for the first two and half hours. Then I passed out. I tried to hang, but I couldn't. By 11:30 (an hour and a half after the party really got started), I'd had three rum and cokes, three gin and tonics, four vodka and orange juices, three whiskey shots, two brandies, and I think two cognacs – I was in a blackout after the second whiskey shot.

All I knew was that one minute I was dancing on the coffee table (with myself) with Greg, Brent, and some others trying to coax me down, and the next, I was lying on Greg's bathroom floor, vomiting up what I was sure was my intestines. After I barfed a couple of times, Greg came in, picked me up (unaware of the vomit that streamed down the front of my once-pretty purple dress as a result of my missing the toilet a few times), and laid me down on his bed. He was heading for the door when I rose my head and slurred out to him to 'stop twirling the god-damn room!' He glanced back at me, gave a little chuckle, and ducked back into the party crowd. I lay there assessing my situation. I felt like shit. I smelled like shit. And I was sure I looked like shit. So I gladly welcomed complete, utter, drunken unconsciousness.

I was awakened by a great commotion. I was lying on the bed on my back, drool sliding down my cheek, when Greg burst into the room, slamming the door into the wall behind it. He'd thrust open the door with such force that when it hit the wall, the doorknob created a gaping hole. I raised my head as much as I could to see what was going on. Greg's left arm hung limp at his side, and his shirt was soaked with some type of liquid. I figured it had probably been caused by a spilled drink – I had no idea it was blood.

'Watz slapin'?' I slurred.

'Mothafuckas want to start some shit,' he growled to no one in particular as he reached into his closet and grabbed a shot-gun, 'then it's gon' be some shit!'

His eyes were bloodshot red, and his face showed pure rage. He stormed out of the room.

Well, whatever it is, I thought, *he's obviously handling it.* I suddenly became conscious of the fact that my head was too heavy to continue holding up. I plopped back down on the bed and passed out again.

The next afternoon, when I came to, I learned what happened.

By midnight, about two hundred more people had shown up wanting to get into the party and get their free drinks. However, there were at least 125 people already inside the house, so Greg refused to let anyone else in. Some of the niggas got upset and tried to force their way in. A shoving match started; shoving escalated to punching. Several fights started. Suddenly, someone pulled out a gun and started shooting. Greg, who was standing in the doorway turning people away, was shot in the arm. But he was too drunk and pissed to think rationally. In his drunken fury, it never occurred to him to shut down the party and call for help. Instead, the alcohol told him to shoot back and 'get them mothafuckas!' That's when I'd seen him dash into the closet to grab his gun.

Later, he was taken to the hospital and patched up. The bullet went clean through his arm. He was the only one shot that night; however, someone else was stabbed, and still others were beaten up pretty bad. But it was unclear who shot whom, who stabbed whom, and who'd been fighting whom. Of course, when the cops tried to interview people, no one knew anything and no one had seen anything.

I didn't give a fuck about the others who'd been hurt. Those niggas ruined my party. I did feel kind of bad for Greg, though. I mean, it *was* my fault that so many people had shown up. But, hell, I figured if I'd passed out three hundred flyers, *maybe* seventy-five people would show up. It never occurred to me that some of those three hundred would tell a friend.

Still, it was a great party. Only thing I hated was that I'd missed most of it and *all* the excitement. Greg didn't harbor any ill feelings toward me. I gave him a dime bag for his troubles, and we were cool. We continued to party together for months to come. But he never again let me use his house. I didn't care. Finding places to party was never a problem.

28

One day, Jr. called to say Grandma had died. I was hungover, so it took me a moment to clear my head and realize what he'd said.

'Grandma's dead?' I asked disbelievingly. He answered that she was.

I cried most of the day. Partly because Granny was gone, but mostly because of the intense guilt I felt. I hardly ever went to see her, using the excuse that I couldn't take seeing her like that. Now that she was gone, I wished I could see her 'like that' or any other way. But I couldn't. Now, I'd never see her again. To help ease the guilt, I got loaded until I passed out.

After Grandma's death, I drank more and more; and my promiscuity increased dramatically. The realization that the only two women I'd ever really loved, my mom and her mom, were gone forever seemed to widen the already huge void I had inside me. However, Daddy didn't understand my need to sleep around. In fact, he firmly instructed both me and Kelly not to have men in our rooms. More important, they were not allowed to stay overnight. But where else was I supposed to take them?

One Saturday morning, Daddy was heading for the golf course. His car wouldn't start, so he came to my room to ask me if he could use mine. He knocked on the door a couple of times, but there was no answer.

I never heard the knock on the door. I was busy.

Daddy knew I was home because my car was in the driveway. So he opened the door and peeked in. He said that all he could see was the covers moving up and down. Every time they moved up, he'd see my toes sticking up. He gasped and shut the door. I never knew he was there.

Daddy decided that he should also check on Kelly. So he went and peeked into her room. Again, all he saw were covers moving up and down. He closed the door and caught a cab to the golf course.

Later that afternoon, when he returned, he called us into the dining room. It was then he informed us that he'd caught us both in the act. We were shocked as we looked at each other.

I started to lie. 'I wasn't fuck – '

'Cup, don't lie to me!' He slammed his fist down on the table. He was really pissed. He said it was disrespectful to him and Lori as parents for me and Kelly to have sex with men in the house.

Let me get this straight, I thought. We *can sell dope, and* you *can have hos, but all of a sudden you don't want* me *fuckin'?*

Daddy continued, 'If them niggas can't afford a hotel, they're not worth it. But in any event, there will be no more men in the bedrooms. Is that understood?'

'Yeah,' we replied with our heads hanging down. I wasn't so upset by knowing Daddy caught me in the act of sex. I was more upset by the fact that I'd have to find another place to do it. I wondered if he really meant what he said. I decided he didn't mean it; he was just trying to be a 'father' in front of Lori.

The next day, tired from playing golf, Daddy was sitting at the kitchen table reading a newspaper. A young black man, wearing nothing but boxer shorts, sauntered into the kitchen, opened the fridge, grabbed two beers, and casually strolled away. The young man saw Daddy, but didn't bother to speak.

Wondering who the young man was and where he was going, Daddy quietly got up and followed him. He watched him walk into my room and close the door.

'Did my daddy see you?' I asked the young man as he entered the room with the beers. His name was Billy, and he lived down the street from us. When I'd sent him to get the beers, I told him to be careful, to be quiet, and to *stay out of my daddy's way.* The last thing I needed was to hear Daddy's mouth.

'Naw,' Billy lied.

Later that day, Daddy called me and Kelly into his room.

'I thought I told you girls I didn't want any more niggas in this house?'

'But—' I started.

'But, my ass!' Daddy screamed, cutting me off before I could finish the lie. 'Now shut up and listen, and listen good. I don't want anyone – man, woman, boy, or girl – to come through that front door without my permission. Now I will never kick you two out into the street, but what I will do is put my foot so far up your asses, it will take a dentist to get my toenails out of your throat! Now get the hell out of here. I'm sick of looking at you both.'

Kelly and I turned and walked out quietly but quickly. Shit, I was scared. The last time I'd seen Daddy that pissed was the day he'd kicked the wall when the doctor told us Momma was dead.

Any doubt I'd had as to whether Daddy was serious about his 'no-boys-in-the-room' rule was now gone. We would definitely have to get another plan.

Kelly and I were sitting at the park, smoking weed and drinking Long Island Iced Teas, trying to decide on what to do.

'Let's move,' I said.

'Move?' she asked. 'How we gon' move? We can't afford to move!'

'Well, you get your welfare check and I still got money from my trust fund. On top of that, I can hustle. Together, we should be able to find *something* we can afford! Besides, think of the fun we'll have in our own place. I've been there before, and trust me, ain't nothing like the freedom of having your own place. Nothing like it!'

She had to think about it only for a moment before she agreed to my plan. We would immediately start looking for a place.

We went home to tell Daddy and Lori that we were moving out. They were lying in their bedroom watching TV. We knocked on the door, and after hearing Lori say, 'Come in,' we walked in and announced that we were giving them two weeks' notice. For a moment, neither of them spoke. Then Daddy got a weird grin on his face. He looked at us, still giving a sarcastic smile, and said, 'Well, since neither one of you pay rent, there is no need to give notice.'

Even we had to chuckle at that one. Daddy continued.

'Now, I would never put you out. But since y'all wanna be

grown, this is probably best. Get your own place, then you can live as you wish. But remember, y'all are leavin' on your own – we ain't puttin' you out.'

We now had Daddy and Lori's blessing. Somehow that made our decision to leave feel right.

At first, we had a hard time finding an apartment. No one wanted to rent to two teenagers – one who listed 'welfare' and the other 'hustlin' ' for income. We knew that any landlord willing to rent to us would have to be someone who wasn't too picky about his or her tenants. I found that landlord back at my old Complex. Actually, I found him *in back of* the Complex – in the two rows of raggedy, dilapidated two-bedroom cottages that stood behind the Complex. Kelly and I rented one of the cottages. We could move in the following week.

'What we gon' do for furniture?' Kelly asked. We were back at Daddy and Lori's, sitting in my room smoking a joint, drinking Brass Monkey, and celebrating our new apartment.

I hadn't thought of that. Shit, the apartment I had when I'd gotten emancipated came furnished. After that, I moved into the Complex with Daddy, who already had furniture. From there, we'd brought our furniture to our current house in Skyline. So, I'd never had to worry about furniture.

'That's a good question,' I replied. I thought about it for a moment, but drew a blank. 'Something will come up,' I said, and took a swig of Monkey. The next day, while tooting lines, it did.

I approached Daddy about loaning us money to buy furniture. Kelly stood behind me. She said she wanted to stand back there so that if Daddy swung on us, I'd get hit first and she'd have time to run.

'Girl, you know y'all ain't got no damn money,' he replied. 'Tell you what, you can take anything you want and need from this house to help you set up your apartment.'

I stood there dazed. 'Anything?' I asked, not sure I'd heard him correctly.

'Anything.'

'Even the TV?'

'Anything, Punkin. You girls can have anything.'

Now that she was sure Daddy wouldn't do any swinging, Kelly stepped out from behind me.

'Even the stereo?' she timidly asked, also thinking she'd heard wrong.

'What the hell is wrong with y'all's ears?' Daddy snapped, obviously irritated. 'Don't you know what 'anything' means? It means anything! Anything you want! Take it! Take it!'

We were shocked and touched. Neither of us could say anything for a moment. Finally, I spoke.

'We didn't think you'd do that.'

Daddy stared at us for a moment before speaking. 'I'm still Daddy, and that will never change. Just because you two disappointed me doesn't mean I don't love you.'

We ran into his arms, crying and grateful that someone *did* love our worthless asses.

Then we did as he said – we took *everything*. Pictures off the walls, pots and pans, trash cans, trash bags, the broom and vacuum cleaner, all of the living-room furniture, both of our bedroom sets, the TV, the stereo, telephones, telephone *cords*, cleaning supplies, lamps, tables, ashtrays, food. Everything and anything that wasn't nailed down or attached to the house was taken. Daddy just sat there and watched us empty his house. Periodically he'd chuckle, but he never said a word. Lori, who always agreed to whatever Daddy wanted, also kept silent.

29

We loved having our own place, though it was much harder than we'd imagined. Kelly paid her share of the rent from her welfare check. I paid mine the best way I could. I'd periodically turn tricks with my male and female partiers, sell dope, or, as a last resort, go into my trust fund, which was dwindling quickly.

We had *planned* to leave Jason with Daddy and Lori and visit him on the weekends. But Daddy was still pissed at Kelly's lying about going to school and tricking them into watching Jason, so we were forced to take him with us. Neither of us knew much about parenting or priorities; our main concerns were booze, drugs, gas (for my gas-guzzling car), clothes (we had to look good), and men. As a result, we didn't have much money left for food. Kelly did receive food stamps from welfare. Luckily, those were one of our constant sources of income. We would sell a hundred dollars' worth of food stamps for seventy dollars cash. This arrangement offered a two-way bargain: as sellers, we got the cash (which we used for drugs, booze, etc.), and the buyer got thirty dollars' worth of food for free. Since someone was always looking to buy food stamps, we rarely used them to buy food. Luckily, grocery stores always had specials on Top Ramen, a type of noodle soup. You could get ten packages for a dollar. We'd buy fifty packages. Then, we'd buy a big box of generic cereal and a huge box of powdered milk (you mixed it with water and voila! – milk. Yes, it was *nasty, chalky* milk, but milk just the same). We figured that as long as Jason was being fed and not being beaten or raped, he was all right. So we actually considered ourselves to be good parents.

We never allowed our nasty living conditions to diminish our positive parental self-image. Kelly, like me, hated to clean – though I was never able to figure out why – it wasn't like Lori had ever *made* her do it. Anyway, because we both hated to clean, our house stayed filthy. Piles of dirty clothes lay everywhere. Bowls with dried-on ramen noodles left in them or bowls of dried-up cereal with paste residue from the powdered milk still clinging to them were piled high in the sink.

Neither did we allow the fact that we lived with rats thwart our first-rate self-image. Actually, we often found the rat episodes comical. For instance, one day, Jason was running barefoot across the living-room floor. Kelly and I and our party friends didn't notice the very frightened rat scurrying by. In fact, no one saw the rat till Jason stepped on it. We were sitting around drinking Heineken, tootin' lines, and smoking blunts when we heard the squeals – Jason's *and* the rat's. The room grew suddenly quiet as we wondered what the hell had just happened.

'Mommy! Auntie Cup! Look!' Jason screamed, his bony finger pointing at the broken slump of fur that lay squirming. We all stood up and gathered around the rat, who still hadn't surrendered to death. We just stood there for a few moments, no one saying a thing. Finally, I broke the silence with a whisper.

'What should we do?' I didn't know why I was whispering.

'Poor thing, we have to have a funeral,' Victor said softly to no one in particular. Victor had been one of our faithful partiers. He'd been a regular at the toga parties, and he'd loyally followed us when we moved out on our own. Now, he looked so sad, like he was about to cry. A huge black man, Victor stood about six three and weighed about 270 pounds. So to see him near tears and speaking softly about a funeral for a dead rat was just too funny.

I looked at Victor and began to laugh. My laughter must have been contagious, because Victor started laughing too. Soon, Kelly and the others joined in. Even Jason joined in, though he really had no idea what was so funny. I don't know if it was the beer we'd drunk, the coke we'd tooted, or the weed we'd smoked, but once we started laughing, we couldn't stop. Even after the rat died and began to ooze yellowish fluid from his eyes and mouth, we cracked up. In fact, for about twenty-five minutes, we lay out on the floor in a circle around the dead rat, laughing our asses off. By the time I was able to get myself together, my eyes were watering so much I could barely see, and my side was killing me.

We never thought twice about the diseases rats carry or about the fact that Jason could have been bitten by it. Actually, whenever someone wanted to get us laughing, they'd bring up the time Jason stepped on a rat.

Being in our own house allowed our partying to escalate. Since most of the other tenants were illegal aliens from Mexico, we never really had to worry about anybody calling the police on us. We immediately changed the venue of the toga parties from the beach to our living room. It was during this time that my heroin use skyrocketed.

I was driving to the store to get more beer, when I happened to notice this guy walking down the street. Normally, I wouldn't have paid him any mind. What caught my attention were the three creases ironed into the back of his shirt – the sign for Eight-Tray Gangsta. But as far as I knew, I was the only Gangsta in San Diego. My heart began to race as anxiety and uncertainty kicked in.

What if it really was one of the homies? Would they remember me? Would I remember them? Would they be after me? I asked myself.

Why would they? I answered myself. *You ain't snitched.* I hadn't. I'd kept my vow of silence.

I slowed down so I could get a better look at the man. As I crept by, he looked up, smiled as he threw up three fingers and hollered, 'What's up, cuzzz?'

It was Bootsey! One of the OGs from the set. We'd done a few crimes and smoked a few live ones together. He was family. I pulled over, almost hitting him, jumped out of the car, and ran to hug him. I jumped into his arms with such force, we both almost fell over as he struggled to catch his balance. 'Damn, cuzzz,' he slurred, obviously loaded, 'you sheem really happy ta shee a nigga!'

I was. At the realization that what I'd found really was one of the homies, all of the fear and anxiety I'd felt just moments before were immediately forgotten. Just that fast, the intense feelings of camaraderie, solidarity, and friendship returned. I felt like I had found a long-lost relative.

'Com' on, cuzzz,' I said. (I hadn't used 'cuzzz' since leaving the set, and I didn't realize how fast, and automatic, the lingo returned.) 'Ride with me to the store to cop some brew.'

On our way to the store he caught me up on what had been happening on the set. He told me which of the homies had gotten killed or jailed since my departure. He said the game had changed – that the little homies comin' up didn't have respect for the game like we'd had. He said the younger homies weren't true to 'the blue' or the set. Their main attention was now focused on 'the green' (money) and 'territory' (drug turf). It seemed more and more of the homies were getting into slangin'. He said it wasn't just the Gangstas either. Every set was turning on the game.

'Remember when niggas used to scrap?' He angrily asked me.

I did remember. I'd been in several scraps myself. I began to fondly reflect back on the night I'd been jumped into the set.

'Well, no more,' he stated irritably, bringing me back to the present. 'Now niggas just shootin'!' I marveled at his extreme anger about the apparent changes the gang environment was going through. I figured this would be a good time to change the subject.

'What about you, cuzzz?' I asked. 'What the hell you doin' in Diego?'

He said he'd had to leave L.A. in a hurry. It seemed he was wanted for questioning for a hoo-ride on some N-Hoods.

Wasn't he just complainin' about niggas shootin'?

I wondered who he'd gotten and if he'd taken anyone out. But I decided not to ask. The less I knew, the better. I already had enough to keep quiet about. He said that since he had family in Diego, he thought it would be a good time to 'take a little vacation.' He was staying with an aunt, who lived about a mile from me. I didn't care why he was there; I was just so glad to see him.

I took him home with me, and of course, we started goin' together. I really enjoyed having him around. For the first time since leaving the set, I was able to reminisce about the good ol' days. Bootsey loved snorting heroin. I did too. So we got along fabulously. Since we spent so much time together, we began snorting more and more.

231

Bootsey hipped me to stealing cars. I'd be the lookout while he'd hop in a car, break off the ignition, and hot-wire it. Sometimes, I'd do the stealing, but I was too slow with the hot-wiring and most times too loaded to remember which wires to twist together to start the ignition. So I preferred stealing those cars in which the owners were stupid enough to leave the keys. Bootsey used to tease me and say I wasn't really a car thief if I had the keys. I didn't care. I was always looking for an easier way to do things.

Once we took the cars, he and his 'friends' stripped them and sold the parts. Sometimes, we'd just take the car to Mexico and sell the whole damn thing. We'd take the money and buy heroin. That's all Bootsey snorted. And since I always followed my man, it soon became all I snorted. Bootsey and I loved, stole, and snorted our way around Diego. But the relationship was short-lived. A couple of months later, Bootsey got busted for a GTA. I was supposed to go with him to steal it, but I'd gotten a little delayed: I'd just snorted a big fat line of heroin and my nose was stinging, my eyes were watering, and my ears were ringing.

'Wait a minute!' I'd yelled after him. 'I'll be ready to go in a minute!'

But his impatience wouldn't allow him to wait for me. He was arrested a few hours later.

When he was arrested, he gave a fake name, but they ran his prints and discovered his true identity – as well as an arrest warrant for attempted murder. He was immediately returned to L.A. I never saw or heard from Bootsey again.

I was sorry to see him go, but I drowned my sorrows in heroin, which thanks to him had become my new favorite. I convinced myself that as long as I didn't slam, I wasn't a dope fiend. I failed to realize that, even though I was only snorting it, I was using much more of it and more frequently than did my friends who did slam it. In fact, *they* started telling me *I* might have a drug problem.

My friends had also begun to nag me about my drinking. I had to kindly remind them that *I* was the one with a college certificate. But to shut them up, I decided to change my drinking habits – I'd only drink beer during the week. I convinced myself that by only drinking hard liquor on the weekends, I could not have a drinking problem. The beer I decided to do the most drinking of was Heineken because Victor said that Heineken was the 'good' beer – the regular favorite of 'high-class' folks. Soon, Heineken became the *only* beer I'd drink. In fact, I'd set a new goal in life. I convinced Kelly, Victor, and our party friends to help me get into the *Guinness Book of World Records* for having the most (empty) Heineken bottles. At first they laughed and dismissed the idea as stupid. But after each one had drunk five beers and smoked a couple of joints, they changed their response to 'willing to listen.' After they'd each had another eight beers and several more joints, they thought it was an excellent idea. Before each of them passed out drunk that night, they were seriously committed to helping me set a record.

We started saving the bottle of every Heineken we drank. We stacked and stored the empty bottles in the six-pack containers. We decided to 'build' the collection along the longest wall in the kitchen. Within four months, there was nothing in the kitchen but empty six-packs of Heineken that stood as high as the refrigerator. As word of the incredible Heineken collection quickly spread throughout the hood, people began asking to see it. Me, being the hustler I was, started charging admission – seventy cents for adults, and fifty cents for kids – to see what was soon being called the 'greatest Heineken collection in the world.' The money I made from admission fees wasn't much, but hey, every little bit counted.

Soon though, the Heineken bottles began to bore me. And the constant trail of people was also causing tension between Kelly and me. Even though the collection was my idea, she somehow thought it was her collection too, and wanted half of the admission money.

But it wasn't just the bottles that caused friction between me and Kelly – we also fought over money. Because of our party-ing, either of us rarely had our respective shares of the rent.

And though it had never been a problem before, dope also became a regular topic for argument. She began accusing me of constantly hogging the straw, joint, bottle, or whatever sub-stance we were consuming. Her nagging pissed me off 'cause hell, *I* wasn't hogging – *she* was a lightweight.

Daddy and Lori decided to move to Chula Vista, the city in

the southern tip of the San Diego area, where I had lived when I'd gotten emancipated. Kelly decided it would be a good decision to go with them, so she moved out. Her departure was quick and uneventful. She came into the house, announced that she was moving back in with Daddy and Lori, hurriedly shoved her and Jason's clothes in a trash bag, and left. I could care less whether she left or not. What I *did* care about was the bitch stuck me with the unpaid rent and the landlord was constantly sweating me about when he was going to get it. I had to do something – and fast.

I decided to deal with my problems like I always did: ignore them. The night Kelly left, I went down to the Oasis nightclub to have a couple of drinks. The place was packed. Good. I could really get my party on when the place was full. As I walked in, the bouncer, Big Red, scowled at me. He knew me well because he'd had to save my ass a couple of times from some nigga I'd pissed off. As I walked by him, he angrily warned: 'Behave yo'-self gurl. I ain't in the mood for no shit tonight.'

'Fuck you,' I retorted. 'I paid my money like everybody else.' If he had understood me, he probably wouldn't have even let me in. But I'd already had several drinks so what he heard was, 'Fwuck sue. I paved ma sunny slike sheveryone selse.' He irritably waved me by.

I went to the bar and ordered a drink – Long Island Iced Tea with no coke and no ice (all booze, baby). I got my drink and stood next to the dance floor so I could check out the crowd – and let them check me out. I knew I looked good in my black miniskirt, gold sequin tube top and matching shiny gold leg warmers (before you go thinking I'm crazy, remember that leg warmers were in in the early eighties).

As I stood against the wall, scanning the room to see who piqued my interest, I saw a tall light-skinned black man standing along the wall directly across from me. He seemed bored as he watched the people on the dance floor. He looked as though he didn't want to be bothered. He looked like a challenge – I loved a challenge.

I sauntered up to him, aware that he was checking me out as I approached. As I got closer, I realized he was more handsome than I'd originally thought. He had a square face, and large sexy lips. When he smiled, his bright white teeth lit up the room. He stood about six feet tall and was very thin. I especially liked the hair on his face: he wore a thin mustache that curved down around his mouth and met a small nicely groomed beard under his chin.

I didn't have to think about what to say to him. I used the same line I used with every man.

'Don't I know you from somewhere?' I knew damn well I didn't know him.

Surprisingly, despite my slurring, he understood me. 'I don't know. Do you?' he quietly replied. A smart-ass. I liked that!

'Probably not, but I'd like to,' I said in the sexiest voice I could muster while giving him a sly grin. He blushed, obviously flattered by my directness.

We stood there for a moment, not saying anything. Finally, I spoke up.

'You wanna dance?' I asked.

'Sure,' he replied.

As we walked to the dance floor I could tell he was checking out my ass. Though I was thin, I made sure to put an extra little switch in my walk.

His name was Tommy. We danced, drank, and talked until the club closed. The first thing I noticed about him was how 'proper' he spoke. He almost sounded as though he were white. I liked hearing him talk, though. So even after the club closed, we sat in my car in the club's parking lot talking. Actually, he did most of the talking; I just listened to the cool way he sounded. All of a sudden, in midsentence, he told me he didn't want to go home.

No problem!

Tommy didn't have a car of his own, so I brought him home with me in mine. I wasn't embarrassed by the fact I lived in a two-room shack. I wasn't embarrassed by the fact that the house was absolutely filthy and smelled like old trash, dirty clothes, and grimy dishes. I didn't care about any of that, since I figured he'd only be there one night – so it wasn't like I had to impress him or anything. Little did I know, he'd be a one-night stand that would last over five years.

30

The next day, it took me a moment to come to. I lay still in the bed as I tried to make myself aware of my surroundings. When I opened my eyes, the light coming in through the tattered, dirty white curtains stung like hell. I shut my eyes and kept them closed. I lay there for a moment to make sure I didn't have to throw up. Once I was sure my stomach wasn't pissed at me, I did what I usually did first thing in the morning: reach under my bed for my weed tray. As I felt around for the tray, I never opened my eyes. I didn't need to see. I could roll a joint with my eyes closed – it was second nature. Feeling my way around the weed tray, I rolled the joint, lit it, took a long hit, and left it hanging out of my mouth as I stumbled out of bed.

I was still physically out of it as I staggered to the fridge to grab a brew. My head was killing me, and my body felt like I'd been in a vicious fight – and lost. I was fussing to myself about my hangovers, which were getting worse and worse.

You gotta stop drinking vodka.

I closed the fridge and leaned up against the door, taking time to gather the strength to make the trek back to my room. I was sure it was vodka that was causing the headaches. I closed my eyes and held the cold beer against my pounding forehead. The coolness seemed to offer momentary relief. With my eyes still closed, I began feeling my way back into the living room; I was trying to decide what booze I should replace vodka with. Because of the throbbing in my forehead and pains racing through the rest of my body, I was walking very slowly, with my head down; joint in one hand, beer in the other. It wasn't until I jammed my foot into the wall that I realized it would probably be a good idea to open my eyes.

Tommy was sitting in the living room, wearing nothing but his underwear, watching my rinky-dink little black-and-white TV. Even though I now had my eyes open, I was so out of it mentally that I didn't see him until I was halfway into the living room. His presence startled me.

'You still here?' I asked irritatedly.

My one-night stands usually slipped out during the night or early in the morning. I didn't care, so long as they were gone by the time I came to. I felt like shit enough without having the object of my exploits hanging around as a remnant.

'Well, I thought I'd wait for you to wake up so we could go and grab some breakfast.'

Breakfast? Who was this idiot? No one ever offered me breakfast! Maybe hush money to ensure my silence in case I ever ran into them with their wives. And, on occasion, a couple of bucks left on the night stand in a desperate attempt to erase their own feelings of dirtiness and shame. But breakfast?

My gaping mouth and bulging eyes must have showed my surprise.

'What's the matter? You act like you've never been to breakfast before!'

With a one-night stand, I hadn't. Disregarding my shock, he continued.

'Come on, girl. Get dressed. I'm hungry! I thought you weren't going to ever wake up!'

Shit, he was serious!

So I got dressed and we went to breakfast. The whole time, I was suspiciously watching him out of the corner of my eye, waiting for him to spring the real reason we were sitting in Bob's Big Boy ordering pancakes and bacon. I figured maybe he'd ask me to run some dope across the border, or maybe he was looking for a chick to boost for him. *Whatever* it was, I wasn't doing it. So I watched him, ate my breakfast, and waited. And waited. And waited.

Though he ran his mouth the entire time, he never asked for a thing. Instead, in his funny-sounding proper English, he told me all about his family. His parents were still married to each other. They, with his younger sister, lived in New York where he was born and raised. He had a full-time job at a warehouse, loading boxes and stuff. It'd been his fourth job in a year. I was impressed by his proper speech and by the fact that he worked, though I didn't let him know it. He ended his story by saying he'd been in California for only a few months.

'You thinking 'bout goin' back to New York anytime soon?' I flippantly asked. He was starting to get on my nerves. He was talking like we were going to be around each other for a while.

'No, I think I found something worth staying around for,' he replied as he winked at me, lazily held back his head, and popped another piece of bacon into his mouth.

Try as I might, I couldn't get rid of Tommy. I thought he'd get tired of my drinking. Instead, he drank with me. I thought he'd get tired of my drug use. Instead, he used with me. I thought he'd get tired of my partying. Instead, he partied with me. We soon became inseparable.

I fell in love with Tommy because he never tried to change me. He never teased me about the ghetto way I talked or the sexy way I dressed. He never complained about my short skirts and high heels. Most important, he never tried to stop me from doing any of the drugs I liked to do, and in fact, was always willing to try new ones. So I was not shocked when, a couple of weeks after we'd been going together, instead of using a straw to toot our coke, he took a little glass pipe out of a small black bag.

'How in the hell am I s'posed to toot with this?' I asked, turning the pipe over to examine it.

'Girl, ain't you never heard of basin'?' Whenever we did drugs or hung with partiers, Tommy used slang. I thought it was kind of cool how he could jump back and forth, at will, from 'white' talk to slang.

But this time, I was too intrigued by the glass pipe and his question to notice he'd jumped into slang. I'd never heard of basin'. And I thought I'd heard of everything.

He said 'freebasing' was a new way of doing coke.

He didn't have to tell me twice. I was always down for something new. So I watched him with great interest.

He said the bag held his 'cooking kit.' In it he kept the glass pipe, a cylinder-shaped glass vial that was about three inches in length, a small container of baking soda, cotton, a pair of pliers, a razor, a thin metal stick, a bottle of 151 proof rum, a copper scouring pad, and a lighter. He laid out the contents as if preparing for surgery. Then he began.

First he put some baking soda into the cylinder-shaped glass vial, took it to the kitchen, and added some water in it. Then he wound several pieces of cotton around the pair of pliers, dipped it into the rum, and lit it with the lighter. The cotton exploded into a small ball of fire. He said this was called a 'torch.' Then, holding the vial slightly at an angle, he began quickly waving the torch under it, gently twirling the vial in a circular motion, all the while never taking his eyes off the contents inside. Slowly the solution began to boil.

I watched in absolute awe because I'd never seen anything like it. He was intently staring at the vial as if it contained something priceless. Small beads of sweat began to appear on his forehead and his breathing started to come in short, quick breaths – almost like he was panting.

'What are you doing?' I asked in a whisper, afraid noise would destroy his scientific undertaking.

'Cooking it,' he replied, also in a whisper. His eyes had grown to the size of large marbles as he continued to wave the torch under the glass vial.

A few minutes later, he blew out the torch. Then, using the thin metal stick (which I later learned was actually a piece of a wire hanger), he reached into the vial and began slowly twirling it around and around. The small amount of white substance inside began to stick to the wire. It reminded me of a cotton-candy machine at the annual county fair. The vendor would stick a white paper cone into the center of the machine, and as the machine twirled, the cotton candy would slowly wrap itself around the cone.

Cotton candy. Fairs. Girl, this ain't no time to be daydreaming, I grumbled to myself as I brought my mind back to the mission at hand.

When Tommy did bring the metal stick out of the vial, a clump of moist white stuff clung to it. It again took me back to my younger days and the milky white paste we used during elementary-school arts-and-crafts sessions. When we were supposed to be making papier-mâché heads, mine ended up looking like a white, sticky deformed fiasco. I hated arts and crafts.

Stay focused, girl, I scolded myself. *Somethin' important's goin' on here.*

Tommy continued with his task. He moved so cautiously, as though he were handling something extremely fragile. He took the wire with the glob of white paste still clinging to it and placed it on my coke mirror – a mirror I kept for coke only, which was no good if it got wet because coke was no good wet. So seeing him place the moist glob on it immediately irritated me. I let out a quick gasp.

Ignoring my irritation, he began to gently blow on the white glob, which began to harden immediately. Within seconds, it had hardened into a shiny white rock about the size of a large marble. I was amazed.

Then he cut a small piece off of the copper scouring pad and placed it into the bowl of the glass pipe.

How much fuckin' preparation does this shit take? He'd been 'preparing' for almost fifteen minutes – hell, I was ready to get high!

Still taking his time, and still moving cautiously, he used the razor to cut a small piece of rock off of the bigger one. He put the small rock into the pipe, redipped the torch into the rum, lit it, and began waving it under the pipe.

For the first time since he'd started cooking, he looked up at me. 'This,' he said, continuing to wave the torch back and forth under the pipe, 'is pure cocaine, baby. Pure coke.' (I later learned that the purpose of cooking is to clean out all impurities.)

Just as the rock began to melt, he put the pipe up to his lips and took a long, slow hit. As he inhaled, small clouds of white smoke began to twirl around inside the glass pipe. I marveled at how pretty the swirling smoke looked.

Once his lungs could take in no more, he took the pipe from his mouth, closed his eyes and held the smoke for what seemed like forever. I understood this concept. It was like smoking weed. The longer you held in the smoke, the higher you got. But I'd never seen anyone hold smoke in *that* long.

Finally, he exhaled – slowly. As he did so, a long stream of white smoke flowed out of his mouth. His eyes turned glassy as his mouth flipped up into a wide grin. One look at the pure euphoria reflected on his face and I knew I needed some of that shit.

'Come on,' I said, still irritated at having to wait so long, 'let me try.'

'Okay, but let me show you how to do it,' he said.

'Nigga, you ain't got to show me shit! I been using for years. Just *give* me the shit!'

'Fine, Ms. Know-It-All,' he snapped. 'Learn the hard way.'

And the hard way I did. The first time I hit it, I did it all wrong. I didn't wait for the coke to melt. I wasn't holding the torch right so it *couldn't* melt. So the first time I hit the pipe, I felt nothing.

'This shit is bunk!' I yelled. 'Ain't you got some plain ol' coke?'

'You didn't do it right!' he yelled, jumping to his feet and protectively snatching the pipe out of my hands as if it were a priceless object. 'And you're wasting it! I told you. You have to let me teach you. Now stop being so fucking hardheaded and listen!'

Determined to do it right, I did listen, and listened well.

That night, I learned how to hold the pipe and the torch so the rock melts correctly. I learned how to inhale slowly. I learned to hold my breath twice as long as I ever had smoking weed. And I learned not to swallow the smoke (swallowing gives you the runs). When I finally did do it right, it was the best feeling I'd ever had in my life. Better than booze or regular coke. Better than meth, sherm, heroin, or uppers. The physical sensation I got from freebasin' is difficult to explain. But let me put it to you like this: think of the happiest, most joyful, blissful moment in your life. Now multiply that feeling by a hundred. That's the ecstasy of basin'. It was simply the most exhilarating and pleasurable sensation I'd ever had. And I didn't want to lose it. I never again reached the same level of ecstasy that the first blast had given me. But I spent the entire night trying.

At first, I always had to wait on Tommy because I didn't know how to cook. This triggered some intense arguments between us because he moved so fucking slowly. So I began to watch him cook

241

very closely and soon learned how to do it myself. Within weeks of taking my first blast, I had my own little cooking kit; though I was never as good at cooking as he was. Once I took that first blast, though, I wouldn't care *who* cooked it, as long as it *got* cooked.

31

Tommy and I were hitting the pipe every opportunity we got. I became obsessed with trying to recapture the golden euphoria of that first hit. We spent every dime we had, and sat there for days on end trying to get back to that place of absolute bliss. It immediately became the most expensive drug I'd ever done.

Tommy began to fuss that I was doing too much *smoking* of dope and not enough *buying* of it. Although I was hustling here and there – robbing, boosting, conducting 'business arrangements' that Tommy didn't know about – it didn't produce enough money, and the money I was able to make wasn't steady. He wanted me to get a job. He broke down all the reasons why:

First, he said it would mean that every payday would provide a guaranteed high.

So far, I liked the plan.

Second, he said that although freebasing could be very addictive, it was completely acceptable and harmless if I had a job. He also said that working was the way to go because no one would notice the drug use if I had a job.

I thought about this for a moment. This wasn't the first time I'd heard this theory. I knew several drug users who weren't considered dope fiends because they got up and went to work every day. In fact, most of our 'real' dope-fiend buddies didn't consider those who had jobs to be real fiends. Maybe Tommy was onto something.

I brought my mind back to the present conversation as Tommy continued with his list of the benefits of working. Finally, he suggested that getting a job would help me with part of my problem.

I didn't ask him what my problem was. Nor did I question his reasoning. Hell, it made sense to me.

'But what kind of job can *I* get?' I asked.

'I don't know,' he replied. He took a hit off the pipe, lay back, and closed his eyes. After a moment, his eyes opened and he sat straight up as he announced he'd thought of a plan. 'Didn't you say you went to college? I'm sure you can do something with that. Anyway, you need to start looking. You can't be sittin' around all day doing nothing.'

I took the pipe, dropped a rock on it, and took a long hit. I closed my eyes as I held my breath and enjoyed my high. 'Okay,' I huffed as I exhaled the smoke, 'I'll get a job.'

Besides, I told myself, *Daddy and Jr. are starting to get on my nerves fussing all the time. Always saying I need to 'do something' with my life. Maybe if I got a job, they'd get off my back.*

'But first, you gotta work on your speech,' Tommy announced.

'What the fuck you mean?' I snapped. Whatever he was hinting at, I decided I didn't like it.

'You gotta quit using slang,' he replied.

'Slang? What's wrong with slang?' Everybody I knew spoke slang.

'They don't use it in the working world. White folks are scared of blacks that use slang. So you're gonna have to learn to enunciate your words.'

'Enuncee – who? What the fuck did you call me?' I assumed my warrior stand: feet shoulder width apart, head cocked to the side, fists balled up ready to pounce.

'I'm not calling you anything, Cup. It's not a *name*, it's a *thing*.' He was again speaking in that 'you fuckin' idiot' tone of voice. 'It means you have to pronounce your words, say the entire word instead of cutting it off at the end.'

The confused look on my face told him I still didn't understand.

'Okay, check this out. You say "ain't"; white folks say "aren't". You say "dat", they say "that". You say "fittin' to", they say "getting ready to". You say "puttin", they say "putting"—'

'Okay, okay,' I snapped. I didn't need any more of his fuckin' examples. I got the picture. I knew what he meant; I just didn't know how I was going to do it. I mean, I'd been talking that way since I *could* talk. How was I supposed to completely and suddenly change something I'd been doing all my life?

He realized what the puzzled look on my face meant.

'You're going to have to practice.'

'Practice?' I asked. I'd never practiced anything in my life.

'Yes, practice. I want you to stand in front of a mirror twice a day, fifteen minutes in the morning and fifteen at night and have a conversation with yourself. Look at yourself and practice saying "isn'*t*", "tha*t*", and "put*ting*". Also, you cuss too much. You need to practice talking without cussing. Pretend you're talking to someone white at an all-white tea party. Practice speaking to them – pronouncing the entire words, the proper words.'

That's it? That's what's going to change my speech – thirty minutes a day? He was truly trippin'!

'Nigga,' I replied, 'I been speaking this way all my life. And I *like* cussing! Cussing makes the sentence *sound* better. It gives true meanings to the words. Besides, if you think thirty minutes a day is gon' turn me 'round, this coke is better than I thought, cuz it's got you trippin' so you done lost yo' crazy-ass mind!'

He didn't say anything for a moment. He just stood looking at me and softly giggling. Then, cautiously, with extreme sensitivity, he explained the other part of his plan.

'No. Thirty minutes a day is only the beginning; it's not *all* you'll have to do. Next, you'll need an incentive to stop cussing and start speaking properly. So this is what else we'll do.'

Who the fuck is we? I asked myself irritably.

He continued. 'We'll tell all our party friends what you're trying to do.'

'What the fuck good is *that* gon' do?' I snapped. 'Them bastards *never* speak right! Besides, all they'll do is laugh at me.'

'You know how much you hate being hit, right?' Well, every time someone around here hears you cuss or say anything slang, they'll punch you. The one catch is, you can't hit back. No matter how hard or how often they hit you. You follow my plan and I guarantee that after three or four weeks and extremely sore arms, legs, and other body parts, you'll start to pay closer attention to what you say and how you say it.'

I thought about what he said for a moment. Tommy hardly ever cussed. And he did speak properly most of the time, though

245

every now and then, mostly when he was high, a slang word would slip out. But his 'properness' is one of the things I liked about him. And he *did* have a job; though he never had one for long. Still, he kept one.

His plan, as crazy as it is, just might work! Besides, the way he's always finding jobs, this little plan must've worked for him.

Tommy's next comment interrupted my thinking: 'Next, you need a résumé.'

'What the fuck am *I* gon' put on a résumé?'

He punched me in the arm. Hard.

'Ow, you son of a bitch!' I screamed as I drew back my right fist to knock the shit out of him.

'Uh, uh, uh!' he chimed, waving his forefinger back and forth in my face as if scolding a child. 'Remember, you can't hit back!'

'What?' I yelled, still pissed and baffled about why I'd gotten hit.

'You were *supposed* to say "What am I supposed to put on a résumé?" Not "What the fuck am I gon' put on a résumé?" Now is as good a time as any to stop cussing and start speaking properly.'

Proper, my ass! I thought, rubbing my arm, which had begun to pulsate with pain. *Maybe this wasn't such a good idea after all!*

But I didn't want to get hit again, so I reasked my question.

'What am I supposed to put on a fuc – I mean, on a résumé?'

'Make it up!' he yelled, as if it should have been obvious. 'They never check that shit.'

And make it up I did. Sharon, a fellow partier, gave me a résumé book she'd stolen while she was robbing a house. Why she'd taken the résumé book, I have no idea; nor did I ask. Personally, I didn't care *why* she'd taken it; I was just glad she had.

Using the examples in the book, I handwrote a résumé. For the section 'Previous Work Experience,' I listed the alarm company, though I used a fake address and phone number, and said that I'd worked there for three years, instead of less than four months. I also listed that I was a college graduate, typed sixty-five words per minute, and took shorthand at seventy words per minute.

I hope they don't test my ass!

246

It'd been awhile since I'd typed or taken shorthand. I could type sort of fast, but my speed was nowhere near sixty-five words per minute, and the text would be full of mistakes. And though I was sure I could take shorthand at a fast pace, I wasn't very good at being able to read what I wrote. And if you couldn't read it back, shorthand was no good.

Nevertheless, I was proud of the résumé I'd created. I looked *good* on paper. I showed it to Tommy.

'When you gon' type it?' he asked.

'Nigga, I used my best fuckin' print!' I snapped.

He balled up his fist in preparation to punch me. Before he could deliver it, I recognized my slip and corrected my statement.

'Boy, I used my best print, handwriting, or whatever it's called!'

'Girl, you can't use a handwritten résumé. You have to type it!' He spoke as if he were talking to a dummy. I hated when people took that tone of voice with me – as if I were stupid or something.

'Don't worry,' he said, seeing the irritation on my face. 'Sharon has a typewriter.'

Luckily, Sharon had stolen a typewriter from the same house she'd stolen the résumé book. She gladly let me use her typewriter to type the résumé. I hadn't used a typewriter since 'graduating' from vocational school, though I still remembered the basic finger placements. Because I was high on uppers, I was able to type quite fast, though not accurately. It took me a few hours and an entire bottle of liquid Wite-Out to type the résumé. When I was done, it looked horrible. I had inserted the paper into the typewriter crookedly, so all the words slanted to the left. There were huge clumps of Wite-Out all over the paper, which I hadn't allowed to dry before retyping. Not realizing I'd had the 'Caps Lock' on, some words were typed in all capital letters. Some words were misspelled; others had letters missing; and still others had two letters on top of each other as a result of my forgetting to hit the space bar.

'I can't use this damn thing!' I yelled, frustrated at the mess I'd made.

'Yes, you can,' Sharon said as she punched me for cussing. 'Just Wite-Out everything that's wrong or messed up. Then,

247

make a copy of it, make corrections and then copy that copy. The final document will look perfect because Wite-Out doesn't show up on copies.'

Who said thieves ain't got no sense?

By the time I was done, the résumé was almost perfect. Though it still had a few misspelled words, and it still sat on the paper crookedly, I decided it was good enough. So I began looking for a job.

For a couple of months, my search turned up nothing. Meanwhile, I stood in the mirror twice a day, every day, and practiced my speech exercises. I found the 'exercises' even more enjoyable when I was high because I could have entire conversations with make-believe people. I began watching 'white shows' and then pretended to be speaking to the rich white folks I'd seen on TV: Tom Brokaw, Dr. Ruth, and Barbara Walters. Tommy was right: they never cussed. Never.

The partiers readily agreed to punch me whenever I cussed or spoke street, mainly because they didn't think I could change. They began to take bets on how long it would take before I got frustrated with 'trying to be white' and quit altogether. Their doubts made me even more determined to make it. Their punches also helped me in my determination. At first, they were punching me all the time. And, they punched really hard, thinking I'd give up so I wouldn't get punched again. But I was adamant about not quitting. I swore to myself that before three months were up, there'd be no more punches. The more they said I couldn't change, the more I wanted to.

They tried everything to deter me.

'You was born a ghetto nigga. And dat's all you ever gon' be is a *ghetto nigga*!' one of them would tease. When those comments didn't sway me, they made others.

'Who ever heard of a dope fiend talking properly?' another would ask as they all busted up laughing.

I remembered Candy and Money, a ho and a pimp, both of whom talked properly. I knew it could be done.

The more they laughed, teased, and challenged me, the more persistent I became. I began to practice more and more. Soon, it wasn't just in front of the mirror in the mornings and evenings, but at the grocery store, talking to the gas-station attendant, even talking to the dope man.

'Yes. I would like a ten-dollar container of marijuana,' I'd request in the most formal, proper voice I could muster.

The dope man would pause for a moment, give me a funny look, and say, 'Girl, why you tryin' to be white?'

Ignoring him, I'd repeat my request. 'Yes, I would like a ten-dollar container of your best marijuana, sir.' And, I'd give him my white smile, which I'd also been practicing. (My white smile was a kind, gentle, all-teeth smile. My 'ghetto' smile was more of an eye-piercing, eyebrows-furrowed and lips-curled, menacing snarl.)

Laughing, the dealer would shove the bag into my hand, 'Here gurl, wit' yo' crazy ass. Looked at your skin lately?'

'Thank you very much, sir,' I'd reply, ignoring his nasty comment and feeling proud of myself for having gone through the whole transaction without using any cusswords or slang.

Tommy was right. The more I practiced, the better I got. I concentrated on completing my words, not cussing, and not using slang. Within a couple of months, the punches reduced from thirty to thirty-five a day, to twenty to twenty-five a day. Within five months, they were less than ten a day.

'I'll be damned,' one of the partiers exclaimed in disbelief. I'd been relentlessly practicing my speech for over six months. A bunch of us were sitting around, drinking, talking, and getting high. All night, I'd properly requested to be handed the joint, a drink, the straw, or the pipe. Each time my request was fulfilled, I politely said, 'Thank you.' And I hadn't said one cussword all night.

'The bitch did it!' the partier continued in disbelief. 'The fuckin' bitch done taught herself to talk "white." Y'all trippin' off dis?' she asked the others, her eyes wide open as if she'd seen a ghost. I wasn't sure if it was the shock of realizing my successful verbal transformation or the effects of freebasing that made her eyes grow so big. Not waiting for an answer, she continued:

'I never thought it could be done. I never thought *she'd* do it. But, the bitch done fuckin' did it!'

I sat back, hit the pipe, and smiled smugly.

However, I never completely and totally spoke properly. I'd always end up throwing in a 'fittin' to' or an 'ain't' somewhere in the conversation. And sometimes I had problems 'translating' words from slang. But for the most part, my speech had improved so much that a person could no longer tell my ethnicity just from talking to me on the phone.

While my speech was drastically and speedily improving, my job search wasn't. I'd been searching for over three months, and the results were disappointing. I searched the newspaper daily looking for legal-secretary positions. I called, using my most formal, whitest voice, to schedule an interview. But once I showed up, everyone wanted at least two or more years of legal experience. At least, that's what they said as they looked me up and down, gawking at my halter top, shiny skintight gold disco pants, and five-inch heels. I decided I should shift from the legal-secretary ads. Three weeks later, I found a job.

A title company was advertising for a word processor for its third shift: 11:00 P.M. to 7:00 A.M. This was perfect for me because I could *stay up until* 7:00 A.M., but I couldn't *get up at* 7:00 A.M. I called and scheduled an interview for the next night.

The title company's word-processing department sat in its own corner of a large building. The 'department' was a small, plain room with six computer stations where the processors – the third shift consisted of all women – sat and typed land descriptions for title insurance policies.

I arrived for the interview a half hour late and was met at the door by a tall white woman who introduced herself as Andrea, the shift supervisor. One look at her and I knew we would get along: her form-fitting blouse with its plunging neckline made her large tits exceptionally obvious. She wore a short miniskirt; her black patent-leather stiletto heels called attention to her long, sexy legs.

We sat at one of the workstations and began to chat. Although she had my résumé in front of her, she didn't ask me anything about it. Instead, she complimented me on my miniskirt and I complimented her on hers. We spent the next half hour talking about where to buy the sexiest minis and halter tops and who had the best prices on stiletto heels. Then the conversation switched to a lengthy discussion of our mutual contempt for those wimpy women who couldn't sport five-inch heels. By the end of the interview, we were laughing and chatting like old friends.

Andrea told me that she loved my style and my carefree personality. She said that I was 'just the type of girl' she'd been looking for, that I would fit into the night shift perfectly, and that if I wanted the job, it was mine.

'Of course, I want it!' I yelped. I couldn't believe my luck – finally, after months of trying, I'd gone on my first interview with a title company and gotten the job, just like that. We agreed I would start the following week.

As I stood to leave, I felt that since she was giving me a chance, I should at least try to be half-assed honest with her.

'Andrea,' I said as we walked toward the door, 'I like you. I really do, and I really need this job. But I feel like it just wouldn't be right if I'm not honest with you.'

She stopped walking, and looked at me, patiently waiting for me to continue.

'I need to tell you that my typing speed is probably a little less than sixty-five words per minute.' I had stopped walking and was standing with my head bowed down.

You idiot! I screamed at myself. *Who the fuck said it pays to be honest?*

I was sure my declaration of truthfulness had just cost me the job. I stood completely still, waiting for her to gruffly inform me that I was not so perfect for the job after all.

Instead, she giggled, gave me a big smile, and looked at me with her big blue eyes.

'Don't worry about it,' she said as she gently placed her hand on my back and resumed escorting me to the door. 'I like you. That's all that matters. Besides, typing is all you'll be doing here, so your speed will increase fast.'

She patted me on my back as I stepped through the door into the cool evening air. I smiled and began to turn and walk away when she tapped me on my shoulder and added: 'Anyway, we've got something for that.' She gave me a coy little wink and quickly closed the door.

What the hell did she mean by that?

It didn't take long for me to find out.

32

Tommy was ecstatic about my getting a job. My party friends couldn't believe it.

'You the luckiest nigga I ever seen in my life!' one of them exclaimed as he took a swig of Wild Turkey.

'Dey say luck is just God's way of being anonymous,' Shelly, a fellow partier, said as she hit the joint.

At the reference to God, the whole room got silent. We never talked about God. It just didn't seem like the appropriate thing to do when getting high – and we were always getting high. Victor broke the uncomfortable silence.

'Where the fuck you learn a big word like "anonymous"?' he shouted at Shelly.

'She been watching Tom Brokaw!' someone else chimed in. Everyone broke out laughing. Shelly smiled sheepishly, but didn't respond. I was glad they'd changed the subject.

'You serious 'bout this working thing, huh?' Victor asked as he passed me a joint.

I was very serious, especially after I'd summed up the people I hung with. They saw people with jobs as 'unique' folks. I didn't know many partiers that had legitimate jobs, but those that did were sort of put in a different category from the rest of us. Working showed dedication and commitment; it somehow made their drug use okay because it wasn't *all* they did. I noticed that those who had jobs were even viewed as though their drug use was acceptable.

I immediately called Daddy and Jr. to tell them I'd gotten a job. Though I spoke with them regularly by phone, I rarely saw either of them. It wasn't that I didn't love them; it was simply because neither of them partied. *All* I *did* was party. Besides, whenever I *did* see them, their fussing spoiled my fun and ruined my high. So I'd check in with them every once in a while, usually by phone. I kept the physical visits to a minimum. So although they knew I'd been looking for a job, they never believed I had taken the issue seriously.

'Cup,' Jr. would say calmly, 'you can't go to a job interview in a halter top.'

So they were *really* surprised upon learning the news that I'd finally gotten a job. In fact, I could *hear* the pride in their voices.

Tommy was right. I thought smugly, satisfied that Daddy and Jr. were *sort of* proud of me. *This job thing is paying off already.*

A few hours before I was to start my first night on the job, Tommy dropped the final 'requirement' of his plan: I'd have to change my past.

'What do you mean 'change my past'?' I snapped.

'The same way you got that résumé,' he snapped back. 'Make it up!'

I still didn't get it.

'Cup, white folks are scared of gangbangers. If you tell them about your gang days, they'll think you still have that type of behavior in you. They'll be afraid you might have a flashback on them. They'll be afraid to be around you. If they know about your robbing and thieving, they'll be afraid you'll steal from them.'

Tommy continued. 'And white folks loathe street people. If you tell them about your homeless days, sleeping in parks and eating out of trash cans, they'll think you're crazy, because only crazy people sleep in parks or eat out of trash cans.'

Not just crazy people – what about desperate *people?*

'White folks are scared of anything that's not nice, prim, and proper,' Tommy said. 'Your past is anything but nice, prim, OR proper. You've got to change it if you want to make it in the working world, which, like it or not, is the white man's world.'

I thought about what he said. I knew a few white folks. 'Dirty white trash' is the phrase they once told me their own folks used to refer to them. I never asked why they were called that. I figured it was because their clothes were dirty most of the time, and they were white. Where the 'trash' part came from, I didn't know, nor did I care. What I *did* care about was that they drank, drugged, and partied. None of them knew my past. They'd never asked either, and I never volunteered.

'But what should I say my past is? And how the fuc – I mean, how do I make it up?'

'Listen, think of the life you always wanted and, well, make it yours! Think of how you would have liked your life to be, and say that's how it was!'

'Wow, that's pretty simple.'

'Simple as one, two, three.'

'So did you make up *your* life? I mean, is what you told me about your mom, dad, and sister real, or was it a fantasy of how you'd have liked your life to be?'

'No, it's all real, just not complete. I left out the messed-up parts, like how my dad used to drink and fight a lot. Like I said, white folks don't like violence, so I left the violent parts out.'

Is it white folks that made you leave out those parts of your past, or is it your own pain in remembering them? Could you be blaming white folks for your own unwillingness or inability to deal with your past?

I didn't give myself time to seriously reflect on these thoughts because, even if Tommy's reticence about his past was really due to his own pain, I understood his point. My past was so fucked up, so full of hurt and things I'd just sooner forget that I figured it would be better for me to create a new and better one too. Again, Tommy was onto something.

But what kind of past should I create?

I kept hearing Tommy say, *Think of the life you've always wanted.*

It wasn't hard. When I was in Lancaster, I used to wish I was Marcia Brady of *The Brady Bunch.*

Hey, don't laugh.

Who wouldn't want to be Marcia? She had two loving parents; brothers and sisters who loved and supported her; no one was raping her or beating her; and she could eat as much as she wanted. And from the looks of it, she ate well – not just rice and beans. Alice was always cooking up all kinds of goodies. She lived in a large, beautiful house. She had the cutest, latest clothes. And, on top of all that, she had a dog *and* a maid! Yup.

Marcia Brady had it going on! If I could have been anyone different or have lived life differently, it would have been as Marcia Brady. Except, instead of a white girl, I would have been a light-skinned black girl with long hair so that I'd be pretty. But I knew that no matter how much I pretended, I wasn't ever going to be light-skinned. My skin color wasn't ever going to change.

I decided it would be better to stick with the parts of the past I *could* change – if only in make-believe. So the Brady story is the story I adopted as my own. But instead of the three brothers and two sisters Marcia had, I told people I had five brothers. I figured that if I really had had five brothers, Pete wouldn't have raped me and Mr Bassinet wouldn't have forced me into cheer-leading practice. And although I would say that my mother had died, I'd leave out the part about finding her. That was still just too painful. And I'd tell them that my daddy, my *real* daddy – *not* the sperm donor – raised me and my brothers, and we all lived happily in a huge house that looked just like the Brady house, except in a black neighborhood. I figured saying we had a maid might have been going too far, so I left that part to the TV show.

A little while later, as we were tooting lines, I recited my freshly created past to Tommy. He liked it instantly. He said it was refreshingly devoid of sex, drugs, and violence – an accept-able, normal, ordinary past.

That night, I started my job as the sixth word processor on the third shift. The other five were white girls ranging from twenty to fifty years old. They all loved miniskirts, tight jeans, sexy blouses, and high heels, though they couldn't wear anything higher than three and a half inches. And, just as Andrea had, they seemed to like me, and I liked them right from the start.

After Andrea introduced me to the girls, she told everyone to 'tell a little something about themselves' so we could all get better acquainted. The girls all pretty much told the same story: where they were from (San Diego, Iowa, Ohio, etc.), how many siblings and children they had, what their parents did (doctors, teachers, businessmen, etc.). When my turn came, I recited my newly created history and waited for their reaction. They listened with what seemed to be minor interest and appeared to accept the story without question. I told myself that night that, from then on, if anyone ever asked me about my childhood, that would be the story I'd tell. Diane, the Bassinets, the Eight-Tray Gangstas, the tricks, violence, crimes, and every other part of my miserable, sordid past would be hidden away, never to be mentioned again.

Because we were the third shift, the whole building was absolutely deserted except for us. The entire third shift loved to party, and they loved to talk about it. All night, all we did was type, talk, and laugh. Type, talk, and laugh. We'd type the property descriptions, talk about our partying escapades, and laugh at the comical parts. (Of course, I left out the stories about my getting beaten up or put out of a club in a drunken stupor.) I used these conversations with the girls to practice speaking properly. So I ended up practicing eight hours a night.

The girls weren't aware of it until one night, as we were discussing how men needed to learn to address women in nightclubs, I blurted out that I had been practicing speaking so I would sound 'right.' I didn't tell them the truth: that I really did it so I could sound 'white.' That just didn't seem like the appropriate thing to say in a room full of white folks.

'But we think you speak just fine,' Tina replied. Tina had been at the title company for a year. She was thin, with dirty-blond hair, and although she was only twenty-years old, she already had three children.

'Yeah, but that's because I've been working on it for a while now, so it's already improved quite a bit. If you'd heard how I talked before this, you'd have been like, 'What the fuc—' I mean, you would not have liked it. Anyway, I can still use improvement so just let me know if you hear me say something that's 'street' or if you hear me cuss.'

'What's 'street'?' Tina asked as she cocked her head to the side – like, somehow by holding it in that position, it would help her understand. 'I mean, like, how will we know whether something is 'street' or not?'

'Yeah,' the others said in unison.

I was amazed at their ignorance.

'I'll tell you what. If you hear a word you don't understand, it's probably street. Just bring it to my attention so that I won't use it again. Okay?'

'Okay,' they replied, again in unison.

'But we aren't going to say anything about your cussing, because hell, we all do it,' Sandra stated moodily. At fifty, Sandra was the oldest of the group. She was grossly overweight, but she never let her weight stop her from wearing skintight clothes; though she would constantly complain that her pants and skirts were cutting off her circulation. I admired her for not being afraid to dress like she was a size 10 when in reality she was a size 20. Nor did the fact that she wore eyeglasses as thick as Coke bottles deter her from her self-image as a beauty queen. She thought she was hot shit, and had no problem telling you so.

Sandra was right about the cussing, though. Not only was cussing allowed during the third shift, it was expected and regularly used – especially when telling stories of hot and wild party adventures. So though the girls never said anything about my cussing, they would correct me whenever I said something street. Soon, it became almost like a language lesson for both sides. Whenever they did bring a slang word to my attention, I had to explain to them what it meant. Then they'd go around all night saying, 'Use it in a sentence!' And once someone did, we'd all crack up laughing. They loved learning the meanings of the slang words, and I appreciated the extra help with practicing the regular use of proper words. It became a game that made the verbal transformation that was transpiring in my life much more pleasurable.

Still, they didn't have to correct me often, since I was practicing on my own regularly. Soon, I could go from talking slang with my friends to using proper speech when at work. I could make the switch at will and without effort, though I never got perfect at proper speech. I had to (and still do) concentrate on what I was saying and constantly remind myself to speak correctly.

I was actually enjoying working – it didn't interfere with my partying, especially since when I was at work I stayed high on coke, meth, black beauties, or other uppers, which provided me with extraordinary energy – that is, when it was good shit. Every so often, I'd cop a 'bad batch,' which is what happened one night shortly after I'd started working. The blow was so bad, it wasn't keeping me up *or* giving me energy. In fact, the only indication I'd snorted anything was the fact that it caused my nose to run nonstop. I walked around constantly sniveling and wiping my nose.

'You got a cold?' Sandra asked gruffly. We were in the bathroom. She was coming out of one of the stalls; I was standing over the sink blowing my nose, trying to get it to dry up. She wasn't trying to be gruff; it's just that she was huffing and puffing from the effort of trying to force her fat ass back into her skintight pants that were two sizes too small. Any other time the sight would have been comical, but with snot flowing out of my nose like Niagara Falls, I didn't have time to take pleasure in it. I was so preoccupied with my nose, that her question caught me off guard.

'What?' I asked, irritated that she'd interrupted my concentration while I was trying to stuff a large piece of twisted tissue up my nose.

'I said, do you have a cold?' she repeated. She'd successfully forced her zipper closed. But her stomach poured out over the top of her pants. Looking at it, it reminded me of how beer foam oozes out over the top of a glass that's been poured too full. She stood there trying to hold in her breath in an effort to relieve some pressure.

'Ah . . . yeah,' I replied, unsure of how to respond.

'Girl, stop lying,' she snapped suddenly. Her direct and firm tone startled me. She seemed to have forgotten about her bulging stomach and was now focusing on me and my nose. My eyes grew wide as I realized she may be a little more hip than I'd originally thought.

Play it cool, girl, I told myself. *Act stupid. Just act stupid!*

'What do you mean?' I asked as I fluttered my eyes and spoke in the most innocent, naive voice I could muster.

'Aw, girl, com' on. Everybody gets high off *something*. Why do you think we run our mouths a mile a minute around here and type like Flash Gordon? Me, myself, I like blow. It looks like you do too, though it looks like you got punked on your last batch.'

I wasn't sure how to deal with her comments. My mind began to race.

Was it a set up by management? Trying to see if they could get me to confess that I did drugs so they could fire me? Or maybe it was a setup by Andrea on behalf of management? Hell, come to think of it, who the fuck was management? Andrea was the only 'authority' person at the title company I'd ever met.

I decided *I* wouldn't admit to shit.

'I . . . I don't know what you're talking about,' I said loud and slow as I looked around the bathroom for the hidden camera. 'No, no drugs here. I'd NEVER do ANYTHING like that,' I said even louder as I walked around checking under stalls, toilets, and sinks for a hidden microphone. I wanted to make sure 'they' could hear me.

'Girl, relax,' Sandra said as she began laughing. 'This ain't no setup, okay? Nobody put me up to this. I've been snorting long enough to know a bad drip when I hear one.'

I stood there silent. Eyes wide. Mind racing. *What the fuck to do? What the fuck to do?*

'Look, try some of this,' she said, pulling a small brown glass bottle from her large watermelon breasts. I instantly knew what was in it. I sometimes used those little bottles myself. They were used for carrying blow or meth. When the lid was unscrewed, it had a tiny spoon attached to it by a short, thin silver chain – the chain was to prevent the spoon from getting misplaced. The spoon came in handy for snorters who had no fingernails with which to hold their blow.

Sandra unscrewed the lid, grabbed the thin chain, and dipped the spoon into the bottle. Making sure the spoon was over-flowing with the shiny white substance, she held it up to the left side of her nose; and holding the right side closed with a finger, she snorted. As she inhaled, the white power vanished up her nose so fast that, if I had blinked, it would have seemed to magically disappear. There was no doubt in my mind – Sandra was a blow pro.

'Now *that's* some good shit!' she exclaimed, as she held back her head, reached up, and pinched her nose to keep any powder from spilling out. She closed her eyes and enjoyed the head rush. After a moment, she handed the bottle and tiny spoon to me.

'Here, you need some *real* stuff to keep you awake; not that fake-ass shit you got.'

Now that she'd done some blow herself, I was feeling more comfortable about the whole situation not being a setup. Besides, the white stuff in the little brown bottle looked good. It *smelled* good. It was calling my name. I decided it was safe. I quickly snorted a heaping spoonful. She was right. It was good. I instantly felt the dope rushing to my brain as my ears began to ring and my eyes began to water.

'Damn, girl!' I yelled. Because my ears were still ringing, sounds were muffled, causing me to speak louder than I realized. She began laughing again.

'Yup,' she said as she laughed at my reaction. 'Told you you needed some *real* shit.'

Sandra and I stayed in the bathroom and continued to 'bond' for a while longer. We took a couple more toots as she hipped me to who on the shift did what. She said that Andrea smoked weed, but her main thing was pills – uppers mostly – beauties and yellow jackets. Tina liked to toot horse. Sandra said that during one of her and Tina's bathroom 'bonding' sessions, Tina told her that as long as she didn't slam heroin, it wasn't addictive.

'Never mind the fact she spends every fucking dime on the shit,' Sandra stated, obviously annoyed at Tina's misguided conceptions. 'She's convinced herself that tooting it is harmless.' Sandra shook her head in disgust as if the blow we were tooting weren't. I didn't understand Sandra's disgust, but I did understand Tina's reasoning. In fact, I agreed with it.

Sandra continued informing me on who did what. She said that she, herself, did anything that was free – a woman after my own heart. However, when spending her own money, she preferred blow.

She kept talking, but I began to ignore her and go into my own little head trip and enjoy my high. The main message I got from her chatter was that everyone on the third shift got high off *something*.

Finally, she shut her mouth for a moment. She sat on the sink, held her head back, and enjoyed her high.

'Girl, we'd better get back,' I said a few minutes later. 'We been in here – I mean, *we've* been in here for quite a while now.'

Sandra's eyes flew open as she looked down at her watch and

screamed, 'Oh, shit. You're right. My break was up thirty minutes ago!'

We jumped up and began preparing to return to our stations: straightening our clothes (I don't know why tweakers do this. But for some reason, we always felt the need to straighten our clothes before reentering the world), and checking ourselves out in the mirror to make sure there was no white residue on our noses.

'Now, look . . .' Sandra stated, checking out her ass in the mirror while running her hands over her large butt in an effort to smooth her skintight pants. Why she felt the need to smooth down the material I could never figure out. It was already stretched so tight there wasn't *space* for a wrinkle.

'. . . this shit ain't any big secret. But look at it sort of like the elephant in the middle of the room.'

'What the fuck does that mean?' I asked.

'What I'm saying is, although we all know we get high, we don't really talk about it. The only thing we talk about openly is drinking and partying at the clubs. Anything else, we just let each other be. Nobody asks questions and nobody gets sweated. Ya got it?'

I laughed to myself at Sandra's use of the word *sweat*. It was one of the slang words I'd taught the crew. To 'sweat' someone meant to bother, question, pester, harass, etc. Now she was using it like an everyday word. They were learning slang almost as well as I was learning proper speech.

'Yeah, I got it,' I slyly replied. And I did. In fact, I wholeheartedly agreed with their little philosophy: don't fuck with them about their using, and they wouldn't fuck with me about mine. Damn, I loved the working world.

So that's how it went. I went to work loaded on uppers, but never drunk. I knew if I got drunk, I'd show up and cuss everybody out. So I never went drunk – only loaded – though never loaded on basin'. I immediately realized that once I started basin' I couldn't stop till all the dope, or money – whichever ran out first – was gone. So I vowed to freebase only on the weekends. But I wasn't the only 'responsible' one. Everyone else on the shift also pretty much shunned alcohol during work hours and only came high – or got high shortly after their arrival – everyone that is, except for Sandra who had no shame in taking

261

a 'couple sips' during lunch. Oftentimes, throughout the shift two or three of us would meet in the bathroom and 'bond.' Other times I went in and 'bonded' by myself.

At first, my typing was horrible. Though it was fast, it was full of mistakes. But as time went on, Andrea was right: my speed and accuracy increased. Typing is the perfect activity to do when speeding because it requires fast, quick movements of the hands. Tweaking on the typewriter soon became one of my favorite things to do, which made the job even more enjoyable.

There were several unexpected benefits that came from working. First, just as Tommy had said, every payday provided a guaranteed high from at least one of my two favorite drugs: basin' or heroin. In between paydays, I did what I had to do to make a little money, which usually meant selling a little dope, shoplifting, driving the getaway car for a homie doing a burglary, or letting a homie stash hot goods at my place – for a fee, of course. These activities, together with the stash supplied by the numerous partiers who were always hanging at my house, was enough to provide a regular source of the less-expensive drugs: meth, pills, acid, dust, weed, and booze. Working also made me feel better about the illegal shit I was doing. I mean, hell, it wasn't like I was a thug or a bum. I had a job, dammit!

33

Everything was going great at my job. Sometimes, I had to miss work because of hangovers or extreme fatigue (every now and then, staying up for days at a time would catch up with me). However, this didn't cause me to suffer any negative repercussions because the girls on the third shift had a secret arrangement. Every now and then, when someone couldn't make it to work or had to leave 'sick,' the others would sign her time card and cover for her. We all knew that sometimes partying got a little out of hand. So when it did, we covered for each other. This allowed the 'sick' girl to miss work and recover without having to worry about using up sick leave or vacation. We didn't have to worry about Andrea finding out – she often took advantage of the arrangement herself. I loved my job.

Tommy and I continued to work different shifts, but we made the time we did have together count: we got high. To allow us even more time together, Tommy left his dumpy hotel room and moved into my dilapidated shack. Even though we were both working steadily, we were getting high steadily. As a result, we were two months behind in the rent. (When Kelly lived with me, I'd at least pay *a portion* of the rent. But I soon quit paying *any* of it.) The landlord, fed up with my never-ending excuses and lies as to why I didn't have his rent, started eviction proceedings. We needed a place to go, and fast.

One Saturday, as we sat around getting high, Nancy, one of our partiers, proudly announced that her Section 8 application had finally come through. She was ecstatic because what that meant was that the government was going to pay $300 of her

$350 rent. Still, the girl had the nerve to complain about having to pay the other $50.

Tommy and I looked at each other. We didn't have to speak – we each knew what the other was thinking. It didn't take long to figure out how much get-high money we'd have if we only had to pay fifty dollars a month. I immediately told Nancy that we would be her roommates for fifty dollars a month.

'Hell, yeah!' she screamed, happy that she wouldn't have to pay *any* rent.

Nancy moved into a small two-bedroom, one-bath apartment. Tommy and I lived in one of the bedrooms; Nancy and her three children lived in the other. The cramped living space didn't bother the adults. Tommy and I worked different shifts, so only two adults (one of us and Nancy) were home at the same time during the week. The children were all school age, so they were in school during the day when Tommy was at work, and in bed at night while I was at work. So the only time all six of us were home simultaneously was on the weekends, which is when we really partied – with at least ten other partiers. The adults were always too loaded to care, or notice, the tight living quarters.

If sharing a room with their mom, the constant presence of drugs and alcohol, or the regular parties bothered Nancy's children, they knew better than to say anything. Nancy ruled with an iron hand. She, like me, had no patience, no tolerance, and couldn't stand noise – not the greatest characteristics for a parent. So her children learned at an early age not to be seen *or* heard when their mom was partying. They were never physically abused, though. I wouldn't have stood for that. One thing I wouldn't tolerate was beating a kid. *Spanking* them was all right. (I'd gotten spanked many times by my mother. I'd been beaten many times by Diane. I knew the difference.) As far as I was concerned, drugs, alcohol, and partying around kids was okay – long as no one was beatin' 'em.

One day, after a wild night of partying, I awoke to Nancy frying chicken. As the hideous smell streamed into my bedroom, my eyes flew wide open, I started sweating profusely, and my stomach started flipflopping like a fish out of water. I threw back the covers, jumped out of bed, and sprinted to the toilet, all the while placing my hand over my mouth in hopes it would keep the vomit down till I got there.

'What's the matter with you?' Tommy asked as he got up and followed me. 'You got a hangover?'

'Yeah!' I screamed as I stuck my head into the toilet to allow the previous night's alcohol, food, and dope to gush out.

After two or three violent heaves, the gushing stopped. I plopped down on the floor and laid my head on the rim of the toilet. The cool porcelain felt good on my feverish skin, but the queasiness was returning. I had to get out of the house. I just couldn't stand the smell. I ran out the front door – panties and all.

'What the hell's the matter with her?' Nancy asked as I flew by with one hand over my mouth and the other over my stomach.

'She's sick,' Tommy replied, opening the fridge and grabbing a beer.

'I done tol' her about mixing drinks,' Nancy stated annoyingly as she wildly waved the fork she was using to turn the chicken. 'Crazy heifer had rum, vodka, gin, beer, wine, *and* tequila! No wonder she sick!'

It was true. I had mixed quite a bit of liquor the night before. But I knew it wasn't the booze – at least not this time. I had some birth-control pills. But, as usual, I'd often forgotten to take them.

I stayed on the porch until Nancy finished cooking the chicken. I used the time to try to remember the last time I'd taken a pill. I wasn't sure if it'd been three, four, or five days. Hell, I didn't even know where they were!

Fuck it! I told myself. *Even if you did know where they were, they ain't gon' do you no damn good now!*

The rumbling in my stomach advising me of hunger interrupted my thoughts. I decided to ignore my 'little problem' for the time being, I went inside and had some of Nancy's delicious fried chicken. (I could *eat* fried chicken, I just couldn't be around when it was being *cooked*.)

Everyone was grubbing on fried chicken. The children were sitting in the living room, glued to the TV cartoons as they ate. The adults sat around the kitchen table, discussing the important topic of which partier had committed to bringing which party favors to that night's festivities. While I had been outside, Tommy said Victor had called and said he'd scored some bomb blow, which he'd be bringing over that night. I figured this was as good a time as any to make my announcement.

'I'm pregnant.'

Tommy and Nancy grew instantly silent. The only noise audible was the sound of the Road Runner's 'beep-beep.' The children never turned from the television. I guess, to them, my proclamation wasn't as interesting as watching Road Runner beat the hell out of Wile E. Coyote.

'Pregnant?!' Tommy exclaimed. He had a look of sheer terror on his face – as if someone told him he'd be dead in forty-eight hours.

'Pregnant?!' Nancy repeated. The look on her face was one of surprise, not terror.

'What the fuck is the matter wit' y'all's ears!' I yelled. 'Yes! Pregnant! You know, as in 'wit child'!' I was pissed. And when I got pissed, *anything* proper went out the window.

Again, the room fell silent.

Wile E. Coyote was laughing out loud as he realized he now had Road Runner where he wanted him.

'What you gon' do?' Nancy asked.

Tommy looked at me as if he were wondering the same thing.

I was waiting to hear the familiar *splat!* that always follows when Wile E. Coyote's traps for Road Runner backfire at the last moment.

'I'm gon' do what I always do. I'm gon' git rid of it.'

'You mean like an abortion?' she asked.

'What the fuck else could I mean?' I snapped.

Boom! Splat! The kids cracked up laughing, confirming that Road Runner had, again, gotten the best of Wile E. Coyote.

'Girl, don't you know what that kid is worth?'

I looked at her in total confusion. 'What the fuck are you talking about?' I had no idea what she meant.

'Girl, welfare! You can get money for that baby!'

Money? For a baby? I'd never thought about it that way.

'Girl, why you think I got all these kids? I get a fat check *and* Uncle Sam pays my rent! I get food stamps, free medical, and I don't have to move my fat ass!' She busted up laughing, obviously very proud of her fringe benefits.

266

'Chile,' she continued while gnawing on a chicken leg, 'you betta git with the game!' Because she had food in her mouth, as she finished her sentence, she spit fried chicken all over the place.

'Cup.' Tommy had finally regrouped himself enough to speak. 'It's not worth it. Think about it! By working you get more money in two weeks than a bitch on welfare gets in a month!'

'Who you callin' a bitch?' Nancy snapped.

Ignoring her, he continued, talking quickly as he laid out the facts. '*Think* about it. You are in no position to have children! You can't stand noise. Children cry all the time! You have no patience. Think about how other people's kids get on your nerves *now*! You barely feed yourself! How are you going to feed a child? Do you really want the responsibility of taking care of someone else *all the time*?'

Tommy was right. I hated cooking, cleaning, noise, and kids. Realizing that he was actually getting through and making me seriously consider his comments, he continued, talking even faster.

'You *hate* people in your business! You hate having to answer to others. If you keep that baby and go on welfare, Uncle Sam will *own* you. He will tell you what you can do and cannot do, where you can do it, and how long to do it! You can own only certain things, and you can't even have a bank account.'

Shit, it's not like I ever have money in *the fucking thing anyhow,* I laughed to myself. It was true. Though I did have a bank account (I only got it because the check-cashing store charged too much to cash my paychecks), there was never any money in it.

Nevertheless, no money in the bank was the least of my problems. I had turned a few tricks here and there when money was low and my need for dope was high. I wasn't sure if the baby I was carrying was even Tommy's. Actually, I didn't know *whose* it was.

What if I kept it and it wasn't Tommy's?

While I was having this intermittent conversation with myself, Tommy went on with his argument.

'And Uncle Sam is nosy as hell. They get all in your business, asking thousands of questions – *regularly.*'

I quickly raised my eyebrows and my eyes grew big at the mention of being questioned. I hated being questioned. I felt like the system had never asked any damn questions – or at least *the right ones* – when they were supposed to. When I was getting raped, molested, beaten, mistreated, shifted from home to home, no one ever said a fuckin' thing. No one ever asked me *why* I ran! They simply labeled me 'hard to place' *because* I ran. And *now* the bastards wanted to ask questions?

Fuck that!

'Nigga,' Nancy interjected, 'you just don't want to have to take care of no babies! This ain't about Uncle Sam controlling her, or about her not wanting a baby. This is about YOU controlling her and not wanting a baby. Cup, don't listen to him.' Her eyes seemed to be pleading with me. 'He's got his own selfish motives. He's thinking of himself! Just like a nigga!' No longer pleading, her eyes now glowed with pure rage.

Regardless of his motives, Tommy had hit a nerve with me. No fuckin' body was gon' tell me what I could and could not do. I *hated* authority, especially the system, which to me, was on the same team with the government.

'Fuck welfare, Nancy. It ain't worth it. That little couple hundred dollars you get a month ain't worth it. The little bastard's gone next week.'

The cool tone of my voice told Nancy I was serious. She dropped the subject.

Five days later, I went back to the same clinic I'd gone to before. If any of the nurses remembered me, they didn't show it. And if the nurse that prepped me was the same one I'd had previously, I was too high to know it. Besides, I didn't care *who* took the baby out as long as it got *out*.

This time the abortion wreaked more havoc on my body. I cramped, ached, and bled for days. Unlike the previous abortions I'd had, I wasn't able to just jump up and party. I was ill and bedridden for five days, and I was forced to call in sick. On the fourth day that I called, Sandra told me that someone 'high up' in the title company had been watching the third-shift crew. Everyone, including Andrea, was scared and nervous. She said that, as a result, our 'arrangement' couldn't be used. I'd have to take all the days as sick leave. I was so sick I didn't care.

I wasn't too sick to get high, though. I just did it in bed. It made the cramps feel better – or least it made me not give a damn that I was cramping. It also made me not give a damn about what I'd done. But there was another reason why I was able to relieve any guilt. Years before in Lancaster, when Connie and the girls had beaten that baby out of me, I swore that that would be the last baby I'd ever keep – or love. Bringing up the anger and resentment of that baby being killed somehow allowed me to feel okay about killing this one – and the ones before it; and if need be, any others after it.

After about a week, I was back up and ready to go.

When I returned to work, though, things had changed drastically. Andrea had been fired. When I asked why, the girls mumbled that they'd been told something about her not being a 'capable supervisor and manager.'

'How can they say that?' I screamed when Sandra told me the news. 'She was great!'

Before Sandra could reply, a tall white man entered the word-processing room. He was dressed in a very nice black suit. He looked like a mortician to me – dressed all in black, with a solemn face. The girls all jumped to attention and started frantically pecking at their keyboards, as if they were working. They were obviously scared. I wondered why.

Who the fuck is *this dude?* I asked myself. No one ever came into the word-processing room during the third shift. And I'd never seen anyone give the girls such a strong and sudden desire to *work*.

The man introduced himself as Mr Collum. He pulled me aside to the same small station I had sat at during my interview with Andrea, almost six months before. Speaking quietly so that only he and I could hear, he said he was the vice president of some department. I didn't catch *which* department because I was too busy staring at his suit. It was very, very, very nice. As I stared at it, I wondered if it was one of those Italian suits I'd heard about. Sometimes, as we sat around getting high, the other partiers and I would play the 'when I get myself together . . .' game. That's when we'd daydream and swear to what we were going to be/do/say/get tomorrow – when we stopped spending *all* our money on dope. I specifically remembered one of them, Spook, declare on several occasions:

'When I get rich, I'm gon' buy me an Italian suit in every color.'

Though he was always *talking* about getting one, I'd never actually seen one. But as I sat there staring at the fine fabric, exquisite design, and precise stitching, I was sure that that's what Mr Collum was wearing.

Mr Collum droned on and on. When I made myself come back to the present conversation, he was saying something about 'cleaning up' and a 'reduction in force.' I chose to ignore his chattering and return my focus to the gorgeous suit.

I wondered what he'd do if I reached over and touched it. I tried to imagine what the beautiful fabric felt like – if it felt as good as it looked. I was almost *drawn* to it; like I was craving up-close and personal contact with it.

Girl, you trippin'! I scolded myself. I had done a couple of lines before walking into work. I figured that's why I had a sudden fascination with Collum's suit.

My mind quickly cleared up and raced back to the immediate conversation when Mr Collum informed me that I was fired. He said it so calmly and nonchalantly, I thought I'd heard him wrong.

'What?' I asked in complete and total surprise.

'You're fired,' he repeated just as calmly as he'd said it the first time. 'I've been going over your file. You miss a lot of work. You're late almost daily and your work is *beneath* substandard.'

How the fuck did he know when I was late? I asked myself.

I wasn't angry about the fact that he'd made the statement about my regular tardiness. I mean, hell, it *was* true. What pissed me off is that he knew – the girls were supposed to be covering for me. But that wasn't the only question that was rushing through my mind.

What the fuck is 'substandard' and how did I get beneath *it?* My eyes quickly darted back and forth as my mind continued to race nervously with unanswered questions.

Still using the same calm voice, he explained that Andrea had been fired. However, before leaving, she'd snitched on the rest of us – about everything. As a result, he said that everyone on the third shift was being let go. He reached inside his coat jacket, pulled out an envelope, and handed it to me. As I looked

270

at it confusedly, he explained the envelope contained a check: they were giving me two weeks' severance pay, as well as unused vacation and sick leave. He said that the company had decided to give me the benefit of the doubt and pay me for all of the vacation and sick leave I had supposedly accumulated *according to the books* – even though they had gone back through each girl's records with Andrea and figured out how much sick leave or vacation we'd really have had it not been for our illegal arrangements. Mr Collum said that if they had used Andrea's reconfigurations, I would have *no* sick leave *or* vacation, and in fact would *owe them* money.

It briefly occurred to me that, as the only black, I was the only one being let go immediately. And it momentarily crossed my mind to ask why; and to ask about the other girls – like if and when were they leaving and how much severance pay they would get. But my mind didn't allow me to focus on those issues; it was more concerned about the check in my hand. My mind was more focused on wondering just how much money the check was for and how much coke, heroin, dust, bo, and booze I would get. I felt like, since my regular payday was still a week away, it was extra money! I'd failed to realize it was the *only* money I'd be getting for a while.

The more I thought about getting high, the faster I wanted out of that place. I jumped up as Mr Collum was saying something about being willing to give me a good reference.

'Oh, okay, thanks!' I responded as I grabbed my jacket and bolted for the door. As I reached it I turned and looked around the word-processing department for the last time. The girls and Mr Collum were looking at me in complete surprise. Andrea's station was still empty and for the first time I noticed two other stations were empty.

Oh well, not my problem!

'See ya!' I yelled as I slipped out the door.

I never saw anyone from that title company again.

That night as I got loaded, the partiers began to tease me about getting fired.

'I knew yo' ass couldn't hold no damn job!' one of them exclaimed as the others laughed.

'And to get fired – that's *embarrassing*!' someone else said, putting great emphasis on the last word.

'Gurl, that's like dey tellin' you to "get the fuck out"!' another chimed in.

'Yeah,' still another said. 'You'd've done better not working at all cuz at least then, you wouldn't of been *thrown out*!' They all laughed.

As I tooted another line and took a swig of Thunderbird, I swore to myself that that would be the last time I'd ever get fired. I told myself that from then on, before getting fired, I'd quit.

'What you gon' do now?' someone else asked, interrupting my thoughts.

'I'm gon' get another job!' I replied indignantly.

'Girl, ain't nobody gon' hire you. You've been FIRED!' Everyone cracked up again.

'Oh, they'll hire me, all right,' I snapped. '*Someone's* gon' hire me!'

'Well, I like her balls,' one of them said.

'Yeah, bitch just won't quit,' another responded.

And I wouldn't. Having a job was very important to me. As long as I had a job, I figured it didn't matter how much I drank, used, or partied. I loved the special status I got among drunks and druggies simply from the fact that I managed to get something few of them ever had or could even *get*.

I *had* to get another job.

Tommy warned that although the title company said they'd give me a good reference, I needed to hurry up and find another job before they changed their mind and told prospective employers the truth. I figured since Tommy had had numerous jobs, he would know. So, taking his advice, I didn't waste any time. I donned my miniskirts, halter tops, five-inch stilettos, and hit the pavement.

34

I found another job a couple of weeks later. It was in the word-processing department of another title company. Although the supervisor, Debra, was a little taken aback by my attire, she was impressed by the fact that I'd previously worked at a title company. She commented that she'd lost three processors suddenly and unexpectedly, and urgently needed someone who was experienced in typing title documents. However, when I asked to be put on the third shift, she told me they had only one shift – the day shift – and that if I wanted the job, that would be the one I'd be working.

Desperately needing word processors, she hired me. Desperately needing a job, I took it.

Unlike my first job, I hated this one. I wasn't a morning person and was still partying throughout the night – every night. As a result, it was very difficult for me to get to work on time. To help me get up, I'd do speed first thing in the morning. Problem was, it took a while to kick in. I was supposed to work 9:00 to 5:00, but was never there before 9:30. Debra tried to work with me. She changed my hours to 9:30 to 5:30. That didn't help; now I was never there before 10:00. So, then she switched me to 10:00 to 5:30, with my agreeing to give up an hour's pay each day. It didn't help, though. No matter what I did, I was always at least a half hour late. But shortly after arriving at work, the dope kicked in and I'd be just fine.

There was another reason I didn't like the job. There wasn't the camaraderie among the word processors like I'd experienced before. Here everybody kind of minded their own business. While we laughed and discussed general topics during work, no one ever really got personal. But I knew a tweaker when I saw one. So although no one ever mentioned tweaking or getting high, I knew we all weren't speeding around that office because of coffee. But as long as they didn't fuck with me about my using, I didn't fuck with them about theirs.

Unlike the first title company, this one paid really close attention to my attendance. At my ninety-day review, I was warned that if my tardiness didn't improve, I'd be fired. I was already doing the best I could so I knew that getting fired was inevitable. Remembering my promise to myself to always quit before being fired, I started looking for another job.

True to my promise, I was never again let go, at least not officially. I always quit first, which meant I quit a lot. The story was always the same. I lied on my résumé about performance and length of time at my previous job. The employer was desperate to hire and I was desperate to work. I only seemed to get offers from the desperate employers. I didn't care – so long as I got the offer.

In between jobs, I lived off the petty crimes I committed. (My trust fund had long since disappeared. I had spent the money so fast, I had no clue where it went.)

Somehow, my persistence in maintaining a job, *any* job, was threatening my relationship with Tommy. The more jobs I got and the more money I brought in, the more insecure he got. He would constantly accuse me of screwing around, or he would say crazy things like I would leave him when the 'right' job came along. I tried to convince him that I loved him and didn't want anyone else. Still, the more I tried to assure Tommy of my love and dedication, the more insecure he got. And the more insecure he got, the more violent he got, though at first it was just pushing and shoving.

One day, we were cruising down the street in my car. Tommy was driving, and I was in the passenger seat looking out the window. I'd quit yet again and was trying to figure out if I should change careers – maybe try for a legal-secretary position again. Though I still didn't have any legal experience, I had managed to gather *some* work experience. I was sure that if I could find a lawyer desperate enough, I could get my foot in the door.

As we rode along, I continued looking out the window and

contemplating my next move. Tommy slowed for a stoplight where there happened to be a guy standing in the direction I was looking. Suddenly, Tommy screamed:

'You want that nigga?'

I didn't know how to respond. Startled by his outburst, I confusedly looked around as I shrieked, 'What the fuck are you talking about?'

'I see you flirting wit' that nigga.' When he was pissed, his proper speech went out the window just as mine did. 'You want that nigga, huh? You want him?'

I had no idea what he was talking about. My eyes got big and my body tensed as I noticed the rage on his face. Before I could respond again, he pushed my head against the window. Hard.

'Nigga, is you crazy?' I yelled.

One thing that remained from my bangin' days was that hitting back and pushing back were natural reflexes. It wasn't even something I had to think about; if you hit me, you were gon' get hit back.

I reached over with both arms and shoved him back as hard as I could.

In response, he slapped me. Hard.

It was on. I started swinging, kicking, cussing, and screaming. He didn't hit me again – not that time. Instead, he tried to grab my arms to keep me from hitting him.

'Wait! Wait!' he yelled as he continued to struggle to dodge my blows. 'I didn't mean to hit you. Wait!'

I wasn't listening. I was in fight mode, so I kept swinging. Finally, he was able to wrap his arms around mine and bind them down. The light turned green and the cars behind us began honking. The honking startled Tommy who immediately let me go. That was the break I needed.

'Fuck you!' I screamed to him as I clambered out of the car, clothes disheveled, hair a complete mess.

'And fuck YOU!' I yelled to the driver in the car behind us. Not satisfied with that little cussing, I added, 'BITCH,' as I tossed up my middle finger. The driver, a middle-aged white woman, obviously was not used to seeing an irate, red-eyed, wild-haired black woman cuss her out and flip her the bird. She looked at me in complete and utter shock – and fear.

'This mothafucka slapped me!' I yelled to no one in particular as I stormed off in complete rage. 'THAT mothafucka slapped me!' I yelled even louder, this time to a small Mexican lady who was walking toward me. Startled by my outburst, she let out a little yelp, but said nothing. Instead, she quickly lowered her head, and sped up her pace, apparently hoping that the crazy black chick would just keep on passing by.

A second later, Tommy came running up alongside me.

'Baby, listen,' he pleaded. 'I'm sorry. I didn't *mean* to hit you. It's just that you make me so *crazy*! I'm sorry. It's just that I'm so afraid of losing you! I swear, I *swear* it'll never happen again!'

If he's here, where the fuck is my car? I asked myself when I realized he was half-walking, half-jogging alongside me. *Fuck the car!* I yelled to myself. *That bastard hit you!*

'Fuck you!' I yelled at him, as I continued stomping to nowhere in particular.

'Baby, PLEASE!' he pleaded. 'Will you just stop for a minute? At least long enough to hear me out?' He was now beginning to pant from the effort of trying to keep up with me.

Ignoring him, I picked up my pace – stomping even faster and harder.

'Damn girl, you sho can move when you want to!' he half-gasped, half-panted as he struggled on.

Realizing he was quickly losing energy, he grabbed my arm and turned me toward him, forcing me to stop.

'Baby, I'm sorry. I SWEAR I am!'

He dropped to his knees and tears began to fall.

I couldn't believe it! He was crying! He was actually crying! I'd never seen Tommy cry before. Actually, I'd hardly seen *any* man cry, except a few times when one of the homies had gotten shot or stabbed. (There's no such thing as machismo when you think you're dying.) And Daddy – the day Momma died and the day his kids were taken away. But I had never seen a man cry over a *woman* – especially ME!

But he *was* crying. The tears were falling like giant raindrops. Through sobs, he assured me again of how sorry he was and how it would never happen again. I took one look at him and instantly calmed down. I was so touched. I mean, a man wouldn't cry if he didn't mean it, right?

I don't know if it was the ignorance of youth, the blindness of love, or the mistaken belief that insecurity is love, but I believed him. I believed him when he said that he was sorry and that he'd never hit me again. So I took him back.

And true to his word, he didn't hit me again – for almost a year.

35

Nancy loved to hit the pipe. And because we lived with her, we hit the pipe every time she did – which was almost every day. My past was littered with other drugs – pills, weed, sherm, coke, heroin, to name a few – but since moving in with Nancy, all I wanted to do was hit the pipe, which was extremely expensive. Realizing my freebasing was getting out of hand, I suggested to Tommy that Nancy was our problem, and if we moved away from her, our basing would trim down. Tommy thought about it and agreed that my theory made sense, so we decided to move out on our own.

Lying on rental applications about our job and rental history, we were finally able to rent a two-bedroom apartment in North Park, a small area in San Diego. At first, our plan seemed to work. We slowed down on the pipe quite a bit, though we still smoked weed, drank, and tooted (however, Tommy tooted only coke and crystal; he refused to toot heroin with me, saying it was addictive. I didn't care – more for me!). On top of that, I regularly popped pills, dropped acid, and smoked dust.

Shortly after moving into our own apartment, I once again realized I was on the verge of getting fired and would be forced to find yet another job. I couldn't figure out for the life of me why I kept going through jobs so fast.

'You need to get married,' Tommy suddenly announced.

He dropped this bomb while we were sitting around having an especially great party. The night before, we'd scored really well on a job – we'd robbed a house that had really great stuff. I did crime only at night; somehow it just seemed like the responsible thing to do, so it wouldn't interfere with my day job. Anyway, I would agree to rob only houses we knew were empty – the knowledge of which we'd discover from doing our homework: having one of the homies without a day job scope the place out long enough to know the 'leave and return' pattern of whoever lived there.

Well, one of the homies had done his homework on the house we'd hit the night before. The owners had tried to fool potential burglars by leaving a couple of lights on, but after three days of the light never going off, it didn't take a genius to figure out the lights were never going off. (Timers never fooled us either – especially if they were set to go off and on every day at the exact same time.) Convinced the house was empty, we hit it. It was an unusually good payoff: stereos, records, plants. We took anything we could carry quickly and quietly. And when robbing a house, anything and everything was game as long as it could be sold or traded to the dope man or the pawnshop. We took the money we got for the loot and copped coke to smoke, heroin to toot, pills to pop, and booze to drink. I was in heaven.

I was just getting ready to put the torch to the pipe when his statement made me freeze. I hardly ever stopped in midhit, mid-snort, mid-*anything*; but that comment *made* me pause for a moment.

Seeing the surprised look on my face, he repeated his statement. 'Yup, you need to get married.'

This nigga is straight trippin'.

'Married? What you mean "married"?' I was astonished. He'd never spoken of marriage before. Hell, he'd never even said the *word* before.

'You heard me. That *is* your problem, you know. Marriage will make you stable, which will make you more attractive to employers because they like stability. It will make you seem more okay with yourself and the world. And it will make me more secure. I won't be afraid of losing you because you'll be mine.'

He paused for a moment as he snorted a line. 'Yup, that's your problem,' he continued as he closed his eyes and held back his head to enjoy the rush. 'You need to get married. *We* should get married.'

I thought about his suggestion. Maybe he was right. I had tried just about everything else, but nothing seemed to make me feel okay – there was always an *if*: if I was prettier, if my skin was lighter, if my hair was longer, if my mom was alive, if my teeth were straight, if I was more popular, if I made more money . . . if I had *any* of those things, I'd be okay.

Maybe marriage is the thing I've been looking for.

My thoughts then turned from the benefits it would provide me to the benefits it would provide Tommy. He was pretty insecure, though I tossed it up to love. I figured he must have really been in love with me to always be so desperately afraid of losing me. And I found it endearing that he accused me of sleeping with every man I looked at.

Most of our friends didn't think his behavior was so cute – especially when he started fights with guys he *swore* were checking me out. We'd be in a club dancing and drinking, when all of a sudden he would say, 'That nigga over there's staring at you. He must want you.'

Knowing what was to come, I'd try to calm him down and say, 'Com'on baby, that dude ain't thinking about me. Let's just have fun.'

He would calm down – for a while. But, like I told you before, alcohol talks to you. And I KNOW his booze was telling him something like: *You* know *that nigga wants your girl. Look, she's checking him out too. If you don't check that nigga, he'll be leaving wit' yo' woman!*

Listening to the gibberish of his alcohol-influenced mind, Tommy would plunge toward the dude, who'd be caught off guard, since he had no idea of the insanity that had been going in Tommy's mind, and a fight would ensue. Club security would come and break it up, and we'd all get put out, only for Tommy to do it again at another club another night.

My friends didn't mind Tommy's insecurity; they just hated getting put out of the clubs. When his behavior started to affect their partying, they finally spoke up.

'Girl, you gotta do something 'bout that nigga,' one of them would say as we were escorted out of the club. 'I hadn't even finished my fucking drink!'

As we'd climb into the car to look for another place to party, I would simply reply, 'Aw, but he *loves* me!'

What could it hurt? I asked myself as I returned to contemplating Tommy's suggestion. *You haven't tried marriage to help*

with Tommy's insecurities, though you've tried everything else.
It was true. I had tried everything to make Tommy realize that
he was the only man for me: not looking out the car window,
not looking at other men, not talking to other men. But nothing
had worked. In fact, his insecurities got worse.

But you haven't tried marriage, my mind repeated.

'What the hell?' I said now as I took a big swig of Jack
Daniel's. 'Let's get married.'

Tommy jumped up, and picked me up in a big bear hug. He
was obviously *way* more excited about the idea than I was.
He immediately started making plans – plans that didn't
necessarily match mine. He wanted a big, fancy wedding. I just
wanted to go to the justice of the peace. He had at least a
hundred friends and family members to invite. The only friends
I had were my party friends. I knew none of them would come
– unless there was free dope and booze. I didn't have any family
except Daddy and Jr.

But Tommy was paying no attention to what I wanted. He
wanted a big wedding. He was the only boy in his family – a
huge family – and he wanted everyone there.

'Whatever,' I flippantly responded. Big, small, I didn't care, so
long as it didn't get in the way of my partying.

I was still looking for a job. But employers didn't seem to be so
desperate anymore, so the offers weren't pouring in. I was
forced to resort to illegal activities more and more to keep me
supplied with the money I needed. But I frantically increased my
job search.

One day while perusing the newspaper, I came across an ad
for a 'legal secretary trainee' position. The ad said 'no experience necessary.'

I called the number in the ad and scheduled an appointment.

The job was for the two-attorney law firm of Jack Baker.
When I entered the office, I was met at the door by Mr
Baker himself. Jack, a thin white man, stood about six foot
three and had a full head of wispy gray hair. He had on a very
nice suit and his shoes shone so brightly they almost sparkled.
His chiseled face and wide, bright smile made him unusually
handsome.

He introduced himself and gave me a firm handshake. 'Why

don't you come into my office?' he said in a manner more like a command than a request.

As we walked along together, I checked out the place. The square footage was sparse. I had entered through the reception area, which was really just a small desk placed directly in front of the door. Directly behind that desk was a small office. Down the hall and to the right of that office was another, slightly larger one, which was Jack's. The large space between the two offices accommodated two computers and several shelves of law books. In the rear corner of the suite was a small kitchen that had a microwave, sink, small refrigerator, and coffeepot.

Jack's office was not very large, but it was very nice. He had a dark brown leather couch that reminded me of the couch the shrink at Hillcrest Receiving Home had had in his office – the shrink bastard that told them to return me to Diane's.

Hillcrest didn't happen! I reminded myself when I realized I was getting angry. *Hillcrest didn't happen! Remember, you have a new past. Marcia Brady. A black Marcia Brady!*

Jack sat down and gestured for me to sit on the couch. As I did, my butt just seemed to sink down into it.

Damn, I'd love to sleep on this thing! I wonder how it'd feel against my bare skin – like on my ass!

Jack interrupted my fantasy about his couch by asking a few questions: where I was from, where I was raised. I gave him my perfect lil Marcia Brady past. He seemed impressed that I had five brothers, all raised by our father. He was also impressed that I'd graduated from legal secretary school with a 'straight-A average.'

After asking a stream of questions, he paused for a moment and looked me up and down. Then he asked me if I always wore my skirts so short.

'You betcha!' I proudly replied.

He smiled nervously and continued. After asking a few more questions about my résumé, he explained what the job would entail. He was looking to hire someone who would be what they used to call a 'Girl Friday' – a receptionist for the office, a file clerk, and a secretary for Todd, the other lawyer in the firm who sat in the small office directly behind the receptionist area. Todd wasn't a partner (which I later learned meant 'owner'), but was an associate (which is just another term for an attorney who wasn't a partner). Jack explained that, as a receptionist, I was to answer the three incoming phone lines, input the attorneys' billing time, make sure the coffeepot was always full and the kitchen was always clean. As a file clerk, I was to maintain all of the client and form files. He said that by maintaining the forms, I'd quickly learn about them. As Todd's secretary, I'd file documents with the court, type letters, do general filing, and whatever else he needed done. He was quick to tell me that I was to be only Todd's secretary – he already had one, Gloria, who'd been working for him for fifteen years. Since she was also the office manager, she would be my supervisor as well as the one who would teach me the ropes.

Once he finished the lengthy job description, he looked at me and asked if I had any questions.

'You know I don't have *any* legal experience, right?' I knew there was no way I could fake having experience with doing all that shit they expected me to do.

'Yes,' he replied, 'but, you've been to school for it. Besides, between me, Todd, and Gloria, we'll teach you everything you need to know.'

He paused for a moment and put his chin in his hands, as if he was trying to remember something. 'Oh, one other thing.'

What now? I thought, but kept silent and just looked at him.

'DO YOU SMOKE?' He bellowed as his eyes grew large and his eyebrows quickly raised. The volume in his voice startled me.

'Nnnnnnooo,' I muttered.

'WHAT?' He bellowed even louder than the first time.

'No!' I replied more loudly.

'Good. Because I HATE smokers.'

I'd obviously given the right answer, but, then the realization of what I'd said hit me. I smoked a pack of cigarettes a day. *How in the fuck am I gon' hide that?*

'I like you,' he suddenly announced. He then said that if I wanted the job, I could have it. At first I was thrilled, till he told me how much it paid. Suddenly I realized why he was so quick to want to hire me – the job paid minimum wage. It would be the lowest-paying job I'd ever had! Still, I knew I needed some type of experience if I wanted to break into the legal field. And for some reason, I really wanted to be in the legal field. 'Legal secretary' sounded so official, so important, so *smart*. So I took the job – and the cut in pay.

At first the job was cool. I was supposed to be there at 9:00, although the office didn't open until 9:30. I was *supposed* to arrive by 9:00 and start the coffee. And in the beginning, I did. But it didn't take long to realize that the phones never rang before 10:30, probably because the others never got in before then. So I started getting in right before they did, usually between 10:15 and 10:20. This plan worked fine, except every now and then before leaving his house Jack would call into the office to see if he had any messages. Of course I was never there to receive his calls. When he would arrive later and ask me why I didn't answer the phones, I'd tell him I was on another line, in the kitchen, or at the copier and couldn't hear it. He always seemed to fall for it.

Once I *did* get in and get the coffee started, my day consisted of doing whatever it was Jack, Todd, or Gloria told me to do, from typing letters to filing legal documents with various courts to inputting the attorneys' time for billing to clients. Unfortunately, the learning process went extremely slowly. I found the never-ending court rules convoluted and confusing. I couldn't seem to type the letters with sufficient accuracy. Luckily, between the computer's spell-check and Gloria's double-check I'd have to redo each letter only three or four times. I was constantly frustrated and irritated at my lack of understanding and inability to catch on, not to mention the constant stress and fear I had of getting fired for yet another screwup. I swore it was only the drugs that allowed me to keep my sanity!

Somehow, the whole office, especially Gloria, maintained extreme patience with me. I don't know if it was because I was working for pennies or because she really needed the help. Whatever the reason, she was always willing to work with me. Like, when I lied and told her that my bad memory was the result of an old head injury, she believed me and even thought of ideas to help me remember stuff. One of her ideas was for me to write court rules on lil Post-its and stick them all over my desk. Soon, my desk and everything around it was completely covered with hundreds of lil yellow Post-its. You couldn't even *see* the desk – all you saw was yellow. Although they weren't very attractive, they were extremely effective.

Every once in a while I would hear Jack complaining to Gloria about the sight of so many Post-its haphazardly stuck around my desk, walls, phone, even on my chair and how 'unprofessional' they made the receptionist area and entire office look. But Gloria would remind him of the consequences of making me remove them: late court filings, rejected court filings, and numerous other time-consuming, and costly, mistakes. Jack would pause for a moment with his chin in his hands as he thought of my past mistakes and what they had cost him in terms of time and money, and suddenly exclaim: 'Let her keep 'em. DEAR GOD, LET HER KEEP THEM!!'

I soon found other uses for the Post-its: though I had learned to *speak* properly, I hadn't learned to *write* or *spell* properly. My grammar was absolutely horrible. Continuing to take me under her wing, Gloria slowly began to teach me grammar, punctuation, and word usage. For some reason, the rules of English came easy to me, so my improvement was quickly noticeable.

The hardest part about working with Jack, though, wasn't the difficulty of learning legal rules and procedures; it was hiding the fact that I smoked cigarettes. Because I was forced to sneak cigarettes throughout the day, my deceit actually caused me to become a chain-smoker. I'd use the fire from the butt of one cigarette to immediately light the next one. In the mornings, before the others arrived, I'd smoke three to four cigarettes. Then, during my ten-minute morning break (which usually lasted twenty minutes), I'd smoke at least four more. Then, during my lunch hour, I'd smoke eight to ten more. Sometimes, I'd be jonesing so bad for a cigarette, I didn't eat during lunch, all I could do was smoke. Then I'd get in another four or five during my afternoon break. Whenever I smoked, I walked around the corner and hid behind a large building pillar or crouched behind a parked car. Then as I made my way back to work, I'd douse myself with perfume and chew three to four sticks of gum. I don't know if they ever caught on to the fact that I smoked. If they did, they never let me know that they knew.

All in all, the learning process at the Baker firm was surprisingly pleasurable. No one in the office ever harassed or hassled me about my continual mistakes, lack of legal experience, or severe forgetfulness. In fact, the whole office learned to work *around* my shortcomings. For example, Todd would file court documents a day or two before they were actually due – he had to, since he quickly learned that I'd inevitably do something wrong that would force us to have to refile them. And like Gloria, Todd would give me helpful suggestions whenever he saw the need – and he was never rude, condescending, or patronizing.

For example, whenever I would take phone messages or talk to clients calling in, I would say 'uh-huh, uh-huh,' to signify to the caller that I was taking down their phone number or that I'd understood the message they wanted me to relay. One day, after listening to me take several calls, Todd came out of his office and softly said:

'Hey, Cup, instead of saying 'uh-huh' when talking on the phone to clients, why don't you try saying 'okay'?'

The next time I took a phone message I tried Todd's suggestion. Sure enough, 'okay' *did* sound better than 'uh-huh.' So I immediately squeezed another Post-it onto my already yellow-covered phone that read 'OKAY' in big letters.

Nor did they ever sweat me about my attire. I guess it was because clients hardly ever came to the office, so they never had to worry about anyone seeing me. Gloria once told me that, of more importance to them, at least for the moment, was teaching me to be a good legal secretary. She said that they'd come to the conclusion that as I began to feel more and more confident about my job, I'd want to, in turn, dress more professionally – at least that was their plan.

Personally, I liked their plan because it seemed to be working, in spite of the fact that it often took me a long time to get stuff. But, once I did get it, I *got* it. Luckily, the court rules didn't change often, which made them easier to remember. And all of those legal documents that seemed so strange at first began to make sense as Gloria explained their purpose. Most important, my spelling of the legal terms got better as they began to sink into my memory.

Shortly after starting work, Gloria took me to the thrift shop and showed me how I could get tons of great clothes for next to nothing. Though I refused to give up miniskirts, she was able to convince me to wear more professional (or what I called more 'skin-covering') tops.

All in all, their patience and persistence, paired with my hard work and determination to learn to do the job, were actually beginning to pay off.

Again, my party friends couldn't believe it. As we sat around one evening getting high, I was talking about how much I'd learned and how well I was doing at work.

'This bitch is amazing!' one of the cokeheads exclaimed.

'Yeah,' Victor, my old faithful get-high buddy, joined in. 'First, she says she's gon' change her speech. But none of us believed her.'

'But the bitch did it!' the cokehead chimed in.

Victor stood up and began to talk in a southern drawl as if imitating a preacher addressing his congregation. 'Yeah,' he continued. 'THEN she say she gon' get a job! Still, no one believed her.'

'Hell, bitch never had no job befo'!' someone else yelled from the back of the room.

'But the bitch did it!' the cokehead chimed in again.

'Shit, she just didn't get ONE, she got SEVERAL fuckin' jobs!' someone else yelled.

'Yeah, and all in a year!' the cokehead chimed in again. Everybody started busting up laughing.

'THEN she say she gon' be a legal secretary!' Victor drawled as he strolled back and forth, continuing his sermon.

'Yeah!' the congregation responded in unison.

'But again, none of us believed her!' He waved his arms across the congregation to explain who he meant by 'us.'

'But the bitch done did that too!' the cokehead chimed in yet again.

'Just goes to show,' Victor continued in his southern-preacher drawl, 'you can do anything – on dope!'

'Amen!' everyone yelled as they cracked up laughing. We continued partying.

I sat back and thought about what they'd said, and realized they were right. Slowly, but surely, I was indeed becoming a mothafuckin' legal secretary – on dope.

36

Around this time, I discovered ready rock. Ready rock is best described as 'freebasin' to go.' Prior to ready rock, a buyer had to take the powdered coke home and cook it up before it could be smoked. But 'ready rock' was just that: cocaine rocks that were ready to smoke. Someone had come up with the ingeniously wonderful idea to do the cooking *before* selling. So all a buyer now had to do was take it home and smoke it. No more cooking kits, no more waiting. Instant high. It was later called 'crack.' Why, I don't know; and personally, I didn't care. All I cared about was that it was wonderfully fast – and cheap. I could get a rock for as lil as ten dollars, whereas with powder, the smallest quantity I could get cost twenty-five dollars.

I instantly fell in love with ready rock. Soon, it was all I was doing. I began missing more work because I couldn't pull myself away from it. In one month, I missed fifteen days. Jack sat me down and, for the first time, seriously threatened to fire me if my attendance didn't improve. I was also spending more money on my new dope preference. I stopped buying food, paying rent, or doing anything else. All I was doing was smoking crack.

One day, Tommy was fussing about how we didn't have one dime saved for our upcoming wedding. He was upset that, although we both had jobs, we didn't have anything to show for it. It was during this conversation that I got a moment of clarity. It occurred to me that maybe the crack smoking might be getting a little out of hand.

I couldn't have a drug problem, could I? I asked myself. I decided there was one way to find out. I'd quit – for a while.

288

I figured that if I could stop smoking crack, say, for a year, I couldn't have a problem, because people with a drug problem can't stop.

'Let's not smoke for a year,' I said suddenly.

Tommy stopped fussing in midsentence, totally surprised at my outburst. He studied my face to see if I was serious (I'd sworn off dope and booze several times before – usually when I was doubled over with stomach pains caused by lack of food, or while hugging the toilet and praying for the room to stop spinning). I stared back just as hard to show him I was. Realizing I really meant it, he didn't think about it for long. For months he'd been complaining about the way I smoked dope. Still, he wasn't quite convinced. But, after a few more assurances, oaths, and promises that I really did mean it this time, he readily agreed. That day, we stopped smoking crack – just like that. Now mind you, I didn't say anything about powder cocaine, angel dust, acid, pills, weed, booze, meth, and heroin – all of which I regularly used. I really believed that if I could stop and start *crack* at will, I couldn't have a problem with *anything*. So I stopped crack, kept up everything else, and continued learning to be a legal secretary.

Meanwhile, Tommy and his family were planning a huge wedding. Still unsure of whether I was doing the right thing, I wanted to wait a couple of years before getting married. But Tommy, afraid I would change my mind, insisted that the wedding take place within six months. When I told him that that wasn't enough time for *me* to plan a wedding, he said it was more than enough time for his mom to do it.

'Fuck it, then,' I snapped at him one day when I had gotten tired of arguing about when we should get married. 'Let yo' momma do it.'

And she did. Although I had never met Tommy's mom in person, every now and then we would talk to each other whenever Tommy called home to check in. As a result, we got along well over the phone, partly because of my attitude – if you didn't sweat me about my lifestyle, I liked you.

Even though she was in New York, she was more than willing to take over the arrangements. Actually, she was ecstatic about the idea of having control over planning the wedding. I was ecstatic that she didn't fuck with me about wedding stuff and, most important, that she didn't let the stupid wedding get in the way of my partying.

The only thing I insisted on doing myself was picking out the wedding dress. I wanted it to have roses – my mother's favorite flowers. Thinking about my mother and her favorite flowers was one of the few times since her death I'd allowed myself to think about her at all. But even for the special event of a wedding, the thought of her was still too painful to do sober. After having a few drinks and tooting a few lines, I and a couple of my female party friends made the trip to the wedding-dress store.

The store was full of young white women smiling, running around the store oohing and aahing as they looked at the beautiful dresses. When we walked in, a sudden hush descended on the entire place. I and my crew sauntered in, talking shit and cussing loudly. Ignoring angry glares, we began milling around, looking at dresses. It didn't take long before it became apparent that none of the salesclerks wanted to assist us. I don't know if it was because we were loud or black or high or drunk, or because we were dressed in miniskirts and tube tops. Maybe it was all those things. Whatever the reason for the clerks' stand-offishness, we didn't care. We were used to being ignored and shunned. But that didn't mean we were going to stand for it.

'Hey, heifer!' one of my girls yelled to the salesclerk standing nearest to us. She was standing so close to a rack of wedding dresses, she looked like she was getting ready to disappear into it. From the look of dread on her face, she was probably wishing she could.

'Get over here and help us!' Lisa, one of my girls, snapped. Though it didn't come out like that. We'd been drinking, and smoking blunts, so Lisa's words were slurred. What actually came out sounded more like, 'Shit sover hur and sep us.' The rest of us cracked up. The salesclerk, however, was not amused. Nevertheless, she reluctantly walked over and offered her assistance. I think she did it to prevent us from causing a scene or making even more of a ruckus (we were obviously scaring the other shoppers). Realizing that we were drunk and high – but harmless – the white women returned to their shopping, but continued to cautiously watch us out of the corners of their eyes.

290

The search for my wedding dress did not go well. I was drunk *and* speeding, which resulted in my constant stumbling as I rushed around trying dresses on. If I did find one I liked, I'd start loudly cussing and complaining that it was too expensive. Tommy's mom had sent me a thousand dollars, with strict instructions to get a 'nice' dress. Oh, I intended to buy something 'nice,' all right; I was going to get the dress for a hundred dollars and use the rest on some 'nice' dope.

After an hour or so of trying on dresses (I ruined two by accidentally poking my five-inch stilettos through the trains), I chose an off-the-shoulder white wedding gown.

'Girl, I KNOW you ain't serious 'bout wearing white!' Lisa shrieked when I announced that I'd found my dress.

'Yeah, and why not?' I retorted.

'Girl, only *virgins* get to wear white!' she snapped back, obviously irritated that I didn't know that.

Sharon, another party friend, spun on Lisa.

'Are YOU a virgin?'

'No,' she replied, lowering her head.

'Well, when you get married are YOU going to wear white?' Sharon asked even louder.

'What the fuck does it matter?' I bellowed before Lisa could answer. Every woman in the store instantly stopped whatever she was doing and silently glared at us. I didn't care. I didn't want me and my girls to start fighting among ourselves – at least, not till I'd gotten drunker and higher so I could enjoy the quarreling. But on top of that, I began to think about how I'd lost my virginity. I never *gave* it to anyone; it was stolen. As I thought back to Pete, Diane, and the system, my anger began to quickly rise. I knew myself well enough to know that if I didn't change my state of mind – and quickly – the booze would intensify my anger and I'd start tearing *something* up.

'Society makes those stupid rules,' I continued, 'and society *sucks*!'

We all seemed to be in agreement about that, so the subject was immediately dropped. Even though it was the cheapest dress in the shop (on sale for a hundred dollars), it was pretty. Standing in front of the store mirror, looking at myself in the long, flowing white dress – just for a moment – I felt like a beautiful princess. But as my mind once again reminded me of my painful past, the beauty soon faded. I began to reflect on how my life had really been. I began to wonder why I had so much anger, hatred, and resentment inside me. Why I couldn't *really* be someone's princess.

Fuck it! I told myself, fighting back tears as I realized that druggies, gangstas, hos, and high-school dropouts didn't make good princesses so *I'd* never really get to be one. *It's just a fucking dress!*

'I'll take it,' I nonchalantly informed the salesclerk.

'You do look beautiful in it,' she said, obviously happy that she'd made a sale and we'd soon be leaving. She never dared asked me to pay for the two dresses I'd ruined with my high heels. I guess she figured our swift departure would be payment enough.

'Yeah, whatever,' I grumbled as I went to take the dress off. But as I came out of the dressing room, I told her that the dress wouldn't do after all, because there were no roses on it. Roses were my momma's favorite flowers, and I wanted roses on my dress. To prevent my having to continue to look at more dresses – which would require us to stay in the store even longer – the salesclerk offered to have roses sewn on for free. Always looking for something for nothing, I took her up on her offer and had three white roses added down the center in back.

'Come on, y'all!' I shouted to my girlfriends as I headed for the door. 'I need a drink.'

'But we just *had* some drinks.' Lisa slurred as she followed me.

Fuckin' lightweights! I hated 'em.

'Why do you drink so much?' she asked.

They didn't want to know.

Once I'd found my dress, I pretty much stayed out of the wedding process. Other than listening to my occasional input about it, Tommy and his mother continued on with their own plans. The one thing I was forced to do was address and send out wedding invitations to my side of the family. I told Tommy's mom that I didn't claim family.

'Everybody's got family,' she replied.

'I didn't say I didn't *have* family,' I angrily retorted. It's just that my daddy and uncle are the only family I *claim*!'

'The only family you claim? How can you disclaim family?'

I couldn't believe how naive people could be. I wanted to scream at her: *It's easy – especially since they'd long ago disclaimed me!* But I kept quiet. She wouldn't understand. Her family had always been there for each other. Mine had deserted me the day my momma died. Still, despite my warnings that no one from my family would show up, she made me agree to send out invitations. Jr. provided me with names and addresses of family members. Tommy and I had each sent out one hundred invitations.

Tommy's mom wanted an outdoor wedding so the event was held in a park located in Lemon Grove, a small city east of San Diego. When the day of the wedding arrived, San Diego provided its famously flawless weather: beautiful, warm, and clear – not a cloud in the sky. The sounds of birds chirping made beautiful music to coincide with the beautiful day. The sun's rays caused a beautiful orange-and-yellow glow to spread across the sky, putting the final touches on the perfect picture.

Tommy's mom had done a beautiful job with the wedding plans. White wooden chairs sat in two columns on the freshly cut green lawn. Since I'd refused to use red as a wedding color, someone had chosen yellow and white. Huge yellow satin bows were placed on each aisle seat. An arch covered in yellow and white roses was centered at the front of the chairs. The minister, dressed in a black suit, stood making small talk with guests waiting for the wedding to start. I had no idea whose minister he was or what church he'd come from.

Nor did I care. I had a horrible hangover and was dead tired from lack of sleep due to my attending a private party the night before. Since we had only a limited amount of people we could invite (apparently, the reception food cost by the plate), we decided not to invite our friends. Knowing there would be no hard liquor there, and that we'd invited a crowd heavily stocked with squares, our friends weren't insulted by being left out. In fact, they'd preferred the idea of having our own lil celebration on the eve of the wedding. And celebrate we did. We stayed up all night partying, drinking, and tooting. By the time we got to sleep, it was 7 A.M. Tommy's dad woke us at 11 A.M. to leave for the park and prepare for our 2 A.M. wedding.

'Y'all ever do anythin' but sleep?' his dad shouted as he

watched us scrambling around, falling over each other in an effort to get our stuff and leave.

My first meeting with his parents had not gone well. They had flown in from New York five days before the wedding so his mom could tighten up the finishing arrangements. Tommy and I had decided it was best they stayed in a hotel. After one look at our dirty, nasty apartment, they readily agreed. Still, even though Tommy's parents were staying in a hotel, his mom managed to find a way to bug me every day about something. I'd only agreed to a big wedding as long as it didn't interfere with *my* life. Now that his parents were in town bossing us around and ordering us to do a bunch of shit for the silly day, I was starting to have second thoughts.

As I arrived at the park, Tommy's mom was obviously irritated.

'You guys are late!' she shouted, shooing me into a dressing room where my dress and bridal party awaited. The 'dressing room' was really just a small room on the side of the park in which several wooden chairs and a mirror were placed to allow the bride and her party to see themselves as they prettied up for the big day. Unfortunately, I wasn't feeling very pretty.

I irritably looked around the room at the three bridesmaids who made up my bridal party. They stood around admiring themselves in their yellow-and-white Cinderella gowns. Actually, the girls in my bridal party weren't even my friends – they were women I'd worked with at different jobs. I'd picked them because I knew: (1) they didn't drink or drug, so I was sure they would be able to afford the $25 rental fee for the bridesmaid dresses, and (2) they were reliable enough to *show up* for the wedding. They were cool – for squares – but at that moment they were irking me because they were smiling too fuckin' much, were talking too fuckin' loud, were just too fuckin' chipper about the occasion, and on top of that, their dresses were just too fuckin' yellow.

I casually strolled into the room, grumbled a 'hi' to the girls, who were standing in a semicircle giggling and admiring themselves. I plopped down into one of the hard wooden chairs and dumped my head in my hands.

'Are you crying?' Gwen, one of the bridesmaids, asked. We'd

worked at the second title company together. Gwen was the shortest of the girls, standing about five one. She had brown skin and wore her hair in a jheri curl. Her large brown eyes and deep dimples complimented her girlish smile and made her look much younger than she was. She was sweet. Square, but sweet.

'No,' I grumbled. Oh, how I wanted to tell her what I was really thinking – that I was trying to figure out how I could get out of getting married.

Just walk out, I thought. *Better yet, tell her the truth. Tell her the only thing you really love is partying.*

Just as I got ready to open my mouth and tell her, Tommy entered the dressing room.

'You can't see the bride before the wedding!' Gwen exclaimed. 'Yeah!' the other girls chimed in as they all stared at Tommy in obvious violation-of-wedding-tradition panic.

'I just came to give her her wedding 'present,' ' he responded, ignoring their nervous expressions.

At the mention of 'present,' my ears perked up. Tommy grabbed my hand and pulled me outside. He looked so handsome in his black-and-gray pinstriped tux – just not handsome enough to marry.

'I know how irritable and rude you are when sober' – he paused for a moment – 'or hungover.' He gave me a sly grin as he placed a small brown paper bag into my hand, kissed me on the cheek, and gleefully jogged away.

I looked inside the bag and instantly began to feel better, happier, more at peace about the occasion. The bag contained a half pint of rum, a fat blunt sprinkled with PCP, and a small brown vial filled with meth. I would have felt better if there'd been a rock in it, but then I remembered that I'd sworn it off for a year. So I gulped downed some rum, lit the joint, tooted some meth and reminded myself that 'beggars can't be choosers.' The rum felt good going down, even though it burned my throat with each swallow. I knew it would have gone down smoother and tasted better if I'd had a lil coke to mix with it.

But hey, I told myself as the alcohol dispersed through my veins and the meth kicked in. *Do what you always do – use what you got.*

When I walked back into the room twenty minutes later, I was a happy, joyous, high bride-to-be.

'Let's get fuckin' married!' I screamed as I began putting on my dress.

'Wow, look how happy her man makes her!' Gwen exclaimed, obviously grateful for my mood turnaround. She had no idea how right she was. Any nigga that brought me booze and dope made me happy.

One hundred people showed up for the wedding. But as I looked out into the crowd from the small dressing room, a heavy sadness came over me. I had sent out one hundred invitations to family members who lived in California. Not counting Daddy and Jr., who were in the wedding, the only people who showed up were my aunt Pam and one of her daughters. I hadn't seen or talked to Aunt Pam since she'd discovered the welts on my back and I was sent off to Hillcrest. Still, I was glad to see her at the wedding. However, that didn't hide the miserable realization that although I had sent out one hundred invitations, only two people thought enough about me to show up.

Tommy had also sent out one hundred invitations – 'cept instead of all of them being sent to relatives in California, his went to family members located in *five different states*. Ninety-eight showed up to see him get married. *Ninety-eight*. Hell, even his ninety-eight-year-old great-aunt made a ten-hour trip from northern California.

Fuck 'em! I sternly commanded myself as I thought about my no-show relatives. The angel dust had kicked in and I couldn't risk getting sad. I hated being sad, but on top of that I knew that dust significantly magnified whatever feelings I was experiencing. I didn't want to have a bad trip and end up having an all-day bawling fest. So I talked myself into being happy.

You DO have family here. You've got Daddy and Jr. here. You've got dope and booze here. That's all the family you need.

I took another gulp of rum and quickly tooted a spoonful of meth. The girls were looking at me in disgust.

'You shouldn't be high on your wedding day,' one of them commented.

'Just start the fucking wedding!' I screamed, spitting rum all over the place and completely disregarding their looks of revulsion. 'Let's get this shit over with!'

Besides my dress, the only other thing I insisted on was that Daddy and Jr. both give me away, since they both had spent time being my daddy. Daddy looked after me till Momma died, then Jr. took over. In fact, while I was running away, living in the streets, and hitchhiking up and down the California coast, only Jr. ever knew where I was – that is, when I wanted him to know. Still, he'd been there for me when no one else could have or would have. Unfortunately, Tommy didn't choose the men in his wedding party based on the same criteria I'd chosen my girls – *reliability*. So, at the last minute the best man – a fellow partier – didn't show. Tommy appointed one of the groomsmen to be his best man.

Tommy's mom started running around frettin', sweatin', and stressin' because Tommy's last-minute best man promotion meant that a bridesmaid would not have a man to escort her down the aisle. To appease Tommy's mom (and because he was always so thoughtful and accommodating), Jr. offered to step in as an escort. I was livid that the wedding party had been re-arranged without my permission. I really wanted Jr. *and* Daddy to walk me down the aisle; but by the time I'd discovered what they'd done, it was too late since the wedding march had begun to play and Daddy and I stood arm-in-arm preparing to walk down the aisle.

My memory lapses were becoming more and more frequent when I was drinking – especially when drinking and using. My wedding day was no different. Just as the wedding march began to play, the rum, dust, weed, and meth converged all at once and in full force, hurling me into a blackout. As a result, I have no memory of the wedding. Nonetheless, I became Mrs Tommy Brown.

I remember coming out of the blackout during the reception as some old black bald guy was shoving a beer into my hand and shouting, 'Congratulations!'

'For what?' I snapped back. He was grinning from ear to ear as if he'd just won the lottery.

'For getting married to my great-nephew!' he exclaimed. Party music blared in the background.

'I did what?' I screamed back. As my mind began to clear, my eyes scanned the room. I had no idea how long I'd been out of it. But obviously it'd been long enough to get a party started. People were everywhere: dancing, drinking, eating, celebrating.

'You's a married woman!' he shouted back at me, while gulping down what was left of his beer. He was obviously very drunk. Not wanting him to drink alone, I tossed back the beer he'd handed me.

Though I had no memory of the wedding, the portion of the reception I *was* mentally present for was great. It was one big party. And anyone who knew me knew that I loved to party.

Tommy's mom walked around admiring the great job she'd done and what a wonderful wedding it turned out to be. Tommy walked around greeting people, giving hugs, and thanking them for coming. I walked around sneaking toots from my lil glass vial and downing the unfinished beers and glasses of wine people left sitting around.

No sense in wasting perfectly good booze, I told myself as I downed what was left of yet another person's wine.

Soon I was loaded and drunk all over again; so it wasn't long before my mind was gone again.

When my mind found its way back, Tommy was saying how nice it was that his work friends had given us a dinner cruise as a wedding present. We were sitting at a table aboard a beautiful boat filled with people I'd never seen before.

What happened to the reception people? I asked myself as I watched the ship's crew milling around setting plates of food in front of everyone.

'You need to eat,' Tommy was saying. 'You haven't eaten all day. All you've been doing is drinking. You're going to get sick.'

I wasn't trying to hear that shit. I leaned over to the lil old white woman who was sitting on the other side of me and asked her where the bar was. I immediately began to make my way toward it.

As I was returning to my seat with my favorite drink in my hand – Long Island Iced Tea, no coke and no ice – a thin white woman approached me from behind.

'Excuse me,' she said very quietly, 'did you sit in something?'

Did I sit in something? I repeated to myself. *Shit, DID I?*

I had no clue. I started to say something smart, like, *Bitch, you brought it up, so you tell me!* but for some reason I decided

298

against it. As I was thinking of something else smart-alecky to say, she whispered, 'I think you should go to the restroom and check it out.'

Why do I have to go to the bathroom to check it out? I asked myself. *And why the fuck is she whispering?*

Deciding it was probably in my best interest not to make a scene in a place where being put out meant being tossed into the bay, I made my way to the restroom. I was horrified when I got there.

The bathroom was full of white women, talking about their husbands, boyfriends, and children; combing their hair; touching up their makeup. When I walked in, all of the chattering suddenly stopped as they stared at me with what looked like colossal shock.

During the reception and still in a blackout, I had changed into a white cocktail dress. I had no memory of changing into the dress or where I'd even gotten it from. Actually, where it'd come from was not important. What *was* important was that the entire back of it was red. I had started my period! I guess I was so out of it, I had no clue – even though the dress was soaked through to the skin.

'Oh, you poor thing,' one of them cried.

Before I could respond, the women got to work, moving as a team. One told me to take off the dress as she began to fill one of the sinks with cold water. Another began to help me pry off the saturated dress while carefully trying not to get blood everywhere. Another went to get the spare shirt and pair of shorts she 'just happened to have' in her bag. Another grabbed the dress, threw it into the sink and began ferociously plunging it up and down in the cold water in an effort to get the blood out. The way they grouped together to help me, you would have thought we were all old friends.

The woman hurriedly returned with the shirt and shorts. As I struggled to keep my balance while putting on the shorts, the women continued to focus on the dress, chattering about various tricks they'd learned or heard about over the years for getting out blood. As I threw on the shirt, I interrupted their chattering and told them that I was on my honeymoon. At that announcement, they seemed even more determined to get me looking right again. Though, I really cared less. What I *did* care about is that I'd learned that their pity for me kept drinks coming.

'What are you drinking?' one of them asked as she dunked my dress in the sink of cold water. 'Long Island Iced Tea – no ice and no coke,' I replied.

'Darn,' the woman who'd given me the spare clothes said, 'I've never heard of *that* before. Long Island Iced Tea. Let's see, that's made with vodka, rum, gin, bourbon, and coke. So if you remove the coke and ice, all you've got is . . . straight alcohol!' Her eyes were wide with amazement.

'Well, this is such a depressing moment,' another chimed in, 'I don't blame her for drinking like that.'

Finally, someone who understands!

'We'll keep your glass full,' she continued as she looked at me compassionately, 'How 'bout that?'

'Shit, fine wit' me,' I replied. But, what I was *thinking* was, *Y'all can HAVE that raggedy-ass dress. Just keep the booze coming!*

And they did.

I returned to the table a while later. The entire time I was in the bathroom, Tommy stayed at the table drinking. He never once came to see what was wrong. Never wondered about why I had taken so long. When I walked over to the table and told him what had happened, he got upset that I was on my period because that meant we couldn't have sex.

'Nigga, I done embarrassed myself by walking around God knows how long soaked to the core in blood and all you care about is you ain't gettin' no pussy!' I screamed at the top of my lungs. I was livid.

'Cup, shut up and sit down,' he said sternly. 'You're making an ass of yourself – as usual.'

What did he say that for? That only pissed me off more.

'Fuck you!' I screamed. 'You been fuckin' me for years and all of a sudden you pissed cuz you can't fuck *now*?' I couldn't believe what I was hearing.

'Cup, I said sit down!' he said louder as he stood up to face me. His eyebrows scrunched and his lips curled.

'You threatening me?' I screamed, bracing myself for a fight. 'You threatening me?' I balled up my fist.

The entire boat became instantly silent. Tommy and I were

the only black people on board. A sea of white faces stared at us in silent amazement.

Realizing I was drunk and aware of how belligerent I became when I was, Tommy immediately changed his stance and lowered his tone.

'Listen, baby, it's all right. Just sit down and we'll talk about it,' he said quietly and slowly, in an obvious effort to calm me down.

'Fuck you,' I screamed. I was pissed. It was too late for talking. It was too late for soothing. He'd gotten my anger boiling, and once it began to boil, I wouldn't stop – I *couldn't* stop because the alcohol took over and was in complete control. The six and a half Long Island Iced Teas I'd drunk had taken over and were talking to me.

You know you shouldn't have married this mothafucka! they were urging. *Cuss his ass out! In fact, cuss everybody out.*

And I did. I cussed Tommy out, calling him everything but a child of God. Then, the booze told me to storm out of the room. And that as I went, I should cuss out everybody I passed. Like a good drunk, I did as commanded.

'What you lookin' at, white woman?' I screamed at one person.

'Bitch, who told you to put yo' fat ass in that dress?' I snapped at another.

The room was completely silent except for my ranting and raving. The ship's crew, obviously uncertain of how to deal with the bizarre situation, just stood aside and, along with everyone else, watched in complete astonishment and disgust. No one within my eyesight was safe from an insult, not even one of the women who'd come to my rescue in the bathroom.

'Thanks for the help, heifer,' I slurred and popped her on the back of the head as I staggered by. On and on I went as I staggered toward the door.

'Boy, who gave you that fucked-up haircut?' I growled at an old white man sitting near the door.

Though he looked at me with obvious distaste, he was the only person who didn't seem shocked by, or afraid of, my behavior. And he was the only person who said something back.

'I hate drunks,' he stated calmly but somberly as he stared up at me with piercing eyes.

'Well, us drunks hate YOU too!' I indignantly yelled back, staggering out the door, losing my balance, and slamming my head against the door frame.

I don't know what happened after I left. I made my way up to the deck where I spent the remainder of the cruise hurling over the side of the ship.

That night was the first time I'd ever admitted to being a drunk. I wouldn't admit it again for a long, long time.

37

Thanks to Tommy's mom, the wedding was a huge success. Unfortunately, the marriage was not. Within a couple of months of getting married, Tommy and I began having ferocious fights – usually because he thought I was flirting with someone. It started with pushing, shoving, and shouting. But his jealous rages began to happen more and more frequently. The pushing and shoving escalated to slaps. I'd slap back, which he said forced the dispute to come to heavier blows.

'If you wouldn't get up in my face like a nigga,' he'd plead the next day while he'd be apologizing for beatin' my ass the night before, 'I wouldn't have to hit you!'

But I couldn't just roll over and do *nothing*. So I'd always hit him back. Even though I knew he was bigger, taller, and stronger than me, and could kick my ass with minimal effort, I couldn't allow him to just hit me without my doing *something*. So I'd rear back, stick out my chest, get in his face, and hit him back, even though the first hit was usually the only one I'd get in. Still, I got one in.

My ignorance of domestic violence prevented me from seeing anything wrong with Tommy's behavior. At first, I justified his behavior by pointing out that he landed only body punches so as not to mess up my face. Of course, once we'd come to stronger blows, that theory went out the window. But ignorance manufactures denial. So though my eyes were sometimes black or swollen, my lips puffy or busted, though I often intentionally wore clothes that would hide the black and blue bruises scattered all over my body, or grit my teeth through the pain in an effort to walk so I could look as if nothing were wrong –

when in fact my entire body was sore – I believed that as long as he didn't break any *bones*, it wasn't really violence.

I further justified the hitting by telling myself that he must *really* love me to be so adamantly vicious about the thought of losing me. I defended his behavior even further by telling myself that it was the dope and booze that caused him to act that way. I came to this conclusion because Tommy was only violent when he was loaded or drunk. Problem was, we were *always* loaded or drunk.

I justified his behavior even further by convincing myself that, other than the violence, he was a good man – he kept a job, he drank, and he drugged – all I ever wanted in a man. I knew nothing about standards, principles, respect, or boundaries. I even began to accept as true his own reasoning: that I deserved to get hit because I insisted on hitting back. No one ever told me that no woman deserves to get hit, period.

The people at work either didn't see the signs of abuse, or ignored them; most likely because, like most people, they didn't want to get involved. Actually, though, making the decision to mind their own business was probably a good thing. Because if they had said something to me, I would have most certainly cussed them out for getting in my business. I absolutely *hated* folks in my business.

Still, no one said anything about the black eyes and busted lips. No one ever told me that I didn't have to live that way or take that shit. Even friends that *knew* about Tommy's behavior failed to school me about domestic violence. Some said nothing at all, others laughed and teased me about it. Take my two closest friends, Mona and Rose, for instance.

Although the three of us had been very close throughout elementary school, we'd all lost contact after graduating sixth grade: I was given to the sperm donor and shipped off to Lancaster; Rose's family moved to Chula Vista, the small town in southern San Diego County where I'd lived when I'd gotten emancipated; and Mona's mom placed her in a school in a distant district. But shortly after Tommy and I had gotten married, I ran into to Rose buying a dime bag. Although we'd both often copped at the same spot, we'd never before run into each other. So, when we first saw each other, we both stopped dead in our tracks, eyes wide as we stood staring, mouth open as if to speak, but unsure of what to say. I finally broke the ice.

'Hey, girl, what's up!'

'Vette?' she asked unbelievingly. 'Is that you?' She paused, then said, 'I heard you died.'

Dead? Me? Who the fuck started that rumor? Then I remembered that in a drunken stupor I had. You see, I sometimes still used 'La'Vette' – usually to disguise myself when engaging in illegal activity – like buying dope (didn't want the lowlifes to know who I *really* was). A few months before, I'd stolen some heroin from a dealer named Sly. Shit, it wasn't like it was *my* fault. He was the one who'd left several balloons out on the table in plain view as he went into the back to get change. Several days later I learned he'd put a five-hundred-dollar hit out on me. I was extremely flattered that someone thought my miserable life was actually worth five hundred dollars. Still, once I'd overheard enough people talking about collecting the money when they found this 'Vette' chick, I took the hit seriously. In an effort to save my ass, I started the rumor that the chick named Vette had been killed by an L.A. dope dealer for stealing his shit. It never occurred to me that people would actually believe it. But listening to Rose, it seemed they had.

'Naw, girl, I ain't dead – 'less you dead too!' We both started crackin' up laughing.

We shared a joint and a couple of 40s as we got caught up on each other. As Rose went through her history, it became apparent that, besides the tragic death of her father who'd been killed shortly before my mom died, she'd had a normal adolescence: boys, high-school dances, zits, etc. She now had a good job working in the plumbing business.

When it came time to catch up on *my* history, I had to make a quick decision as to which story to tell: the hellacious truth or the 'Marcia Brady' version. It took only a second to decide which it would be because talking with Rose, reminiscing about the 'good ol' days,' brought up warm, happy feelings. Sitting there, gettin' high, turnin' up 40s, laughin', and kickin' it with an old friend – a friend who knew me *before* Lancaster – I didn't want to fuck up the moment, so I gave her the 'Marcia Brady' tale. Like everyone else, she fell for it. I also told her about my decision to take back my original birth name.

Once we'd caught up with each other, she asked if I'd kept up with Mona. I told her I didn't know where Mona, or anybody else, was for that matter. Nor did I care.

'Cup!' she yelped, obviously stunned by my callousness. 'How can you be so heartless?'

'Friends are like buses,' I uncaringly replied as I took a hit off the joint, 'if you miss one, sooner or later, another will come. The names of the routes change, but the *destinations* don't. It will always cost *something* to ride – nobody rides for free. And, they'll leave your ass if you don't get with the schedule.'

Realizing I was telling the truth, or maybe it was the Old 8, Rose cracked up laughing. Her laughter was contagious, so I joined in. Soon, we were both laughing so hard, tears were streaming down our faces. We laughed loud and hard for what seemed like forever.

Once we were able to compose ourselves, she told me what she knew about Mona. She said Mona's mom still lived in the same house she did when we were in elementary school. We decided to roll by and see if Mona wanted to smoke a joint with us. We stopped and scooped up Tommy (who had been angrily sitting at home waiting for me to return with the weed) and drove to Mona's mom's house.

Mona's mom said that Mona had gotten married and moved to an apartment with her husband, James. She called Mona, who squealed when I got on the phone. She gave us directions and made us promise to come right over. We showed up at her apartment, where I, Rose, Tommy, Mona, and James all got acquainted and reacquainted while smoking blunts and drinking bourbon, vodka, and gin.

That night, while drinking and getting high, I looked around the room at my new crew. I decided that Mona, Rose, and James would be good friends for Tommy and me to have – especially since, like us, they all had jobs and so were also 'responsible.' I immediately cut loose all of my 'loser,' non-working friends. I, Mona, and Rose became inseparable.

The new crew worked out great: we all worked, and got high regularly and constantly, though at first all they did was smoke weed and drink.

But even Rose and Mona, my two closest friends, failed to school me about domestic violence. I think partly because our constant boozing and doping caused them to not take my and

Tommy's fighting seriously. On top of that, they never actually saw any physical abuse – at least, not at first. The only clue that I'd been in some kind of physical altercation was the fact that I sometimes walked very slowly, as if I were very sore or in great pain. I being the mean, fighting drunk that I was, Mona and Rose chalked it up to another ass-whuppin' I'd gotten from callin' out some big dude at a club, or to another one of my frequent drunken tumbles. They had no idea that Tommy was the big dude doing the ass-whuppin'.

I can't blame them for their naïveté because I never admitted to any abuse – at least, not at first – mostly because I was too embarrassed. I prided myself on being streetwise, for having raised myself from the age of eleven, and for successfully surviving the game. And being from one of the downest sets in South Central, L.A., there was no way I could admit to an ass-whuppin'. Besides Tommy wasn't always the one doing the hitting. Sometimes, *he* had to struggle to keep *me* from beating the shit out of *him* because there were plenty of times when I was drunk, angry, and in my renowned 'fuck-the-world-and-you-too' mood. During those times, I was suicidal, in that I didn't care if I lived or died; as well as homicidal, in that I wanted to take someone with me. Unfortunately for Tommy, that 'someone' was usually him. So he'd spend the night fighting me off and being afraid to go to sleep (I'd told him of my previous attempts to kill both Larry and Diane). Our relationship was so toxic and unhealthy that we took turns being the batterer. The fight's aggressor was determined by who was the highest, drunkest, most jealous, or angry. Although we took turns throwing blows, I usually got the worst of it. Still, we managed to keep the violence a secret for a while.

But it soon became impossible to hide the black eyes and bloody lips. When James figured out what was going on, he said that 'grown men shouldn't get in other grown men's business.' He never said another word to me or Tommy about our fighting, except to joke that Tommy shouldn't let me 'whup on him like that.'

When Rose learned what was going on, she kept quiet. She understood both my hitting Tommy and his hitting me. She'd watched family members endure physical abuse, and yet they had stayed in the relationships. Those experiences taught her to 'shut her mouth and mind her own business.' When Mona found out, she just teased me about it – trying to make me smile.

Problem was, I was usually in too much pain to smile. Despite the violence, I refused to leave Tommy – for good, anyway. In my mind, *my* hitting *him* wasn't a reason to leave. *His* hitting *me* was another story. Oh, don't get me wrong; I left his ass all right. In fact, I left him every time he hit me. I packed up all of my raggedy shit and took off for Mona's or Rose's, who would put me up for a few days. But I was *always* home by Thursday, because Tommy got paid on Thursdays and I knew we'd be getting high.

And get high I did. Shortly after establishing my new crew, I decided that my year hiatus from crack should be up. I hadn't stopped for a whole year; it was more like ten months. Still, I was proud of myself for having restrained from the drug for that long. So I began hitting the pipe again, it quickly got out of hand. I figured I just needed to try something different.

'Maybe we should switch between premos and the pipe,' Tommy announced one day. (Premos are crack-laced blunts.)

Shit, his idea made sense to me.

'Let's try it,' I said firmly, mistakenly believing that altering *how* I did a drug would allow me to control *using* it.

What I hadn't yet realized, though, was that the type of drug I used and how I used it didn't matter. Once I started getting high on anything, I could not stop. But I was determined to control it.

Within months, my crack use was right where it was when I'd stopped ten months before, and getting worse. It wasn't long until, just as before, every dime I had was going toward it – regardless of what form it was in – and all my time was spent smoking it, including time I was supposed to be spending at work. Jack finally became completely fed up with my absenteeism and tardiness; not to mention my frequent mistakes. It got so bad that he said I was no longer even worth the pennies he was paying me.

Infuriated that I'd missed six days in less than two weeks, Jack fired me, but not before angrily warning me that I had a 'serious problem' and needed 'serious help.' However, he said he felt sorry for me, and since I'd worked for him so hard for almost a year, he wanted to help me out a little. So he decided to be nice and not fire me right away. Instead, he informed me that he was giving me two weeks' notice.

'What's that mean?' I snapped. I'd never before received a 'notice' so I was unsure as to what that entailed. Jack gladly told me what it meant – I'd be fired in two weeks. I wasn't angry. In fact, I was grateful for the 'help,' especially since, in my mind, if I could find another job before the two weeks were up, I could quit! Keeping my vow to never again be fired, I immediately set out to find another job.

Dave Curnow was a partner in a law firm located in the office building directly across the street from Jack's. Dave, in dire need of a secretary, placed a newspaper ad, which I came across while sitting at the corner bar checking the classifieds. So I doctored up my résumé, extended the length of time I'd actually worked for Jack to three years, lied about the length of my stay at other jobs, and set up an interview.

Unlike Jack's office, which was only one of several small suites on the floor, Dave's firm took up four entire floors. And unlike at Jack's firm, where I worked in the dual capacities of receptionist and secretary, Dave's firm had a real receptionist – a pretty young white girl. All she did was sit behind a huge beautiful desk, answer the firm's numerous phone lines, and greet clients.

She looked at me nastily when I asked for the office manager. I don't know if it was my constant sniffing and wiping my nose (I'd tooted right before arriving) or my miniskirt that made her scrunch up her nose and look at me as if I'd pissed in her breakfast. Whatever the reason, I immediately got the message that she didn't like me.

'Does she know what this is concerning?' she snapped as she stood up from her seat to glare more closely at my miniskirt and wrinkled blouse.

'Does she know you got on all that damn makeup?' I snapped back as I leaned over the large desk to glare at her much-too-heavily-applied cosmetics.

She sucked her teeth and threw a finger at one of the big soft leather chairs that sat around the waiting area. I decided that I should probably wait till after I got the job to start a fight. I plopped down on one of the chairs and waited for the office manager. When she arrived, she seemed to be a bit taken aback by my attire, but she shook my hand and led me to Dave's office. As we walked through the hallway, I was impressed with the decor. This was a real law office. The corridors were lined with the large offices of the attorneys. Directly across from each office was a secretary's station.

She led me into a very nice office with a big desk, fancy chairs, and a large bookshelf that held lots of books. Behind the desk sat a handsome white man who looked to be in his early forties, gray strands streaking his thick black beard and thinning hair. But instead of appearing old, the gray actually made him look very distinguished. His nice physique was also immediately obvious. I figured he must regularly work out. Although he was noticeably well built, he didn't appear to be very tall. So when he stood to shake my hand, I was shocked at his height. He was at least six one.

Tall, built, and handsome! I shamelessly said to myself as he gave me a wide, warm smile and introduced himself as Dave Curnow.

Dave wasted no time jumping into the interview. He seemed absolutely thrilled with my résumé – and the three letters of reference I'd created, but I got the feeling that he was not as impressed with my attire. In fact, I began to believe it made him a little uncomfortable because he kept shifting in his seat, clearing his throat, playing with the pens on his desk, and making an obvious effort not to look at my legs protruding out from under the miniskirt.

After going over my résumé, there were a few moments of uncomfortable silence. Then he suddenly asked why I wanted to leave Jack's. I replied that I was looking for more of a challenge – and more money. I lied about the amount of money I'd earned at Jack's, raising my salary by five dollars an hour. I made it very clear that I wasn't willing to take less money than I was already making. Dave said he understood. After a few more moments of uncomfortable silence, he stated that he was also impressed with my communication skills and professional attitude. However, he said, he was still interviewing, so someone from the firm would get back to me within a couple of weeks.

I guessed that not a lot of people were busting down Dave's

door for the position because three days later, the firm's office manager called and offered me the job. And the office manager had even *more* good news: to ensure I'd take the job, they offered me a dollar more an hour than what I'd told them I'd been making at Jack's. Hot damn! In less than two weeks, I'd gotten a position with a larger, more prestigious firm AND gotten myself a six-dollar-an-hour raise.

I immediately quit Jack's and started with Dave. Not being one for long good-byes or staying in touch with folks, I walked in, announced that I quit, turned on my heels, and walked out before anyone could respond.

I never saw Jack, Todd, or Gloria again.

Damn, gurl, you're good! I told myself that night while smoking premos and drinking bourbon. I'd lasted longer with Jack than I had with any other employer. I was definitely getting better; there was NO way I could have a drug or alcohol problem.

Little did I know, I was plummeting myself into an even deeper living hell.

38

The violence between me and Tommy was getting worse. So was our drinking and using. We were forced to move to different apartments almost every six to eight months. We were always late on bills. We never had any money. We never had any food. We never went anywhere. We never did anything except drink, use, party, and occasionally, work. We needed a plan. It wasn't long before one came to me.

I was talking to Daddy one day when he blurted out that he was sick of living with Lori. Kelly's son, Jason, was spoiled rotten; Lori gave him full rein and let him wreak havoc throughout the house. Kelly was still living with them for free, and refused to work or go to school. Daddy said that he was tired of taking care of grown folks. On top of that, he'd rekindled his relationships wit' ho's – though just for sexual relations this time around; he wasn't dealing or having 'business arrangements.' Still, he knew that to enjoy complete, continual fun, he needed to get out of his marriage. Being the fast thinker and opportunist that I was, I spoke up immediately.

'What about moving in with me and Tommy?' I asked. I didn't bother talking to Tommy about it. No need to. Since being married, we'd moved at least three times because we'd smoked up the rent money. And we were getting ready to be evicted yet again. So I knew Tommy would be down for any plan that reduced the amount of money we'd end up paying for rent. Daddy said he'd think about it and would get back to me.

The following month, we moved. Two weeks later, Daddy moved in with us. Daddy's moving in didn't require us to change our lifestyle at all. I never felt like I had to hide my drinking and using. I was grown and in my own home. *Nobody* told me what to do in my own home. Besides, it wasn't as though Daddy didn't know about my lifestyle. Anyway, he wasn't worried about us. He was dating hos again. So I stayed out of his business and he stayed out of mine – including my and Tommy's ferocious fights. Though Daddy never actually saw Tommy hit me, he heard the hollering, heard furniture breaking, and saw the police making their way up our walkway.

'You're [They're] grown and you're [they're] married,' he would respond when I (or the police) would ask why he never intervened to stop us from fighting.

Daddy was smart to stay out of our fights. If he had interfered, I'd have cussed his ass out, just like I did the police when they showed up at my door, talking about 'somebody's complaining about the noise and fighting.' The police never did anything. Realizing we were both drunk and high, the police would just calm us down, admonish Tommy to 'behave himself,' then leave, warning us to 'keep it quiet.' And we would – for a while.

I liked the way the police handled our fights. I hated and distrusted cops, and didn't want them at my house for any reason. Even my 'business partners' weren't allowed in my home. But it wouldn't be long before Tommy's violence would escalate to a point where I was no longer cussing out the police, I was calling them.

Tommy and I were trying to live with some sort of normalcy. With Daddy's help on the rent, we weren't officially evicted anymore. Actually, we just made sure to move *before* getting the eviction notice. That way, Daddy never caught on to why we were moving. He just knew we sometimes moved quickly and quietly. He never questioned and we never volunteered anything. I'd just come home one day and say, 'com' on, Daddy, we found something better.' And we'd pack up our shit and move; though Daddy's helping with the rent allowed us to stay put a lot longer than usual.

Soon, all of the pretty new furniture Tommy and I had bought to celebrate our new jobs disappeared. In a crack-induced frenzy, we'd sold it for a third of what it was worth and used the money to buy more crack. Within two months of starting our new jobs, our house was completely empty – again.

Daddy often noticed that furniture and other items would be there one day and gone the next. But he never questioned us about it. 'You guys were grown!' he told me years later when I asked him why he never said anything. He was right.

Besides, one time one of his hos stole our shit. It was a chick named Tina. Daddy really liked her and brought her home more than the others. Tina and I got along fabulously, so I didn't complain when she began to stay days at a time. I even began to consider her a friend – something you don't do with dope fiends. But I was high all the time and was slippin' on my street rules. One day we came home from work, and all our shit was gone – TV, stereo, even Daddy's gun. Now, I was known for selling my shit, but I knew I hadn't sold it this time. Come to find out, Tina had stolen it while we were at work. We knew it was she because a little neighbor kid saw her and identified her for the police. The police said Tina and her crew had hit three houses in the area in two weeks.

'I'll be damned!' I shouted when Daddy told me the kid had identified Tina. 'How could the bitch rob ME? I shared my dope with her! I shared my Schlitz with her!'

But after thinking about it for a while, I realized that I'd actually been kind of lucky because, after all of the houses I'd robbed, this was the first time it'd ever happened to me. So actually, I couldn't really get mad. I guessed what they said was true – 'What goes around comes around.' But I vowed if I ever saw that bitch, I'd whup her ass. Fortunately for her, I never saw her again. Several days later Daddy and the cops set up a sting and Tina was arrested. She copped a plea bargain and pled guilty to that charge and the burglary of two other houses. In exchange, they dropped several warrants and failures to appear in court. Her plea got her a reduced sentence and she was shipped off to prison.

I think I was more pissed off by the fact that in stealing my shit, Tina was able to sell it for dope, robbing me of the 'right' to do it instead. But something good came out of Tina's burglary. Unbeknownst to us, we had renter's insurance. Tommy was complaining to our agent that we didn't have the money for that month's car insurance because our apartment had been robbed. It was then that our agent stated that, just the previous month, we'd added a renter's insurance policy. Luckily for us, we hadn't had it long enough to lose it because of our failure to pay. The agent said that if there was a police report, the insurance would replace everything that was taken. Tina's robbery was perfect timing. Of course we claimed things that we never had and Tina never took: we claimed three TVs, VCRs, and stereos (one of each for the living room, our room, and Daddy's room), telephones, two microwaves, blenders, pictures, etc. Without question, the insurance replaced it all. So through Tina's robbery, we ended up with three times as much stuff. Of course, we sat looking at all our new stuff and swore that *this time,* we wouldn't sell *any* of it. And we didn't – for almost three months.

I liked working for Dave. He was a litigator like Todd. But, unlike Todd, he was a partner, which meant he had more pull. Though I made a lot more money working for Dave than for Todd, I did a lot less work – for several reasons. First, he did most of his own work as did the female associate, Rhoda, who worked with him. Every now and then they'd ask me to file something with the court or finalize a letter, but they were pretty much self-sufficient – which meant we got along fabulously. And unlike at Jack's firm, where I had to answer all of the phones, with Dave's firm, the full-time receptionist did that. And the firm had a file clerk whose sole job was to update the files. They even had calendar clerks who kept up with essential deadlines and reminded attorneys of court appearances.

Still, *some* work from me was required. But, this wasn't a problem. Doing speed made working no problem. The only problem I had with working with Dave was that, sometimes, I had absolutely *nothing* to do; though no one ever knew it because of the way I scurried from here to there, moving fast, talking fast, and sweating a lot. In fact, I stayed 'on the go' so much, everyone else really thought I was busy.

Though I was able to fool people about my workload, I wasn't able to fool them about my size. People soon began commenting on my astonishing thinness: I was 5 feet, 5½ inches tall, weighed about 120 pounds, and wore a size 4. I started trying to disguise my size and weight by wearing two sets of pants or oversized dresses. But no matter what I tried, my thinness showed through. I was well aware that one of the side effects of speed was loss of appetite, but I was still convinced that, since I wasn't 'hooked' on speed, it couldn't possibly have been the cause of my thinness. So whenever I was questioned about it, I'd shrug my shoulders and respond that I honestly didn't know why I was so thin. One day, Shirley, a coworker, told me she knew why.

I was standing in the kitchen washing coffee cups. It wasn't my job to clean the staff kitchen. The firm actually had a full-time person to do that. But I was bored and tweaking and needed something to do with my hands. I'd wandered into the kitchen, saw the dirty dishes, and thought, *What the hell, washing can be fun!*

Why I had no problem washing other people's dishes when I refused to wash my own, I'll never know.

Unbeknownst to me, Shirley had been standing in the doorway watching me for a while. She startled me by asking how I stayed so thin. When I shrugged and said I didn't know why, she responded that she knew why, all right.

Her comment startled me so bad that I had to stop washing dishes. I turned and stared at her.

Did she know about the crack, crank, and pills? I held my breath as I waited for her answer.

'It's your metabolism!' she exclaimed. 'Of course, that's it! You have a high metabolism!'

Metabo-who? I was used to people making snide comments about my weight. I couldn't see anything wrong with my size – I thought 'thin was in' – so I usually just ignored them or blew them off as being jealous.

'That and the way you run around!' she continued, excited that she'd solved the puzzle. 'I've watched you move. You don't just stand up. You JUMP up!'

So that's it, I thought. *Sure, it all makes sense now. That's why I'm so skinny. I've got a high metabo-something!*

From that day forward, it was the answer I gave when questioned about my size. And it was an answer that everyone seemed to accept and no one ever questioned – including me.

The best thing about working at a large firm was that I got more vacation and sick time. Instead of the one-week vacation I got at Jack's, I got two weeks at Dave's. And my sick days more than doubled, from five to twelve! *Plus,* I got three 'personal days,' which I could use for personal reasons, like doctor appointments or a sick spouse. I also got two floating holidays: my birthday and my annual anniversary date, which I could use any time I wanted. And on top of that, the office was closed for *every* state *and* federal holiday. All in all (not even counting bereavement leave and holidays), I could legally take off twenty-seven days a year! Of course, with my frequent need for time off that wasn't nearly enough time. Still, it was three times as many days as I'd gotten at any of my previous gigs. But, it wasn't just the fewer job tasks and additional days off that made me like my new job. I also liked Dave as a person. He was very easy-going and seemed to accept me just the way I was. He soon got used to my dressing style and once even stuck up for me when he'd heard that other staff and attorneys were complaining about my inappropriate attire, my extremely loud voice, and periodically foul attitude. So like everything else new in my life, things went well for a little while.

It wasn't long before the extra money at Dave's wasn't enough. I had to come up with another hustle. The one I found I wasn't even looking for; *it* came to me: credit cards.

Yes, credit cards! Somehow, credit card companies discovered that not only did I have a legitimate job that paid money, but that I didn't have any debt. They started sending me 'pre-approved' credit card applications for every type of card – department store cards, gas cards, jewelry cards – all of which I gladly accepted. I fell in love with them. It was like getting stuff for free – you walked into a store, bought whatever you wanted, flashed your card, and walked out with the booty. Then, when the bill came, you didn't have to pay what the merchandise actually cost, you only had to make a minimum payment! What a concept!

Unfortunately, the gas and light and telephone company didn't take department store or gas credit cards. And my party-ing soon prevented me from paying those bills. One day, I came home and the lights wouldn't come on. At first, I thought the lamp just needed another light bulb.

'Cup, *every* bulb couldn't have blown out!' Tommy screamed, obviously blaming me for the complete darkness, 'They've cut the fucking lights off!'

'Well, don't blame me!' I screamed. We started arguing over whose fault it was that the bill hadn't gotten paid. I stormed outside to get some air. Immediately next to our apartment was the building's laundry room. Since the apartment building only housed six apartments, the laundry room wasn't very big; it held one washer and one dryer. I hopped up on the washer and began to think. How the fuck were we going to get electricity with no money? As I pondered my dilemma, my eyes scanned the small room. That's when it came to me.

I rushed inside and began scrambling through the junk drawer in the kitchen. Luckily, it was still light enough outside to provide enough light for me to see.

'What are you doing?' Tommy snapped.

Ignoring him, I kept rummaging. Finally, I found what I was looking for – an extension cord. I hoped it was long enough for my purpose.

I ran back outside with the extension cord and plugged it into the outlet in the wash house and walked back into the house with the other end. It came to rest just inside the front door. But, there was still a problem: the cord was so thick, it prevented the door from closing all the way.

'Oh, great, genius!' Tommy sarcastically snapped, 'We'll have electricity but get killed by the burglar who gets in through the open door!'

His sarcasm was pissing me off. Besides, I thought I'd come up with a great idea – free electricity.

'You got a better idea!' I screamed as I slammed the television plug into the extension cord. He paused for a second. We didn't have *any* money. It didn't take him long to admit that we had no other choice.

For the next couple of nights, we used the laundry room outlets for our source of electricity. Although we did pay the light bill when Tommy got paid, our drugging and boozing forced us to take advantage of laundry room electricity many more times. In fact, it became our fall back plan when we intentionally smoked and drank up all of the gas and light money. I went to the thrift shop and stocked up on extension cords so that whenever our lights got cut off, the house was full of cords. Each bedroom and bathroom had two extension cords into which all electrical items were plugged. The living room and kitchen each had three. The numerous cords sprawled all over the house looked like piles of lil brown spider webs that haphazardly coiled into one long one leading out to the wash house.

It took a while for the neighbors to catch on to what we were doing. Once they did, they kept quiet and like good neighbors minded their own business. No one ever complained to the owners and no one ever said a word to us about our 'secondary' electricity source. And I, of course, thought I was a genius!

My genius didn't last long. I thought I had all of my shit together, but my life was quickly spiraling down a slippery slide. The first push down the slide was bereavement leave, which I'd never heard of until I got to Dave's firm. I was walking the halls looking for something to do with my hands when I overheard two employees talking about another employee whose mother had died. It was during that discussion that I learned about bereavement leave – paid time off I could take whenever a relative died. The downside was that it only applied to close relatives: parents, grandparents, children, and siblings. The upside was there was no limit to the number of times an employee could take it. And if the deceased family member lived in another state, the employee was given even more time off for traveling. Of course, most people don't have such bad luck that they needed more than one stint of bereavement leave a year. But then again, I wasn't most people.

I immediately set a plan in motion to use my newly dis-covered information, though I promised myself to never kill off anyone I loved. So my mother, her mother, and Jr. were off-limits. As for 'father,' well, every birth certificate has a place for 'father,' never for 'daddy.' Since I loved my *daddy*, I couldn't kill him off, but my 'father' – the sperm donor – was open game. I decided to kill him first.

Within the next ten months, I missed around fifty-five days of work due to several serious 'illnesses' and a rash of out-of-state tragic deaths: I lost my father, his mother *and* father, and a brother – all of whom lived in the eastern portion of the country. Dave was always very understanding and com-passionate. He even gave me money to help with traveling expenses when my father and each of my grandparents died. Others in the firm, however, weren't so sympathetic. The secretaries, who in my opinion paid entirely too much attention to *my* attendance, complained about my excessive absenteeism. The partners, always cognizant of employee time off, resented me for taking so much paid time off. But what could the firm do – tell my family not to die?

At first, Dave tried to stick up for me. Whenever they pressured him to get rid of me, he fought on my behalf by insisting that they were mistaken about me and that I was a good worker when I was there. Then, to console them, he'd call me into his office and give me a 'straighten up and fly right' speech. He'd start out by saying how sorry he was for whatever tragedy I'd suffered that month. Then he'd go into a 'pep' talk by telling me how much the firm depended on me, how much *he* needed me to be present, and how difficult it was for him when I wasn't. He always looked so sincere during those speeches that I'd resolve to do better. And I really meant it. And for a couple of weeks, sometimes even months, I would do better. But then the boozing and drugging would take over, and my behavior would slack off again – to the point where either I was late every day or not there at all. Sometimes I offered an excuse – sickness, death in the family, stalled car – most times I didn't.

Finally, though, the firm had had enough. None of Dave's backing or persuasion could change their minds. They were adamant that I be put on probation. Dave, being the kind-hearted, compassionate soul that he was, insisted that he be the one to do it.

When he called me into his office to give me the news, he looked so bleak. He instructed me to sit down, shoved a document in front of me, and told me to read and sign it. I'd come to work exhausted from drinking and partying the night before. To 'pep' me up, I'd popped some black beauties and tooted a lil meth at lunch. During the meeting with Dave, the speed kicked in. My mind was racing a mile a minute. My eyes kept darting from side to side, and sweat was streaming down my face. My heart was pounding so fast and so hard, I was afraid it would jump out of my chest. I usually loved these physical effects of speed, but Dave looked serious. I knew I really needed to concentrate but the speed wouldn't allow me to. My eyes began darting about even faster. I couldn't keep them still enough, or focused enough, to read anything.

'I can't read this!' I exclaimed as I realized Dave was watching me suspiciously. 'I'm just too nervous!'

That explanation seemed acceptable to Dave. Always the understanding one, he took the paper from me and explained what it said. I was being put on a ninety-day probation. If I came in late for more than two consecutive days, and if I missed any days without a doctor's excuse, I'd be fired.

As serious as Dave looked and sounded when discussing the probation, I didn't take it seriously. He'd always protected me. I figured he'd continue to do the same. And I knew several crooked doctors. So getting a doctor's excuse would not be a problem. Still, I really liked Dave and didn't want to cause him any unnecessary pressure. So I promised him I would behave. And I really intended to try like hell to do so. There was no way I could have known of the horrible tragedy that lay ahead.

39

Dave was in such good shape because he was a triathlete. He'd begun competing in 1981 and had been in over twenty-four triathlons. During the first thirty days of the probation period, I did great. I came in on time (usually by a hair), and I didn't miss any work (though I did have to leave early a couple of times for 'doctor appointments'). Anyway, the firm seemed to be content with my minimal improvement.

Six weeks after being forced to put me on probation, Dave was training for the biking portion of an upcoming triathlon. He was riding his eighteen-speed road bike in the bike lane on Highway 101 in Cardiff-by-the-Sea, a small town in north San Diego County. Concentrating on his speed, Dave was going around twenty miles an hour. He was riding with traffic so he didn't see the car approaching behind him. Something distracted the driver who drifted into the bike lane and plowed into Dave.

Dave slid across the hood. His head hit the windshield on the passenger's side. His body went over the roof, across the trunk, and fell by the roadside just short of the bridge that crossed the lagoon outlet to the ocean.

Dave was rushed to the hospital. The doctors didn't know if he was going to make it. His condition was up in the air for weeks. His neck was broken at the C5-6 level and he had a compound fracture of his left leg. Luckily, he was wearing a helmet so there was minimal brain injury.

I got the news when I arrived at work the next day. I was hungover from my birthday celebration the night before and the black beauties I'd taken hadn't kicked in yet, so it took a moment for me to understand what the office manager was saying.

'What do you mean "hit"?' I snapped. My head was pounding, my stomach ached, and I felt like I had to barf. I was in no mood for games.

'He was riding his bike and was hit by a car. He's in intensive care. Cup, his neck is broken,' she replied softly.

I felt my legs go numb. I would have fallen to the floor, except she caught me and helped me to a chair. I put my head in my hands and started crying. The officer manager suggested maybe I should take the rest of the day off. No one *ever* had to tell me those words twice. I immediately left the office and went to the corner bar. It was one of my 'regular' spots when my speed supply got low, so the bartender knew me.

'Hey, Cup, your usual?' he asked as he began making the Long Island Iced Tea with no coke and no ice.

I couldn't respond. All I could do was cry. Not wanting to pry, he let me cry. And I cried and cried and cried. I cried for Dave and his family. I cried for me (I didn't have any money and didn't know how I was going to pay for those damn drinks!). The drunker I got, the more I cried. The drunker I got, the louder I cried. It wasn't very long before I was very drunk and wailing fiercely. Tears gushed down my face. Wide, black mascara streaks made my face look like I'd stuck it up against freshly painted bars, but had failed to see the 'wet paint' sign. Snot flowed out my nose with each wail and spit flew from my mouth with each yell. I'd begun to cuss out loud to no one in particular. I was cussing out the bastard who'd hit Dave. Luckily, it was early morning, so the bar was pretty much empty.

Still, the bartender was well aware of how I could be when I was drunk, so he let me sit and cuss and vent my grief. Cussing was one thing, but once I started throwing empty drink glasses (I *never* threw *full* glasses), he refused to serve me any more alcohol, telling me that I needed to go home. And he meant it too – that is, until I told him the whole tragic story. Feeling sorry for Dave (and for me), he agreed to keep the drinks coming, except he made me switch to vodka. He also said that having to deal with something like that, the drinks were on him.

After several more drinks, I was good and drunk. I decided to return to work (the alcohol told me to go back and see if I could be of help somehow). This time, though, instead of being irate about my being drunk during work hours, the firm seemed to understand. As she put me in a cab, the office manager told me they realized that I'd gotten drunk because I couldn't handle Dave's accident.

Dave's accident was tragic for everyone. And everyone seemed to expect me to take it hard. Now, it really wasn't my intention to take advantage of Dave's misfortune. But once I realized it provided me with the firm's understanding and, most important, acceptability of my drunkenness and tardiness, I went to work drunk and late for the next several weeks. At first, the firm put up with it, believing I was drinking my grief away. But after about a month, they decided I'd grieved enough. I was warned not to come to work drunk again.

'No problem,' I flippantly replied and switched back to speed.

The doctors determined that Dave would live, although he would be paralyzed from the neck down. He was in intensive care for three months. I wasn't able to visit him during this time because only close family was allowed into the intensive-care unit. So I just kept up my usual routine and waited. I hated going to work without Dave there. He was really the only person that liked me. Everyone else thought I was weird and mean. (Okay, I usually *was* mean. But I wasn't weird!) Not wanting to be at work made it easier not to show up. During the next four months, I called in sick at least fifteen times, killed off two relatives, and was late almost every other day. Still no one said anything. I figured that with Dave's tragedy and all, they'd forgotten I'd been put on probation. What I didn't know is that they were just giving me enough rope to let me hang myself.

After intensive care, Dave was moved to a rehabilitation facility. I went to visit him a few times. Each time I went, I was loaded, though he was too sedated to know it. But his wife and the hospital staff did. The nurses were sick of me. If I was speeding, I'd be rushing from room to room, talking a mile a minute to patients I didn't even know, fucking with the controls on their televisions or automatic beds. If I was drunk, I was loud, obnoxious, and staggering along the halls. If I was on downers, I cried the entire time I was there. I even cried at commercials. At the end of my third visit, his wife informed me that if I came back drunk or loaded, I would not be able to see Dave. I told her to 'kiss my ass' and stomped off.

I really tried not to get loaded the next time I went to visit Dave. But no matter how I tried to not drink or use, I couldn't. I don't know where I lost control. One day, I thought the booze and drugs were providing me with the peace and solitude I needed to get through the day. The next, they were working *against* me, flooding me with anxiety and depression and leaving me with increasingly severe hangovers. I didn't want to get drunk or loaded, but I couldn't stop. Try as I might to stay sober, I always ended up drunk. Dave's situation wouldn't, in fact *couldn't,* change that. Unsurprisingly, the next time I went to visit Dave I showed up drunk. His wife refused to let me in. I cussed everybody out and left. I wouldn't see or talk to Dave again for over twelve years.

It was inevitable that the firm's patience and sympathy would run out. Several months after Dave's accident, the firm notified me that I had two weeks to find another job. They said they weren't firing me; they were 'letting me go' because, with Dave gone, there wasn't enough work to justify keeping me around. I suspected what they really meant was that, with Dave gone, there wasn't enough *protection* to keep me around.

Even though I'd been with Dave's firm longer than I'd been at any job, I couldn't believe I was already being forced to look for another one. But I knew I had to find one. The only semblance of normalcy in my life was my job. All around me, friends were losing control of their drug use. But I kept myself fooled because I had a job and the uncanny ability to periodically 'fix up' my life to resemble normalcy. My life was a mess, but I refused to see it.

I just had to get another job.

40

Although I was sick of having to find yet another job, I got busy doing so. I got the paper and perused ad after endless ad trying to figure out which position I should apply for. I really wasn't too particular about where my next job would be. Nor was I ever concerned that I wouldn't get one. The shit on my résumé was just too damn good – it didn't *need* checking. Besides, I never had a problem *getting* a job; my problem was *keeping* one.

After four months of looking, my patience with a job search and checking ads started wearing thin. The meth I'd snorted earlier kicked in full swing, causing my eyes to move across the paper so fast, all of the ads began to blur into one. As the speed zoomed my heartbeat into overtime, I began breathing heavily and sweating profusely. I wasn't going to be able to sit still much longer.

Fuck it! I screamed to myself. I closed my eyes and slammed my finger into the paper. When I raised it, it was pointing to an ad placed by one of the oldest firms in San Diego. I decided that firm would do. I called the number and scheduled an interview for the following week.

You'd think that, as many job interviews as I'd been on, I would no longer be nervous about the process. But I was. I entered the building, frightened and doubtful as to whether I would actually be able to keep up the charade I'd been putting on for years.

I got into the elevator and pushed the round button marked 19. As the elevator jerked up toward the nineteenth floor, I considered my situation. I was applying for yet another job. I never seemed to be able to keep one longer than a year, most times even less. The gentle Voice that had been quiet for years now, speaking up only now and then to warn me not to go down a certain street or not to buy dope, now began to talk to me. It hinted that maybe things weren't as good as I'd been trying to convince myself they were.

Maybe, just maybe, the Voice calmly stated, *things are actually getting worse. And maybe,* just maybe, *it's time you thought about doing something about it.*

The elevator reached the nineteenth floor, and I stepped out into the pretty oak-paneled hallway that led from the elevators into the firm's reception area. I hardly noticed the expensive art that lined the walls, or the large fancy silver sign informing me that I was about to enter the office of 'the firm.'

Could the Voice be right? I asked myself as I stood in the center of the hall. I still didn't question where the Voice came from. Nor did I care. Since I was little, I just called it 'the Voice.' Besides, *who* was talking was never important to me – *what* it said usually was. I remained as still as a statue while I stood in the center of the hall staring down at the floor in deep, deep thought about the Voice's suggestion.

Naw, that's not it, I suddenly replied to myself.

Then what is *it?* the Voice asked.

I thought hard for another few minutes. Then it came to me. It was just nerves! That's all it was – nerves!

Gurl, you trippin'! I scolded myself. *You just need a lil somethin' to ease your nerves and you'll be all right. You are fine! Look at you!* You're on a job interview! *Do people with drug problems go on job interviews? Do people with booze problems change their speech?*

Fuck no! I yelled to myself.

Yup, that was it – nerves! I just needed to do something about my nerves. I asked the receptionist to show me to the bathroom.

Sitting on a toilet in one of the stalls, I tooted what was left of the meth I'd bought the night before and popped a black beauty, forcing it down my dry throat. (I no longer needed water to take pills. I could dry mouth *any* pill – upper or downer.) The meth seemed to instantly take effect. I sat and waited for the beauty to kick in.

I'd entered the bathroom scared, doubtful, unsure, and

pondering my life. A few minutes later, however, I emerged confident, secure about my life *and* my employability, and prepared to let the firm know that they should be happy I was even *in* their legal establishment.

How silly of me to think I could have a problem with anything!

I skipped up to the receptionist and proudly and loudly informed her that she could announce my arrival. Obviously not as impressed with me as *I* was, she nonchalantly buzzed the officer manager.

The office manager was a black chick named Rhonda. I was surprised to see a black woman managing such a large firm. She gave me the usual grimace as she scanned me up and down, but admitted that she was impressed with my résumé. That's when I decided she was cool.

She led me to the office of the attorney whom I'd be working for, a lawyer named Ken Rose. I was used to a large, pretty firm. So the walk down the corridor to the lawyer's office wasn't as impressive as it had been when I'd interviewed at Dave's firm.

As Rhonda guided me into the office, a tall handsome man stood up, gave me a firm handshake, and instructed me to sit down in one of the two chairs in front of his desk.

I sat in one of the chairs and Rhonda sat in the other. No one said a word as Ken looked over my résumé.

'I must tell you,' he stated, once he finally looked up, 'your résumé is quite impressive.'

Of course it is! I smugly said to myself. I'd gotten very good at forging résumés and was quite proud of my ability to do so.

'But,' Ken continued, 'I'm quite uncomfortable calling you "Cupcake".'

I didn't understand his hesitation. No one ever had a problem with my name – my attire, yes; my drinking, yes; my attitude while drinking, yes; my tardiness, yes; my absenteeism, yes. But never my name. I didn't know how to respond.

'You see,' he explained, 'I'm an employment lawyer. Do you know what that is?'

The quizzical look on my face told him I didn't.

'I represent employers in labor- and employment-related matters, like wrongful termination, sexual harassment, etc. So you can see the problem it might cause if a client hears me calling you 'Cupcake.' '

Personally, I still didn't see the problem. I wasn't sure of what 'sexual harassment' was. But, I surely knew what sex was, and during all of my years of 'business partners' up and down the California coast, no one had ever found my name to be a problem.

'Is there another name you go by?' he asked.

I was insulted by the question.

'Cupcake is my name!' I sternly replied.

'I didn't mean to offend you,' he calmly stated. 'But, 'Cupcake' will definitely take some getting used to. Do you have a middle name?'

Did I? I had to think about it for a moment. Then it came to me.

'La'Vette.' My stomach jumped and my forehead furrowed just at the mention of the name. I still hated it, and I still hated the sperm-donor-asshole who'd given it to me.

'Then, IF you're hired, that's what *I'll* call you.'

Well then, this sho in hell ain't gon' work! I told myself.

Ken changed the subject and began to discuss how impressed he was with my shorthand and typing speeds. I was enjoying his praise until he said that, if I was hired, he actually intended to use my shorthand skills.

Use *them*? I bolted straight up in my chair. No one ever 'used' my shorthand. All my previous employers just noticed it on the résumé and were impressed by the fact that it was there.

I hadn't used my shorthand in *years*! Sure, I still remembered some of it and could probably even take some stuff down. But there was no way in hell I would ever be able to transcribe what I'd written!

'You look surprised,' Ken stated as he sat staring at me suspiciously.

'Uh, y-y-yeah,' I stuttered.

Think fast, Cup. Think fast!

'It's just that my last two employers never used my shorthand, so I'm probably a little slow. But I've already signed up for a refresher class at a community college, so I'm sure my speed will increase quickly.'

Thank goodness for uppers. Not only did they make me move fast, they also helped me to *think* fast.

'That's fine,' he replied. 'I admire the fact that you took it upon yourself to take a class to improve your skills.'

Shit, I did too.

Obviously satisfied with the explanation, he sat back in his chair and continued going over my résumé.

'If you're hired, I'll give you a couple of months before I expect you to be able to take dictation at a decent speed. But I DO expect you to be able to take it.'

I got excited because he sounded as if he intended to hire me.

'One more thing,' he said.

Aw, shit. Here we go.

'I'll need to see some past performance reviews from prior employers. Can you get them?' he asked.

Is this dude serious? I asked myself. But the more pressing question was, *Could I?*

'S-s-s-ure,' I replied slowly. All the while my mind was racing.

The interview went on a few minutes more, then Ken stood up, letting me know it was over.

Rhonda grabbed my arm and led me to the door.

'Get us those reviews and we'll get back to you,' she said as I stepped into the elevator.

Once at home while smoking a joint and drinking bourbon, I pondered my situation. It seemed I had two problems. If I got the job, I'd have to find a night-time shorthand course. But first and foremost, I had to get my hands on some performance reviews.

I damn sure couldn't use any of my own.

I thought and thought and thought. Nothing came to me – at first. Then, just as I was getting ready to toot some meth, an idea did come. Actually, the higher I got and the more I thought about it, the solution became quite simple. I just hoped it would work.

The next day, I called my old friend Sara. She still worked in the vocational school's administration office. Just as I suspected, she confirmed that the school conducted annual reviews of its teachers. And she just *happened* to have the forms on her computer. She said that, for fifty dollars, she could get me four review forms.

Fifty bucks! Ouch! That was a half gram of coke!

Perceiving myself to be a clever businesswoman, I countered Sara's offer.

'How about twenty-five dollars for two?'

Being the good dope fiend that she was, and in need of money, she accepted.

With me standing over her shoulder, we created performance reviews. Of course, we had to make minor adjustments to some of the categories on the forms – like instead of 'interaction with students,' we changed it to 'interaction with others.' And instead of 'ability to encourage students to learn,' we changed it to 'ambitious and quick to learn.' Soon, we'd properly fixed all of the categories.

Because the rest of the form needed to be filled out by hand, I no longer needed Sara's computer skills. Her job was done. I paid her her money and left. I did the rest of the job at home since the only thing left was to complete my 'ratings.' Each category required the 'employee' to be rated from one to ten, with ten being the highest. Not wanting to brag on myself too much, I went down each form and inserted a mixture of nines and tens. I signed Dave's name to one. Then, so both forms would not have identical penmanship, I had one of the partiers sign Jack's name to the other. When I was done, I admired my work. Just as I'd done with my résumés, they looked authentic and credible.

'Damn, I'm good!' I said as I patted myself on the back and took a swig off a 40 of Schlitz Malt Liquor. It felt good going down as a chaser for the bourbon, which was burning my throat.

'You sure the fuck are!' the partier who'd signed Jack's name shouted as he took a long hit off a joint.

I loved impressing my party friends. It always felt g___ __o amaze the lil people.

A couple of days later, I dropped off the review___ ___ who I assume gave them to Ken. Two week___ ___ called and offered me the job.

I didn't say anything at first. I was th___ ___ should accept or not, especially know___ being called 'La'Vette' all day, eve___

Sensing my hesitation, Rho___

'Oh, and we're willing to pay you two dollars more an hour than you currently make.'

That instantly removed all hesitation.

'When can I start?' I immediately asked.

We agreed I'd start in two weeks – and that only Ken would call me La'Vette. I never even returned to Dave's firm. I called them on the phone, told them I quit, and instructed them to mail me my final check.

'What "final" check?' Sandy asked. She seemed extremely aggravated by the question. Sandy was in the human-resources department and in charge of vacation and sick-leave benefits. We never got along, especially since she constantly complained about my missing so much time from work – time she *swore* I never had on the books. She was such a bitch. I hated her.

'You're ten days in the hole!' she yelled.

'What's that mean?' I yelled back. I started to add 'bitch' to the end of the question, but decided I probably shouldn't piss her off *before* I'd gotten my money.

'It means you've already taken vacation and sick days that you didn't have on the books.'

'So?'

'So, YOU owe US money!' she snapped. 'I don't know why they kept you around this long.' She continued ranting on and on about how I'd taken advantage of the system and how it wasn't fair to the other employees and how I should be reported to the 'proper authorities.'

I wasn't in the mood to hear her shit. Anyway, it wasn't MY fault the other employees were too stupid to take advantage of leave policies. I mean, hell, that is why it's called 'LEAVE'! Besides, her blabbering was fucking up my high, and since it was obvious that she wasn't gon' give me any money, I could dispense with the pleasantries.

'Fuck you – bitch!' I yelled, and slammed down the phone.

I never saw anyone from there again. I didn't care. *Good riddance!* was my attitude. I was on to bigger, better, and higher-paying things.

The following week, Tommy got good news too. Through a ⌐kup with a fellow partier, he'd landed a good job delivering ⌐or a major department store. On top of finding a job, he'd gotten one that paid more money and had opportunity for advancement. (Of course, we didn't give a fuck about any advancement. All we cared about was more money.)

We were back on top. That weekend, we celebrated our new jobs and unexpected higher salaries by charging new furniture, housewares, pictures, and even some new clothes. For the first time in a long time, we fixed up everything – including ourselves – really nice and pretty. So we ran up the charge cards, swore off crack, and vowed to do only 'good' drugs: coke, meth, weed, pills, booze, and of course, PCP – at least, for me – every now and then. As usual, we charged the stuff with honest intentions of paying for it (despite the fact some of the cards were obtained using aliases). We planned to use the higher salaries to pay bills and get our lives in order.

I hated working for Ken at first, and he wasn't so happy about it either, though he continued to demonstrate extreme patience – most likely because he was well aware of the legal-secretary shortage. Still, it was immediately obvious that my knowledge of court rules was a little lacking. I gave him the story about a prior head injury that caused periodic memory loss.

'Well, you've been a legal secretary for years now. How have you *been* managing with your "bad" memory?' he asked suspiciously. I explained how previous employers allowed me to supplement my memory by writing things down on Post-its. 'Well, did you bring those Post-its WITH YOU?' he snapped.

I explained that I hadn't because I was unsure of how he would respond to a bunch of Post-its stuck all over my desk.

'Whatever it takes!' he yelled. 'Do whatever it takes!'

I did. And so did the firm, by assigning one of the more experienced legal secretaries to assist me in 'learning the ropes.' The woman named Maria was an older white lady. As she taught me the firm's policies and procedures, and 'refreshed' me about court rules, I made notes on little yellow Post-its. During our first session, we went through an entire packet of Post-its. It wasn't long before my desk, ledge, and entire cubicle were covered with Post-its.

Ken also expected me to work way more than any other boss. Even though the firm had a full-time receptionist, Ken required me to answer all of his incoming calls and place all of his

333

outgoing ones. At first I was nervous about having to have such extensive phone interaction, fearing I'd have periodic slips of slang. And I also had to watch *how* I talked, since I had a habit of talking loud – very loud – partly because my voice was just naturally loud, but mostly because I spent so much time partying where there was loud-playing music.

While I worried about speaking softly and properly, Ken worried about how his clients would react to my name – especially since, when making his outgoing calls, I'd have to state my name and on whose behalf I was placing the call. I told Ken that I understood why he couldn't call me Cupcake, so I was willing to compromise and allow him to call me La'Vette. But, no one else could refer to me by that name. I didn't go into specifics as to why; I just determinedly stated that I disliked the name. Seeing my seriousness about the issue, we agreed that only he would use La'Vette. I would be introduced to everyone else as Cupcake. At first, people were a little taken aback when I said 'Cupcake,' often asking me to spell the name because they were unsure of what I said. But I was so friendly, courteous, and talkative, they usually responded positively. As callers slowly became used to it, my name wasn't much of a shocker anymore.

My nervousness quickly vanished, and I soon loved the phone contact because when speeding I loved to run my mouth; and talking to opposing counsel and to clients provided me the regular opportunity to do so. My conversations were unusually uninhibited, since I was unaware of the unspoken rule that a secretary was supposed to be reserved or conservative when talking on the phone. I talked to everyone who called – about everything and anything. I'd regularly ask about their well-being, their families, what they had planned for the weekend, or anything else that happened to be on my mind at the time. Although they may have been initially surprised by my talkativeness, soon people actually started chatting with me for a little while before asking to be put through to Ken. It didn't take long before I'd developed a great rapport with everyone who called. As caller after caller began telling Ken how terrific I was and how much they enjoyed talking to me, his discomfort about my name diminished.

Ken really liked the fact that I typed so fast. What he didn't know was that coke, crystal, and other uppers provided me with incredible typing speed. On top of that, the extensive typing that had been required when I was a word processor had provided me the essential practice to improve my accuracy.

Shorthand was another story. I wasn't fast or accurate. So shortly after starting work with Ken, I started taking a class at night school. I loved that shorthand class and immediately remembered why I'd picked it up so easily in the first place: it was a great way to tweak. And Ken was impressed that I had signed up for a refresher class at night. He saw it as true dedication and commitment to my job (I tried to keep a straight face when he said that). Daddy and Jr. were also happy that I was taking a night class. I didn't tell them it was only a short-hand class and that it wasn't for credit; I just told them that I was going to school at night. Still, they were proud of my 'efforts' to better my life and viewed my night class as a sign that I was really trying to get myself together.

I did too.

I was drinking and using way more than when I'd taken shorthand at the vocational college, so I was having a hard time remembering all the symbols. To rectify this, I made up a few of my own. By the end of the class, using a combination of official shorthand symbols and those I'd created, my speed greatly improved. Soon, I actually began to truly enjoy working for Ken because between running my mouth a mile a minute on the phone, taking shorthand, and typing, I had plenty to tweak with all day. And the extra responsibility and higher pay further solidified my belief that I had my shit together.

Ken's clients were constantly telling him how friendly and polite I was and how much they liked me; and he observed the effort I put into trying to be a good secretary. All of these factors combined caused him to like me even more – which is probably why he stood up for me when the complaints started rolling in. Almost immediately, the other secretaries began to complain about me. They nagged Rhonda, the other lawyers, Ken, and anyone else who would listen.

They started with my attire. While I was working for Jack's firm, I'd trimmed down wearing miniskirts and halter tops. But this time it wasn't my *style* of clothes that was being criticized, but rather their condition: most times they were dirty, but not filthy. Sometimes they were wrinkled and disheveled, but at least they matched.

Then, they complained about my hygiene – or lack thereof – I never brushed my teeth (hell, they were crooked and ugly; I thought people brushed only pretty teeth); I came to work with sleep and other sticky gook in my eyes (if I had even slept the night before); and rarely combed my frenzied, unkempt hair (I'd justify it by saying I was going for the 'natural' look; problem was, there was nothing 'natural' about my uncombed hair). But hell, no one told me that good hygiene was a requirement for working. And my attitude was if you didn't like my breath, my unwashed face, or my tousled hair, stay the fuck away from me – no problem.

They also made a ruckus about my total lack of work ethic. Though I hadn't yet gotten into my usual habitual absences, I was late every day.

Y'all oughta be happy I'm even HERE! I'd grumble to myself as I stumbled in twenty to thirty minutes late.

As I tottered past the other secretaries, they'd frown at me with *You're late again* glaring in their eyes. All of the secretaries, that is, except Maria, the woman who'd been assigned to teach me the ropes. She always seemed to be glad just to see me. No matter how late I came in, she greeted with me a wide, warm smile. It seemed liked the more negatively the other secretaries talked about and judged me, the more patience and kindness Maria showed me. I once asked her why she hadn't jumped on the 'Let's hate Cupcake' bandwagon. She stood for a moment pondering the question and then softly replied that 'God' had instructed her to love me. That's when I realized that Maria was nuts.

Still, the other secretaries nagged on. Next, they bitched about my cluttered work space. They complained about the number of lil yellow Post-its covering my cubicle; they nagged about the fact that my desk stayed cluttered with papers, that I was constantly disorganized, that my voice was too loud, and that I ate at my desk – and smacked my lips when I ate. (What they didn't realize, or know, was that I *had* to eat at my desk. Any money I got was seldom spent on food, so the snacks the firm supplied in the break rooms provided me breakfast and lunch every day. But I couldn't eat breakfast *before* work because I was usually late *to* work, which meant I didn't have time to eat it in the break room. And I couldn't eat during my lunch hour because I usually spent that time using or sleeping. So the only time I had to eat was at my desk).

At least Ken was pleased with me. He didn't seem to notice my unprofessional attire, my unusually loud voice, my noisy smacking, or my messy desk. All he seemed to care about was that I did what he asked and his clients loved me.

Meanwhile, Tommy was also doing really well at his new job. In addition to just being a deliveryman, the department store began teaching him how to drive their trucks – the big trucks – eighteen-wheelers. It seemed Tommy picked up the skills easily and quickly. His supervisor told him that if he continued to catch on like he did, he'd be able to obtain the special license in no time. The supervisor also told him that with that special license came even more money. That was all the incentive Tommy needed. Within a few months, he'd taken and passed the test and was no longer riding in the large moving trucks, but driving them – severely hungover or high as hell.

41

In my mind, every category of drug had a medicinal purpose, and I used them like medication. I would self-prescribe a fat blunt to relax me or increase my appetite (most times both). Speed gave me energy, a pep in my step, and a head rush that was out of this world. Alcohol gave me courage, made me dance like Michael Jackson, and in the wee hours of the morning was the only thing that could slow me down when hours of doing speed had sped me up too much. And downers calmed my sometimes uncontrollable anger and helped me sleep.

Every drug had its purpose, but if I had to pick a favorite, it would be crack. I loved everything about it: the smell, the texture of the small white rocks, the way the smoke curled up inside the glass pipe, and the feeling of that first hit. But that was the problem with crack: I was never able to regain the euphoria of the first hit. And worse still was the dreaded 'come-down.' Crack gave me such a feeling of ecstasy that coming down was like barreling down a ninety-degree slope at two hundred miles an hour – with no brakes. Losing the elation was so gloomy and miserably depressing, it was called 'crashing.' The compulsion to avoid crashing generated its own desperation: desperation to keep the intense high, desperation to keep the heart beating so fast that it felt like it was going to jump out of your chest, and desperation to maintain the astounding euphoric sensation. It is this extreme desperation that compels the most calm, passive, peaceful person to abruptly and unexpectedly turn into an aggressive, brutally violent criminal willing to do anything – rob, steal, and even kill – to keep from crashing. That is why it was such an expensive drug: I never wanted to come down. Never.

But I wasn't rich, so each time the money ran out, I was forced to crash. And it was during the crash that I had to face the financial damage I'd done during that run: spending the rent money, smoking up the phone bill that was already two months overdue, looking at spaces that used to hold something but were empty because we'd sold whatever had been there to the dope man or the pawnshop. And it was always during the crash that I'd swear off crack. I swore that that would be the last time I'd lose control. I swore to learn to control my smoking. I'd convince myself that the next time, I'd only do a hundred dollars and that would be it! And I meant it with every fiber of my soul.

As our crack use increased, we were forced to develop new ways to make money. Since dumping most of our party friends and vowing to generally hang with partiers who had jobs, I refused to do anything really illegal, which meant that burglaries were now out, though shoplifting remained open game. Problem with that was stores were getting smarter and installing cameras everywhere, so it wasn't as easy as it used to be. And although the working group was hauling in several paychecks, with all of us constantly smoking, we never had enough money or dope.

It's amazing how creative dope fiends can be. It didn't take me long before I discovered several hustles – furniture-rental centers and gift certificates – each of which came by mistake.

One day a doper had come to our house to party. Seeing that we were sitting on large sleeping bags thrown around the room, she told us about furniture-rental centers: places where you could actually go and rent furniture.

Tommy was hesitant at first. Always being the rational one, he pointed out that we were barely paying the bills we had, so maybe it wasn't a good idea to go creating more. Ignoring him, I wasted no time getting to the place the doper told us about. Sure enough, they rented us a houseful of furniture: living-room, bedroom, even dining-room sets. They were so impressed by our jobs and salaries, they even rented us a twenty-five-inch TV, a VCR, and a microwave.

When we had the stuff in the apartment, Tommy's hesitancy disappeared. Once again we knew we were 'coming up.' Surely this time it would stick because now we had stuff we didn't own, so we couldn't sell it – so I thought.

It turns out that the dope man even took rental furniture. I found that out by accident. We'd beeped Rafael, one of our dealers to bring over a '50-cent piece' (a half gram of crack). (Back then, once you became a 'regular customer,' the dealer would deliver. We'd just beep him on a pager and when he returned our call, we told him how much dope we wanted, which he'd bring over.) Problem this night was we were ten dollars short. I was reminding Rafael of what loyal customers we'd been and began begging him to give us a break. Ignoring my pleas, he looked around the room and suddenly said:

'I'll give you a hundred dollars' worth of dope for the TV.'

'A hundred bucks!' Tommy yelled. 'Man, that's a twenty-five-inch color! It's worth at least three hundred!'

'A hundred,' Rafael repeated slowly and firmly.

We'd been broke for several days. All I'd done was weed and booze. Although they were fine in a crunch, I was dying for a hit.

'Sell it to him!' I yelled. I really wanted to get high.

'Cup, it's not even *ours*!' Tommy yelled back. 'It's *rented*, remember?!'

I had forgotten. We'd had the stuff for less than two months, and I'd already forgotten it wasn't mine.

The room went silent for a moment, and then Rafael spoke, again in that low, firm voice. 'Man, that's not *my* problem.'

Shit, if he didn't mind if it was rented, *I* sure as hell didn't!

Rafael took the TV that night. And we got high that night.

The next night we sold the VCR and the microwave to him. Two days later we sold the whole living-room set to another dealer. The dining-room and bedroom sets were gone in the following weeks.

Of course we quit paying the furniture-rental bill. Shit, I figured I was justified in not paying for stuff I no longer had. The phone had gotten turned off, so we didn't have to worry about any harassing calls, and we ignored the 'final notice' threats we regularly received in the mail. Each time they caught me at work, I promised to send a payment in a few days. Of course I never did. Soon they just stopped calling. I don't know if they ever came to repossess the furniture because we were evicted shortly thereafter and were forced to move. Naturally, we didn't leave a forwarding address. In fact, we never left a forwarding address – either because we didn't want creditors and former landlords to find us, or, at the time of eviction, we didn't know where our next address would be. This time, it was both.

We did find another apartment, though. Vowing again to 'start over' and get our lives together, we went to a different rental place. Why they rented to us, I don't know. Whether the previous place had put anything on our credit reports, I had no idea. All I know is that, once we showed two recent check stubs, they rented us a TV, microwave, *and* VCR. We swore not to sell them this time. And we didn't – at first. Instead, I discovered the benefit of gift certificates. Again, by accident.

I'd gone to a department store and, using one of my numerous charge cards, charged a $50 gift certificate, which I made out to myself. My plan was to charge a $50 leather purse which I'd then sell to the dope man, or his woman, for $10 worth of dope (the dope man never paid full value for anything). When I went to pay for it, the clerk opened the cash register drawer to return the unused amount to me.

'You mean if I buy something for less than the amount of the gift certificate I get the difference in *cash*?!' I asked with total shock.

'Why yes,' she replied. She seemed surprised at my ignorance of gift certificates. As she continued counting the change, she asked 'Is there anything else I can do for you?'

Fuck yeah!!

My mind raced with ideas about what to do with the luck I'd just been handed. I immediately changed my mind about the purse. Hell, it cost too much.

'Uh. . . . yes.' I stammered. I was trying hard to contain my excitement and keep my composure. My eyes darted around the department looking for something small – something cheap. They quickly locked onto a $3.00 pair of earrings.

'I'll take these instead!' I yelped.

She gladly gave me the earrings and almost $46 in cash. I gladly got high.

Over the next several months I ran up thousands of dollars on the charge cards, solely on gift certificates. I'd charge a $100 gift certificate and then buy the cheapest item I could find.

341

I seemed to never run out of charge cards. Once I ran one up to its limit, I'd quit paying on it and open others using aliases, which allowed me to get even more cards. Whenever the dope man wouldn't buy my goods, I switched to pawnshops. Pawnshops took *anything* – furniture, clothing, jewelry – which allowed me to expand my hustle. Between the rental furniture, gift certificates, pawn shops, and full-time jobs, money was good – for a while. Sometimes I told Tommy about the extra money. Most times I didn't.

For a while I was able to keep a vow never to drink during the day. I wanted to make the job with Ken last. But as usual, I was only able to fake it for so long. It didn't take long for me to start calling in sick and killing off relatives so that I could take bereavement leave. My using was increasing exponentially. I was forced to revise my vow: now it was to never drink before noon because I began needing a drink or two in the morning to help steady my shaking hands and slow down my racing heart. After smoking crack or using various forms of speed all night, my heart would be beating so hard and so fast that it felt like it was going to (literally) explode. My eyes would be trying to see everything everywhere at once, and my body would be zooming. Because of these 'health reasons,' I allowed myself to drink in the mornings. And when I couldn't get away long enough to sneak a couple of drinks, I'd pop reds, T's, blues, or valium. Of course the downers and booze did what they were supposed to: calmed my body down, slowed my heart rate, and steadied my eyes. Problem was, they slowed everything down so much that I'd damn near fall asleep at my desk, in the bathroom, or wherever I happened to be when they kicked in. So to counter-act the booze I'd toot some crank or pop some beauties or yellow jackets at lunch. They lifted me up and gave me the oomph I needed to make it through the afternoon. It was an ingenious schedule.

The violence between Tommy and me was getting worse. The combination of mind-altering drugs and extreme insecurities was a dangerous one. The higher Tommy got, the more he became convinced that I was screwing around. And when he became insecure, he became violent.

He also became violent when he thought I'd hidden or stashed dope. He was usually right, but I never admitted it. He always forced me to be the one to go cop more dope. It would be three in the morning and I'd be the one that had to go re-up. I never realized how dangerous it was: a young woman alone in crack-infested territory in the wee hours of the morning. But I wasn't scared. Fear of physical harm never occurred to me. The only fear I had was of the police. I'd escaped jail all of my life and intended to continue to do so.

Once I copped the dope, I'd immediately cut off a small piece and stash it. Then I'd happily head home to get high with my husband. We'd get high and be happy – till the dope ran out. If we had more money or something to sell, I took off again to re-up. But once the money ran out, the arguing would start: who'd gotten the biggest pieces, who'd wasted more dope by inhaling wrong, or who'd hidden dope. Then the fighting would start. No matter how hard or how many times Tommy hit me, I'd never own up to the piece of rock stashed in my shoe, shirt, or panties. After kicking my ass, he'd crash. Once he crashed, I'd sneak into the bathroom, pull out the piece I'd hidden, and get high, laughing to myself at how I'd fooled him yet again.

Sometimes though, the fighting was not over drugs, but his insecurities, which were getting insanely out of hand. I still remember his craziest delusion. We'd moved yet again. This time we lived right across the street from a liquor store. It was a Friday night and I'd just gotten paid. Paydays were no big thing in our minds. The only thing different about them was that they guaranteed a get-high for the night – but only for the night. I'd leave work with a full paycheck and, by the next morning, wouldn't have enough left to make a twenty-cent phone call. But the night was early and we still had money, so the get-high was 'gettin' good.'

We'd run out of rubbing alcohol. We no longer used rum to burn the torch because it cost too much. Rubbing alcohol served the same purpose and was a third of the cost. Only problem was, it turned the pipe black. I hated black pipes because I couldn't see the smoke swirling inside. But we'd taken care of that problem because we no longer used glass pipes. They'd also become too expensive (though I loved watching the smoke curl and dance inside the pipe as I took a hit, once I realized that the less money we spent on paraphernalia, the more money we'd have for dope, I gladly gave it up). So we switched to metal car antennas. I don't know who discovered that those slim metal antennas were a perfect and cheap substitute for glass pipes: they were hollow so they smoked just like a pipe ('cept they got hot too fast); and the best part was that, unlike expensive glass pipes, they were free – you just snapped them off a car – *any* car, and there was an unlimited supply.

Anyway, we were on our third run of hundred-dollar rocks when Tommy announced that we were out of alcohol. He ran across the street to the store to get some more. What happened next is bewildering.

Our apartment complex was very small, and the units were very close to each other. They were so close that front doors were literally side by side. Our next door neighbor, Debra, 'entertained' a lot and always had a different guy visiting her. If a person wasn't careful, or wasn't paying close attention, he could easily think that someone who was coming out of Debra's apartment was coming out of ours instead. That's exactly what Tommy thought as he returned from the store and saw a man leaving Debra's apartment. The dope convinced Tommy that the man was leaving our place.

'You got that nigga in here?' he hollered as he came bolting through the door, slamming the small brown bag containing the alcohol on the table. Or what we used as a table. We'd recently sold our dining-room set, so the table was just a card table with two folding chairs. I didn't care. It did its job – it held the mirror, which held the dope.

The whole five minutes he'd been gone, I was on the floor on my hands and knees searching for lost rocks. (I called it 'cleaning the carpet.' For some reason, I believed – or rather hoped – that during the night, I'd spilled some crumbs onto the floor. So once the dope was gone, or in between hits, I'd get down on the floor on all fours and literally pick at anything in hopes of finding a rock. I'd be down there for hours, sweating, eyes dilated enormously, in a crack-induced trance, picking at the carpet. I never found anything, but that never stopped me from looking.)

Tommy's yelling startled me out of my trance. I had dope but, without a torch, had no way to smoke it. Needless to say, I'd become extremely antsy while waiting on him to return with the

344

alcohol so I could resume smoking. I was in no mood for his shit.

'What the hell are you talking about?' I snapped as I jumped to my feet and reached for the alcohol.

'I saw that nigga come out of here. You snuck him in here and fucked him, didn't you?'

This nigga's trippin'! I told myself. How in the hell could I have called a guy, sneaked him in, and fucked in the five minutes it took Tommy to go to the store?

'Nigga, you trippin',' I nonchalantly responded as I began wrapping a piece of cotton around the pliers to form a torch. I was so focused on the torch, I didn't see the punch coming.

Pow! He punched me in the arm. I, being the Gangsta I was, stood up and swung back. We'd fought for only a few seconds when I realized I was losing. I decided a good run was better than a bad stand any day. I bolted for the door, screaming at the top of my lungs, with Tommy quick on my heels.

Our neighbors were used to the fighting, screaming, and sounds of smashing furniture. That night was no different. So they reacted as they normally did – ignored us. One of them did shout for us to 'shut the fuck up!'

Ignoring the irate neighbor, I ran down the stairs two at a time and headed straight for the iron gate that guarded the entrance to the complex. Normally, I was glad for that gate because without a key, a person had to be buzzed in. However, now that I needed to get *out* really, really fast, the damn thing was in my fucking way. Still traveling at full speed, I reached for the knob but I was too high to be able to perform the required coordination of pushing the gate and turning the handle at the same time. So instead of going *through* the gate, I clumsily smashed my body into it.

'Shit!' I screamed as the coldness of the metal slammed through my body.

I was struggling to get the gate open when Tommy came running up behind me.

'Bitch!'

He grabbed me by my hair. Luckily for me I didn't take care of my hair, so it was constantly breaking off at uneven lengths. Unfortunately for Tommy, he grabbed at a short portion and my head easily slipped through his hands. Realizing he'd missed, and I had another chance, I continued struggling with the metal knob. I couldn't believe how much trouble I was having turning and pushing at the same time.

'Damn you!' I screamed to the gate, hoping that cussing it out would somehow force it open.

This time, Tommy decided to go for my head instead of my hair. I had never realized how large his hands were. His right hand cupped the back of my head easily. Once he knew he had a good grip, he began squeezing his hand around my head.

What's he gon' do? I asked myself. *Squeeze my head till it pops?* I laughed to myself at the vision that appeared in my mind: some horror flick with 'Jason' or 'Michael Myers' squeezing their victims' heads till the eyes popped out, and blood, veins, and other carnage gushed every which way. But I didn't have time to enjoy my comedic imagination. I had to save my life.

'You want that nigga?' he yelled. His hand squeezed around my head even tighter. The pressure was starting to mess up my high and give me a headache.

'I *said* do you want that nigga?' he asked again, this time through clenched teeth. Before I could answer, he yanked my head back and with all his might *slammed* my face into the gate, which swung open from the impact.

Oh, NOW the mothafucka opens!

Jets of pain, corresponding to each metal bar, shot through my face. Ignoring the pain, I dashed through the open gate and bolted down the street. Tommy started to run after me, but he was high too and his coordination was off. Instead of running through the open gate, he lost his balance and he fell face-first through it. I turned just in time to see his forehead smash into the ground.

'That's what you get, mothafucka!' I yelled. Wanting to enjoy his pain but unable to waste precious time, I turned and began to run with all my might.

'Ughhhhhhh,' I heard him moan in frustration and pain. He didn't stay down long. He got up and continued after me.

Tommy was fast, but not fast enough. He lost me as I jumped into the backyard of a neighboring house. Determined to give me an ass-whuppin', he started roaming through the neighborhood, screaming my name at the top of his lungs. From the faraway sound of his voice, I knew he wasn't close. So I doubled back to our apartment, ran up the stairs, bolted through the door, and dialed 911. (Funny how the tables turned. There was a time when I *hated* the police. I hated them in my house and in my business. But the violence in my marriage had escalated to such a degree that I'd begun calling them, *begging* them, to come to my house and get in my business!)

'Nine-one-one emergency,' a female operator said casually.

'This is Cupcake Brown.' Huff, huff. I was so out of breath I was having trouble talking. 'Send the police!' Huff, huff. 'My husband's trying to kill me!'

Using the same casual voice, the operator began asking a bunch of questions like 'Is there a gun in the house?'; 'Does he have any weapons on him?' I didn't have time to answer a bunch of fucking questions. But I needed help, so I tried to answer them quickly, all the while watching the door, afraid that Tommy would come busting through at any moment.

'No. No.' Finally, she'd worked my last nerve. 'Just git me some fuckin' help!' I yelled and slammed down the phone. My face was killing me. I reached up to feel my nose, which felt broken. It wasn't. Luckily, when Tommy smashed my face into the gate, my nose went *in between* the bars. If it had hit a bar head-on, it would surely have broken my nose.

At that moment, Daddy came out of his room. My relationship with Daddy had long since changed. We didn't talk the way we used to. And although he lived with us, he rarely came out of his room when Tommy and I were home. At the time I thought he didn't come out because he usually had some ho in there with him. But years later he told me he stayed in his room because he didn't want to see us fight or he didn't want to see us getting high. And we were always doing one or the other.

For a few seconds, he just stood staring at me with a shocked expression, not saying a word. He later described to me what he saw at that moment. My chest was heaving up and down because I was out of breath. Each strand of my uncombed, tousled, jagged hair danced wildly in the air. My eyes had grown to the size of large marbles because of the crack, and I was sweating profusely. I hadn't bathed in two days, so I smelled funky. That funk, mixed with the tons of sweat leaking from every pore, caused an awful smell to emanate from my body. The look in Daddy's eyes changed from shock to disgust.

'Punkin,' he said, 'I'm sick of this shit! All y'all do is get high and fight! Get high and fight! Can't you two see what that shit is doing to your lives?'

How could he preach *at a time like this?* I was shocked at his notion that the situation was somehow caused by drugs.

'Daddy, how could you *say* such a thing! This has *nothing* to do with crack! Any *idiot* can see that this is all because of Tommy's insane jealousies and psychotic possessiveness!'

'Well, I don't give a damn if y'all kill each other!' He coolly turned and went back to his room. Right before slamming his door, he hollered, 'You'd better put that shit away fo the cops git here!'

I looked on the table and yelped at the small white rocks that were lying openly on the mirror. I didn't have time to trip with Daddy anymore. First, I had to stash the dope (in case the cops *did* come), and then I had to figure out an escape. I grabbed the mirror and cupping the several white rocks so they wouldn't spill, quickly slipped them oh-so-carefully into a kitchen cabinet. I turned my focus back to escape and began to consider my choices. Since our two-bedroom apartment was located on the second floor, there were only two ways out: the front door and a balcony off the master bedroom. I knew the front door was out, since Tommy would be charging through it any moment.

Could I jump off a second-floor balcony? I asked myself, sprinting toward our bedroom.

Sure you can! the crack I'd been smoking all night replied. *You know how to jump don'tcha? Just jump!*

Hell, it made sense to me. *Besides, the second floor wasn't that high! It wasn't like jumping from a high-rise . . .*

On my way to the bedroom, I caught a glimpse of myself in the bathroom mirror. My cheek was starting to bruise from its date with the gate. My lip had a small cut in it from which a trickle of blood ran down into my mouth. And though my nose wasn't broken, it hurt like hell. I reached up with my tongue and quickly licked the blood away. Ignoring the ghastly sight in the mirror, I ran through our bedroom and straight to the sliding glass doors that led out to the balcony. The cool night air felt good on my skin and especially cool on my lip, from which I could feel blood dripping again. I was trying to figure out where I should land when I heard a voice from the living room.

'Hello? San Diego Police. Is anyone home?'

Oh, good. I'm safe!

I ran into the living room to be met by two cops – one white and one Mexican. The Mexican was in the lead and had his gun drawn. Upon seeing me, he put it away. They knew I wasn't dangerous. Our house was on their regular beat, so they'd been there before because of our fighting. Actually, they knew Tommy and me by first names.

'Cupcake, you guys at it again?' the white one asked. Any other time, I'd have gotten smart. But this time I needed them.

'That mothafucka's crazy!' I screamed. That scream seemed to wake up my facial muscles that hadn't realized they'd hit the gate. Because my whole face started killing me.

The Mexican spoke this time. 'Okay, Cupcake, where is he?'

I told them I didn't know. That Tommy had taken off running. I pointed in the direction he'd run. After asking me if I wanted to press charges, they called a backup unit to help them look for him.

I was instructed not to move until they returned. And, I didn't – except for periodic trips to the bathroom to sneak hits and wipe my lip.

By the time the cops returned, I'd lost track of time. So I have no idea how long they were gone. Nor did I care because I was feeling pretty good, I had only one concern.

'Did y'all get that mothafucka?!'

Don't get me wrong. I really didn't care whether they got *him* or not. All I cared about was that they *kept him away* long enough for me to finish the dope I had left in the bathroom and the rock I had hidden in my shoe.

They had him, all right – in the hospital. Once they left the house, several cops began scanning the neighborhood looking for Tommy. They spotted him heading back toward the house. Upon seeing them, Tommy took off running. The cops took off after him. In an attempt to lose them (as I'd lost him), he jumped a fence. Problem was, it was one of those metal fences where the top of each pole ends in the shape of an arrowhead. Believing he could get high enough to clear the sharp points, he jumped. Unfortunately, he misjudged his landing and grazed an arrowhead, which punctured one of his lungs.

The cops told me which hospital he'd been taken to and gave me a number to call if I had any questions. I didn't.

I didn't go to the hospital that night and never gave Tommy a second thought. I stayed home and finished off the crack in the bathroom and in my shoe.

The next day I did go to the hospital to see Tommy. Not to see how he was doing, but to get some money. What little money we had was in his pocket when he hopped the fence. I was out of dope and needed that cash. We never discussed the fight that night. It was as if it never happened. The only topic of discussion was getting high – which is why Tommy refused to give me any money – he wanted me to wait until he was out so that we could get high together.

The problem with that was, he wasn't scheduled to be released for at least another week.

'Nigga, I ain't waitin' for you!' I yelled, horrified at the thought. There was *no way* I could wait a week! A day was pushing it. But a week? Never. I angrily informed him that if he didn't give me some money, I'd sell everything in the house. He didn't believe me. I left cussin'.

A few hours later Tommy called home and Daddy answered the phone. This is the conversation as Daddy later relayed it to me:

'Pops,' Tommy said, 'is Cup there?' Daddy told him he hadn't seen me since the fight the night before.

'Well, she told me that if I didn't give her any money she was going to sell the microwave.'

'Aw, she wouldn't do that,' Daddy replied. 'She was probably just blowing off steam.'

'Well, do me a favor. Go check and see if it's there.'

Daddy put down the phone. A few seconds later, Daddy hollered, 'Aw, shit!'

He returned to the phone and said, 'Yup, it's gone.'

'What about the stereo?'

Daddy went and checked the entertainment center, which was completely empty.

'Yup, it's gone. So is the TV and VCR.'

They talked for a little longer, but not about our drug use or our violent fights; Daddy knew broaching such subjects would be a losing battle. Instead, they engaged in small talk about Tommy's health and when he'd be coming home.

Later that day, when I returned home with a pocket full of dope I'd gotten in exchange for the electronics and the microwave, Daddy told me about his conversation with Tommy. My reaction was blasé. I felt no guilt about selling that stuff: not about the fact that it wasn't even ours (it was rented), nor about the fact that I smoked up all the dope bought with it by myself. Actually, I blamed Tommy. My thinking was that, if he had given me the money I demanded, I could have gotten high with *that*. Then we could've sold that stuff together – at another time when money was low. So see, it wasn't my fault that I did what I did. It was Tommy's. That was my thinking about all of the problems in my fucked-up life. They were somebody else's fault. It was *always* somebody else's fault. Always.

42

I was using more and more, drinking more and more, and working less and less. Ken was beginning to complain about my absenteeism, which had increased drastically: using bereavement leave, I was killing off relatives left and right; I was sick with some ailment several times a month; and I was late every day. When I was there, I wasn't worth a shit. I was either hungover, exhausted from days without sleep, or so buzzed on speed I didn't know (or care) which day it was. Though clients still loved me, my work quality and quantity plummeted. I was making a lot of mistakes: failing to file court documents, failing to send out mail on time, misfiling and misplacing documents. Luckily, nothing too major was ever done that couldn't be corrected. Ken, who didn't micromanage, was unaware of most of these fuckups. He still assumed I was a great secretary and that everything was being done correctly and on time. I didn't want to shatter his assumptions.

Keeping unfinished assignments from Ken was another story. One day, his son, Robert, provided me with a solution. Robert was the cutest little three-year-old I'd ever seen. He had big brown eyes, and short curly, curly brown hair. Robert wasn't tall enough to be seen over the ledges of the secretarial cubicles that lined the firm's hallways. But you didn't have to *see* Robert to know he was in the office. You could *hear* him as he went stomping by. Robert loved to run, and he ran everywhere he went. Whenever Ken brought him into the office, Robert would endlessly run up and down the hallways. But it wasn't just his looks that made him cute. Being only three and still learning to talk, he couldn't yet pronounce his 'r's' properly. So when asked his name, he'd look up with those big brown eyes, give you a wide grin with a few missing teeth, and say 'Wabert Wose!' It was cute and funny as hell. I loved hearing him say it and just couldn't get enough of it. So we'd spend all day with me saying, 'What's your name?' And him replying, and with a big grin, 'Wabert Wose!' I'd bust up laughing, which made him laugh.

One day Robert was running laps around the floor at top speed. On one of his laps, he stopped at my desk because my in-box caught his attention.

'What's this?' he asked, looking up at me with those big, beautiful brown eyes.

'That's my in-box,' I replied. 'That's where your daddy puts work he wants me to do.'

'Can I play with it?' he asked.

I thought about this for a moment. Whatever Robert played with, Robert lost, tore up, or destroyed.

'Sure you can, baby!' I exclaimed as I almost threw the stack of work at him. Robert snatched it and took off around the corner. When he returned a little while later, he was throwing shreds of paper in the air shouting, 'Popcorn! It's popcorn!' I had no idea what he meant. Nor did I care. What I *did* care about was that he'd gotten rid of my work. Of course, when Ken discovered what had happened, he was livid. But, shit, he couldn't get mad at me. It was his son! That incident took my and Robert's relationship to a whole new and wonderful level. Whenever he came into the office, I persuaded him to play with my in-box because, by his doing so, he got rid of assignments Ken had given me that I hadn't yet done; as opposed to letting him play with my out-box, which contained work I'd already completed. Ken was always pissed when this happened because he was the one who was forced to redo the work. He'd angrily admonish me not to let Robert play with my in-box. Of course, I played dumb and acted like I was unaware that Robert was anywhere near the damn thing. As Ken stomped off to his office to try to re-create the work Robert had destroyed, I'd sit smugly at my desk, tickled pink because I had more time to hide or fix all my other mistakes.

I was starting to feel the physical effects of using. Oh, they'd been fuckin' up my body for years. I was just starting to *feel* them. Like one day, I began sweating cocaine! No, I'm serious.

I was at my desk trying to figure out what I was *supposed* to be doing. Ken was standing behind me, looking through some file cabinets for something. All of a sudden, I started sweating profusely. Now, I was used to sweating (it was a side effect of speed), but this time I could actually *smell* cocaine in my sweat. It had that unique smell that crack has when the torch hits it and it begins to melt. Petrified, I looked around to see if Ken smelled it too. If he did, he didn't let on. He continued rummaging through the files, muttering about what bad shape they were in and how it was my responsibility to keep them up. I began sweating even more as my heart rate increased from the panic.

What should I do? I asked myself. I'd never encountered this situation before. My mind began racing with questions.

Will I start sweating bourbon or Long Island Iced Teas? What about acid or dust?

My fear turned to silent laughter at the thought. Then my laughter turned to innovation as I began to wonder if there was a way I could somehow save the 'coke sweat' and smoke it later.

Other physical things were happening to me. The days without eating and sleeping were starting to take a toll on my body. Popping speed during the day was no longer helping. One day I was so tired, I told the receptionist that I was going to spend my lunch hour napping in one of the empty offices. To prevent me from oversleeping, I asked her to wake me. I went into an empty office and passed out, spread-eagle, on the floor. When the receptionist tried to wake me, she was unable to. She shook me, yelled in my ear, pinched me, and even pulled my clothes and hair, but it was useless. I was dead to the world. Unfortunately, her dumb ass thought I was *really* dead and dialed 911. I awoke to find two paramedics walking around me, taking vitals.

'What's hap'nin'?' I sleepily asked. I was startled by their presence and scared on seeing several secretaries huddled in the doorway, staring at me with terrified looks on their faces. I later learned that while waiting for the paramedics, they too, *as a group,* had tried to awaken me, to no avail.

'What's the problem?' I asked again. I *felt* fine, except I was still dog-tired. I felt like I could sleep for days.

Ignoring me, the medics continued with their checks. Though they couldn't find anything wrong, they insisted I take a trip to the hospital. I refused to go with them right then, but promised to take myself in my own car. And I did. At the hospital, numerous tests were run. The only thing they could find was that I was hypoglycemic, which was explained to me as low blood sugar. The doctors accounted for my inability to waken with the explanation that blood-sugar levels could drop so low as to cause a person to become sort of comatose. They figured that's what had occurred to me. Personally, I didn't care what had happened. All I needed was a medical reason for it to take back to work, since I knew I couldn't tell them the truth – that I'd passed out because I hadn't slept in over two days from smoking crack at night and popping uppers during the day. 'Hypogl – *whatever*' sounded medical enough for me. So when I returned to work three days later (of course I milked the medical condition to the fullest) it was the excuse I gave and the excuse the firm bought, without question.

My excessive absenteeism continued causing problems. Rhonda, the office manager I'd interviewed with, left the firm. Her replacement was a tall white woman named Dorothy, who liked to rule with a strict hand. Dorothy believed in following the rules. Since I constantly broke all of the rules, she didn't like me and often complained to Ken about my attendance, attire, and attitude; she was furious that I was able to get away with so much. Ken tried to stand up for me, but it wasn't long before he too got fed up with my behavior. He put me on probation twice. Each time, I cleaned up my act for a while. But, as usual, I returned to my old ways.

My using caused me to be out all times of the night. On one such occasion, I was out copping a ten-dollar rock at around three-thirty in the morning. As I turned the corner from the dope spot, I was pulled over by the police. A short, stocky black cop walked up to my window and requested my driver's license and registration. He informed me that he'd pulled me over because I'd failed to yield the right-of-way. But I knew it was because he saw me leaving the dope street. As he turned to head back to his car, I noticed the name on his badge. A small gold cross was pinned next to his badge. The cross made me wonder if he was the cop known on the streets as 'Preacher.' Personally, I'd never met him before, but knew a few users who had dealt with him. He had a reputation as being nice – the type who said, 'Watch your head,' as he put you into the back of the squad car so you wouldn't bang it on the roof of the car (most cops were known to bang your head on purpose), or he would loosen handcuffs if someone complained that they were too tight (other cops were known to make them even tighter if you complained). He was also known as a righteous cop, a fair cop. I was hoping he was in a 'righteous' and 'fair' mood that night.

After confirming that I had a valid license and that my registration was current, he asked me if I wanted to 'take a little ride.' Now, although I'd never been beat up by cops myself, I had plenty of homies and knew many young black and Mexican boys who had. Their stories and experiences told me that when cops say that, they mean they're gon' take you somewhere and beat yo' ass. Thinking that's what this cop meant, I got scared and started sweating, stuttering, and shaking uncontrollably in my seat. My high was gone instantly. The cop must have recognized my fear. In an attempt to calm me down, he immediately promised that he wasn't going to hurt me, that he just wanted to 'talk business.' That calmed me, all right, because I knew what *that* meant.

Why not? I asked myself. I could use another 'business partner.' Especially since the two I had hadn't been around much lately, and *both* had failed to come to my rescue one night when I was almost arrested for drunk driving.

He instructed me to follow him. And I did for about a mile or so, when he pulled over.

What the fuck we doin' here? I asked myself. There was nothing around but a gas station and a bus stop with an old beat-up bench.

He got out of his car and told me to get out of mine. He walked over and sat on the bus-stop bench. As I got out and followed him, two thoughts went through my mind. The first was that it was pathetic that Tommy probably wasn't even worried about where I was. He couldn't be too worried, since he was always quick to send me out to dope spots at three and four in the morning to cop. Besides, as long as he had residue to smoke, he'd be fine. He wouldn't start to miss me till he was completely out and started Jonesing. My second thought was, *We gon' do it at the bus stop?* Usually, a cop wanted to be somewhere secluded or isolated.

'Come and sit down,' he beckoned me. I obeyed. All of a sudden memories of Mr Bassinet and 'cheerleading practice' entered my mind. It had been years since I'd thought of him or those horrible days. But, for some reason, they popped up. I felt the hair on the back of my neck rise.

I sat next to him, leaving a foot or so between us. He didn't ask me to move closer, and he didn't move or speak for almost ten minutes. He just sat there with his eyes closed, his head tilted back.

Maybe he wants me to make the first move, I told myself. *Hell, maybe he's crazy. Maybe he gon' kill yo' ass right here at this bus stop.*

Shut up! I screamed to myself. I had to shut my mind up because it was starting to freak me out.

I sat quietly and tried to keep my mind quiet.

Finally, he spoke.

'You know you don't belong out here.' His voice was quiet and calm, like he was talking to an old, dear friend.

'Now don't get me wrong,' he continued. 'Nobody *belongs* out here. But some people . . . well, they need to be here. They don't want anything better for themselves. They're too far gone. They don't *want* to come back.'

Come back from where? I wondered. I started to ask, but the earnest look on his face told me I should probably hold all questions for the moment.

'They rarely make it out. They don't even *want* out.'

Out of where? His ambiguity was starting to work my nerves. On top of that, I remembered that I had a ten-dollar rock in my sock. All of a sudden, his speech became very boring – and too damn lengthy.

Because his eyes were still closed and his face still pointed toward the sky, I knew he was unaware of my impatience. Without opening his eyes, he jabbed me in the chest with his finger as he continued, 'But *you,* you really don't belong here. There's something special about you. I can't put my finger on it, but I know that God's got a job for you.'

Aw, shit. Here we go with this 'God' shit.

'Now, I don't know you or anything about you.'

You got THAT shit right!

'But, God has told me that you've been through hell.'

What the fuck God doin' tellin' you my business. And while He was 'tellin','' why didn't He tell you that I hate people in my business!

'Yeah, you've been through a lot, all right. More than you should have for someone your age. Hell, for *any* age. But there's a reason you've gone through what you have. Don't you see? Everybody isn't strong enough to overcome that kind of stuff. But you are. You've survived!' For the first time since sitting on the bench, he moved. His eyes flew open, and like a shot he slid over to me and grabbed me by my arms. He began shaking me as if to make me understand. His fingers wound tightly around my arms. His eyes had an intensely crazy stare. All of a sudden, a tear began to roll down his right check. That's when I realized he actually looked, well, *serious.*

Okay, he's definitely nuts. Just play along. Nod at the appropriate times and hope you get the fuck out of here alive.

'Uh-huh,' I said, all the while slowly wriggling my body in an effort to try to ease the pressure his fingers were putting on my arms. If he noticed my movement, he didn't let on. He didn't ease his grip. And he didn't let go.

'Listen to me!' He was now talking through clenched teeth. 'You of all people don't belong here! You've got to get out! You've got to do what you were put here to do!' He was so intense.

'Okay, I will,' I answered softly.

'But it will get worse before it gets better. And you will go down. Fast. Very fast. But don't worry. It's all part of the plan.' He paused for a moment, giving me more time to think.

What fucking plan? I wanted to scream at him. *There IS no fucking plan!* As usual, the mention of God had pissed me off and got my mind to going.

'Yup, you *will* go down. You will go *underneath* the bottom. So far beneath that it will seem there's no way up.'

Was this supposed to be a pep *talk?*

'But that's when God will step in. And *if you let Him,* not only will He bring you up, but He will propel you to unimaginable heights. He will take you to such triumphs that no one – *not even you* – will be able to deny that it was Him.'

Finally, he let go of my arms. As he did so, his shoulders sagged and his hands heavily dropped into his lap, as if he were exhausted.

Nutso. Yup, this one's nuts.

'I know you think I'm crazy.' He was speaking quietly and slowly. 'I'm not. Just remember what I'm telling you here today, okay?' He looked up at me and seemed to be pleading with his eyes.

'O-okay,' I stammered.

'Remember it. Just *remember.*'

He stood up and began walking back to his car.

'That's it?' I yelled behind him. *No 'business'? No 'cheerleading practice'?*

'That's it,' he said. He got into his squad car and drove off.

I went home. When I walked in, Tommy started yelling and fussing about where I'd been and what nigga I'd been with. But when I told him he could have the whole ten-dollar rock to himself, he quit fussing and immediately starting smoking. I didn't want to smoke anymore that night. I was spooked thinking about what Preacher had said. I kept hearing his words over and over in my head, as if I were being forced to memorize them. No matter how I tried, I couldn't get what he said out of my mind. I started drinking gin hoping it would shut my head up. It took awhile, but finally I drank enough to enable me to pass out.

Although we would never again spend that much time together, I saw Preacher three more times during the next year when I'd been busted buying dope. On each occasion, he mysteriously showed up.

'I'll take care of this one,' he'd tell the other cops. If anyone balked, he'd pull the officer aside. Because the two of them would be at a distance and talking low, I never knew what he said. *Whatever* he told the other cop, he or she went for it. Then he'd cuff me and put me in the back of his car as if I were going to jail. But I never went to jail. Instead, he'd take me around the corner and let me out. As he took off the handcuffs, he'd lean over and whisper, 'Remember!' Then he'd get back in his car and take off. He never tried anything with me and never asked for anything.

He was actually starting to freak me out. So much so that jail was starting to sound pretty good as opposed to going with him. After the second time, I tried to convince the cops to just take me to jail. But whatever Preacher was telling them must've been compelling because they *insisted* that I go with him.

Actually, it was a good thing Preacher came into my life when he did. Because my other two cop 'business partners' just dropped out of sight. They never again showed up to 'take care of me' or to conduct 'business' with me.

One morning, Ken called the office and told me that his wife, who had been pregnant, had had a girl.

He said he was taking off work for a few days to help with the baby. Of course, I figured since *he* wasn't in the office, there was no sense in my being there either. So I also took off a couple of days, blaming it on a horrible cold. When he returned, Dorothy was waiting in his office. She angrily reminded him that I was on probation and that my recent time off had violated it. Still on cloud nine from the birth of his daughter, he waved her out of his office, instructing her to 'just forget about it.'

It worked for me. It pissed her off. As she stormed past my desk she growled, 'I'm watching you.'

You ought to be watching whoever gave you that fucked-up haircut! I wanted to scream back at her. But I decided to keep quiet. I couldn't keep the laughter in, though. I started cracking up.

Hearing my laughter, she stomped back to my desk with her hands on her hips.

'Is something funny?' she snapped.

'Nice haircut,' I said as I continued laughing. Unsure of whether it was an insult or not, she gave me a nasty look, spun on her heels, and walked away.

43

The physical effects of the drugs on my and Tommy's bodies were getting worse. Though dealers always used a number of things to cut dope with to increase the quantity, the main 'cutter' was laxative. Cooking the dope was *supposed* to remove all the impurities. Nevertheless, I think remnants of the laxatives remained, because it got to the point where whenever Tommy hit the pipe he had to do so sitting on the toilet because he couldn't control his bowels.

The physical effects on me were different, but no better. I'd lose control of all of my facial muscles. I couldn't keep my lips closed. They'd just hang open and I'd slobber and drool uncontrollably. My eyes, which would grow to the size of large olives, darted frantically from side to side, so much so that I'd often get a headache just from their rapid, frenzied, nonstop movement. Try as I might, I couldn't keep them still. Then I'd begin sweating so much that within a half hour of getting high, my clothes would be *completely* soaked.

There were also mental effects. For no particular reason, in between taking hits, I liked to make obscene phone calls or call strangers and cuss them out. I'd get the phone book and just start calling people. The problem was, most people didn't even know I was an obscene caller. Because of my uncontrollable lip muscles and constant drooling, all they heard was slurring, slobbering, and spitting. So instead of being insulted, most people just got pissed, cussed *me* out, and hung up.

And still, I got high. But I was no longer enjoying it. In fact, every day I *swore* I'd never get high again. Every day I swore I'd get my life together.

Tomorrow will be different, I'd tell myself. At the time, I believed it and I meant it. But with each 'tomorrow,' it was like my car had a mind of its own and it would drive straight to the dope man. Before I knew it, I'd be high – or drunk – again.

Tommy and I were so far gone on dope that we actually gave up a car simply because of gas. During one of our 'coming up' attempts, we'd purchased a second car: a 1986 Nissan Maxima. We were on our way to cop in the Maxima when it ran out of gas. Leaving it on the side of the road, we had Daddy pick us up in our other car and take us to get our dope. I had every intention of going back to get the Maxima. The problem was that every time I got gas money I had to choose between using it for gas or using it for dope. Each time, dope won. Before I knew it, days went by and we still hadn't returned for the Maxima. I never went back for it, actually. I guess somebody finally towed it. I didn't know and didn't care. We just showed our paycheck stubs to get another car. Because of our bad credit, it wasn't as nice. But I didn't need 'nice.' All I needed was a ride to the dope man.

I wasn't even getting 'high' anymore. No matter how much I smoked, popped, snorted, or drank, I couldn't get high. But I couldn't stop. I hated what it was doing to my body. But I couldn't stop. I hated what it was doing to my life. But I couldn't stop.

Nothing worked. Absolutely nothing.

So I began soliciting suggestions on how to control my drinking and using. Someone suggested that I switch from hard liquor to beer and wine only. That worked for a while. Problem was it took three times as much beer and wine to get the feeling hard liquor provided.

I did finally get some advice that pacified me, temporarily. One day while on a run I ran into Slim, one of daddy's former hos. I hadn't seen her since Daddy and I moved out of the Complex. Now, we were interacting as if we'd kept in touch all along. We spent a moment engaging in the usual small talk (like which dope spot gave the largest portions, who we'd each previously gotten bum shit from, who died, who was in jail). As we were preparing to go our separate ways, I asked her opinion about how to control using.

'Why?' she asked.

'Because I don't want to be a dope fiend,' I replied.

She put her finger to her chin, tilted her head to the side as if she was deep in thought. Suddenly she straightened her head, looked me directly in the eye, and calmly said, 'You ain't no dope fiend.'

'I'm not?'

'No. You don't slam anything, right. You just smoke and snort, don't cha?'

I nodded that I did.

'Then you ain't no "fiend." '

She seemed so sure of herself. I'd long since theorized that *real* dope fiends shot up. And now, here was a real dope fiend confirming that theory.

'Are you sure?' I asked.

'Long as you don't *slam,*' she continued, 'You'll be all right. But once you start slamming, you'll be a dope fiend *and* an addict. You'll be as fucked up as me.' She looked both serious and dismal as she stated the last sentence.

I thanked her and went on my way with my dope. What we'd failed to realize was that I was *already* fucked up like her: we were both alarmingly thin; we both were at the point where neither of us could stop; and most important, we both lived, ate, and breathed for dope. The only difference between me and her was *how* we did it.

Still, her explanation pacified me temporarily. But soon I couldn't deny the fact that I was getting worse. Much worse.

One day, Daddy and Jr. were discussing my and Tommy's drug problem and whether they could help us. Someone had told Jr. about a 12-step program geared especially toward cocaine addicts. Armed with the information about that program, Daddy and Jr. sat me and Tommy down and did what they said was called an 'intervention.'

'Sounds more like *meddlin'* to me,' I growled.

Ignoring my snide remark, they talked for more than an hour about how Tommy and I were heading for deep trouble with our drug use, that everybody (but us) knew we were hooked, and that we needed some serious help. Their badgering was getting on my nerves, so I allowed my mind to wander, thinking of how I could come up with some money to score. Tommy, on the other hand, was really listening to what they were saying. He even admitted that he wanted help, that he needed help.

Wimp!

'Cup.' Daddy turned to me. 'What about you? You know they say before getting help you have to admit you need it. Do you need it?' The room was silent as all three men stared at me, waiting for a response. I still thought that because I didn't slam I wasn't a dope fiend. Obviously, they weren't familiar with that rule. They were so pathetic. But I'd do anything to shut them up and end the intervention session. So I told them what they wanted to hear.

'Yeah, okay.'

That satisfied them. Using a meeting schedule Jr. had gotten from his friend, Daddy and Jr. found a meeting for us to attend. Believing it was better to separate us, Jr. went with Tommy and Daddy went with me.

Oh, great, I thought as Daddy drove to the meeting, *I've got to spend an hour with a bunch of fucking sicko dopers!*

The meeting was in the back of a recreation center located in a large park. At first we had trouble finding it. Personally, I wasn't *trying* to find it. But Daddy was. He kept stopping people and asking them if they knew where the 'cocaine meeting' was. I was so embarrassed.

'Daddy!' I yelled. 'Do you *have* to tell people what we're looking for?'

'Cup,' he snapped back, 'every day you buy dope like it ain't shit. When you go to cop, you don't care *who* sees you. When you sellin' your TV and shit, you don't care *who* sees you. And now that we're trying to save your life, you want to be incognito?'

'Let's get this over with,' I growled when we finally entered the meeting room. I couldn't wait for the fucking night to be over.

There were a variety of people in the room, various ages and races. They all looked normal. I don't know what I expected. I guess I expected the addicts I saw on the corner. You know – dirty, begging for money. I always loved to look down on those people and sometimes would even give them a nickel to make myself feel better. But none of the people in the room were dirty. In fact, some of them were well dressed. As we walked in, a tall black man approached us, introduced himself as Reggie, and asked if we were new.

Mind your fuckin' business! I screamed at him in my mind. *I don't want anyone talking to me. I don't need you people, and I don't want to get to know any of you – it ain't like we ever gon' see each other again!*

'Why, yes we are,' Daddy kindly replied. 'My name is Tim, but everybody calls me 'Pops.' This is my daughter—'

'Tina,' I interrupted. I didn't want that fool knowing my real name. Daddy looked at me with bewilderment, but kept silent.

'Well, welcome Pops and Tina,' Reggie said. He showed us where the coffee was and instructed us to have a seat.

The meeting was interesting. They read literature about the characteristics of cocaine addicts. How they spent all their money on it.

Yeah, that's me, I thought grudgingly.

How they couldn't stop using no matter how hard they tried.

Been there, done that.

How it destroyed relationships with family and friends.

What family? Those sorry mothafuckas . . .

How they would pick at the carpet looking and hoping for dope – which was never found, yet they'd stay down there for hours anyway.

Oh, yeah. Cleaning the carpet! I knew that one well.

It seemed that just about everything they read and said, I could relate to. But then one woman said something that made me realize I wasn't like them after all. She talked about how her using was so bad, it prevented her from being able to work. Well, *I* had a job! And not only did I have one, but I had a *good* one: I worked for a prestigious lawyer, at one of the oldest firms in San Diego, and I made good money! That was the distinction I needed. I was convinced that I couldn't possibly be one of them.

After the meeting, Reggie handed me a hardcover book with a blue-and-white cover. He said they called it the 'Big Book.' I had no idea know why, since it wasn't very big. Nor did I care. But before I could tell him so, he told me I should read it and come back to the meeting next week.

Don't count on it.

Daddy thanked him and we went on our way.

When we got home, Daddy, Tommy, and Jr. discussed their experiences at the meetings. I went into Tommy's and my bedroom to have a drink. I didn't care about Tommy and Jr.'s meeting. All I cared about was mine, and my meeting convinced me that I wasn't an addict.

Tommy quit using for one day. I guess something that was said in his meeting got him to thinking. He didn't think long, though, because when I came home with dope that night, he smoked it.

We never attended any more meetings, and Daddy and Jr. didn't try any more interventions. But you know, that 'Big Book' did come in handy. I discovered it provided a perfectly smooth, nonstick surface for cutting up my dope.

44

For the first time in my life, I stole from someone I loved.

Daddy's father died and he had to go to Tennessee for the funeral. As Tommy and I drove him to the airport, he informed us that he'd left five hundred dollars in an envelope under his bed. He said that the money was the result of a sympathy collection taken by his coworkers to help him with travel expenses. He told us that although he didn't take the money with him, he would definitely need it when he returned. He said he was telling us about it only because if something happened to him while he was gone he wanted us to know it was there. He made me promise I wouldn't touch it. I promised. And I meant it. I really did.

We dropped Daddy off at the airport. As he boarded his plane, I again promised not to touch it. Tommy and I left the airport and went home. As we entered the house, I, moving almost mechanically, walked into Daddy's room, located the envelope under his bed, and took fifty dollars.

'Let's go,' I told Tommy.

'Where we going?' he asked, truly surprised at my statement.

'To score.'

'With what? We don't have any money. I don't get paid till Thursday, and there's nothing in here left to sell.'

'I've got fifty dollars of Daddy's money,' I answered matter-of-factly.

'Cup! That's not our money. You promised him we wouldn't touch it.'

'Aw, come on, it's only fifty dollars! We'll put it back when you get paid.'

'Cup, that money is so your dad could go to his father's FUNERAL! God, woman. Have you no limits?'

'Fuck you, then,' I snapped. 'You'd better not ask me for a hit when I get back!' I walked out the door and headed for the car.

Tommy thought about it for a moment. Realizing that there was no way there would be dope in that house without his smoking it, he changed his mind. He sprinted up to the car just as I was getting ready to take off. He had a look of shame on his face. I felt as though I should console him about what we were about to do.

'We're only going to spend this fifty dollars,' I told him in an effort to make us both feel better. He readily agreed.

Before Daddy's plane landed in Tennessee, the envelope was empty.

When Daddy got home, I, sobbing terribly, told him what I'd done. Instead of being angry, he was heartbroken. He informed us that he was moving out; he couldn't live with us anymore. It was his turn to cry as he said that he couldn't watch us kill ourselves.

I really was sad to see Daddy go, though not for the reasons I should have been. I was sad because it was only because of him that most times Tommy and I made sure the lights stayed on and the rent got paid. Now that he was gone, we had no reason to even *try* to be responsible. The shit was bound to hit the fan.

A couple months after Daddy left, we smoked up the rent money and, as a result, got put out. My attitude was pretty much like, 'Fuck it.'

We got lucky and had to sleep in our ramshackle car for only two days before we found someone willing to rent to us. It was a dump, since, as our bad credit had caught up with us, our choices got worse. I didn't care. I was no longer picky. My motto was, 'Anything is better than the car.'

Ken had no idea about the insanity that was happening in my personal life. All he knew was that the competence of my work performance was decreasing while my absenteeism was increasing. I was again counseled about my attendance. I again promised to do better.

Shortly after we moved into the new apartment, I left Tommy. Not because of the violence, but because he was in my way. What'd I need him for? Not for protection. I mean, hell, he sent

368

me out alone in the wee hours of the morning to re-up. And definitely not for his money. The paychecks he brought in were next to *nothing*, since he was also missing tons of work and had no sick leave. No, I left him because he was smoking too much dope. I figured I could get higher by myself. The requirements for my minimum daily consumption of drugs and alcohol had increased drastically. Tommy's using was dipping into that minimum, so, like anything else that interfered with my using, he had to go.

Tommy wasn't letting go easily. Although he didn't hit me, he tried to scare and intimidate me into staying, even threatening to track me down and kill me. I ignored his threats. My mind was made up.

Once he realized that his physical violence and threats were futile, he tried a new tactic – he gave me an ultimatum.

'If you leave here, you leave with the clothes on your back.'

His announcement shocked me. I turned to look at him to see if he was serious. He stared at me with piercing eyes and an evil sneer. 'You take nothing, you hear me? Absolutely nothing goes with you. Nothing – including the car.'

I paused to look around the small, shabby apartment. It actually looked kind of nice because, once again, we'd 'come up' a little. We'd managed to get another department-store credit card and had used it to charge new furniture. But I knew that, although the place looked nice at the moment, it wouldn't be like that for long. Then my mind turned to the car. It was shabby, but it did run. I pondered my predicament for a moment.

'Fuck it,' I snapped as I turned to walk out the door. 'Keep the shit.'

I walked the few miles to Mona and James's and told them I'd left Tommy for good. I asked if I could move in with them just till I could get on my feet. At first they didn't believe I'd really left Tommy. Though I'd gone to their house before saying I'd left him, I always returned to him when he got paid. However, I'd never before said it was 'for good.' Those words, together with the determined look on my face must have convinced them that I was serious. They were hesitant for obvious reasons, but they were both well aware of my violent marriage and recognized my desperate need for a place to stay.

They excused themselves and went into their bedroom to discuss it. I couldn't understand what they were saying; all I could hear was a bunch of whispering.

After a few moments, they re-emerged. Mona said I could rent their spare room on three conditions. First, I had to agree to let them control my drinking.

'What do you mean?' I asked, truly ignorant to what they had in mind.

Mona explained that anyone who'd ever partied with me knew that I drank too much. And when I did, I got out of control. So as long as I lived with them, they would pour my drinks and they would determine when I'd had enough.

Yeah, right. I chuckled to myself. I had no problem with that condition because there was a simple solution: I'd just hide booze in my room.

'No problem,' I readily agreed.

Their second condition: no crack in the house. I could do any other drug, but no crack.

'You've got to be kidding!' I yelped, jumping to my feet. My mind start racing with arguments. *Shit, that's why I left Tommy – so I could smoke crack whenever, however, and as much as I wanted without interference, intrusion, or interruption!*

I tried to convince them that they should revise that condition. I suggested cutting out all the other drugs, and changing the 'no crack' rule to 'a few hits a week.' But they stood firm.

This second condition was too much. Believing it wouldn't work, I was getting ready to walk out and say 'fuck it.' Just as I got ready to tell them to forget it, my mind came up with a solution for that one too.

Calm down, girl. Just like you'll hide the booze in your room, hide the dope in there too!

I instantly calmed down and agreed.

Their third condition was the easiest. I had to keep a job and be working at all times.

I moved in. Because I'd left Tommy, taking nothing but the clothes on my back, Mona took me to a thrift shop and bought me some things to wear. Personally, I didn't care. People at my job were long used to me wearing the same things over and over, sometimes for several days in a row. The staff had given up complaining.

The hardest part about leaving Tommy was not having a car. Since he'd kept ours, I was forced to learn how to get around on the bus and to hitchhike. I quickly learned to prefer the latter because it was free and often provided a little money on the side.

'No one hitchhikes anymore!' Mona yelled in shock. She was on her way to the store when she passed me standing in the street with my thumb out. So, to prevent me from hitchhiking anymore (and possibly getting killed), she would often let me borrow her car, though I still had to take the bus to work. Which wasn't really a bad thing since a 'late bus' became a regular excuse for my tardiness.

Things at Mona's went well for a while. I'd drink with them and when they cut me off, I'd retire to my room and continue drinking there. Because I was alone in my room, there was no one to fight or cuss out; so I never got violent. I just drank till I passed out.

As for crack, that went well too – at first. Whenever I was home, if we weren't drinking, I spent most of my time in my room. So they thought nothing of it when I'd be in there for hours. And since they rarely came into my room, getting high in there was easy. I'd just put a towel under the door to prevent the smoke and smell from getting out. And voilà! I could smoke to my heart's content!

I still saw Tommy every now and then. He'd gotten evicted from the apartment because he'd smoked up the rent money. He stored everything in a friend's garage and, like me, was renting a room from friends. He still believed we could save our marriage and was always asking to see me. I always refused, unless he had some dope. So whenever he got some money, we'd meet up, get a cheap hotel room and get high. But as our high intensified, we'd start arguing, cussing, and fighting. By the time the money was gone, we'd be stomping off in opposite directions; but we never physically fought again.

Things at work were getting worse. Though I liked my job and really loved working for Ken, he was starting to discover the mistakes I'd hidden. And he was beginning to complain more and more about my behavior, work quality, and attendance. But he was the least of my worries.

It was taking record amounts of speed to be able to gather the energy I needed to make it through the day. It was taking more and more to get me high and the compulsion to use was

371

increasing. The problem was, my money supply stayed the same. Needless to say, it wasn't enough.

I was miserable. I couldn't get high and I couldn't quit, though I was desperate as ever to find a way to do so. One day while on an intense crash a solution came to mind: I could commit suicide.

Suicide? I asked myself. I'd never really thought about it before. *Could I really do it?*

The more I thought about it, the more it seemed to be the only rational answer. I couldn't stop using. I constantly felt that I was in an endless hell: If I wasn't high, I was depressed because I wasn't high. If I was high, I was depressed because I was high. Living had finally become a complete hell, maybe dying would be better. But how? I considered my options. I couldn't shoot myself because I wanted an open casket (hey, just because I was a dope fiend didn't mean I didn't have vanity). I thought about OD'ing, but quickly decided against it once I realized it would result in a wasted high (and I *never* wasted dope). I thought about cutting my wrists, but that seemed like such a wimpy way to go. (Though I hadn't banged in years, I still considered myself a Gangsta. And Gangstas weren't wimps.)

No guns, dope, or knives. What was left?

I'd need to find another way – a way that would make people feel sorry for me.

A few days later, as I made my way to a dope spot, I was still trying to figure out how to kill myself. As I'd come to that morning, I'd sworn off dope and alcohol, but as usual, as soon as I got off work, I was compelled to go by the dope man. I caught the bus to my favorite spot – one worked by a dealer I'd known for a while. I think that since I'd copped from him for some time and was one of his regulars, he sort of trusted me, because he left a few fifty-dollar rocks on the coffee table as he went to the back to get me the ten-dollar rock I'd come for. I looked at the rocks on the table and then looked down the hall in the direction he'd disappeared.

Should I take one? I asked myself.

Naw, take two! the dope seemed to be shouting to me.

I was well aware that I could get killed for stealing from a dope man, and in fact remembered the hit that had been put out on me years before for doing just that. But the dope was calling me, and I surely didn't have enough money to get a fifty-dollar rock. I looked down the hall again. Empty. I quickly reached over to the table and grabbed two rocks.

Where should I hide them? I asked myself in a panic. *In my drawers or in my shoe?* I couldn't decide. Figuring there were too many holes for the rocks to fall through if I put them in my drawers, I decided on the shoes. I bent over and quickly dropped them in. When the dope man returned, he handed me my rock. As he did so, he glanced over at the coffee table. I stood there, shifting from foot to foot, hoping he wouldn't notice the missing rocks. I turned toward the door, as if to leave.

BAM! He backhanded me. The blow knocked me into the wall five feet away.

'Where's my dope, bitch?' he yelled as he came after me. Ignoring the stinging in my face, I tried to run, but wasn't fast enough. He grabbed me by my head and slammed my face into the wall. I turned my head ever so slightly, so the impact missed my nose, but caught the entire left side of my face. I dropped to my knees from the pain. I was sure my cheekbone was broken.

Grabbing my hair and jerking my face up to his, he repeated his question through clenched teeth. 'Where's my dope, *bitch*?' I wasn't sure if his eyes were bloodshot from rage or getting high.

'I . . . I . . . I don't know what you're talking about!' I sobbed. My face hurt like hell.

I hope these damned tennis shoes stay on!

'Oh, you a smart-ass?!' He reached into the back of his pants and pulled out a .45 Magnum and placed it against my right temple.

'If you don't give me my dope, I'm going to blow yo' crack-ass up!' he hissed.

My mind was racing as to how to get out of this situation. Either way, I was dead. If I gave him the dope, that would be admitting stealing, and he'd kill me. If I continued to deny it, he'd beat me till he found it, and then he'd kill me. Then an idea hit me.

Maybe this is the way I should go! Instead of suicide, I could let him kill me. Then people would feel sorry for ME! I could go with dignity! In that split second, I thought about it and decided that letting *him* kill me would be the best way to go.

Fuck an open casket, I told myself. *In fact, keeping it closed will bring even MORE sympathy!*

'Go ahead,' I said softly, as I pressed my head against the gun.

The cold steel felt odd against my skin. 'Kill me. You'd be doing me a favor.'

He hesitated for a moment, unsure of what I'd said.

'What the fuck did you say?' he snapped, tightening his grip on the gun.

I repeated my request. I told him that I was so fucked up, I'd been contemplating suicide but couldn't figure out the best way to do it. So his killing me would be better than my doing it myself – and I'd die with sympathy.

For a few moments he said nothing. He looked at me in astonishment.

'Crazy bitch!' he screamed.

Then everything went black.

When I came to, it was still dark. I was lying behind a Dumpster. My whole body ached. There was an extremely intense pain coming from between my legs. That particular pain felt familiar, but I couldn't remember why. Then it came to me. Pete! I hadn't felt that kind of pain since being raped by Pete.

Have I been raped? I asked myself. I reached down and felt where my underwear should have been. They were ripped apart, but the elastic waistband was still intact.

I must have been raped. But by who? I had no idea. I couldn't remember where I'd been the night before, let alone with whom.

This must be some hangover, I told myself as I struggled to regain my memory. *You've had some bad ones before, but never like this!* Not only was my body aching, the pain between my legs was brutally throbbing and my head felt like it would explode.

What the fuck happened to my head? I asked myself as I reached up to rub my right temple, where it seemed to hurt the most. I didn't feel any blood, but it was tender to the touch. Still, my mind drew a blank.

Unable to answer my own questions, I decided to try to stand up. Unfortunately, my legs weren't quite ready to get up. They instantly buckled, forcing me to the ground with a thud. I decided to take a moment to get my thoughts together. I sat up, leaning my back against the Dumpster for support.

Where the fuck am I? I looked around in bewilderment. It took a moment, but then I recognized the street. I was in an area of San Diego called the Coast.

But how did I get here? Shit, I hated it when I couldn't remember the events of the night before. Though it happened all the time, I still hated it. I concentrated with all my might.

The coolness of the metal Dumpster felt good against my back. Then, like a flood, it all came back to me: copping the dope, stealing the dope, the gun to my head and . . . blackness.

He must have knocked me out.

'But I'm supposed to be dead!' I yelled out loud to no one in particular. The intense pain coming from every part of my body told me I was definitely alive. It also told me that screaming was a bad, and painful, idea.

Fuck! I yelled at myself. *You can't even get KILLED right!*

Disgusted with my failure at bringing about my death, I tried to stand again, this time using the rail of the Dumpster for support. My legs cooperated and I got to my feet. Pain shot through every inch of my body. I stood for a moment and made sure my legs wouldn't give way. Once I was sure they'd hold up, I began walking in the direction I thought was home. I'd taken only a few steps when I felt something inside my shoe. I reached down and, lo and behold, the two rocks were still there! All of a sudden, I felt better.

I felt so much better that I walked all the way home.

'Cup, you been out all night?' Mona asked in amazement when I walked through the door.

Ignoring her, I went straight to my room. Just before I closed the door she said, 'Don't go to sleep. You know you'll oversleep and you'll be late for work.'

Work!

Like a bullet, I shot out of the room. 'What day is it?' I frantically asked.

'It's Friday. Girl, you partied so hard, you done forgot what day it is?' She shook her head – though I wasn't sure if she did so in amazement or disgust.

I knew I couldn't go to work in the condition I was in. Besides, I had two rocks in my shoe! There was no way *in hell* I was going to work when there was dope left to be smoked! But I was on probation, so I needed a good excuse. I thought about it for a moment and then called Ken. I told him that I'd been vomiting and bleeding through the night and that I was going to the hospital for testing.

He seemed shocked at the symptoms and said he understood my need to go to the hospital right away. 'Well, take care of yourself, Cup,' he said before hanging up.

I went into my room and got high. Then, to be able to forget the shame from the night before and go to sleep, I got drunk.

I needed a disease. I'd told Ken I was going to the hospital with horrible symptoms. You can't have symptoms like that without having some kind of disease.

But which disease should I give myself?

I didn't know much about diseases. I knew about Alzheimer's. My grandmother had had that. I couldn't fake that. Besides, I was too young. I'd heard about strokes and heart attacks. But I knew I was too young to be able to fake those. Then I was watching television, and someone mentioned colon cancer.

That's what I'll have! I told myself as I jumped to my feet with excitement. *Colon cancer! That's gotta be good for . . . what . . . three, four days off?* It was an excellent plan.

As I prepared to go to work that following Monday, I realized that there was one problem with my plan. I had no idea where the colon was. I mean, I'd surely have to bind it or rub it when I went into Ken's office to give him a report on my condition. Sitting on the bus on the way to work, I realized this was a difficult obstacle.

Where IS the colon? I seriously had no clue.

Who would know? I looked around the bus to see who I could question. Everyone looked as if they didn't want to be bothered.

Fuck 'em, I told myself. *You don't need them. You're smart enough to figure this out on your own.* And I was.

Luckily, when I got in, Ken wasn't in the office yet and Dorothy had called in sick. I sat at my desk and continued contemplating. While thinking, I just happened to look at my typewriter. There was a key for the colon and the semicolon. I stared at the tiny image of the colon. Its shape was vertical – straight up and down. So I figured the colon in the body also had to be somewhere where it could sit vertically.

But where can anything sit vertically? I asked myself. I put my chin in my hand and began to think. Then it hit me.

The throat! I excitedly answered myself. *Of course! The*

colon HAS to be in the throat. It's the only place that can hold a vertical organ!

I was so proud of myself for having figured it out all on my own. I immediately reached into my bag and grabbed the scarf I'd brought along to wrap around the colon area once I'd figured out where it was. I quickly wrapped the scarf around my neck and got into character: I began coughing, put a sad, sick look on my face, and began rubbing the scarf.

That's what Ken saw when he came in about an hour later.

'How are you feeling, Cup?' he asked appearing genuinely concerned. I didn't respond, but motioned toward his office, signaling that I wanted to talk in private.

We went into his office where I explained that the diagnosis wasn't for sure yet, but they thought I had colon cancer. I rubbed my neck and coughed as I said 'colon cancer.' Ken asked a few more questions like, 'What are they going to do?'; 'When will they know for sure?' I told him I didn't know, but would let him know when I did.

'Well, take care of yourself,' he said. 'I need you around here.'

That was the end of it. He never asked me about the scarf around my neck or the cough. He never questioned why, if I had colon cancer, I was rubbing my neck.

Dorothy let me know that she had her doubts, but she knew better than to voice them to anyone other than me. To harass an employee with cancer would be going too far, and she knew it. So she kept her mouth shut.

Of course, I played the cancer out as long as I could; it afforded me at least a week and a half off with pay. Afterward, I told Ken the 'spots' were 'noncancerous.' He smiled, mumbled something about that being a 'good result,' and waved me out of his office. He never mentioned it again. And neither did I.

During the 'cancer' period, I was still trying to figure out a way to commit suicide. I was convinced more than ever that that was the only way out. I'd quit talking to Daddy and Jr. because all we did was argue: they fussed about how I was fucking up my life, and I wanted to know if they had any money I could borrow. In my mind, unless they had money to give, we had nothing to talk about.

Mona and James caught me hitting the pipe. They had suspected my breaking the rules for a few weeks. One night,

Mona decided to follow up on those suspicions and just busted into my room. When she came in, I was too busy loading a hit on the pipe to stop and act innocent, and too busy trying to get high to care about being caught. Of course, she was livid. She yelled and fussed about how they had agreed to let me stay with them because they were trying to help me out and how I was blatantly spitting in their faces for it. I was truly sorry for violating their trust and told them so. I put on my 'pathetic' face, bawled and cried, and explained to her that I was trying to stop but couldn't. I begged her to give me another chance. Feeling sorry for me, she agreed to let me stay, but warned me that no more rule infractions would be tolerated.

I was more convinced than ever that the only way out of my miserable life was suicide, but still wasn't sure how to do it. Then, as usual, I got a bright idea. One night while doing crank and drinking gin, I saw an AIDS TV special. The story featured people who had contracted the disease in various ways: a little boy who'd gotten it through a blood transfusion, an infant through his infected mother, a young woman who had gotten it from her husband who, unbeknownst to her, liked to have sex with other women; a teenage girl had gotten it from slamming, etc. Their stories touched me. They were people from all walks of life who, under various circumstances, had contracted a horrible disease for which there was no known cure. That night, before passing out drunk, I got an idea about how to end living in the hellhole that was my life.

Sure, I convinced myself, *people will feel sorry for you because there's no cure and it won't be your fault. That way, you can die with dignity.*

I had made up my mind about how I would die. I would get AIDS.

The TV show said you could get AIDS only by having unprotected sex with an infected person, through blood transfusions, or by using dirty needles. Deciding which method I'd use to get infected wasn't difficult. I didn't foresee any blood transfusions in my near future, and I definitely wasn't doing any slamming (only dope fiends did that). But sex, well, *that* was no problem. No problem at all.

I began picking up men. Any man. Every night, once I ran out

378

of whatever dope I'd been able to score, I went to a club, got drunk, and picked up a different guy. The TV show said I couldn't look at someone and tell whether he had AIDS, so I just picked the drunkest man in the place. I figured if he drank like me, he also used drugs like me. I'd sneak the guy into my room while Mona and James were asleep, then sneak him out before they awoke for work. I figured it would take three, four weeks tops, of trying for HIV before I'd get it.

During the fourth week of my 'suicide mission,' Mona caught me hitting the pipe for the third time. On previous occasions when I'd been caught, I was able to cry, moan, and whine my way out of getting thrown out. But she'd had it with me. I had to go. She was in anguish about having to throw me out, but she was also extremely angry and hurt that I had again violated house rules. Through tears, she screamed at me that, although she loved me, she couldn't, and indeed wouldn't, allow me to bring my destructive and detrimental behavior into her home. It was very apparent that no amount of my crying and snotting was going to make her change her mind this time. It was only Monday and normally I would have been broke, but I'd had a few 'business arrangements' the night before. As a result, I had money, a brand-new fifth of gin that was still in the paper sack, rocks on my mirror, and a rock in my pipe (I'd dropped it in just as Mona busted into my room). Unlike on previous occasions, when the threat of having no place to live made me regretful and remorseful, this time the money, the gin, and the dope made me cocky.

Fuck her, the gin told me. *You don't need her. She's just jealous.*

Convinced that *Mona* was my problem, and not wanting to stop getting high to fight with her, I left without making trouble.

'Aren't you going to take your things?' she asked. 'At least some clothes?' I was wearing only a thin light green tank top–style summer dress and some flat, enclosed fake-leather shoes. I told her I'd be back for my measly belongings in a few days. I had a fifth of gin in one hand, a pipe in the other, and rocks in my shoes. As far as I was concerned, I had everything I needed.

'You'll at least need a jacket,' she said as she went to the closet to get a coat. Before she returned, I was gone.

I began walking, to nowhere in particular because I was

unsure of where I was going. I just knew I had to get somewhere where I could drink and smoke in peace – without people fucking with me about how I was living my life.

It ain't like I'm not trying to do something about it, I angrily told myself. *I mean, I was trying to commit suicide and end it all. If only she'd've waited another week or so, I'd surely have gotten HIV and coulda been on my way outta here! Now what am I going to do?*

I was pissed that Mona had fucked up my plan. I continued walking, being careful not to crush the rocks between my toes, all the while fussing to myself and taking a swig of gin every now and then. I needed a place of peace. Where could I find peace? Then I remembered the Dumpster I'd been dumped behind the night I'd stolen from the dope man. It occurred to me that I'd been behind it, unconscious, for hours. I probably could have lain there for days without anyone finding me.

Remembering the Dumpster brought up no feelings about the rape. Like every other negative event in my life, I tossed it aside and kept going. The only thing on my mind was finding a nice, quiet, hidden place where I could do my dope and drink my drink. I decided the type of seclusion provided by the Dumpster would be an ideal place to get high, especially since no one looks for anyone in the trash.

I walked to the Dumpster, squatted down behind it, and began hitting the pipe, which was actually the metal antenna I'd broken off a parked car. The sole purpose for the gin was to pacify me when I was 'in between' hits and to stop my hands that sometimes shook uncontrollably in the mornings. So the gin was really just a filler. When out of dope or in between runs, I gulped gin. It no longer burned to drink alcohol without chasers or mixers. In fact, that's the only way I got any effect from booze – I had to drink a lot of it – *straight.*

I hadn't planned on being behind the Dumpster for longer than a couple of hours. I figured I'd finish the dope and then figure out what to do with my life. But I didn't do much figuring because each time I ran out of dope, the only thing on my mind was getting more. As usual, the compulsion to use was overpowering; I didn't try to fight it. I figured I was finally at the point of no return. The only thing on my mind was doing whatever it took to stay high. So I stayed behind the Dumpster, leaving only to turn a trick to get the money to buy more dope.

In my mind, however, I wasn't actually prostituting because I didn't stand on a corner; I did what I always did – stuck out my thumb to hitch a ride. Just as they had been when I was a child hitching up and down the California coast, rides were always looking for 'business arrangements.' After handling my business, I'd have the ride drop me off at the closest dope spot. I'd cop and then return to my Dumpster.

I didn't call work and let Ken know I wasn't coming back. I didn't call Daddy, Jr., or anyone else to let them know where I was. I didn't eat and I drank only booze. I no longer cared about anyone or anything – except getting high. All I did was get high, drink, and turn tricks; get high, drink, and turn tricks.

I was making my way to hitch another ride. I had no idea how many rides I'd had, nor did I care. The only thing on my mind was getting another one so I could get more money for dope. I was walking down the street in no particular direction. My left hand was stretched out into the street with my thumb stuck up, my right hand was swinging a half-full pint of gin. I didn't remember when my money had run so low that I had been forced to switch from fifths to pints. Personally, it didn't matter since I didn't care how big the bottle was, as long as there was something *in* it. As I walked, my head hung down, deep in thought as to where I'd cop my next rock. The last one had been kind of small. I wanted to go somewhere where they were givin' out fat ones! I walked past a gas station with a large plate-glass window. It was then that I just happened to look up. What I saw stopped me in my tracks.

My hair stood up on my head, each strand sprawled in its own haphazard direction. Staring at myself in the window's reflection, I realized I looked like Don King, though my hair was so outrageously wild that any comparison of me to Don King would have probably been considered an insult to *him*.

Compared to the rest of me, my hair actually looked *good*. My eyeballs were bloodshot and bulging; my sockets seemed to be sunk into my head. My lips were scabbed and burnt from the metal antenna I'd been using for a crack pipe. One of the scabs had bled. I guess I'd been picking at it. I swiped my tongue across my bottom lip in an attempt to wipe away the blood. But it had long since dried, so the odd-shaped brownish-red spot didn't come off.

The lime green dress I had on when I'd left Mona's was now soiled black with filth and grime. I was used to filth, but not that filthy. And I stank. A nasty, putrid smell consisting of days of body odor, garbage, sweat, and filth. I don't know why I'd never smelled myself before then. Maybe I hadn't *wanted* to smell it. But now the stench was overpowering. I was funky as hell.

But the rancid smell of my body is not what stunned me. What shocked me most was the thin figure in the window. I'd been extremely slim for years, but was always able to fool myself and others by wearing several layers of clothes and blaming my thinness on my metabolism. But there was no fooling the horrid reflection that was staring back at me. For the first time, I saw myself. I mean really *saw* myself: my arms looked like toothpicks, and my legs were as thin as rails. I slowly reached up and touched my arm, watching the reflection do the same thing. All I felt was *bone*. No meat. Just bone. Unconcerned about who was looking, I raised my dress to look at my stomach. I gasped at what I saw. I could literally see the bones that formed my ribs.

You look like one of those starving children in Africa, I told myself. Honestly, those children looked healthier than I did at that moment.

It was then I noticed that I didn't have on any shoes. I wracked my brain trying to remember what the hell happened to my shoes. I had no clue whether I'd lost them, sold them, walked out of them, or what. I couldn't remember the last time I'd eaten. I hadn't *wanted* to eat. Hadn't brushed my teeth or washed my ass. Hadn't combed my hair or changed my clothes. All I'd been doing was turning tricks, drinking, getting high, and living – no, *existing* – behind the Dumpster. I hadn't been living as a human. Shit, the thing staring back at me barely looked human. There was no more pretending – I'd become an animal.

Oh shit! I thought gloomily. *I'm dying. After all these years of drinking and using, you can't deny it anymore,* I fussed at myself. *Congratulations. You're literally smoking yourself to death.*

What was even worse than realizing that I was 'smoked out' was realizing that I was completely powerless to do anything about it. I felt absolutely hopeless. I was despondent, disconsolate, and in total despair.

But what could I do? I knew of no one who could help me. Daddy and Jr. had tried, but to no avail. I myself had tried. I'd tried working, marriage, moving to different apartments, moving to different areas, getting different friends, switching drugs, *alternating* drugs, vowing to never drink in the morning (which didn't last long), switching from beer to wine, switching from bourbon to brandy. The list was endless. Nothing could stop me from drinking and using. Nothing.

What about God? the Voice quietly asked.

God! I surprisingly replied. *Are you kidding me? How in the fuck am I gon' talk to God?*

Try, the Voice urged.

'Look at me!' I screamed out loud to the horrid reflection in the mirror. 'Look at me!' I screamed again through the tears that had begun streaming down my face. 'Look at me!' I yelled again as I glared with dismay at the thing in the window.

Try.

How do I talk to God?

I had no idea. I didn't know a single religious verse, prayer, or adage.

I stood there for a few moments contemplating my dilemma, when suddenly I remembered talking to Him when I'd gotten shot.

I didn't know any religious sayings then either, I wasn't any particular religion, and wasn't spiritual in the least; yet He still heard me, didn't He?

Suddenly, I was filled with hope. But my hope quickly vanished as I realized God was probably pissed at me.

Why? the Voice asked.

Because I didn't keep my part of the bargain, I replied.

I stood there for a few moments and thought about that conversation I'd had with God in the hospital so many years before. I went over every single detail of the deal I made. As I did so, a thought came to me. The deal I'd made wasn't that I'd stay 'good,' the deal was that I'd get out of the gang – which I had. I never said anything about drugs, sex, crime, or alcohol.

So actually, I did *keep my part of the bargain!* I proudly realized. I figured I'd try that route again – I'd bargain.

But, as I looked up at the wretched thing in the glass I knew I couldn't afford to bargain. What was surprising was that suddenly I was so horribly despondent and dismayed that I didn't *want* to bargain. I just needed help – anyway I could get it and from whomever I could get it. So I decided to talk to God right then and there. Just like I was. No religion, no prayers or holy verses, no rules, no deals, no bargains. Just me, with all sincerity, asking for help. I really didn't have a choice because if He couldn't help me, I was surely fucked.

I didn't look up or down. I didn't get on my knees, I didn't try to speak eloquently or use fancy words. I simply closed my eyes, took a deep breath and with all earnestness and sincerity I could muster, whispered two words.

'Help me.'

Dead silence for a few moments. Then the same calm Voice that had been talking to me for years now responded with a simple statement.

You'll have to quit your job.

What? I screamed in my mind. My face grimaced with confusion. *What the hell does that have to do with me getting help?*

As soon as the question came out, a thought suddenly came to me (another one of my moments of clarity). My job had been my only attachment to normalcy. I'd never been willing to quit a job without immediately getting another one because, in my mind, it made everything okay. I truly believed that addicts and alcoholics didn't, *couldn't,* have jobs.

Could it be that, by being willing to quit my job, I was finally admitting that I had a problem?

I believed so.

'Okay,' I said out loud, softly. 'I'll quit. I'll call Ken and tell him I quit.'

'Go see him,' the Voice quietly instructed.

Now the Voice was starting to get on my nerves.

Why did I have to tell Ken in person? Why couldn't I just call and give him the news. Admitting my problem in person would be embarrassing. Besides, look at me! I was filthy and I stunk.

'Why?' I screamed out loud looking around frantically to see if the Voice would speak again. It didn't.

'Why?' I screamed again.

Still no response.

I was pissed. I'd asked for help and instead was instructed to embarrass the hell out of myself by going and personally informing Ken that I was quitting because of drugs. If I hadn't known it before, I knew it now – God was nuts.

Crazy thing was, I had no other choice. I didn't know what else to do. I *had* to do as instructed, even though it didn't make a bit of sense.

It was 5:30 in the morning and not many people were out. I was in south-east San Diego and Ken's office was in downtown San Diego, about sixty *long* blocks away. I took a deep breath, a swig of gin, and began the long walk to Ken's office.

The going was slow because I was still loaded. On top of that, being shoeless forced me to have to carefully watch my steps. I'd never before noticed the glass, trash, and other debris that cluttered the sidewalk. In some places it was so bad that, to get around it, I had to walk in the street. The gin was also slowing me down because the more I walked, the more nervous I got; the worse my nerves got, the more I drank.

So I walked and drank, slowly but steadily. With my head held down and absolutely nothing on my mind, I walked and drank. Halfway to Ken's, most of the gin was gone. I started to wait until the liquor store opened so I could 're-up' before resuming my trip, but decided against it.

Keep walking, I told myself. *You've still got about half a bottle left. And the gin's effect should last at least a couple of hours. After you get to Ken's and quit, you can work on getting more gin.*

I kept walking. A few hours later, I arrived at Ken's building. I don't know what took me so long. Somewhere along the way, I'd lost track of time.

Who cares how long it took me to get here? Shit, at least I'm finally here!

I was tired and my feet hurt; still, I'd made it. As I stood at the building's entrance, I hesitated.

What do I say to him? How do I say it? What will he say? Will he yell at me? Would he have me arrested? Was being an addict a crime?

Unanswered questions were flying through my mind. I was scared. But I was more afraid of what would happen if I *didn't* get help.

You can't go on living the way you are, I scolded myself.

So I chugged down the rest of the gin, tossed the bottle into a nearby trash can, took a deep breath, and entered the building.

As I stepped out of the elevator onto the firm's floor, my heart began pounding. The gin helped me forget the image I'd seen in the window. As I walked by the receptionist, she looked up and began to speak but stopped in midsentence.

'Oh, hi, Cup—' She sat frozen, staring at me. I wasn't sure if her expression was one of shock, disgust, fear, or all of the above.

I didn't have time to worry about her. I was on a mission. I continued on toward Ken's office. As I passed each secretarial cubicle, I barely noticed the dropped jaws, frightened gasps, and alarm-filled stares.

I kept walking.

As usual, Ken's office door was open. I looked in and saw Ken sitting at his desk, signing some papers. What I didn't know was that the papers he was signing were for my termination.

I stood at Ken's door and waited for him to notice me. I'd been standing there for a few seconds when he finally looked up. What he saw must have startled him because he dropped his pen, his mouth fell open, and he looked like he'd seen a ghost.

'Cup?' he asked disbelievingly as he stared at what he thought was his secretary standing before him. I'd always hidden my thinness by layering long-sleeve shirts and wearing several pairs of pants. But, wearing the thin, lime green tank dress, he couldn't help but notice my sickeningly thin outline. For the first time, he was really seeing *me* – not the facade I'd been wearing for the past year.

'Cup?' he repeated, unsure if it was really me.

I didn't respond to his queries. I walked up to his desk and said, 'Ken, I've got a drug problem. I just came to tell you I quit so I can go get some help.'

I was crying, partly from shame and partly because, for the first time in my life, I'd admitted I had a problem. A problem I hated to admit having.

Ken didn't respond. I figured he didn't have anything to say. What could he say? I turned to walk out. I didn't know where I was going. I just felt I had to get the hell out of there.

Just before I reached the door, he spoke.

'Cup,' he said softly, 'don't quit. There's *something* about you worth saving.'

I stopped in my tracks and turned to look at him. I wasn't shocked by what he said. I had already decided that I was worth saving when I'd stared at my horrific reflection and prayed for help. But I did view his comment as confirmation of my decision.

Ignoring my look of astonishment, he took the papers he'd just signed and tore them up. As he did so, he said, 'I knew there was *something* wrong with you, but I didn't know what!'

He instructed me to sit down and I did. It was then that he told me the papers he'd ripped up were for my termination.

'You were firing me?' I asked

'Cup, you've been gone for *four* days!' he exclaimed. 'You didn't call in. Nothing. You know you're on probation and not supposed to miss *any* days and you've missed *four*! Cup, I had to let you go!'

I sat quietly with my head down. I was in shock, not because he had been getting ready to fire me, but because of the information I'd just learned.

I've been behind the Dumpster for four days? I couldn't believe it. I had totally lost track of time – and life.

Ken interrupted my thoughts by telling me that instead of firing me he was going to assist me in my decision to get help.

I was still speechless. Besides, what do you say when someone you've taken advantage of, lied to, and totally played, turns around and, instead of being angry – which he had every right to be – says he's going to try and help you? I was at a loss, so I sat there silently. Unsure of what to do Ken called Dorothy, who came right up to his office. Dorothy's brother was recovering from addiction, so she had some experience with the disease. She told Ken that I should probably be put in the hosptial so that I could detox under medical supervision. She gave him a list of hospitals with rehab units.

Ken immediately got on the phone and began calling the hospitals on the list. He called five or six. Although every one of them had a rehab unit, each told him they were filled to capacity and had no room for me. They each suggested he call back in a few days. The last hospital he called, Mesa Vista, was well known for its drug and alcohol recovery program. But they, too, had no room for me. Discouraged, Ken hung up the phone and informed me that we'd have to wait a few day before getting me in somewhere that could help.

'Ken,' I said, 'if y'all don't get me in someplace today, I'm not going.' Though I was still a little high from my four-day crack binge, and under the influence of the gin, I knew that as I began to come down, I would convince myself that I didn't really have a problem; that I'd just been "trippin".

He looked at me helplessly. Dorothy let out a quiet sigh of despair.

'I mean it,' I repeated. 'If not today, then *never*.' The room grew eerily silent.

Just then the phone rang, startling all of us. Ken quickly picked it up. It was a nurse from Mesa Vista Hospital saying they'd just had a cancellation. They instructed Ken to bring me in right away.

Ken was working on a brief and couldn't leave right away. As the firm administrator, Dorothy couldn't leave either. However, she said she knew someone who would probably be willing to take me: Sheila, another secretary at the firm, who had undergone similar drug treatment. She had over a year clean.

Bullshit.

Dorothy asked if I'd be okay with Sheila's taking me to the hospital. I knew of Sheila, though we'd never talked much. Like most of the secretaries, she didn't fuck with me and I didn't fuck with her. Still, I told Dorothy that I didn't care who drove.

As Dorothy left to talk to Sheila, Ken gave me a little pep talk. He told me to go and take care of myself and not to worry about my job – that it would be there when I got out.

'The most important thing,' he said, 'is that you get better. That *you* take care of *you*.'

Just as Ken was finishing his talk, his office door opened and Sheila came bouncing in.

'Let's go, Cup,' she said. Dorothy must have already filled her in because she seemed so damned happy about taking me to the hospital.

I, on the other hand, began to sweat.

Aw, shit, I told myself, *this is really happening!* All of a sudden I changed my mind. I began convincing myself of reasons why I didn't need help.

I ain't got no 'problem' with drugs. I just use too much every now and then. I just need to learn how to control it. Yeah, that's all I needed: learn to CONTROL my using! Girl, you was just trippin'!

I realized I couldn't go to any damn hospital! I also realized that going to Ken was a bad idea.

Damn that Voice! I screamed to myself. I had to get out of this!

Ken, Dorothy, and Sheila were heading for the door.

'I can't go!' I suddenly yelled.

They all stopped in their tracks; the agitation in my voice apparently startled them. Almost in unison, they turned toward me and eyed me suspiciously.

Dorothy was the first to speak.

'Why?'

'Because I don't have any cigarettes.' I could smell the gin on my breath. I wondered if they could. If they did, they didn't let on.

Although at the time I smoked, I *never* had cigarettes, unless I bummed them or stole them, because every dime I had went to drugs and booze. But all of a sudden, at that moment, it became VERY important that I had some cigarettes.

'I'll get the cigarettes,' Sheila said.

Shit!

But they weren't dealing with an amateur. Before they could reach for the doorknob I spoke up again.

'I can't go.'

'Why?' they all asked at once. They were all obviously fed up with my excuses: Dorothy's arms dropped to her sides as she gave a heavy sigh; Sheila threw her arms up in the air with a groan of frustration; Ken glared at me and said, 'You'd better have a good reason!'

Oh, I got a good reason, all right. The hospital said they would keep me anywhere from two weeks to thirty days. I didn't have any time on the books, so I wouldn't get paid.

'I don't have any sick leave. I can't *afford* to go!'

I'd failed to realize the audaciousness of that statement. Less than an hour before, I was about to be fired. And I *never* had sick leave or vacation. If I earned one day, I took three.

They all stood silently for a moment; Ken lowered his head into his hands, as if in deep thought. Suddenly he turned to me.

'Cup,' he said, 'I'm going to GIVE you the time off with pay. Don't worry about your job; it will be there when you get out. You just take care of your life.

'Now,' he asked slowly, 'is there anything else you need?'

I sat there quietly contemplating the question, my hands racing up and down the chair's arm rests. My mind raced frantically for an excuse. I kept coming up blank.

'Okay,' I quietly muttered. I stood up, but my head hung down with what I thought was shame, but later learned was humility. 'Let's go.'

Sheila and I took off for the hospital; Dorothy stayed behind to gather the insurance information the hospital had asked for; Ken went back to his brief.

We stopped by Mona's to pick up what few clothes I had and headed for the hospital.

'What kind do you smoke?' she asked.

'Wh-what?' I stammered. Her question threw me off.

'Cigarettes. What kind do you smoke?'

I'd completely forgotten about my alleged need for cigarettes, or that she had volunteered to buy me some. I told her my brand. She didn't respond. She just kept on driving.

A few minutes later, she pulled over to a liquor store and went in.

Fuck the cigarettes. I hope she's buying something to drink, I thought as I sat in the car, waiting for her to return. I'd lost my high on the way to the hospital and was dying for a drink, a snort, something.

A minute later, she returned with a brown paper bag. I felt my spirits lift because I'd convinced myself that there would be booze in it. She got into the car and pulled a carton of cigarettes out of the bag.

'Are these the right ones?' she asked.

I nodded.

She winked at me and nodded her approval as she pulled into traffic and headed for the hospital.

She seemed so happy about the whole hospital thing. I, on the other hand, was scared to death.

45

As Sheila pulled into the parking lot at Mesa Vista, I felt like I was going to the electric chair. I was scared to death. Dozens of questions were running through my mind.

What could they possibly do to me or tell me to make me not drink and use – I'd been high off *something* almost every day since I was eleven.

Sheila found a parking space and turned off the car.

'You ready?' she asked.

Hell, no! I wanted to yell.

Instead, I slowly nodded my head. A tear began to work its way down my face.

'Why are you crying?' she asked gently.

'I don't know.' I really didn't.

'Don't cry. We're here to save your life. Trust me. About a year ago, I was exactly where you are, and I can honestly tell you, it's the best thing that ever happened to me.'

I really wasn't trying to hear that shit. Then a new thought popped up in my head.

Maybe the hospital will teach me how to control my drinking and using! Not quit, just get it under control. All of a sudden, the hospital didn't seem so scary – in fact, I wanted to go in. I'd seriously convinced myself that they wouldn't try to make me stop, they would just teach me how to do it right.

'Let's go!' I said as I hopped out of the car and almost ran to the front door. Surprised at my abrupt attitude change, Sheila scurried behind me.

At the reception area a short white woman approached and introduced herself as Sam. She said she was an intake counselor

391

and was the one who would assess my condition to determine where I should go.

With Sam leading, me following, and Sheila bringing up the rear, we walked down the hall to a small office that had a chair sitting outside the door. Sam gently escorted me into the office, but when Sheila started to enter, she held up her hand. Explaining that the process was quite personal, she asked Sheila to sit in the chair until she had completed checking me in. I didn't want Sheila to stay outside, but before I could protest, Sam had closed the door and plopped down in the chair behind her desk. She instructed me to sit in either one of the two chairs in front of it. She pulled out a clipboard with some forms attached to it. Grabbing a pen, she began asking questions.

'Name? Age? Birth date? Social Security number?' Each time I gave her an answer, she feverishly scribbled it onto the paper. I was glad *she* was doing the writing. There was no way I could have written the answers myself. I was too pissed to write. I hated folks in my business and that woman was all in my business. The questions seemed endless.

I needed a drink badly.

As the questions continued, they got much more personal. She wanted to know if I had any sexually transmitted diseases.

'Do you mean now or ever?'

For the first time since she'd begun asking questions, she looked up at me. She had a puzzled look on her face. Apparently *she* wasn't even sure which one she meant. After thinking about it for a moment, she decided she wanted both.

'Let's see,' I said as I began to think back. 'I don't remember much. But I do remember having crabs. And I've had gonorrhea. Twice, I think. Oh, yeah, and recently I tried to get AIDS, but I don't know if I was successful.'

Her head bolted up as she stared at me in horror.

'Are you saying you *tried* to get AIDS?' she asked.

'Yeah,' I replied. 'I wanted to commit suicide and it was the best I could think of.'

Her stunned look told me Sam didn't understand my reasoning. She was already too much in my business, so I chose not to explain it to her.

'Are you *still* suicidal?' She asked slowly, studying me carefully.

'Well, I don't know.'

'Well, let me ask you this. Would you consider yourself suicidal or homicidal?'

That one was easy.

'I guess right now, I'd have to say I'm homicidal 'cause before I kill me, I'll kill you!' I cracked up laughing.

She didn't laugh with me; she just sat there with a baffled look on her face. She obviously failed to appreciate my humor.

'Let's continue,' she said, apparently deciding not to push the issue. 'What is your "problem"?'

My 'problem'?! Bitch, you my 'problem'! I wanted to shout. She was wrecking my nerves. All of a sudden, treatment didn't sound so good.

'With drugs, I mean,' she said as if that clarified the question. 'What drug are you here for?'

I get to PICK one? I asked myself. *What, you got different treatments for different drugs?*

I took a moment and thought about it. Maybe the drugs I listed would be those they would teach me to control. Shit, I wanted to learn how to control ALL of them. So I proudly listed all of them.

'All four of the white girls: crack, coke, meth, heroin, and of course acid and dust. Can't leave out dust. Ummmm, let's see. Oh, yeah, pills.'

'What kind of pills?'

'Shit, ANY kind: uppers, downers. And let's see, what else? Oh, weed. Can't forget weed. It *relaxes* me.' I gave her a sly grin and a coy wink. She didn't grin or wink back. She just kept writing.

'Booze, of course. We can't forget booze. Hell, that's what I can get when I can't get nothing else. If all else fails, I can always steal a can of beer or bottle of wine.'

'Which one is your favorite?' she asked.

That question puzzled me. No one had ever asked me that before. I really didn't have a favorite. Whatever was *free* was my favorite. But deep in my heart, if I had my choice, I knew crack would definitely be at the top of the list.

'Crack,' I replied.

Next she wanted to know how long I'd been using.

How long had I been using? I'd never really thought about it.

But now that I was, it seemed like I had been using forever. I sat quietly thinking about it. She sat quietly watching me.

My mind flashed back over my life and stopped at Pete and the first time he'd raped me. He'd given me a drink of some sort.

But, what was it? I don't know why all of a sudden I needed to remember what kind of drink it was. I just did.

It was rum and coke. Yup, that's what it was. Rum and coke.

That wasn't the first time I'd ever had alcohol, though. Daddy would give me sips of his beer every now and then. But that wasn't important because alcohol wasn't a drug – least I didn't think it was; and she'd asked when I started *using*, not drinking. Like a flood, the memories came back: Candy, the weed, more booze, my first trick. I was eleven years old then. Along with the memories came the shameful feelings – reminding me of why I never looked back.

'Eleven,' I whispered.

'Eleven?' she repeated, unsure of what she'd heard. 'Did you say "eleven"?'

'Yeah,' I said.

She sat motionless.

I wasn't offering any explanations. Personally, I didn't want to talk about it. Never wanted to talk about it.

No sense in dwelling on the past. What's done is done.

'Can we move on?' I asked, irritated by the uncomfortable silence and the forced memories.

'Ah, y-yeah,' Sam stammered as she squirmed around in her chair in an attempt to regroup herself. She returned to the questions on her sheet.

'When was the last time you used?'

'My last hit was around four or four-thirty this morning.' Since she'd asked about 'using' and not 'drinking,' I didn't mention the gin I guzzled during my walk to Ken's office.

She made a notation on her sheet.

'And I'm way past due for another one,' I said smugly. I'd long since become proud of how hardcore I was; I took sort of a perverse pride in being more widely and deeply into drugs and alcohol than anyone I knew. The dope world was one I knew well, and using was something I was good at – the *only* thing I was good at. So I guess I was showing off now that I had a chance to talk about it. At the same time, I truly believed I was beyond redemption; there was no coming back from the wretched hell I'd spiraled into.

The checking-in process was wrecking my nerves, what with all of the childhood-memory recalls and the questions. No wonder I was having trouble deciphering whether I was talking to myself or talking out loud. I needed a drink, a hit, a toot, a ... *something*.

I looked up and was surprised to see Sam staring at me, as if she were trying to read my mind. I smiled sheepishly and gazed down at the carpet. Neither of us said anything for a few moments.

Finally, Sam broke the uncomfortable silence. 'Well, that's why you're here, isn't it?'

I'm here to learn to do it right.

'So, there won't be any more 'hits,' right?'

No more hits!

She stood up and announced that the questioning was over. And not a moment too soon, as far as I was concerned. As we walked out of her office, Sheila stood to greet us. Sam politely informed her that there was nothing else she could do; I was now in the hospital's care, so she could leave. Sheila gave me a long, warm hug, and told me that everything would be all right.

Once Sheila disappeared out the front door, Sam gently nudged me and said we had to finish checking me in.

She shuffled me off to another room where the physical part of the check-in began. In a daze, I did what I was told to do and sat where I was told to sit while a nurse checked my blood pressure and took my temperature. For the whole time, I remained silent and my facial expression remained blank. My mind was going numb from the sudden tedium after all of the day's craziness, until it was time for me to be weighed. I stepped on the scale and watched the thin black needle swing back and forth until it finally stopped just before 100.

'I weigh ninety-nine pounds?' I was in shock. I'd never weighed myself. Oh, I knew I was thin; I just never realized how thin.

'Ninety-eight,' the nurse corrected me. Her disinterested facial expression never changed as she wrote the numbers down on her chart.

'Shit!' I said. 'I'm a skinny shit!'

'Oh, girl,' she said casually, 'I've seen them thinner.'

'You've seen people thinner than *me*?' I asked in disbelief.

She nodded and finished her checkup.

I was then passed on to another nurse who showed me around the unit and introduced me to the staff. She also informed me of the rules: drinking alcohol or using any drugs would result in my immediate discharge. Any and all prescription drugs would be handed out by hospital staff.

Oh, so y'all DO have drugs here? I was starting to perk up; maybe rehab wouldn't be so bad.

Continuing with the rules, the nurse told me that I was not to leave the facility for any reason. When I did leave, I'd have to get a pass. Passes were given by merit, not as a matter of right. I had to attend all 12-step meetings held at the facility. I would also have daily 'group' meetings, as well as daily one-on-one counseling sessions.

Shit, I wasn't this busy at work!

The nurse still wasn't finished. We could receive or make phone calls only during certain times in the mornings and evenings, and all calls were limited to ten minutes. When I wasn't in a meeting, group session, or individual counseling, I would be given, and expected to do, various reading and writing assignments. Visitors were allowed only during visiting hours, and all visitors had to sign in and were subject to being searched.

To be sure I wouldn't forget what she'd told me, the nurse gave me a paper with all of the rules written on it. I had to sign another paper to acknowledge I'd been informed of the rules and received a copy of them.

After being allowed to take a shower, I was taken to my room. It was a plain hospital room: two twin beds, one dresser with eight drawers (four on each side), and a nightstand for each bed. Normally, there were two women or men in each room; but my roommate wasn't coming for a day or two, so I'd have the entire room to myself for a while, which was good. I wasn't in the mood for company. I plopped down on one of the beds and looked at the clock on the dresser. The bright red numbers informed me it was 4:15 P.M.

With a sigh, I asked the nurse what else I had to do. She said the rest of the night was mine to do what I pleased. She suggested I unpack my things and put them away and then try and get some rest because the next day would be a busy one.

I unpacked my raggedy clothes. Once my things were put away, I lay down and tried to get some sleep. I tossed and turned and tossed and turned. I knew I was exhausted; I hadn't slept in days. My body was tired, my eyes were tired. Hell, even my *mind* seemed tired. But, try as I might, I couldn't sleep. Frustrated, I tried counting sheep. When that didn't work, I tried counting blunts. Then beers. Then lines. After a while, I sat up in the bed. The small radio clock on the nightstand informed me it was 12:30 in the morning. It had almost been twenty-four hours since I'd had anything to drink or use.

What the fuck are you doing here? I asked myself.

You need help, I answered.

Help with what? Girl, you're fine.

No, I'm not.

Yes, you are.

No, I'm NOT! I haven't slept in days and I STILL can't get to sleep!

Girl, you're FINE. You just need to learn control.

Oh, what the fuck do YOU know!

I realized I was losing it. Not only was I talking to myself, I was arguing with myself.

I was agitated. The room was too quiet. My thoughts were too loud. Suddenly I noticed that the room had grown cold. I put on a sweater. Minutes later, I was burning up. I threw it on the floor. My legs felt cramped, so I jumped up and began to walk around the room to stretch them. Then they started shaking and felt weak, so I sat down.

What's happening to me?

I'd never felt that way before. I looked down at my hands. They were shaking too. But that didn't surprise me; I'd seen them do that before – usually first thing in the morning before I'd had a drink. Experience had taught me that it was only after I'd had that first drink that my hands would stop shaking. All of a sudden I really needed a drink. It wasn't just a desire for one; it was more like an intense compulsion.

'I gotta get outta here! I gotta get outta here!' I started shouting over and over again.

397

Seconds later, the door flew open and two nurses came running in.

'Are you all right?' one of them asked as she placed her hand against my forehead. The other immediately grabbed my arm and began to take my blood pressure.

I don't need my blood pressure taken, you idiot! I wanted to scream. *I need a drink!*

'Some-something's wrong,' I stammered. 'I don't feel so well.'

'How long has it been since you used or drank anything?' one of them asked.

What the fuck does that have to do with anything?

'I don't know. Sometime early yesterday morning,' I replied irately.

My heart was pounding a mile a minute, and the shaking in my hands was getting worse. I'd started sweating profusely, and my legs were wobbly. Something was happening to me, and I didn't know what it was. I was scared.

'You're probably starting withdrawals,' one of the nurses said.

'Starting?' I asked.

'Yeah, sweetie. It will get worse before it gets better.'

Where had I heard that before?

She suggested I try to get some sleep.

'I tried to sleep!' I yelled. 'I can't sleep! I've been trying for hours now!'

One of the nurses darted out of the room. The other tried to convince me to sit down. Once I did, she began rubbing my back while softly talking to me. She explained that part of getting clean meant that my body would have to go through a physical withdrawal period – a period that obviously had already started. When I asked if such a thing was normal, she replied that different people 'kicked' differently: some could go days without drinking and using before experiencing any withdrawal symptoms, some only hours, and still some never felt anything at all. She surmised that, since I was starting withdrawal so soon, I must have been using 'quite a bit for quite a long time.'

The other nurse returned with both her hands full: one held a small plastic cup filled with water; the other held a small paper cup containing two small pills. She handed me the paper cup with the pills. I didn't ask what they were; I didn't *care,* as long as they were drugs. As she handed me the plastic cup of water she said that the pills would 'help me sleep,' or at the least, help me relax.

I quickly tossed back the pills, and then lay down and stared at the ceiling. Slowly the pills took effect and I drifted off to sleep.

It seemed like no sooner than I'd fallen asleep the lights flashed on and a nurse was happily informing me it was time to get up.

'What time is it?' I asked as I sat up in bed, rubbing my eyes.

'Six o'clock!' she replied joyfully.

I was not joyful. I was tired.

'Listen, I haven't slept in four days. I couldn't get to sleep last night. And the minute I did start catching some shut-eye, yo' happy ass busted in here and woke me up. Now, I'm tired and I'm sleepy, so I'm going back to sleep. If you don't like it, you can put me out. But, you'll have to do it once I wake up, 'cause if anyone wakes me up again, I'm goin' the fuck off!'

I turned over and put the covers over my head. She scampered out of the room.

I later learned that she had spoken with the head nurse about how to handle the situation. The head nurse talked with the nurses who'd given me the pills the night before. They confirmed that I hadn't been able to sleep and seemed to be in the beginning stages of withdrawal. Then the head nurse spoke with Sam, the woman who had checked me in. She confirmed that I had indeed been up smoking crack for four consecutive days. It was then that she told the nurses that it was probably best to let me sleep, especially since I wouldn't be able to digest any 'recovery' if I was dog-tired.

I slept all that day and into the night; I slept straight through without waking once. The nurses took turns checking on me. I didn't change positions; I didn't go to the bathroom. I never moved. I was dead to the world.

By my third night, I began to see things – spiders, specifically. Hundreds and hundreds of little *purple* spiders with *red* legs. They were marching all over the place singing, 'We will, we will, rock you!' Each time they sang 'rock,' they'd throw up a small crack rock. At first, I watched in amazement as they began marching up the curtains, dresser, and nightstands while throwing their little rocks in the air like confetti. I even began swaying to their music and singing along with them. It wasn't till they began marching toward *me* that I lost it.

'Get away from me! Get away from me!' I screamed, frantically swiping and swatting at them. There were too many of them. Soon, they were marching along my arms and legs, crawling up my back, even going into my ears.

My screams of 'Get away from me!' quickly changed to 'Get off of me!'

Hearing my screams, nurses rushed in and found me clawing at my body.

'Get 'em off me! Help get these lil fuckas offa me!' I continued screaming as I clawed and scratched at the spiders that, unbeknownst to me, only *I* could see. My fingernails were digging into my skin so deep that, in some places, they had drawn blood.

Having seen this scene before, the nurses immediately jumped into action. To keep me from hurting myself any more, they tied me down and gave me a shot, which I later learned was some sort of sedative. As the medicine took effect and I began to drift off, I remember shivering in fear, crying, and begging to the nurses to untie me because, if the little spiders returned, I wouldn't be able to get them because my hands were tied down. The nurses pacified me by promising that, if my spiders returned, they'd help me stomp the shit out of them.

Slowly, the DTs reduced in intensity and occurrence, though it took several days before they stopped completely. I went from seeing invisible spiders and clawing at myself to hiding in a corner, curled into a fetal position and bawling uncontrollably to sweating so much that by the end of each day my clothes would be soaked completely through. At night I had to lie on top of towels to help absorb the sweat.

During my first counseling session, after the DTs had stopped for good, I learned that the DTs were a part of the alcohol (and sometimes drug) withdrawal process, and that they're often accompanied by hallucinations. The counselor warned me to remember the whole horrible experience whenever I thought about taking another drink. I wasn't sure if a fear of DTs would stop me from drinking, but I surely wouldn't forget them.

One of my first assignments at Mesa Vista was to write a good-bye letter to my drug of choice. I refused to do it because, as I explained to my counselor, I really didn't have a 'favorite' drug – my favorite was whatever was free. To prove my point, I listed all of the different drugs I used at least occasionally. Once I finished my list, I proudly showed it to him, expecting him to be impressed. He reviewed the list and handed it back to me disinterestedly. He explained to me that I was what they called a 'trash-can junkie' – someone that would, and did, do any drug. I actually liked this label because it described me accurately. Still, he said I could pick only one drug for the letter. I still refused, and we argued back and forth about the issue. Finally, we came to a compromise and agreed to a slight change in the assignment: I would write *two* good-bye letters – one to every drug I'd ever done, and one specifically to crack because it was the one I preferred when I had money, and it was the one that had brought me to my last residence: a Dumpster.

Writing those letters was an eye-opener. I spent hours on them. I finally got brutally honest about my using. I talked about the effect they'd had on my life, my mind, my body, and my family. The letters helped me see the progression of my using as well as its treacherous end. As I got deeper into the letters, it all started becoming clear: there was no longer any denying it because it was laid out in front of me in black and white and in my own handwriting. Job or no job, school or no school, married or unmarried, I was definitely an addict. By the end of the second letter, I was crying so hard, my tears were smearing the ink on the paper.

The revelations in those letters helped me fight cravings to use. While I was in the hospital I didn't get many cravings, but the few I did have were immediately put to rest when I reread the good-bye letters. But the letters alone weren't enough to completely stop my cravings. Luckily, the hospital's rehab program was so intense that, most of the time, I was too busy to have a craving – between attending group sessions and individual counseling sessions, doing my writing and reading assignments and going to meetings, both on and off site – my day was so full, I usually plopped into bed totally exhausted. The totality of it all

– the hospital's controlled environment, the intense daily schedule, and the camaraderie and support of being with other patients fighting the same struggle – helped me successfully fight the few cravings I did have.

Besides writing the letters, I had to write about the effort getting high took. At first, I didn't think it took effort, but the more I wrote, the more I realized that staying high wasn't easy. It took work – constant work and hard work: locating dope; trying to avoid getting bunk dope; hustling and bustling trying to get the best deal; ditching cops; lying, robbing, and stealing for get-high money; the necessity of suspiciously watching doper friends as vigilantly as they were watching me.

It was at Mesa Vista that I started attending 12-step meetings, though it was a few days into my stay before I got to one. I first had to get over the DTs to the point where I could sit still and concentrate. As soon as I was better, I was put on a strict recovery regime, which included attendance of all 12-step meetings 'on site,' which was a separate, classroom-size building located on the rear acreage of the hospital. None of the 12-step meetings were sanctioned by the hospital, which simply meant that the hospital wasn't responsible for any of the 12-step meetings. The meeting groups just rented space from Mesa Vista, and each meeting chose its own format, etc. The majority of the attendees weren't even hospital patients.

To get to the meeting building from the hospital, you had to go through a delightfully tranquil Japanese-style garden. The garden was one of my favorite places in the hospital. It was filled with marvelously fragrant flowers, a Japanese pond filled with colorful fish, and several benches placed here and there for patients to use when visiting with family and friends, sitting and meditating, enjoying the melody of the chirping birds, or just taking pleasure in the warm Southern California sun. Also in the garden, close to the meeting facility's entranceway, stood a large beautiful tree. Its thick brown branches stretched out over the garden like a maze suspended in air, providing shade to anyone who sat under them.

At first, I didn't want to go to any meetings. I remembered the 12-step meeting Daddy had taken me to, and I remembered that it didn't work. In fact, that same night I'd gotten high using their book to cut my dope on. But when I tried to ditch the meetings, a counselor told me that I didn't have a choice – they were mandatory.

The first meeting I went to only intensified my initial hesitance. First, the room was full of white folks. Although there were several minority patients in rehab with me, everyone from the 'outside' who attended the meeting that night was white. There were men and women of various ages, shapes, and sizes – but all of them were white. As I stood in the building's doorway, looking around, I couldn't help but see one particular guy on the far side of the room. He was a burly fellow with a wide friendly smile – a smile he gave to everyone who walked through the door, including me. His dark brown mustache and goatee all matched the dark brown hair on his head – at least the hair that stuck out from under his hat. Although it was his friendly smile that caught my attention, it was his hat that kept it. He wore a red baseball cap with 'SICK FUCKER' in bold white letters on the front. My eyes bulged when I saw it. But they damn near jumped out of my head when I noticed what he was doing with his hands. He was playing with a rope, and it looked like he was trying to form a noose at one of the ends. It was at that moment that I refused to move any farther into the building. All I kept thinking was that those white folks and 'Sick Fucker' were going to use that noose to hang me from that big ol' tree in the garden.

One of the patients standing behind me gently nudged me in the back and whispered for me to 'keep going.' I looked behind me and was shocked to see a line of patients waiting to get inside. I thought about stepping aside, letting them enter, and then making my way back to my room. But just then, one of the nurses began making her way to the front of the line to find out what was causing the holdup. Seeing her moving so fast and the annoyed look on her face told me that I couldn't turn back. Yet I didn't want to go in. Before I could think of an escape, the nurse was in my face. Through clenched teeth, she instructed me to find a seat. I had no choice. I had to go in. But, I decided to keep my eye on Sick Fucker.

Twenty minutes into the meeting I was glad I hadn't turned around. In fact, I was thankful the nurse had forced me inside because I actually enjoyed the meeting. Even though I was one of only a few black people in the room, I still felt connected to everything being said. I understood each hellacious story of detriment and degradation caused by drugs. As people talked about their using behavior, I was forced to remember my own similar accounts of things that drugs had compelled me to do – things I never imagined I'd do, and things I'd swore I'd never do.

At first, I suspected that Daddy or Ken had paid the people in the meeting to be there and to say the things they said in order to convince me that I had a drug problem. But as I listened to them and their stories, I knew they were talking from experience. These people weren't acting. They were bona fide dope fiends – just like me.

Out of everyone at the entire meeting, I liked Sick Fucker most of all. He said he'd been clean for several years. He welcomed the new people (he looked at me when he said that) and told us that we never had to use again. That sentence blew me away, especially since he said it with such plainspoken seriousness and sincerity. But I didn't believe he'd really been *completely* clean for years. Everybody I knew did *something*. I was sure he did too. Still, he was funny and friendly – even his burliness made him appear cute and cuddly, sort of like Santa Claus. By the end of the meeting, I was no longer afraid of him. I was no longer afraid of the rope. In fact, I was no longer afraid of any of those white people. I actually wanted to hang with them.

As usual, I took it too far: that night I decided that black folks were my problem. Every bad thing that had happened to me had been done by a black person – the sperm donor, Pete, Diane and her sick-ass daughter, Mr and Mrs Bassinet, the Gangstas, the Rollin' 60's who shot me, the dope men, the dope friends, Tommy – every single one of them had been black ('business arrangements' didn't count – that was business). I convinced myself that if I stayed away from black folks and just stuck with white folks, I could get my life together. I'd be all right.

After that I loved going to the meetings. I especially loved hearing everyone in the room scream 'Hi, Cupcake!' when I introduced myself. As crazy as it sounds, I used to cry when I heard the theme song from the television show 'Cheers':

Wouldn't you like to go where everybody knows your name?

404

And they're always glad you came . . .

For years, I'd longed for a place where I could go and be a part of it; where people knew my name and were glad to see me. The dope man didn't want to know my name, and he was only glad to see me if I had money in hand. I didn't want other dopers to know my name, and they were only glad to see me if I came with a free high for them. In fact, in street life, no one was ever glad to see anyone coming – unless you had money, dope, or both. But the people at the meetings were different. They all knew my name and always seemed so damned happy to see me. And I didn't have a pot to piss in or a window to throw it out of.

A couple of weeks after starting treatment, I began to get passes to attend meetings off site. I didn't have a car, so I was forced to go with a patient that did. A white girl named Karen had been at Mesa Vista a few days longer than me and loved going to outside meetings. Figuring that, as a white person, she knew where the white folks hung out, I trailed behind her every chance I got.

One day, as we hopped into her car, she announced that we were going to a new meeting.

'Cool,' I replied as I strapped on my seat belt. Since swearing off blacks, I was always down for meeting new white folks. As she drove, I closed my eyes and enjoyed the ride. As a result, I didn't pay much attention to where she was going. The next thing I knew, she pulled up in front of a little brown building on Imperial Avenue in an area of San Diego known as Southeast, where the majority population is black and Mexican. The sign on the front of the building read 'Southeast Alano Club' in large letters.

'What the fuck is an "Alano Club"?' I asked as she gleefully hopped out of the car.

'Come on!' she yelled as she skipped up to the door. 'You'll love this place. My friend said they got the *bomb* recovery!'

Okay. But what's a bunch of white folks doing in Southeast? I asked myself as I hopped out of the car and scurried to catch up with Karen.

As we entered the building, the room was full of people and the meeting was already in progress. We had to weave in and out of closely packed rows of people, all the while whispering, 'Excuse me, excuse me,' as we ducked in front of people, knocked some on the head, or stepped on their feet trying to find two empty seats. Once we finally found seats, I was able to get a good look around the room. I saw nothing but a sea of black faces. Tons of black people: fat, skinny, short, tall, dark-skinned, light-skinned, old, young. Everywhere I looked, there was nothing but black folks.

Aw, shit! I exclaimed to myself. *This is just my fuckin' luck!*

'Girl,' I leaned over and whispered to Karen, 'these people are all BLACK!'

Karen glanced around the room.

'I know!' she exclaimed. 'Isn't it great!' She was smiling like a kid in a fucking candy store.

'Hell, no!' I angrily whispered back. The last thing I needed in my life was black folks.

'I'm outta here,' I snapped. I *had* to go. Black folks were my problem, and because of some crazy white girl I was suddenly *surrounded* by them.

I stood up and began to weave my way in between the rows to make my way back to the door. As I struggled through the crowd to get out, a tall, slender light-skinned woman was making her way to the microphone. The microphone sat on top of a podium that was placed in the center of the room on an elevated stage. Apparently, anyone who wanted to speak had to do so from the podium. She reached the mic as I was just about six feet away from the door. I heard her say, 'My name is Venita and I'm a sober alcoholic and drug addict.' That was no big surprise. I'd been to enough meetings to know that that was the normal introduction. In unison, the entire room yelled back, 'Hi, Venita.'

I kept moving.

As I reached for the doorknob, I heard her say,

'And I used to feel ugly.'

I stopped in my tracks. I turned around to look at her – my hand still on the doorknob. She was *beautiful*. She was everything I'd ever wanted to be. She had a nice slender build. But, most important, she was light-skinned with long hair, the ideal woman in my eyes.

What the fuck?

I was so taken aback by Venita that I began to sit down right where I was, not knowing, or caring, that there was nothing beneath me. However, a young black man had been standing next to me and watching me. He must have seen the astonishment on my face and somehow noticed that I was too flabbergasted to care about the fact that I was bending down to sit with nothing to sit on. As my body headed downward, he deftly slid a chair beneath me, saving my tailbone from ramming into the floor.

I sat there in bewilderment. And I listened. I hung on to every word she said because I understood every word she said. I *felt* every word she said. She described a lifetime of feeling ugly and that, all of her life, she wanted to be dark-skinned. *She* wanted to be *dark*!

I'll be a mothafucka! All of my life I wanted to be her, and she wanted to be me? *I'll be a mothafucka!*

She talked about wanting to be a part of something, wanting to be desired, to be 'special,' craving to be loved. She talked about experiencing the kind of loneliness so immense it could swallow you up. She called it 'loneliness that crowds couldn't cure.' I felt like she was reading my mind. Even though the things she spoke of were painful, she spoke eloquently and with such confidence. Like she knew what she was talking about. Like she'd actually experienced these things; they weren't just something she'd read about in a book or learned about in 'group.'

I didn't move. The whole time she was up there, I *couldn't* move. After about five minutes, she was through and I didn't take my eyes off her, even when she walked back to her seat. I was in awe. I had never met anyone who could relay my feelings back to me like that. And she was light-skinned with long hair – I just couldn't get over that. I'd always put those kind of girls in a different, idealistic category. And now, here was one who could have been my emotional twin.

I stayed for the rest of the meeting, though I couldn't tell you what anybody else said. I spent the rest of the meeting staring at Venita and hearing her words cycling over and over again in my head. Wondering who she was and how she knew the things she did. Wondering if someone like her would talk to someone like me.

In the meetings I'd been to already, the group had strongly

suggested that I get a sponsor. It was explained that a sponsor was someone who'd been clean and sober longer than me, someone who had a working knowledge of the 12 steps, someone I could relate to and trust. At first, I looked for a male sponsor, figuring I'd get along better with a man. But when one of the white women heard me asking Sick Fucker to be my sponsor she quickly pulled me aside and informed me that women worked with women and men worked with men, meaning I had to get a woman for a sponsor. I knew I was fucked, because I hated women and really didn't want to be bothered with them – especially *black* women – until now. There was something about Venita, though I couldn't quite put my finger on it. All I knew was that she, with her words, had touched me like no man *or* woman – drunk or sober – ever had. If I were to get a sponsor, it would have to be Venita.

As soon as the meeting was over, several women swarmed around her. I didn't blame them. I wanted to get close to her too. I just didn't know how. It was then I realized that I was afraid. Without the false courage of alcohol or drugs to break the ice, I didn't know how to befriend people, didn't know what to say.

As I stood there contemplating my next move, Karen interrupted my thoughts. She informed me that we had to go. With off-site meeting passes, we were allotted so much time to get to and from the hospital. If we didn't leave right away, we'd get back late – the punishment of which would be losing our pass privileges for a few days.

'Then let's go!' I yelled as I grabbed her arm and began dragging her toward the car. I didn't want to be late because I didn't want to lose my next pass. I couldn't lose it – I intended to use it to come back to the Southeast Alano Club and see Venita. I didn't know why, but I just had to see her again. I hoped that she would talk again. And I hoped that maybe I'd get the nerve to ask her to be my sponsor. And maybe, just maybe, she'd say yes.

The next day, I requested and was granted an off-site meeting pass. Karen had gotten one too, but she was into 'meeting hopping' and wanted to try another Alano Club she'd heard about. I told her to go on. *I* was going to the Southeast Alano Club. I really didn't have a choice. It was almost like I was *compelled* to go; so I gladly made the two-hour bus ride from the hospital to the club.

All the way there, I was hoping Venita would be there.

Please let her be there, I begged. *Please.*

I really didn't know whom I was talking to. I figured it might be God. I hadn't talked to Him much since being in the hospital. Actually, I hadn't talked to Him at all since that day I saw my reflection in the plate-glass window and I'd asked for help. I still hadn't learned how to pray, let alone how to pray 'right,' and I still didn't know any religious rules, songs, verses, or sayings. So I wasn't really sure if I was talking *to* Him. And even if I was, I wasn't sure if He was *listening.* I began pondering the situation in my mind.

Maybe the first time someone talked to God without 'rules' was a 'freebie.' Maybe after that, you were expected to know and follow the 'rules.'

Nevertheless, I wanted to give it a try. I figured I'd just ask Him and see if He'd respond – like before.

'Please let her be there,' I said quietly. I waited, expecting to hear something from the Voice – some profound articulation of the magnificent miracle that was to come.

Nothing.

All the way there on the bus, I waited for the Voice to speak.

It never said a word. The only noise I heard was my own mind running crazy with questions.

How are you going to talk to her? What are you going to say? You don't even know if she's going to be there. You've been to several different meetings and heard many different women – some of which you could also relate to. What's so special about her?

I didn't know. But I had to see her again.

Am I gay? my mind continued. *Could that be it? Was I hot for this chick?* I'd been with women before, sure, but always as a part of a 'business arrangement.'

Naw, that's not it. But what IS it?

What the fuck is wrong with you? I screamed to myself. *She's just a woman!*

I didn't care. I had to see her again. Hear her again.

The dumb-ass bus driver missed my stop. I ran the two blocks back to the club. I threw open the door and looked around. Just as it was the first time, the room was full of blacks. I looked over the sea of blackness and saw faces of various shades, sizes, shapes, and ages, but I didn't see Venita. I scanned the room a second time. She was nowhere to be found.

'Do you want to sit down?' an older black woman asked, startling me.

All of a sudden, people started piling in through the door. The older lady grabbed my arm and quickly led me to a nearby chair to get me out of the way as we made room for the incoming crowd.

I miserably plopped down on the chair. I was let down and embittered. I began to fuss at myself, telling myself that I had been a fool.

You know better than to get your hopes up about anything.

I sat in the chair with my head down and began to cry. I was so disheartened. For the first time since going into the hospital, I felt . . . hopeless. I quickly wiped away the tears, not wanting anyone to think I was a punk or weak. I stared at the floor, wondering when would be the right moment to get up and leave. I wouldn't be coming back to the Southeast Alano Club. In fact, I wasn't going back to *any* meetings.

What's the use? I told myself. *It will never work for* you.

I continued staring at the floor. My sadness slowly began to turn to anger. I was pissed at myself for coming all that way for some black chick that probably wouldn't have given me the time of day anyway. And I was pissed at myself for *trying* to believe in a God after everything I'd been through. The tears began falling faster than I could wipe them away.

Just then, the person in charge of the meeting stood up and spoke into the microphone.

'Venita, would you like to share?'

Venita? My head shot straight up. *Did he say 'Venita'?* No longer caring about who saw my tears, I began frantically searching the room for her. It took me a moment, but soon I spotted her long hair bouncing up and down as she climbed the stairs to the stage.

She's here! I shouted to myself in delight.

Had I somehow overlooked her when I first came in? I couldn't have. I'd searched that room carefully – face by face. The tears really began pouring down my face, but I really didn't care who saw them now, because they were no longer tears of sorrow. They were tears of joy. I don't know why I was so happy to see her. I just was.

She started speaking. First, she apologized for being late.

So I hadn't overlooked her! She wasn't here! She must have walked in when my head was down, when I was busy doubting God.

I shut my mind up, sat on the edge of my chair, and listened. Again, she touched me with her words. I knew that I wanted what she had. I didn't know how she got 'it' or if I could get 'it.' But I had to try.

Once she finished speaking, she went and sat down. Again, I just stared at her. I spent the rest of the meeting talking to myself about how to approach her and what to say. When the meeting was over, she was again swarmed by a group of women. I wanted to go up to her so badly, but I didn't have the courage. All of a sudden, I wanted a drink. I knew that a drink would give me the courage to talk to her. A few drinks and I'd push all 'dem bitches outta my way,' hog her to myself, and kick anybody's ass who complained about it.

There was one problem with that plan: I wasn't supposed to drink. I hadn't had a drink or any nonprescribed drug in almost a month. Shoot, the hospital had even taken me off sleeping pills and sedatives my second week there.

But how else was I going to be able to talk to her?

I decided that I would try one more time the next day. If I failed to do it then, I'd get the courage from my old friend, gin.

The next day, I repeated the pattern. I got an off-site pass and made the two-hour bus trek to the Alano Club. On the way there, I again had a short, quiet talk in my mind with someone I hoped was God. First I apologized for doubting Him the day before. Then I simply asked Him to let Venita be there. I thought about it for a few moments and then quietly added the request that, if she *was* there, He give me the courage to say something – anything – to her. If God heard me, He didn't respond. There were no soft replies of encouragement. No gentle voice telling me not to be afraid. Nothing. Complete silence.

When I entered the club, the meeting had already started. A

411

young black man was at the podium. I had no idea what he was saying, nor did I care. I scanned the room. My eyes immediately locked on to Venita. She was sitting in the middle of the room. As I walked past, she looked up and smiled at me. Damn, she was pretty. I sheepishly smiled back and quickly found a seat behind her. I was angry at myself for being late.

What if she's already talked? I asked myself, terrified at the thought. I hoped she hadn't. And if she hadn't, I hoped she would speak.

'God, I hope she talks today,' I whispered.

'Did you say something, honey,' an older black woman who was sitting next to me asked. I recognized her as the same woman who'd grabbed me out of the way the day before. I later learned her name was Chaney.

'Uh-uhhh,' I stammered, 'n-no. I was just talking to myself.'

She smiled and returned her attention to the man at the podium.

I was hoping he would shut up. The longer he talked, the more time he took from Venita – if she talked.

God, if you can hear me, PLEASE let her talk, I pleaded again, though this time, I made sure to say it to myself. I looked at Chaney to be sure I hadn't spoken aloud. She didn't look my way.

Three more people were called on to speak. I sat there, my patience spent and feeling about ready to jump out of my seat. Although I related to the things they said, it just wasn't the same as when Venita spoke. Finally, the speaker called on her. She seemed to glide to the podium. She walked with such assurance and confidence, I knew there was no way she could have ever done the things I'd done. She couldn't have used drugs or drank the way I had.

Still, she again touched me with her words. She talked about selling furniture, microwaves, and televisions for dope. She talked about living in the dark because she'd spent the light and gas money on dope. She talked about eating Top Ramen for days on end because they were twelve for a dollar. It was like she'd been following me with a hidden camera for the previous fourteen years.

At the end of the meeting, I whispered another little prayer – or something – and approached her. There were no women around her this time. In fact, no one was surrounding her, which is a good thing because if there had been, I probably wouldn't have had the nerve.

I slowly walked toward her, all the while practicing in my mind what I was going to say.

Do I say my name first? Introduce myself, or just come straight out and ask her to be my sponsor? What if she doesn't sponsor dark girls? What if she doesn't sponsor ugly girls? I couldn't shut up my mind. But my feet kept moving.

She stood there, almost as if she were waiting for me. Finally, we were face-to-face. I looked at her, but was unable to speak. I was scared to death. Luckily, she spoke first.

'Hi!'

I meant to say 'hi' back, but I was so nervous all that came out was a mumbled 'huh.' I stared at the ground.

'You're new here, aren't you?' she asked.

'Uhhh, yeah.'

Damn, girl. Pull yourself together. Act cool. You been cool all your life. You know how to be 'cool,' don't ya?

Without a drink or drug, I didn't.

'My name's Venita. What's yours?'

'Cup – Cup—' I stuttered as I continued staring at the ground.

Come on, girl. You know your name! Sure I *knew* it, but I was so nervous, I couldn't *say* it!

'Your name is "Cup"?' she asked.

'Cupcake!' I yelled. I didn't care that I'd said it so loud. I was just glad to get it out. If the sudden elevation in my voice startled her, she didn't show it.

'Cupcake? Is that your birth name?' She was bending down trying to look up into my face, which was still aimed down at the ground.

'Yeah,' I replied.

'That's cute.'

I still couldn't look up.

'How much time do you have?' she asked.

'Time? What do you mean "time"?' I'd heard that term before in meetings but I was usually biting my nails, daydreaming, or doing something else with my mind. Now, I'd wished I'd paid attention so I'd have known what she was talking about.

413

'How long have you been sober? When did you last drink or use?'

I hadn't really thought about it. Although I'd heard other people count the number of days they'd been sober, I never really believed I would stay sober, so I felt like keeping count would be a waste of time. But, since she was asking, I wanted to give her an answer. I took a moment to count back the days since I'd entered the hospital.

'I think about twenty days,' I proudly replied.

She smiled approvingly.

'Will you be my sponsor?' I blurted out. I had to get the question out before I scared myself into not asking. I sheepishly looked up at her and held my breath waiting for her response, which I was sure would be no.

'You don't have a sponsor?'

I shook my head.

'Well, I'm serious about recovery and I only work with people who are just as serious. Are you serious about staying clean?'

Too nervous to speak or afraid I'd say something to make her change her mind, I nodded my head yes.

'Okay, good. Call me tonight,' she said as she took out a piece of paper and wrote her number on it.

I took the paper and bolted for the door. I wanted to get out before she changed her mind. Once outside, I paused for a moment, reflecting on what had just happened.

'She said yes!' I shouted to the sky, startling an old black man passing by. 'She said yes!'

My simple prayer had been answered.

'Thank you,' I whispered as I stood staring at the piece of paper with Venita's number on it.

46

I called Venita that night. I didn't have any money, but the nurse on duty was so ecstatic to hear I'd finally found a sponsor, she gave me a dollar's worth of dimes. As I picked up the pay phone, I was so nervous my hands were shaking and sweating. I forced myself to dial the number, using one hand to steady the shaking one so that I would hit the right buttons.

I was worried for nothing. She had the same sweet voice, and the same pleasant and friendly personality she'd shown me at the meeting. She told me she'd been clean for five years. Five years! That seemed like a lifetime. I hoped I could get to five *weeks*! But knowing that she'd been clean that long, I was even more eager to work with her because she obviously knew what she was talking about.

Phone calls were usually limited to ten minutes, but considering it an extra-special call, the nurse said I could have twenty. It wasn't a lot of time, but it was long enough for Venita to give me an earful. First, she laid down the rules.

She said that if she was to be my sponsor, there were several things I would have to do from the start and continue to do them. First, I had to go to 12-step meetings every day. Second, while at those meetings I had to get women's phone numbers (preferably women who had been sober at least six months) and then call one of them every day. Third, I had to be willing to go to any length to stay clean and sober. She said this meant that I would have to put the same energy into staying clean as I used to put into staying high.

I really didn't have a problem with requirements one and three. But calling other *women*? I quickly informed Venita that

I didn't like that one. Without skipping a beat, she replied that I didn't have to *like* it; I just had to *do* it.

'But what do I say to them?'

Just the thought of talking to another woman was causing fear to form a large, dry lump in my throat.

'Just tell them your sponsor told you to call. They'll take it from there. Trust me.'

There was an uncomfortable silence as I sat thinking about whether I could actually do it.

'If you want what I have,' she said, 'you'll have to do what I did to get it. So what's it gonna be?'

I quickly thought about it. There was no doubt in my mind that I wanted what Venita had. She was so confident and self-assured. She seemed to really like who she was. I admired her beauty and her intelligence. But most important, I wanted her *recovery*. I had never been able to stop using. I couldn't. Even when I didn't want to use, I *had* to. More than anything, I wanted to stay clean.

'I'll do it,' I answered.

Next, she warned me that she could not keep me clean or sober. To do that, I would have to have a power greater than myself. I'd heard that phrase in the meetings. I wasn't sure what it meant, but every time someone mentioned it, they seemed to be talking about God. I didn't do God – at least not in the religious sense – I wasn't any particular religion and knew no religious rules.

'But, I'm not religious,' I blurted. As soon as the words came out, I regretted them. Maybe not having a religion would make her not want to be my sponsor.

'I didn't say anything about religion,' she calmly replied. 'Cupcake, listen to me and listen good.' The intensity in her voice made me listen. 'I only require that you believe in and depend on a power greater than yourself. Remember, alcoholism and addiction are diseases – diseases that are cunning, baffling, and powerful. Too powerful for man. And by 'man' I mean 'human.' Recovery has *nothing* to do with willpower, being weak, or a lack of self-control. Not even love can do it. Think about it. How many parents, grandparents, family members, friends do you know who, if they could, would use love to get their loved ones off of drugs and alcohol?'

416

My mind instantly brought up Daddy and Jr., – about how much they loved me and about how badly they'd tried to get me clean, but to no avail. Venita was right, if their love couldn't get me clean, no one's could – at least no human's.

'I'm not promoting religion or any particular concept of "God." And personally don't care what religion you are or aren't, whether you're an atheist or whether you believe one giant cosmic boom created the earth. The only thing I care about is that you realize that you're going to *have* to learn how to trust and rely on a power greater than yourself because unless you do, you WILL get loaded. So you will begin your mornings by asking this power for help to stay clean, and say thank you at night for doing so.'

She continued with her requirements by telling me that I had to call her every day. If she wasn't home, I was to leave a message.

Finally, she ended our conversation by telling me that I never had to drink and use again – even if I wanted to.

That was the craziest thing I'd ever heard.

'You mean even if I *want* to use, I don't have to?' I repeated in disbelief. The concept of *not* acting on a desire to use had never occurred to me.

'Even if you want to,' she answered matter-of-factly.

I wanted to ask her more questions, but the nurse walked by and tapped her watch, informing me that my phone time was up. When I told Venita, she made me quickly run through the rules to make sure I had them all. I did.

She told me she loved me, and hung up. For a while, I just stood staring at the phone.

Did she just tell me that she loved me?

I must have heard wrong. She didn't know me or anything about me. Surely if she knew the real Cup – the things I had done – she wouldn't have said that.

But she did say it.

Maybe she saw something I didn't. I decided right then and there not to question Venita, her rules, or what she said.

From that day on, Venita was my sponsor. I did everything she instructed: I called her every day; went to meetings every day; and worked on building a relationship with a higher power whom in the mornings I'd pray to, asking for help with not

417

using, and at night, giving thanks for it doing so. And, as much as I hated it, I called a woman every day.

At first I was petrified of calling the women. I'd dial the number, praying their answering machine would come on. Most times it did. When it didn't, however, I just blurted out my name, said I was new, and that my sponsor told me to call women.

Venita was right. As soon as I informed the women that my sponsor was forcing me to call, they'd start running their mouths. Most times, I had to cut them off just to get off the phone. I began developing friendships with some of the women I called. Others were just too damn chatty.

A month or so later Venita explained the reasoning behind this exercise.

'When you want to get loaded, the hardest thing to do is pick up the phone and ask for help – to dial a number and tell the person on the other end that you feel like using. This way, you get used to picking up the phone so when the time comes that you *really* need to do it, and trust me, the time will come, the receiver won't be so heavy.'

It made perfect sense. She was making me practice asking for help. No wonder she had five years clean.

Besides Venita (whose family and friends – which now included me – called her 'V'), I regularly talked to two people when I was in the hospital: Daddy and Jr. I did talk to Ken once to give him a brief rundown of what I was doing and how I was doing. He said, 'Take care of yourself, Cup.'

As usual, Daddy and Jr. were behind me 100 percent, and provided constant encouragement. When I first got to the hospital, I called them to let them know where I was. Thereafter, I called them often with updates on my progress. They even came to visit me once. We sat out in the garden, enjoying the sunshine. No one said anything for a while. It was an uncomfortable silence. I broke it by retelling them all that I'd been doing in rehab. They patiently listened and responded that they would do anything to help me stay clean, but that I had to want to be clean and I'd have to be serious about it. I told them I was. That seemed to break the ice. We engaged in some small talk for a while, being careful not to

418

bring up any drunk stories or any of my swindles, scams, or rip-offs.

Before I realized it, my release date was approaching and it dawned on me that I had nowhere to go. I couldn't live with Tommy. I didn't even know where he was and hadn't spoken to him since several days before I'd gone on my four-day run. I didn't want to live with him anyway. And even though Daddy hoped I would stay clean, he had no desire to live with me again. Jr. was too much like a parent. I'd go crazy if I had to live with him. The only other choice I had was Mona.

I was nervous about calling Mona, but had no choice. I said a small prayer, asking for her understanding and willingness to take me in, and dialed her number. She hadn't talked to me since the day she put me out; I expected her to hang up on me. She didn't. In fact, she was happy to hear from me and said she'd been worried about me. She'd called my job, but they wouldn't tell her whether I was dead or alive. The receptionist simply said that I 'wasn't there.' She was glad to hear I was in rehab and said she hoped nothing but the best for me.

After a few moments of silence, I told her why I'd called.

'Mona, I need a place to stay. I get out of here tomorrow and I have no place to go.'

I couldn't believe I had the audacity to ask her to let me come back. When she'd allowed me to live with her before, she'd given me several chances and on each occasion I blatantly disrespected her rules, her house, her marriage, and her trust. I figured she'd cuss me out and slam down the phone. I waited for the sound of a dial tone.

'Girl, you know you can stay here,' she said without hesitation. 'But the rules are the same. No getting high, 'kay?'

'Okay,' I whispered, still in shock that she would let me come back. I started to ask her why she'd done it, but thought better of it. No need in giving her cause to think about what she'd just done.

Even though my living-quarters problem was now taken care of, I still didn't want to leave the hospital. I felt safe there. Safe from dope dealers and liquor stores, safe from friends pushing joints into my mouth, shoving mirrors under my nose, and putting drinks into my hand. Safe from *me*.

Like she would do so many times after that, V walked me

through the fear of leaving. She reminded me that only *I* could get me loaded – not the people or places from my past. Me. 'The first drink is up to you – besides, you can't stay in that hospital forever. You've got to leave sooner or later.'

I knew she was right. I just wished it was later.

47

I soon realized several unanticipated benefits of being free from the hospital. First, I was able to talk to V as long as I wanted and as much as I wanted. No longer under a ten-minute phone limit, we could and would stay on the phone for hours. It was during these conversations that she began to walk me through what seemed to be innumerable fears. V explained that the fears were the result of experiencing life clean for the first time. Fear was only one of many emotions I'd re-experience in my new lifestyle.

I explained to V that it wasn't that I didn't like being clean; I just didn't like all of the *feelings:* I didn't like being afraid; I didn't like feeling nervous, panicky, or uneasy; I didn't like feeling unsure.

'I've always been the cool one,' I said with a hint of arrogance. 'I've always been in control.'

'You *thought* you were cool and in control,' she replied. 'Most times you were probably making a damn fool of yourself.'

I had to think about what she'd said for only a moment to realize it was true.

As if reading my mind, she continued. 'Because that's the insanity of the disease of addiction. You'd swear the drugs were working. You believe that, if only everyone else would just leave you alone and mind their own business, you'd be okay; you wouldn't have as many problems. Even now, you probably have doubts as to how bad your using really was. That's because you have a disease that tells you you don't have a disease.'

She told me not to try to understand everything at once. She encouraged me to stick around and 'don't quit five minutes before the miracle happens.'

There's gonna be a miracle? I've never seen a miracle. I wonder what one looks like?

She ended the conversation by promising that, if I stayed clean and continued on the road to recovery, everything would begin to make sense. So I did what I was told.

The second benefit of being out of the hospital was that I was able to go to any meeting I wanted and stay as long as I wanted. Without being under the hospital's strict time schedule, I got to meetings early or stayed late, which allowed me to get to know others struggling with the same addiction, the same feelings, and the same problems.

But the best benefit of all was getting away from all of that damn food. Because the hospital prepared delicious meals three times a day, because I could eat as much as I wanted, and because I was finally sober enough to realize I was hungry, I ate like there was no tomorrow. As a result, I quickly put on weight. I was there only a month, during which I'd gained almost seventeen pounds. By the time I left the hospital, the clothes I had brought, my size 1s, were too tight. I wasn't used to seeing myself with weight, I thought I looked like a moose.

'You could use some weight!' Daddy exclaimed when I complained to him about gaining weight and feeling fat. 'Hell, you need to put on some more weight! Punkin, you looked like a *string*!'

So I continued to eat – and fear.

My fear wouldn't allow me to go anywhere except 12-step meetings. I talked to no one except Daddy, Jr., and V. I kept my conversations with everyone else to a minimum, including Mona and James. And I did nothing except pray I wouldn't use that day. I'd learned the 'one day at a time' concept in the meetings and V constantly drilled it into my head.

'Don't worry about yesterday, it's already gone. There's nothing you can do about it. And tomorrow isn't here yet. Just don't use *today*. You can do anything for one day.'

I tried it and, surprisingly, it worked. Though it didn't take the fear away, it kept me clean because whenever I got the urge to use I'd tell myself, *You can get loaded* tomorrow, *but not* today.

I soon realized why this plan worked so well: it is always 'today.'

It wasn't long before I had to return to work – which I was also afraid to do.

Did the other employees know where I'd been?

When I was drunk or loaded, I never cared what people thought about me. Hell, the thought never crossed my mind. Why I cared so much now that I was sober, I didn't know. I just did. I especially cared about what Ken thought. He'd seen me at my worst. How could I ever look him in the eye again?

Again, V walked me through the fear and uncertainty. She made me realize that if Ken had wanted to toss me to the curb he would have done so when he saw the scrawny, dirty, stinky, drunken dope fiend standing in his office doorway.

'Obviously, he cares about you.'

Again, V was right. My fears about Ken were totally unfounded. My first day back at work, he welcomed me with a big hug and a wide smile. He seemed genuinely happy to see me. And I was shocked at how happy I was to see him.

The first time Robert came into the office, he leaped into my arms and gave me a big ol' hug.

'Hi, Cup!' he exclaimed. 'Where ya been?' He looked up at me, his brown eyes wide in anticipation, as if waiting for an explanation. The concern on his small face turned up toward mine told me he had been genuinely worried about why I'd been gone. I decided he didn't need to know why I'd left, but I wanted to be sure he knew I was glad to be back. So I sat him on my lap and ruffled my hands through his curly, curly brown hair as I told him that I'd missed him. And I had.

Since I was no longer messin' up my mind with dope and booze, my work quality increased significantly. I was amazed at how getting sleep and being in my right mind, i.e., a clean and sober mind, made me a better employee. The reduced number of mistakes was instantly noticeable, so was my attendance: I was on time every day, had no sudden deaths in my family requiring bereavement leave, and didn't call in sick once. Ken noticed my seemingly overnight improvement, and as a consequence began to give me more responsibility, which I gladly took on.

It was amazing how 'uneventful' my life became once I stopped the drugs and alcohol.

I didn't live with Mona long before it became apparent that I couldn't stay there: she and her husband still smoked weed and drank. They tried to respect me by not doing it in front of me. But I still knew they were doing it – I could smell the weed coming from under their bedroom door. The same bedroom door that I used to block to keep the smell of my crack from getting out. On top of that, I'd started getting cravings, and the awareness that there was dope and booze in the next room only made the cravings stronger.

'You gotta get out of that house,' V warned one day when we were having our daily check-in discussion. She said that I should never, ever be around drugs.

'What about booze?' I asked. She replied that, one day, I would be able to go wherever I wanted (even places where alcohol was being served), as long as I had a reason to be there. However, she cautioned that, at this point in my recovery, I was still too new and too weak to be around drugs *or* alcohol. Problem was that my credit was so bad and I had so many evictions on my credit report that no one would rent to me.

'Have you prayed about it?' V asked when I told her my dilemma.

'Pray for an apartment?' I asked. At this point I was only praying about my cravings. Besides, an apartment seemed so menial. 'Don'tcha think God got better things to do?'

'You should pray about *everything*,' V replied. 'How else are you going to build trust in God if you don't try Him?'

Why not? I asked myself. I had been talking to my 'Higher Power,' but kept the conversations short and simple. I first decided my Higher Power would be of the male persuasion (a decision which seemed to come naturally and just felt right). In the mornings, I asked Him to help me stay clean. And at night, I thanked Him for doing so. I said the prayers, but still wasn't sure if He heard me, if He was really helping me stay clean, or if He even existed. But that wasn't my immediate concern. My immediate concern was finding someone willing to rent to me despite my horrible credit; which brought me to my next concern: how was I supposed to ask for an apartment? I still didn't know any religious rules, sayings, or songs; and I had no desire to learn any. I wasn't reading any religious materials and, again, had no desire to do so. I tossed the question around in my mind until I got a headache. Aggravated at the thought of needing instructions about how to talk to God, I defiantly decided I'd just talk to Him like I talked to Daddy – straight out. If He was nearby, He should be able to hear.

That night, as I lay in bed, I thanked Him for another day clean and asked Him to help me find an apartment. I thought about it for a moment, and then quickly added, 'One I can afford.'

A week later, I still was at Mona's. I was getting discouraged and losing faith. V continued to encourage me. 'You've got to learn to trust Him, Cup. You're not always going to be able to see the big picture. But you've got to know that, no matter what, you'll be okay. Keep praying. Stay clean. And stay sober.'

I did.

Three days later, my prayer was answered, though at first I didn't realize it. I went to view a place that was advertised as 'a small one-bedroom cottage.' Once inside the place, it was apparent that 'small' was an understatement. It was tiny! Tiny and plain. No dishwasher. No garbage disposal. Not even a laundry room on site. A dirty, torn oversized couch sat rather prominently in the center of the unusually small living room. The owner explained that it had been left by the prior tenant. Looking around the cottage, I knew that it wasn't what I had in mind. Still, it was cheap and I needed a place to stay. So I applied for it.

Two days later, the owner called and said I could have the place if I wanted it. I felt as if I'd won the lottery. When I told him I'd take it, he said he was having the Goodwill come and pick up the dirty ol' raggedy couch and that it would be gone before I moved in that weekend. Realizing I had absolutely no furniture, I asked him if I could have it. Even though a moment before he was going to throw it away, once the bastard realized I wanted it, it suddenly became worth something. He replied that he'd *sell* it to me for twenty-five dollars. Unfortunately, I didn't have a choice. So I agreed – at least I'd have something to sit and sleep on.

I'd abandoned everything when I'd left Tommy – and,

frankly, because of our drug use, there really wasn't much to leave. I had absolutely nothing to my name, so moving was effortless. I did it in ten minutes.

On our way to the cottage, Mona took me by Kmart where I bought a set of pots and pans and looked for a cover for the couch. There wasn't much of a selection. I chose a country-looking one: it had large brown and beige flowers printed all over a slate-blue background. Brown lace and ruffles along the edges completed the country look. Upon leaving Kmart, we went to the grocery store so I could get a few groceries and a bus pass. When it was all said and done, I had twenty-five dollars to my name.

When we got to the apartment, I put my lil groceries away and put the cover on the couch. I had to admit that, with the cover, it actually looked kinda nice. The ruffles gave it a dainty ladylike appearance. Mona gave me a big hug, told me I was in for a 'new adventure,' and left. I didn't realize how silent silence was. I didn't have a television, record player, radio, anything. I looked around the shabby cottage.

What a dump!

I had nothing. And if that wasn't bad enough, I was stuck, *all alone,* in a tiny, shabby apartment with nothing but an old, ugly, USED couch. I began to feel sorry for myself and my pathetic predicament.

Why did I get stuck with such a sorry-ass place to live?

Just before a tear began to fall, my mind was suddenly (and surprisingly) hurled back to just a month or so before when I'd been crouched behind a Dumpster with nothing but a fifth of gin and a crack pipe. My mind flashed to the sickeningly thin woman with the dirty green dress and no shoes. And I remembered her prayer for help.

I'd gotten that help.

Then I remembered my prayers to stay clean. I'd been clean now for something like forty days.

I had prayed for an apartment – an *affordable* one – which is what I'd gotten. I glanced around the tiny apartment again. This time, it didn't look so shabby (at least it wasn't a Dumpster). And the couch didn't look so old and raggedy (at least with the soft, country-style cover, it was clean). The apartment may have been small, but it was mine and I was clean and sober. All of a

426

sudden, I forgot that there was no noise or music. I was instantly filled with such gratitude that I didn't *need* any. I began dancing to my own music.

Imitating Jennifer Beals in *Flash Dance,* I danced in the lil living room, moving my legs and feet as fast as I could and with all my might. Then I did the running man into the kitchen. Once there, I threw up my right leg in a kick, imitating Michael Jackson.

This one's for you, Michael!

After a few moments, I cha-chaed into the bedroom. There was absolutely nothing in it, so I did a cartwheel. However, even empty the room was only large enough to do *one* complete cartwheel without smashing into the wall. So, I did one – over and over and over. Then, I did the bump with the walls as I made my way into the little bathroom.

I danced a joy dance in every room. As I danced, the tears fell because *I remembered.*

When I could dance no more, I plopped down on the couch with a new understanding of my situation: I was clean and sober, I had a little bit of money, I had my own place, and I had a couch. These few things were better than gold to me.

Seeing as how He'd come through on the apartment, that night, before plunging into sleep, I asked God if He could somehow get me some bedroom furniture and some dishes. I reminded Him that it had taken every dime I had to get the apartment, and what little money I had left over was spent on pots, the couch cover, a bus pass, and food. All I had till payday was twenty-five dollars. I ended my prayers by telling Him that if He couldn't do it, it was cool because I was grateful for what He *had* done. I again thanked Him for those things – especially recovery.

For the first time in fifteen years I slept in total peace and with absolute serenity, in that little shabby apartment, on that ol' beat-up couch, completely clean and sober.

Several days later, Maria, the older white lady who'd trained me when I first began working at the firm, blessed me. I hadn't talked to her much since I initially started working at the firm – she was nice to me, but I thought she was nuts. Plus, she'd eventually learned to treat me the way a china serving platter treats a bull in the shop. I was sitting in the break room, worrying about how I was going to live on my limited funds in a completely empty apartment, when she walked in and sat down. I looked at her suspiciously, waiting for her to state what she wanted.

She said she'd heard that I'd recently gotten sober. I froze when she said that. I wasn't sure if she was coming to complain about my stealing from her (I'd stolen from so many people, I'd long since lost track), or to demand money that I'd borrowed from her but never repaid (I owed so many folks money, I'd also lost track). My mind raced frantically trying to decide what scam or rip-off I'd pulled on her. Interrupting my panic-stricken thoughts, she said that she had a set of dishes she had planned to give to the Goodwill, but that if I wanted them I could have them.

I sat staring at her disbelievingly.

I just prayed for some dishes! This is happening too soon! This has to be coincidence!

She continued, saying that the dishes were still in pretty good condition, and very pretty. She said what she had was a complete setting for four: plates, bowls, cups, saucers. She said there were even serving bowls and a gravy boat.

I don't need no damn boat. But I do need those dishes!

She said she wasn't trying to offend me, but figured I could use some housewares.

'Sure, I'll take them,' I said without hesitation or pride as I reflected on what V was always telling me: there was nothing wrong with asking for, or accepting, help.

Maria left the room saying she'd bring the dishes to my house.

M-m-my house?

At the thought of someone seeing my house, I felt the panic and shame return. I didn't want Maria at my house. I didn't want anyone at my house. There was nothing in my house except that ol' raggedy couch. I was too embarrassed for anyone to see the squalor I was living in. (Ain't it funny how quickly pride erased gratitude?)

As I jumped up to catch Maria to tell her she couldn't come to my house, Sylvia, another secretary walked up and suddenly grabbed my arm. I knew her, but, as with everyone else at the firm, I'd never talked to her unless I had something smart or nasty to say. I looked down at her hand firmly grasping my arm and started to say something smart like, *Bitch, git yo' hands off me!* But before I could speak, she did.

'I've got a nineteen-inch color TV. There's nothing wrong with it. It's just that I've bought another one and I have no place to put this one. I'm thinking about selling it. Do you want it?'

'Wh-whaaat?' I stuttered. She'd caught me completely off guard.

'The TV,' she repeated. 'Do you want to buy the TV?'

I thought about it for a moment. It was a dilemma.

If I say yes, but she wanted too much money, I'd be embarrassed and angry thinking she fronted me off on purpose. On the other hand, if I said no, I might be letting my pride make me miss out on a great deal.

What should I do?

She stood looking at me, unsure of why I was so confused about such a simple question.

'How much do you want for it?' I asked with a puzzled look, expecting to hear some astronomical amount.

'Oh, I don't know. It's only five years old, and it still plays really good and clear.'

Here we go. She's pumping up all the reasons why it's worth a couple hundred dollars.

'We bought it brand-new. It's a Sony, you know. Top of the line.'

'How much?' She was starting to get on my nerves.

'Oh, I don't know. How about . . . let's say . . . ummmm . . . fifty dollars?'

Fifty bucks? Was she joking?

'All I have is twenty-five dollars. I can give you twenty-five now and the rest on payday.'

'That's okay,' she said.

I turned to walk away, angry at myself for falling for her ploy.

'Just give me the twenty-five dollars.'

I stopped dead in my tracks – left foot still in midair.

'What did you say?' I asked softly as I lowered my foot and slowly turned around to face her.

'It's cool. Just give me the twenty-five now and we'll call it even.'

I didn't know what to say, so I just stood there staring at her.

'No, really. I just want to get rid of it because I have no place to put it. So just give me the twenty-five dollars, and you can have it today, if you want.'

I felt like crying. I didn't know whether to hug her, kiss her, or shake her hand. So I handed her the money and just stood there. I explained to her that I didn't have a car and so I wouldn't be able to pick it up. She walked away saying something about getting together with me later to figure out how to get it to me. I really wasn't paying her any attention at that point. I just stood there with my mouth open.

Later that afternoon I was still in shock from the TV incident when Maria came to my desk and asked for my address so she could deliver the dishes. I refused to give it to her, insisting that she bring them to work instead. Confused at my sudden change in behavior, she walked away mumbling something about trying again the next day.

That night during my usual conversation with V, I told her all that had happened that day.

'I don't want her to see where I live!' I cried as I tried to explain why I wasn't letting Maria, or anyone else, come to my apartment.

'Cup, if someone is your friend because of where you live or what you have, they're not your friend. Those are the kind of people we dealt with in the *streets* – people who only hung with us because of what we had or what we could do for them. But remember, in recovery, we're changing our friends, our surroundings, our lives. She wants to help you, Cup. And you *need* help! It's okay to need help. Besides, I truly believe she doesn't care where you live or what your apartment looks like. Give her a chance. What's the worst that could happen?'

She had a point. Still, I was afraid of being judged and rejected. I didn't want anyone at my house till I had it 'pimped out.' However, with my current finances, that would take awhile and I couldn't wait. I needed something to eat off now. So after giving it some serious thought, I had to admit that, as usual, V made sense.

I gave Maria my address and told her that she could bring the dishes to my house that weekend. As I was doing so, Sylvia just happened to approach my desk and ask me what I wanted to do as far as making arrangements to get the TV. Before I could respond, Maria said that, since she was already coming to my house to bring the dishes, she would be willing to also bring the TV. We were all in agreement that that was a good idea.

That Saturday, I tried to clean my apartment and get it as ready for company as best I could. There wasn't much in it, so there wasn't much to do to get it ready. I swept the carpeted floors (I didn't have a vacuum cleaner), and straightened the cover on the couch. Then I sat down and waited, all the while trying to determine how Maria would react once she saw my menial living quarters.

She'll probably start shunning you at work, I convinced myself. *Or maybe she'll go tell all the other secretaries what a deplorable, pathetic life you live. Or maybe she'll tell them that God is punishing you for all the shitty things you've done, for all the stuff you've stolen, all the gang fights and shootings, the 'business arrangements'* . . .

By the time Maria and her husband were making their way to my door, I was sitting on the couch rocking my body back and forth. They knocked at the door, startling me. I sat perfectly still, hoping they'd figure I wasn't home and go away.

They didn't.

Again they knocked, this time much louder.

'I *know* she's in there!' I heard Maria say. She was holding the TV while standing on her tiptoes trying to peek into the window. Realizing they weren't leaving, I reluctantly opened the door; my head lowered in embarrassment.

'What a cute little place!' Maria exclaimed as she entered. She set the TV down in the middle of the floor and looked around the tiny apartment.

'It's got such character! There's so much you could do with it!' she said with apparent genuineness. She didn't seem to be making an effort to fight back a laugh. She wasn't making any snide comments about the size or emptiness. I was speechless.

She cheerfully introduced her husband, Brian. He was a large, heavily built man with a deep, husky voice and a large warm smile. He apologized for not being able to shake my hand and nodded toward the large, and apparently heavy, box he was holding.

'Oh, honey!' Maria exclaimed as she realized her husband

was having difficulty keeping the box balanced. 'Let me help you with that.'

He huffed in appreciation. I don't know what she meant by 'help' because she never reached for the box. Instead, she simply led him to the tiny kitchen, which was visible from the small living room. As I followed, I started to ask if they wanted a tour, but realized it wasn't necessary: one could stand in the middle of the living room, make a 360-degree turn, and see the entire place and all of its contents.

Brian set the box on the counter and began rubbing his arms, as if to soothe them. Ignoring his apparent pain, Maria began removing its contents.

'Here are the plates,' she announced happily as she handed one to me. I reached for it and studied it inquisitively. It was white with yellow daisies all around the rim. I turned it over and a stamp informed me it was 'fine china.'

'This is *china*?' I asked as I continued to look the plate over. I'd seen, and cleaned, china before – both Diane and Mrs Bassinet had the best money could buy – but I'd never owned any myself.

'Yeah. It's a really nice set, huh?'

Why would someone want to give me *something so nice – and for FREE?*

'What's wrong with them?' I asked, eyeing her suspiciously.

'Nothing, honey!' she chimed. 'I just bought myself a brand-new set. I don't need TWO! So I figured I'd give them to someone who could use them. You *can* use them, can't ya?' Now she was looking at me suspiciously.

'Hell, yeah!' I shrieked. I didn't mean to cuss, but I was excited and didn't want her to change her mind. I was beginning to recognize blessings when I saw them.

She didn't seem to mind the cussword.

I didn't cook and so had no intention of using the serving platters, boat, or any of that other stuff. All I really needed were the dinner plates and salad bowls – but for cereal, not salads. Still, I'd never had china before. So I graciously took it and kept my mouth shut.

'We gotta go!' Maria almost sang to her husband as she turned and began walking toward the front door.

I sort of wanted them to stay. Now that I realized that they weren't judging me, I could have used the company. But fear of rejection wouldn't allow me to say anything.

Besides, just because she likes the place doesn't mean she wants to stay in it.

Damn, I wished my mind would shut up sometimes!

'Bye,' Brian said brusquely as he stepped onto the porch and out into the California sun. He was a giant of a man, but not intimidating or threatening in the least. He was more like a gentle giant. He stood for a moment with his massive face to the sky as if soaking up its warmth. Suddenly, he gave me a wink and a smile and walked (or more like stomped) to their car. Just before stepping out onto the porch to follow him, Maria turned to me.

'I always knew there was something special about you.'

I kept quiet, but gave her a slight smile.

'I'm so glad you're getting better. I bet you've been through things that others can only imagine. You have been places others never return from. That is why you are going to touch so many people.'

Before I could sarcastically respond that people rarely wanted to 'touch' me, she turned and skipped to the car. I'd never seen a fifty-plus woman skipping before. It was a surprisingly pleasant sight. I couldn't remember the last time I'd skipped. Maybe I'd try it one day.

In a flash, they were gone. She never asked for money for the dishes and she never made me feel ashamed about needing them. I was flabbergasted at the ease of it all.

What did she mean by that 'touch people' stuff? I didn't want to touch nobody and I really didn't want nobody touching me. Remembering that she was nuts, my mind changed thoughts. I had a TV *and* some dishes!

Could it really be that, just like that, my prayer had been answered? Well, wait a minute. I didn't ask for a TV!

It all just seemed too easy.

Quit trippin' girl! I scolded myself. *Now you've got something to eat on and something to watch while you eat!*

I didn't have a stand to put the TV on. I didn't care. It was just as beautiful sitting on the floor.

I returned to the kitchen and begin putting my new china away. As I did so, I felt as though I'd won the lottery – again.

Moments after I had all of the china put in the cabinet, Jr. called and said he'd been going through his garage and found an old mattress and box spring that belonged to my mother. He asked if I could use it.

'I just prayed for a mattress!' I shrieked into his ear. I couldn't believe it. 'Yeah, I can use it! I need it!'

He said he'd use his van to bring it over.

A little while later, Jr. came over with the furniture. To my surprise, not only did he bring the mattress and box spring, but he also brought a dresser and a small stand. He said he didn't know if I could use the stand, but he saw it and thought he'd bring it anyway. Lo and behold, the television fit the stand perfectly – almost as if the stand was made to hold it!

I was in heaven. In one day, both my prayers had been answered. *And,* I'd gotten a TV – something I didn't even ask for.

That night, I made up my mind about the whole situation. This was no coincidence.

48

My relationship with 12-step meetings had gone from in-difference to boredom to obligation to love. I hadn't been able to find such genuine camaraderie and solidarity since bangin'. Everyone at the meetings was working on a relationship with 'God,' though each viewed Him (or Her) in his or her own way. There were Catholics, Baptists, Jews, Buddhists, Muslims, and people of other faiths I'd never heard of; there were agnostics and even atheists. What I thought was the coolest was that everyone respected everyone else's belief – even if it didn't agree with their own. And regardless of one's religious/spiritual beliefs (or lack thereof), everyone seemed to genuinely want everyone else to stay clean and sober. Unlike most religious folks I'd heard about, the people in the meetings never judged anyone else about their beliefs, nonbeliefs, or life/criminal history.

The meetings were occasionally repetitive, but that didn't make them any less fascinating. The stories people shared had common elements that cropped up again and again. For instance, I heard one person after another talking about how they could no longer hang with friends who were still using, and were no longer able to hang out at places where dope was present. I heard them, but I paid them no attention.

V also continually warned me to watch whom I hung with, the places I hung out at, and the things I did when I hung out. She warned that the company I kept would determine the activity I participated in. I paid her warnings no mind.

I wasn't worrying about getting loaded anymore. Since getting out of the hospital, I'd been able to fight off urges to use by doing the 'one day at a time' thing. But V gave me several

435

other tools because she assured me that the overwhelming urge to use would hit me sooner or later. The first thing to do, no matter what, was to pray. Then, depending on the situation, I could do one or all of the following. If I was in a slippery place, I was to get out of there immediately. Next, I should call someone – V, or another person in recovery – and then I was to get to a meeting as soon as possible. V said that every situation would be different so, except for praying first, I wouldn't necessarily use these tools in a particular order, or at all – the order wasn't what was important; what was important is that I used the tools. Again, I paid her warnings no mind.

She also warned me that if I had any reservations, I wasn't ready for recovery. I thought about it. I didn't *really* have any reservations. Well, maybe one: I didn't think I was an alcoholic.

I was nothing like the people in the meetings. *Those* people talked about having gone to jail for DUIs. *I'd* never had a DUI. *Those* people talked about not being able to hold a job because of drinking. *I* kept a job! I didn't do any of the things they did: I never sat on a corner begging for money to buy booze; I didn't drink every day (okay, I *had* drunk every day, but only to calm my nerves).

Still, I smiled and told V that I didn't have any reservations.

'Cup, are you sure? Remember, reservations get us loaded.'

'Y-yes,' I stammered.

Shortly after I returned to work, Tommy started calling me again. I told him I'd been in rehab and was no longer getting high. He said he'd quit using too, that he'd even quit smoking cigarettes, and that he just wanted to be friends. Though I liked my new, clean friends, I missed my old, get-high ones. I felt like they knew me. I'd convinced myself that they loved me. So, convincing myself that I needed to be around such familiar people, I let Tommy pick me up every once in a while. We'd hang out or go to a meeting. Although Tommy hated 12-step programs, he'd endure a meeting for me. He thought that, by going, he'd have a better chance of getting back with me.

I didn't see Mona much, but I had begun hanging out with Rose. Though Rose and I used to smoke crack together, I felt she was now safe to be around. She'd quit smoking the moment she found out she was pregnant. That child, a boy, was almost six months old now, and Rose had stayed clean. I was proud of her. So we often hung out, which meant hitting the local swap meets.

Before I knew it, me, Tommy, and Rose were hanging out every weekend. I didn't see anything wrong with it. In fact, I believed they were safe because they knew I'd been in rehab and wasn't supposed to get high.

Because they hung with me so much during my first couple of months out of the hospital, Tommy and Rose often got to see me at my worst – usually as a result of withdrawal. Although I didn't have any more DTs, I still experienced various physical effects that I later learned were the result of my body still withdrawing: headaches, shivers, sudden sweating, and mood swings. But the most dangerous withdrawal effect of all was my uncontrollable anger, which usually manifested when I was silently fighting the urge to use. (It would be a while before I realized that the anger and the urge to use always occurred simultaneously.)

We decided to go to a Dairy Queen to get some ice cream. It was an abnormally hot September day. I, Tommy, Rose, and her baby, Kevin, had spent the day hanging out. Kevin sat in his stroller, seemingly oblivious to the heat, while we adults were fanning ourselves with anything we could find in an effort to fight off the sweltering heat. I'd been thinking about how pleasant a nice cold beer would be. Though I was thinking it, I dared not say anything about it. I thought it was a no-no to *think* about drinking. So I kept quiet and silently continued trying to fight the urge to buy a beer instead of an ice cream cone.

We walked into the Dairy Queen and immediately became grateful for the blasting air conditioner. Two young girls were working behind the counter, one white and one black. Rose ordered an ice cream, and Tommy ordered some sort of ice-cream drink. The white girl ran off to start making their orders, leaving the black girl to take mine. I told her that all I wanted was a sundae. A simple banana split. That's it. She nodded her head and turned away from me. But she didn't start making my split. It was as if, for some reason, she hadn't understood what I'd said. I watched patiently as she slowly sauntered here and there behind the counter, doing what, I didn't know. All I knew was that she was moving too damn slow and she wasn't making my sundae. Suddenly, my patience ran out and I went off.

'Bitch!' I screamed, startling Tommy, Rose, and even little Kevin, who stopped inspecting his feet to look up and see what all of the commotion was about. Several patrons looked up from their various frozen treats.

'I *said* I wanted a banana split. Do you not speak fuckin' English?' I yelled. The young black girl, who looked to be about fifteen or so, stopped suddenly in her tracks and gasped at me, apparently in shock. The restaurant, moments ago filled with laughter and chatter, suddenly became eerily quiet.

'Aw, shit,' I heard Tommy grumble under his breath next to me. 'Here we go again.'

'A sundae, bitch!' I screamed, ignoring Tommy's comment. 'All I want is a fuckin' split! Do you know what that is?' Without waiting for her to answer, I told her.

'It's a fuckin' dish with bananas, ice cream, syrup, nuts, and whipped cream! Now do you think you can do that?' I was fuming.

The girl still didn't move. I wasn't sure if it was fear, shock, or both that kept her frozen in place. Nor did I care. All I cared about was getting my fuckin' split. And for some odd reason, this chick was taking forever to make it.

Suddenly, I decided to make it myself. And told her so.

'Move! Shit!' I hollered as I hopped the counter, pushed her out of the way, and began opening containers, slamming cabinets, and throwing stuff, trying to find what I wanted for my sundae. Suddenly, I started crying, not from sadness, but from rage. 'I'll make it myself!' I screamed through snot and tears.

The white girl, who was coming out from the back with a slushy cup in one hand and a can of whipped cream in the other, stopped in her tracks. Where she stopped, she just happened to be standing next to the black girl. Both of them stared at me in disbelief.

The place was so quiet, you could have heard a pin drop – well, that is, you could have if it hadn't been for my ranting and raving, slamming, throwing, and cussing.

'Where's the fuckin' cherries?' I yelled, continuing to stomp around searching for ingredients for my sundae. The only kind of ice cream I could find was vanilla. I wanted strawberry.

'Is this the only kind of ice cream you got?' I don't know why I kept asking questions. No one was answering them.

Being unable to find everything I needed pissed me off even more. So I threw whatever I didn't want. I found some pineapple syrup. It wasn't what I was looking for. I threw it up against the wall. As the syrup flew across the room, every eye in the place followed it until it splattered. I continued searching, cussing, throwing, and slamming. Holding the place at bay, my whole ordeal lasted about two minutes.

Finally, my banana split was finished, although it didn't *look* like one. It looked like a mess from the haphazard way I'd thrown it all together into the little banana-shaped bowl. Satisfied with my creation, I hopped back over the counter, sat at a nearby table, and began eating it, as if my actions had been completely natural.

Finally, someone spoke.

'Call the police,' the white girl tried to whisper. Her nervousness made her voice louder than she planned.

'What'd you say?' I snapped as I jumped to my feet. 'Fuck the police. Come outside bitch and I'll whup yo' ass!'

The white girl picked up the phone and started dialing.

'Aw, shit,' Tommy grumbled. 'Cup, let's go,' he snapped as he began dragging me toward the door. 'Everything can't be handled by fighting!'

Why can't it? I wondered.

Once we were in the car pulling off, Rose finally spoke.

'Girl, you acted a fuckin' fool back there!' she said with disgust. 'And I'm here with my baby and everything. I can't be fighting with my baby!'

'No one asked *you* to fight!' I snapped.

'Girl, you know I ain't gon' let you get into no shit without having yo' back. What if that white girl had jumped in? I'd've had to whup her ass. Girl, we too old for this shit.'

Damn, I wished she'd shut up. She didn't.

'Cup, you've got to grow up. You've got to change your ways. You're not fifteen anymore. You're twenty-five and you need to start acting like it!'

Tommy readily agreed. They then began talking about my previous debacles. Of course, Tommy brought up the dinner cruise on our honeymoon.

'Yeah,' Rose replied, 'but she was drunk then. She's sober now and still acting a fuckin' fool.'

I was still pissed and so pretty much ignored them.

They dropped me off and drove off, angry. Neither of them would talk to me or hang with me. I didn't care. I didn't see anything wrong with what I'd done. That is, until the next day when I told V about it. She went off on me.

'Who the fuck do you think you are?' she shouted. We were having our daily telephone check-in, so, although I couldn't see her, I could envision her facial expression: eyebrows all scrunched, mouth in a scowl, eyes glaring with anger. 'You think rules don't apply to *you*?'

'But, she was moving too slo – ' I tried to interject to explain why I'd done what I'd done. V angrily cut me off.

'I don't give a fuck what she was doing. Recovery is about changing *your* ways, not someone else's. You can't control what other people do. But you can control what you do. Cup, that type of behavior is unacceptable. I know that in the streets, cussing and fighting are tools of the trade. But you're no longer in the streets. It's time to find a "new trade." Furthermore, and more important, you're no longer a child, so those temper tantrums are unacceptable.'

Is that what I was doing? Throwing a temper tantrum?

'It's time for you to grow up and learn to be responsible for your actions.'

She was totally intolerant of my behavior. On and on she went, fussing at me for almost a half hour. When she was finally done, I felt an inch tall. For the first time in years, I was ashamed and embarrassed by my behavior, partly because I wasn't drunk, so I remembered everything I'd done, and partly because my conscience had sobered up and woken up – and it was telling me I was wrong.

V then asked if I'd been thinking about drinking or using when I'd gone off like that. I lied and said I hadn't.

'Are you sure? Because it sounds like you were craving and didn't know how to handle it.'

Again I lied and said I wasn't thinking about drinking.

'Well, if you do think about drinking, it's okay. I mean, you've been drinking and using since you were eleven. It's unnatural to think it will never pop up again. It will. And when it does, you need to get that shit out. You hear me? Tell someone.'

I told her I would, but knew I wouldn't. My ego wouldn't allow me to admit I still wanted to drink.

V then announced that I'd have to return to Dairy Queen and make amends to the two girls.

'What the fuck is an 'amend'?' I asked suspiciously. V explained that it was an apology. A *sincere* apology.

'Can't I just call 'em?' I whined. I did not want to go back there.

'Oh, *now* you're concerned about how you look?' she asked sarcastically. 'You weren't concerned when you were throwing shit, acting a damn fool!'

She was right.

'No. You must make direct amends,' she stated firmly. 'From now on, *whenever* you wrong someone, you must make direct amends. The amends are for you, not them.'

'But how will I know when I've wronged someone?'

'Well, this time, it's pretty obvious,' she replied. But she did explain that I would eventually get to a step that would require me to take daily stock of my actions and conduct, and if I realized I'd harmed someone, I'd have to make direct amends.

The next day, V took me back to the Dairy Queen to make amends. Approaching the glass door, I could see the same two girls were working. They looked up and gasped when they saw me come in. The white girl grabbed the phone and got her finger ready to start punching buttons.

'Wait! Wait!' I yelled as I ran up to the counter. Startled, she held the phone tightly in her hand, her forefinger pointed at the dial pad, ready to go. Quietly, but sincerely, I apologized for my previous behavior. I started crying. I really did feel bad about the way I'd acted. I admitted that my conduct was unacceptable and wouldn't happen again. Then, I laid a twenty-dollar bill on the counter and explained that it was in payment for my sundae as well as Tommy and Rose's treats (since we'd left without paying). Our order together couldn't have cost more than five or six dollars. But the remaining fourteen or fifteen dollars was nowhere near what they should have been paid for what they'd had to endure. Still, it was a small attempt on my part to show my sincere remorse. Surprised at my apology, neither girl touched the money, but stood staring at me, eyes bulging, mouths open. Humbled and humiliated, I turned and walked out.

V then made me make amends to Tommy and Rose. I hated apologizing to them even more than the girls at Dairy Queen because they'd seen me act a fool for years and I'd never apologized before. In fact, it was something we usually laughed about the next day. But, sick of my behavior, Tommy and Rose were no longer amused; their laughter had turned to disgust.

With V by my side urging me on, I apologized for my behavior and acknowledged it was unacceptable. They each smiled, but said nothing. They didn't believe I could keep my word. They'd seen me go off too many times. Little did they know, this time I meant it.

Years later, someone told me that the hardest lessons learned are the best lessons learned. Well, that episode at the Dairy Queen turned out to be my best lesson in anger management. From that day forward, I've never acted like that again. Oh, I still get pissed and you'll still hear me cussing every now and then. But no more physical violence, though I have often had to sit on my hands or literally leave the room to keep from fighting. I just didn't like the way belligerent behavior made me feel. I didn't like remembering my ignorant conduct. More important, I hated making amends.

A couple of weeks later, Rose and Tommy started hanging out with me again. V again warned me about hanging with old friends, but I figured she couldn't have meant Tommy and Rose. They were safe. They were also the people I wanted to be with to celebrate having achieved sixty-nine days clean and sober. (There was nothing really special about sixty-nine days. Most people celebrated ninety days clean. I decided to be different and celebrate sixty-nine.)

'Let's really celebrate!' Rose said. She, Tommy, and I were hanging out in my living room. Bored.

'You know I can't do no stuff!' I snapped.

'Girl, ain't nobody said nothing 'bout dope. I'm talkin' 'bout going out – to a club! Let's go dancing!'

I hadn't been to a club since getting clean. I loved to dance and I loved to club. It sounded like fun.

Something told me I should have called V and told her about

what I was contemplating. Something also told me to pray. But I didn't want to bother God.

Besides, what could it hurt? So we got dressed and went out.

We decided to go to a juke joint called the Chat-N-Chew, a small hole in the wall located in an area of San Diego known as Barrio Logan. The Chat-N-Chew had been around for years – and it looked like it. The dirty old dilapidated shack looked like something left over from slavery. The windows were so dirty folks on the outside couldn't see in. Those inside could see out – that is, if they could see over the loads of cardboard boxes, trash, and other junk that were kept piled up along the building's exterior. Despite the dirt on the outside, the inside was kept pretty clean – at least the drinking glasses were.

In addition to being shabby and grubby, the Chat-N-Chew was also very small. Packed inside were a dirty brown counter that served as the bar, a few small round tables, and chairs. A pool table sat in one corner. A rusty old juke-box, which looked like it had played its last song, stood in another corner. The place wasn't large enough for a dance floor, so people danced wherever they wanted and wherever they stood. There was never a DJ – there was no *room*. Actually, a DJ wasn't necessary since the rotting ol' jukebox was filled with golden oldies: the songs of Smokey Robinson, Marvin Gaye, Etta James, Bobby 'Blue' Bland, and numerous other blues and R&B artists blared from its tattered speakers, taking patrons back to 'the good ol' days' and keeping them dancing all night.

Anyone who wasn't familiar with the hood would probably have been afraid to enter the Chat-N-Chew. Hell, most people that lived in the hood wouldn't go there. It was known as a rough spot where fights and brawls could (and often did) break out at any moment. It was my kind of place! The only thing *I* didn't like about it was that it didn't sell hard liquor – only beer and wine. So when I used to drink, before rehab, it was only a *starting* place for partying.

But this particular night, drinking, or rather *taking* a drink, was the farthest thing from my mind. I mean, I *was* thinking about alcohol, but only because its absence was the reason for the celebration – sixty-nine days of continued sobriety!

I walked into the Chat-N-Chew, smelling good, looking fly,

and feeling fine. It was still early, so it wasn't very crowded yet. Rose spotted her aunt and some friends at one of the tables. We pulled up a table and joined them. Soon, a waitress came to take drink orders. Everyone began ordering. Rose's aunt and her friends ordered more beer. Tommy ordered himself a beer and Rose a glass of wine.

'What do you want, Cup?' he asked. Without hesitation, I replied, 'A coke.'

Drinking wasn't on my mind.

I engaged in small talk with those around me. I asked Rose's aunt about her children, listened to someone's story about a fight that had broken out at the Chat-N-Chew the night before. Then someone else chimed in that they could top that and told about a stabbing two nights before. We laughed and talked and enjoyed the music. We were talking and laughing loudly when the waitress returned with a small round tray loaded with drinks. As she sat down the bottles of beer and glasses of wine, I marveled at myself and how easily I'd ordered that coke.

Could an alcoholic have done that? No way! They sit on corners, begging for booze. They can't stop drinking! I've stopped and stayed stopped. I'd even ordered coke! What drunk orders a coke? Girl, you ain't no alcoholic. You just can't do dope!

Just like that, my mind flipped on me.

I wonder if this is what V meant when she asked whether I had any reservations? I asked myself.

Naw, she meant any reservations about dope. I answered. *You've admitted you're a dope fiend. We're talking about drinking!*

Who the fuck is 'we'?

My mind was trippin'. Suddenly, I wanted a drink. I *needed* a drink.

Maybe you should call someone, the quiet Voice said.

I ignored it.

'Hey, y'all,' I said loudly. Everyone around the tables had been laughing and chatting. At my announcement, everyone grew quiet.

'Y'all know I've been sober for sixty-nine days.'

'Yeah, yeah,' everyone acknowledged. Some nodded their heads. Whether they really knew it or not, I didn't know.

Nor did I care. That wasn't the focus of my announcement.

'Girl, I'm proud of you,' Rose said as she gulped down some wine. 'You was fucked up!' Everyone busted out laughing.

'Well, I've got some more good news.' At the mention of 'news' the crowd grew silent, expecting to hear about yet another ghetto 'throw-down.'

'My sponsor said I can have white wine.' Their dazed looks told me they had no idea about what I was talking about. The way they immediately returned to their conversations told me that they didn't care what I was talking about. But Tommy and Rose did.

'I thought you said you weren't supposed to drink,' Rose said. Tommy nodded in agreement.

I didn't respond. Hell, I didn't have a response. After I'd been released from the hospital and was still beaming with the excitement of my newfound sobriety, I'd shared with them that having the disease of addiction meant that I wasn't supposed to do drugs *or* drink. However, it never occurred to me that they'd actually been listening to me.

Think fast, girl. Think fast.

Suddenly, an answer came to me.

'Ah, oh, ummmm, yeah. Yeah. I did tell you that. But, that's because when you first get sober, they tell you that you can't drink because they don't want you to get too carried away. So, they wait until you get sixty-nine days clean before telling you that you can drink. Just today, in fact, V, my sponsor – you guys have heard me talk about V, right? – well, today, I'm celebrating sixty-nine days, and today, she told me that I could drink.'

They stared at me; quizzical looks still on their faces. They weren't falling for it.

'But I can only have wine.'

That limitation seemed to satisfy their doubts. So I continued while I was hot.

'And, it has to be *natural* wine.'

'Well, then,' Rose announced, obviously satisfied with my clarification. 'Let's see if they got some natural wine here!' She stood up, spotted the waitress, and flagged her over to our table. The waitress angrily held up one finger informing us that she'd be over 'in a minute.' What, she really meant was, *I'll get there when I fuckin' feel like it.*

445

I sat for a few moments, trying to be patient. I had butterflies in my stomach and my mouth was suddenly very, very dry. I really needed a drink.

Maybe you should call V, the Voice again quietly stated. *Maybe you should call someone in recovery.*

Again, I ignored it.

All I could think about was getting a sip of wine. That's all I wanted – a sip. I'd just take a sip and leave the rest in the glass. I could control it. I mean, it wasn't like I was an *alcoholic* or anything. . . .

The more and more I thought about it, the more and more I wanted it. After about ten minutes, my patience had run out. I couldn't take it anymore; I felt like I would explode with excited anticipation.

Just as I stood up to go get the damn wine myself, I spotted the waitress walking toward our table.

'Yeah?' she snapped as she approached.

'You got any natural wine?' Rose asked.

'We got wine,' the waitress impatiently replied.

'Yeah, but do you have *natural* wine?' Rose asked with such sincerity. 'It's got to be *natural* wine.'

I didn't care whether it was natural or not. But it was too late, I'd already told them it had to be natural. 'I'll bring you the bottle and you can see for yo'self,' the waitress growled as she walked away.

Damn, I hope that fuckin' label says 'natural' somewhere on it!

'She'll bring us the bottle,' Rose informed me – as if I hadn't heard the waitress myself. I sat for what seemed like forever. I thought the heifer would never return. But, I forced myself to sit still. I didn't want to seem too eager.

Finally, the waitress returned with a bottle of white wine. There on the label in large green letters it read, 'Natural White Wine.'

Hot damn! I could barely contain my excitement.

Rose took the bottle and carefully examined the label. I quickly pointed out the word *natural*.

'Uh-huh,' she acknowledged as she continued her vigilant inspection of the bottle's content.

'Okay. It's natural, all right,' she announced with finality, obviously satisfied with what the label revealed. 'Here you go!' she chimed happily as she handed me a glass and began pouring me a drink.

I held the glass tightly so it wouldn't tip over as she filled it. The wine looked so beautiful, so *alive* as it splashed its way into the glass.

You should call V, the Voice calmly stated once again.

Ignoring it, I gulped down the wine. The Voice didn't speak again.

The wine was warm going down. It was *good* going down. Suddenly I remembered why I loved to drink. Why I had to drink. Instantly, I was happy. Confident and self-assured. I was hip, slick, and cool – once more. Sh-i-t! I wasn't an alcoholic!

I downed that glass of wine and quickly poured another. No one saw me gulp the second glass. They were all up on their feet, slurring, 'Dat's ma jam!' as Billie Holiday begged for someone to give her a 'pig foot and a bottle of beer.' Sitting there watching everyone dance and feel good, feel good and dance, I began to drink even faster. I had to catch up with them – they'd all been drinking for a while and were already high.

Before Billie was through singing, I'd finished off the bottle of 'natural wine.' Since I couldn't find the waitress to order another one, I began finishing off the drinks others had left on the table. As Billie went off and the O'Jays came on talkin' 'bout how they loved music, I was on my feet, heading for the table next to ours where I'd spotted three unfinished beers and a half glass of wine. Before the O'Jays' stopped singing, I'd finished every bottle of beer or glass of wine whose owner was not sitting in front of it.

Luckily for me, everyone was so drunk, no one realized their glasses were empty. If they did, they didn't say anything.

Before long, I was bored.

'Let's go,' I slurred. The wine was kicking in, but I'd need something stronger if I was to get my high on for the night. 'Let's go where they got some *real* booze!'

Rose and Tommy readily agreed.

I came to the next morning with a hell of a hangover. It had been a couple of months since I'd suffered a hangover. As I squeezed my head in an effort to stop the pain, I remembered how much I hated them. At first, I was disoriented and didn't know where I was. After a moment of lying there and looking around the room, familiarity began to return. I was in my own living room on my raggedy couch.

But how'd I get here?

My mind was reeling, trying to remember what had happened the night before. I couldn't. All I remembered was having a glass of wine at the Chat-N-Chew. The rest of the night was a blur. I tried to sit up, but the throbbing in my head and the way the room was spinning told me to lay my ass back down. So I lay there hoping that my memory would return, that the room would stop spinning, and that I wouldn't throw up.

Just then Tommy walked in.

'I see you're awake,' he said solemnly.

'Stop your fuckin' screamin'!' I didn't know why he was yelling. I was less than two feet in front of him.

'I'm not screaming, Cup. You are.'

It hurt to talk. All I could do was groan.

'It's no wonder you feel, look, and smell like shit,' he said with a hint of disgust.

I didn't notice any peculiar smell until he brought it up. Once he did, I became aware of a putrid smell. I looked down and saw dried vomit all over the front of my dress. There I was, afraid I'd throw up and, apparently, I'd already done so.

'I threw up on myself?' I asked. Now it was my turn to be disgusted.

'You did more than that. You pissed on yourself as well.'

I had no memory of either event. Before I could speak, Rose came bouncing into the living room.

'What's up, girl?' she asked. She was working my nerves. She was too damn happy.

I just groaned. After Tommy put an ice pack on my head and gave me two aspirin, I lay on the couch as he and Rose relayed to me what I'd forgotten.

They said that, at my insistence, we'd left the Chat-N-Chew and gone to another club. While there, I'd had several (Tommy believed it was three, but Rose swore it was at least four) gin and tonics. Then some fat chick, who was trying to squeeze past me, made me spill my drink. Apparently, THAT was a no-no. So I socked her. A fight ensued. I got put out.

'We started to act like we didn't know your ass and kept on partying,' Tommy said. 'All the way out the door, you were obnoxiously loud and ghetto.'

'Yeah,' Rose agreed. 'It was truly embarrassing.'

'Problem is,' Tommy continued, 'we love yo' crazy ass. And more importantly, we didn't know what additional trouble you'd get into. So we felt compelled to leave with you.'

I could see the hurt and anger in their faces as they talked about the embarrassment of watching me get put out. Shit, I didn't care – getting putting out never stopped me from drinking. Only two things stopped me from drinking: running out of money or passing out. And though I was forced to leave, I was still awake (though in a blackout), and Tommy still had money. So I was ready to keep drinking and partying. Tommy said that he and Rose tried to convince me to call it a night, but I refused. I kept screaming that I wanted to dance. So, to pacify me, we went to another club where I gulped down four and a half Long Island Iced Teas, Cupcake-style: no ice and no coke. Tommy said he added the 'half,' because before I had a chance to finish the fifth drink, I loudly announced that I had to piss like a race-horse. Though I really wanted to go to the bathroom, my legs wouldn't cooperate, forcing him and Rose to half-carry, half-drag me there. Unfortunately, my bladder couldn't, or wouldn't, wait. So, my mind said, *Fuck it,* and I pissed on myself. Then, I threw up on some fat guy and cussed out the bouncer. Again, we got put out.

I passed out in the car shortly thereafter.

I sat there in awe.

What had happened? I walked into that club knowing I had a drinking problem. And, at the snap of a finger, I was drunk. What the hell happened?

Any reservations I had before were damn sho gone – I was an alcoholic.

I decided to call V. I expected her to cuss me out and say she didn't want to work with me anymore because she'd conclude that if I drank, I wasn't serious about recovery. But she didn't cuss me out. And she didn't say she didn't want to work with me anymore. Nor did she accuse me of not being serious about recovery. Seriously, yet tenderly, she reminded me that alcoholism and addiction are diseases of the mind.

'Think about it, Cup. Where did the idea to drink first originate?'

I sat for a moment contemplating her question, replaying what I could about the night before. I saw myself sitting at the table and all of a sudden *thinking* that I didn't have a drinking problem.

'It had started with a thought!' I exclaimed. 'I knew I was a dope fiend, but I'd convinced myself that I didn't have a problem with booze.'

'That's what I meant when I said that we have a disease that tells us we don't have a disease.'

Now I understood.

'And it's the *first* drink that gets you drunk,' she continued.

'What?' I didn't understand, especially since with my high tolerance, it was usually the tenth or eleventh drink that got me drunk.

'If you never take that first drink, you'll never get drunk. Because you know that once you take the first drink, you won't stop until you're drunk.'

She was right. Once I started *anything*, I couldn't stop. My relapse proved that.

V told me not to beat myself up for falling off the wagon.

'It's okay to fall. Just get back on!' she urged.

She then instructed me to go to three meetings that day. And at each meeting I had to announce myself as a newcomer. This, I didn't like at all. In 12-step programs, once you had achieved thirty days of continuous sobriety, you no longer had to introduce yourself as a newcomer. The last time I'd been in a meeting, I had had sixty-nine days. So what if I drank? In my mind, I was no longer a newcomer. Besides, introducing myself as a newcomer would let everyone know that I'd relapsed, and that would be embarrassing.

'Obviously, you haven't been listening for the last sixty-nine days, since if you had, you wouldn't have gotten drunk,' V responded when I balked about having to tell everyone I'd gotten drunk. 'Or, you would have at least called me *before* you drank.

Something did tell me to call her. But I ignored it.

'Besides, you need the humility, Cup.'

'Humility? Why do I need humility?'

'Because pride gets us drunk. Ego keeps us drunk. Humility allows us to ask for help; it enables us to get honest about what's really going on inside.'

I nodded as if I understood, but I didn't. In fact, it would be awhile before I really began understanding all of the things V said. But she told me that I didn't have to, and shouldn't expect to, understand everything immediately. She promised that, if I kept working the 12-step program, continued attending meetings, continued to build my trust in and relationship with God, everything would soon begin to make sense. But willingness was the key.

Sitting on the couch, I reflected on what had happened the night before. It didn't take me long to get honest with myself and realize that I wanted to stay sober. You see, all my life I had been coming to. But for those sixty-nine days I'd been clean; I had been 'awakening' – and I liked it. I liked remembering what I'd done the night before. During those sixty-nine days, I hadn't pissed on myself or thrown up on anyone. I liked being in control of my bodily functions. During that time, I hadn't missed one day of work. I hadn't even been late for work. I'd been happy, gained weight, and began looking human again. As I sat there thinking about my sixty-nine sweet days, I got a moment of clarity: I didn't want to come to anymore. I decided that I wanted to spend the rest of my life awakening.

I wanted it more than anything. Right then and there, I said a prayer. During those sixty-nine days, I'd talked to my concept of 'God' enough to know that no special physical position was required. I also knew that my words didn't have to be anything fancy or eloquent. I'd just talk to Him like I'd done since the day behind the Dumpster: straight out and sincere. So, quietly and with all the genuineness I could muster, I promised God (and myself) that *with His help,* I would never, ever come to again.

I had no idea it was a promise we both would keep.

49

Having made a promise to truly try to get a grip around recovery, I was like a pit bull – I refused to let go. I did everything V told me to do. Oh, don't get me wrong; I balked, whined, moaned, bitched, cried, and complained. But still, I did it – beginning with her directive to me the morning I called her to tell her I'd relapsed the night before. She instructed me to attend three meetings that day. Though I consented, I insisted on one change: since I didn't get drunk alone, I felt that I shouldn't have to go through the embarrassment of announcing my relapse alone. So I forced Rose and Tommy to go with me. We went to four meetings. At each one, I raised my hand and announced myself as a newcomer. Then, I shared about what happened the night before. Throughout the story, people in the meeting would bust out laughing or nodding their heads with familiarity, especially when I got to the part about convincing Rose and Tommy that the wine had to be 'natural.' Through it all, though, Rose and Tommy never laughed. Rose later told me that she didn't laugh because, every time I told the story (especially the part about my being able to have 'natural' wine), she felt dumber and dumber.

The last meeting we went to was at Mesa Vista. I especially didn't want to go there, since I'd just gotten out of their rehab program. The people at those meetings watched me go from one day to sixty-nine days, sober. I felt that it would be especially humiliating to have to tell them that I, again, had only one day. I didn't want to do it. But I kept hearing V warn that *staying* sober would require me to do a lot of things I didn't want to. So I took a deep breath, placed (or actually forced) one foot in front of the other, and walked in.

As usual, my fears were unwarranted. Upon learning that I'd relapsed, no one cussed me out, called me a failure, or put me down. Instead, they welcomed me with caring hugs and friendly smiles and told me to 'keep coming back.' I vowed I would.

It was during that meeting that I noticed a handsome black man staring at me. I didn't know why he was staring at me. I didn't recognize him as anyone I knew. I mean, it was possible I'd robbed him, cussed him out while drunk, copped from him, or sold to him. Or, hell, he could have been a 'business partner.' I honestly didn't know. What I *did* know was that every time I looked at him, he was looking at me. He was about five seven, with a stocky build. He had a weird sort of sly but friendly smile. The way he smiled told me that if we had crossed each other's paths previously, it must have been a friendly encounter. No one I'd ever done wrong smiled at me – unless they did it while beatin' my ass.

After the meeting, Rose went up to the man and began talking to him. I could tell from the way they greeted each other that they knew each other. I was dying to know who he was. Tommy impatiently informed me that he was ready to go. He said he'd had enough fuckin' 'program' for one day. I reminded him that we couldn't leave without Rose, and suggested he wait in the car while I fetched her.

As soon as Tommy was out of the room, I sauntered up to Rose and her friend. She introduced me as her 'homegirl from way back.' She said his name was Brett and that they worked together. As usual, he asked the routine question.

'Cupcake? Is that your real name?' As usual, I gave the short answer of 'yes.'

No one said anything for a few moments. Brett and I stood facing each other, looking each other up and down. I don't know what was going through his mind, but I was admiring his physique. He was very well built. It was obvious he worked out. His arms were muscular and well-defined. His hard, husky chest stuck out like a proud lion's. And although he had on long pants, the muscles in his thighs and calves were easily observable.

Rose must have felt the magnetic attraction that was happening because she gave some excuse about needing to go to the bathroom. She quickly disappeared, though a few moments passed before I noticed she had.

Brett and I engaged in small talk for a little while. He said that he was in Mesa Vista's thirty-day program and had been sober for about twenty days. I had to, once again, admit that since I'd just relapsed the previous night, I had less than twenty-four hours. He reminded me that he already knew about it because he'd heard me talk about it during the meeting.

Damn you, Cup! Why'd you have to be so honest!

But then he went on to tell me how much he liked and appreciated the openness I'd displayed as I talked about relapse and the humorous way I'd relayed it.

'I wish I could be that honest and straight out like that.' He looked at me with what appeared to be genuine admiration.

Shit, it does *pay to be honest!*

I could have stayed there and heard Brett compliment me all night. But I suddenly remembered Tommy was waiting in the car. Although I knew it was over between us, Tommy still hoped otherwise. I didn't know what he'd do if he saw me flirting. Besides, I couldn't afford to piss him off – he was my ride. I quickly gave Brett a lame excuse about having to go find Rose and took off for the door. Just as I reached for the doorknob, Brett sprinted up from behind me and leapt toward the door, startling me.

'As long as *I'm* around,' he said softly as he gently removed my hand from the knob and replaced it with his, 'you'll never have to open another door.' His mouth turned up into a big smile as he bent over, giving me a majestic bow while simultaneously waving me through the doorway. I didn't move. I *couldn't* move. I was too shocked. The only men who had ever opened a door for me were my daddy and Jr. And it'd been years since either of them had done it.

'Well, I can't hold it open forever!' he said. 'You comin' through or what?'

Realizing I was frozen in place, I forced myself to snap out of it and walk through the door, feeling like a queen.

Brett asked for my number. At first I hesitated. Though he was kind of cute and well built, I wasn't really interested in getting involved. The only thing on my mind was staying sober. Besides, for most of my life, I'd viewed men as nothing but

454

dollar signs – and I didn't need any money – at least not right then. But I gave him my number anyway; maybe it was his polite disposition and his soft, gentle voice. Or maybe it was because he was so gentlemanly. I honestly couldn't put my finger on it.

Besides, I thought as I walked to the car where Tommy sat, his impatience growing, *what could it hurt?* Folks rarely stuck around me for long.

'Who's your friend?' Tommy snapped as I got into the car. He'd obviously been watching me.

I told him that Brett was just Rose's friend from work, and then quickly lied about how the entire conversation had been about recovery.

'But why – ' he began when Rose hopped into the car, cutting him off.

'Let's go, y'all!' she almost sang as she buckled her seat belt. For whatever reason, Tommy decided to leave the issue alone, for which I was none too sad. He started the car and took us home.

Brett called me the next day and we talked for four hours. When I asked him how he was able to stay on the phone so long in light of the hospital's time limit, he said that he'd bribed folks for their phone time. I never found out if he was joking or not. But whenever he called me, he was never restricted to the ten-minute phone limit I'd had when I was there.

I was glad he didn't have a phone limit, though, because I enjoyed talking to him. He was very easy to talk to and quite comical. He told me all about his extremely large family – fifteen children from the same mother and father. He told me the age, occupation, and a little bit of personality background of each of his siblings. He proudly told me that his father stuck around and took care of his kids until he'd died in a car accident, when Brett was about sixteen. He was still very close to his mother, who lived in the same house he was raised in.

Next, the conversation moved on to our jobs and our bosses, where we had great differences. He said he liked his job, but wasn't crazy about his boss. I told him I loved my boss and my job. Once I told him about Ken, he was very impressed with him and how he'd helped me in my time of need. Brett told me that his drug of choice had been crack and he'd been using since he was about twenty. He proudly announced that he'd kept a job during the entire time. I told him what I'd learned in rehab: that I was a trash-can junkie, but that I, too, had been able to maintain a job. It sounded to me as though he had the same erroneous belief I'd had – that having a job prevented one from being an addict.

'We know that's a lie now, don't we?' I asked sternly. He readily agreed. That was a lie neither of us believed, and could no longer tell.

When it was my time to talk about my past, I decided to tell the 'Marcia Brady' version. I swore I'd never tell the real one to *anyone*.

Even with our very different pasts, we kept coming back to the one important thing we had in common: the disease of addiction. We spent a lot of time talking about the horrors of drug addiction and the way it fooled us into believing we'd had everybody else fooled. We talked about how it'd started innocently (we both started out 'just' smoking weed and drinking), and how it progressed to our spending every dime we had on dope and selling everything we owned to get high. What I liked most about Brett was that no matter how difficult or embarrassing the topic of discussion, he spoke in the same soft, calm voice he'd used the night we'd met. He never got upset or angry. Never raised his voice or even cursed – and he'd been raised in the hood. I hung up feeling that he was unlike any other man I'd ever met.

I was soon crazy about him. We talked on the phone every day, each time for hours. The only time we weren't on the phone was when we were at work or at a meeting. Once he got out of rehab, we began coordinating our meetings so that we'd end up at the same one.

Before my relapse, V suggested that I not get into a relationship during my first year of recovery. After my relapse, the suggestion was repeated. At first I was willing – until I met Brett. I felt that Brett was just too good to pass up. I'd been through so many (and I mean *many*) unhealthy relationships, I believed it was time for someone to treat me like a queen, which Brett always did. So he just had to be sent especially for me.

Once she realized that I wasn't going to follow the no-relationship-for-a-year rule, she gave me two warnings.

'Just make sure you keep recovery first. And don't make him your god!'

When I told her that I didn't understand what she meant, she explained that people with addictive behaviors, especially women, have a tendency to put a man before their own well-being, so much so that they stop taking care of themselves. If they exercised regularly, they'd stop once a man came along. If they had friends, they forgot about them once a man appeared. If a woman was self-sufficient and self-assured, she'd get a man and suddenly become insecure and needy. I still didn't understand what she was talkin' about.

I was still pondering her comments, when she hit me with the bomb. She said that the only time a woman is ready for a man in her life is when she didn't need one.

Well, I must not be ready then, I thought. *'Cause I damn sho need one! And this one is too good to pass up!* I smiled and nodded, but kept my mouth shut.

'You were fine before him,' she continued. 'Remember that you'll be fine *after* him! You can do without a man, Cup. It's recovery you can't do without.'

I really wasn't trying to hear her preaching. So I promised that I wouldn't make Brett my 'god.' And she promised not to let me.

I hadn't planned on falling in love with Brett. But he was so charming and charismatic, it was inevitable.

Just days after we'd begun dating, the receptionist called me and said there was a package for me at the front desk.

'What kind of 'package'?' I asked suspiciously. My mind raced, trying to figure out who I'd screwed over in the past who might now be trying to get revenge.

'Is it a bomb?' I slowly asked.

'Girl, you're so crazy!' she replied. 'Just get up here!'

I was about ten feet from the receptionist's desk when I looked up – the sight made me freeze in my tracks. Feeling a scream coming on, I quickly reached up and covered my mouth to stifle it. There on her desk, in a beautiful crystal vase, sat a dozen long-stemmed red roses.

'Are – are – are – ' I was stuttering so much, I couldn't get any words out.

'Yes, they're for you!' she exclaimed, answering the question I wasn't able to ask. She jumped up, grabbed the roses, and brought them over to me.

'Here, there's a card. Read it!'

I still didn't move. I just stood there staring at the roses.

'Aren't you going to open it?' she asked. 'Com' on! I'm dying to know who they're from!'

Shit, so am I.

I wondered if it were possible to hide a bomb in roses. I wouldn't put *anything* past dope fiends.

Some of the other secretaries who'd heard the receptionist's squeals ran up to her desk. They gathered around us and began talking all at once.

'Oh my God! They're beautiful!'

'Look how *red* they are!'

'Look how *big* they are!'

'I've never seen roses that perfect!'

'Who are they for?'

'I think they're for Cup.'

'Cup? Who sent them?'

'I don't know.'

'I didn't know she had a boyfriend.'

'Boyfriend! Isn't she married?'

They were talking as though I weren't there.

Still, I didn't move and didn't say a word.

Roses? Who in the fuck would send me *roses?*

'I think she's in shock,' one of the secretaries said.

'Aw, shit! Last time she was in shock, we had to call an ambulance!' someone else said.

'That wasn't shock, you idiot! She was in a diabetic coma!'

They continued bickering over why the ambulance had been called.

I was just passed out, you dumb shits! I wanted to scream at them. *I hadn't slept in days! I had stayed high on every drug known to man. I was fucked up, you idiots! Git your heads out of your asses!* But I didn't. I could handle only one thing at a time, and I was still in shock over the roses.

'Cup,' Maria said quietly as she slowly approached me and began rubbing my arm, 'would you like me to open the card?' She sounded so sweet.

In anticipation of my response, the crowd of women became deathly quiet. I looked up at Maria. I could see the concern in her eyes. Sweet, charming Maria. I hadn't talked to her since she'd brought the TV and dishes to my house. Though I still thought she was nuts, I liked her. Even though she'd seen my shabby little empty apartment, she'd never said anything negative about it to anyone. In fact, she'd never mentioned the fact that she'd been there. What I liked most about her was that she never tried to force her friendship on me. She'd speak and give me a warm, loving smile. But after that, she'd just leave me alone; and I appreciated her giving me my space. But she was now volunteering for something that I never imagined needing help with. Still, I didn't respond.

'Cup,' she said again quietly, 'would you like for me to read the card?'

I looked at her again.

How do I warn her? If I tell her it might be a bomb, will she think I'm crazy? Can I warn them without revealing my criminal history? Would the bomb kill all of us? Am I crazy? Can you put a bomb in a card?

My mind was racing frantically. Actually, my mind was *tripping*. I had never, ever had flowers delivered to me. I honestly did not know how to react to the situation.

'Cup,' Maria said again.

I liked Maria, but I figured if there *was* a bomb in there, better her than me.

'Yea – yeah,' I replied, as I quickly took three large steps back.

The women looked at me as though they thought I was nuts. Fortunately, they were used to my exhibiting strange behavior, so they spent only a moment being baffled by my conduct before quickly turning to give their full attention to Maria, who was opening the card.

'To a special lady,' she read. 'A *real* lady. Lovingly, Brett.'

'Awww,' the women sighed in unison.

Brett? These are from Brett? He doesn't even know me. I was bewildered. *A lady? He called me a 'lady'?* Tears began to fall down my cheeks.

'Why is she crying?' someone whispered.

'I don't know. She's so weird!'

459

'I'd love to get flowers, and here she is *crying*!'

'Maybe they're tears of joy.'

'She doesn't *look* happy!'

They were still talking about me as if I weren't there. I didn't care. My mind was a million miles away.

Just then, Ken came around the corner. He saw the women gathered around me and tears streaming down my face and immediately became concerned. He didn't know why I was crying; he just knew he didn't like my doing it.

'What's going on here?' he sternly asked no one in particular.

'Look, Cup got roses!' The look on his face told me that he could care less about the flowers.

'Cup, are you okay?' he asked as he approached me and began rubbing my shoulder. When I didn't respond, he lifted my head forcing me to face him.

I nodded my head to signal that I was, though I remained silent and the tears kept falling.

'Come on,' he said as he gently grabbed my arm, 'let's go into my office.'

I didn't say a word and allowed him to lead me away.

'I'll put these on her desk for her,' Maria said as she grabbed the roses and followed us.

Once inside Ken's office, I was finally able to speak. I shared with him my surprise that not only had Brett sent me flowers, but he'd called me a 'lady.' I didn't think I deserved such a gracious title.

'I know your life hasn't been easy. I don't know the particulars. But I know it couldn't have been easy.'

'But, you don't—' I started to protest when he cut me off.

'*Whatever* you used to be, *whoever* you used to be, is irrelevant. You're a lady *now*. And you, yourself said it: if you stay clean, it can only go up from here.'

I looked up at Ken and wondered if he were high.

Later that day, Daddy and Jr. called on a three-way line. They said they were just checking on me. After we chatted for a few moments, I told them about the roses. They said that they weren't surprised that I'd received them; they were surprised only that Brett had the good sense to send them.

'And,' Daddy quickly added, 'he should have sent *two* dozen!'

Later that evening, during our routine check-in, I shared the day's events with V.

'You deserve it, Cup,' she said.

Why is no one surprised about these fuckin' flowers 'cept me?

I couldn't understand it, but decided to let it go – for the moment. Besides, something else had come to mind. I'd realized two things. First, each of the people in my circle had said those wonderful things because they loved me. Why? I had no clue. Hell, I still don't know. What I *do* know is that love, real love, true unconditional love, transcends age, race, and religious beliefs. It sees the good, focuses on the good, and constantly emphasizes it. Second, they weren't a 'circle' at all. They were family. Sure, folks say that family is supposed to be blood. But out of those people who were loving me, supporting me, believing in me, and encouraging me, only Jr. was actually blood. Yet, the others didn't love me any less than he did. That's when I realized that a family doesn't have to be people you're related to. Family are people who love you – whoever that may be. I warned myself not to miss my blessing of a new family just because we weren't related by blood. We were related by *love*.

I cried myself to sleep that night thanking my Higher Power for my 'family' – and their love. And the family was still growing.

Shortly after my relapse, I found out I was pregnant. I didn't take a pregnancy test; didn't need to. My usual test did the trick: I was over at V's house and she was frying chicken. I immediately got nauseous and had to run outside to barf. Concerned, V followed me and asked what was wrong. She thought maybe it was some form of alcohol-related withdrawal lingering from my relapse. Luckily, my relapse didn't produce any kind of withdrawal symptoms. I assured V that the problem wasn't withdrawal symptoms, but pregnancy symptoms. She didn't believe me and urged me to go to the doctor – a medical professional – and let him decide. Several days later the doctor confirmed what I already knew. I was pregnant – almost three months.

The thought of having a baby scared me. First of all, I didn't know whose it was. The four days at the Dumpster had

461

involved several 'business partners,' not to mention my attempts at contracting HIV. More important, I was just beginning to get myself together. I was nowhere near ready for a child.

I screamed at the doctor that I wanted an abortion. Unsurprised by my sudden outburst, the doctor asked if I'd ever had one. When I told him I had, he asked how many. I had to sit for a moment and think about it before responding I *believed* it to have been three or four, but I couldn't remember. I quickly explained that I was drunk and loaded most of the time. Unimpressed by my newfound sobriety, he refused to give me an abortion stating that three was the limit. He made it clear that whether I'd had three or four, I was at the limit. I jumped up and left. I didn't need him. Now that I knew what the limit was, I knew the lie I'd have to tell.

That night during my daily check in I told V. As usual, she didn't pass judgment or belittle me. Instead, she told me that because it was my life and my body, the decision was mine. I pondered over it all night, but no matter how I looked at it, I knew what I had to do.

Several days later, I sat in a nearby clinic filling out paperwork. When they questioned me about how many abortions I'd already had, I lied and said two. The following day, I had the abortion, although it wasn't as easy as it had been before; I didn't have any drugs or alcohol to numb the guilt and shame. But I never regretted my decision. I knew I was in no way ready to be a mother, and no baby of mine was going into the same system that helped fuck me up. Besides, I had to focus on me. I had to focus on recovery. But, I promised myself that that would be the last abortion I would ever have.

It was yet another promise I would keep.

After the abortion, I continued my efforts at living sober, though there was a lot to learn. V never made me feel bad about the way I was feeling – *whatever* I happened to be feeling. And, being clean and sober opened my mind and body up to a never-ending wave of emotions and feelings that felt new. I'd spent so much time numbing myself from feeling anything that I'd forgotten how raw emotions can be. The first – and the worst – was fear. When I left the hospital, I was consumed with it. Without the false courage of alcohol and dope, I realized I was afraid of everything – afraid to be outside, afraid of other people, hell, I was afraid of myself. V suggested I practice turning my fears over to my Higher Power.

I responded that the problem was that I'd been by myself for so long, I didn't trust God or anyone else.

She gave me a coy smile. She never tried to force me to do or think anything; she just gave those strong suggestions. This time, she 'suggested' that I try and get to know a God 'of my own understanding' – whoever that may be. She suggested I take it slow so I wouldn't get overwhelmed. She promised that, as I stayed clean and worked with the 12-step program, I'd develop, enhance, and amplify my own concept in, and relationship with, a Higher Power. I smiled and said I'd try. And I did.

For the next year and a half, I received roses from Brett on a regular basis. No special occasion was needed – the card would read 'Just because.' It got so that, after a while, the deliveryman wouldn't even have to say my name. As soon as the receptionist saw him coming, she'd be calling me on the phone informing me that another bouquet was up front.

Brett was the first gentleman I'd ever had in my life. Not only did he send me roses, but he was the first man, besides my daddy, to open the car door for me. At first, I wasn't used to it.

'Will you just wait!' he'd holler as I hopped out of the car before he could get around to my side to let me out.

'You move too damn slow!' I was so impatient. It was ironic that, although I'd quit using speed, I still moved like I did.

'Cup, why don't you just let someone be good to you?' V fussed one night when I complained about Brett getting angry that I wouldn't wait for him to let me out of the car. 'You're fighting it because you feel like you don't deserve it. But you do! Let someone love you!'

I promised her I'd try. And slowly, I did. Within a couple of months, Brett didn't have to sprint around to my side of the car; I'd patiently wait on him. In fact, I began to *expect* it. But he never seemed to mind. He never allowed me to touch a door – any door.

Besides being the first man to treat me like a lady, Brett was around to share many of the countless firsts I experienced clean and sober. He was with me the first time I saw a movie sober. It was the first time I wasn't screaming at the screen in a drunken rage. We attended our first dance together, and he helped me get over the nervousness of dancing sober – which I hadn't done since I was eleven years old. Shit, the drugs and booze always told me I danced like Debbie Allen. However, having learned about how ridiculously silly I behaved when I was drunk, I now realize that I probably danced more like Woody Allen. Still, I danced anyway, and for the first time, I didn't get put out of the establishment.

Learning to have fun without a drink or drug wasn't as hard as I thought it would be. In fact, being sober allowed the fun to last longer because I wasn't getting into fights or getting thrown out. More important, the next day I could remember the good time I had.

Brett was also with me when I took my first HIV test. I'd told V about my suicide plan. Of course she was shocked, but not surprised. She said she understood the desperation that addiction could put a person in. Nevertheless, she said I'd have to go get tested.

I didn't want to get tested. What if my suicide plan had been successful? Now that I was clean and sober, had a good man, a great job, and was just beginning to learn to truly enjoy life, I no longer wanted to die. But V said recovery also entailed responsibility, and getting tested was the responsible thing to do. Brett, being the ever-supportive man he was, agreed to get tested with me. Though I appreciated his support, he wasn't aware of how different and scary the process was for me. He didn't know that I'd *tried* to get AIDS. I couldn't tell him that. I didn't know how. Luckily, V said it wasn't important that he know. What was important was my HIV status. So Brett and I tramped down to the health clinic and got tested.

Two weeks later, Brett and I both learned we were negative. I wish I could tell you the scariness of the whole ordeal made me immediately start using condoms. I wish I could, but I can't.

Still, I got tested every six months for the next several years and each time the result was negative. It would be years later, when a close friend contracted the disease, before I really and truly woke up and started practicing safe sex.

* * *

After my relapse, one of the main things I was afraid of was having to go through the DTs again. Luckily, I didn't. Still, the relapse provided several blessings in disguise. First, it forced me to admit that I was an alcoholic. You see, when I initially got sober, my mind continually tried to convince me (and often still does) that I wasn't an alcoholic. Just like it did the night of my relapse, my mind insists that although my problems with drugs are clear, I really have no issue with alcohol. Whenever that fallacy emerges, I just reflect back on my relapse and any doubt as to my inability to drink like a normal person quickly goes out the window.

Another unexpected blessing is that I was scared something awful. For the first few months after my relapse, I only allowed myself to go to work and meetings for fear that if I dared venture anywhere else, my feet would head straight to the dope man or liquor store.

Although I never again got the *compulsion* to drink or use, I frequently got the desire to do so. Keeping at the forefront of my mind the promise I made to God (and myself) to never come to again, I'd fight these desires in myriad ways: from praying to crying, to picking up the phone calling person after person in recovery until the desire passed, to literally sitting on my hands to keep them from shaking with the anticipation of getting high. Sometimes I'd sit for hours rocking back and forth, sobbing and crying, my whole body shaking, my clothes soaked with sweat as I pleaded over and over and over, 'Please don't let me get loaded. Please don't let me get loaded.'

But fear will only work for so long, and I couldn't stay hidden from the world forever. So, as the fear began to dissipate, I got busy. I chased recovery like I chased booze and drugs. I put everything I had into it. It was difficult because it took dedication and commitment – two traits I knew about, but didn't realize I had. Everything I'd done in my life up until that point had taken dedication and commitment. It took dedication and commitment to learn to be a Gangsta. Before joining the gang, I knew nothing about gangs; hell, I'd never even heard of them. Now, I'm an 'OG.' Dedication and commitment are what it took to get money to find drugs, cop them (all the while dodging the police), and keep a decent supply of them. I did whatever it took to stay high. So I took that same energy and focused it

465

on recovery. V started me on working the 12 steps (up until this point, all I'd done was attend meetings and started building a support group, but hadn't begun working my way through the steps). I continued to stay sober and continued to recover in 12-step programs.

Unfortunately, Brett didn't have the same commitment to recovery that he had to chivalry. Three months after getting out of Mesa Vista, he got loaded. He'd said he was on his way home from work when his mind gently suggested he cop a twenty-dollar rock. He briefly thought about calling someone and gave an even briefer thought to going to a meeting. His mind again suggested, more strongly this time, that he cop a little something. Before he knew it, he'd convinced himself that since he'd been clean for over three months, he could handle one lil twenty-dollar rock. He copped that twenty-dollars' worth and didn't stop smoking until all of his money was gone.

I wasn't shocked when I learned that Brett had relapsed. Hell, I'd recently done it myself. So I tried to offer him as much understanding and support as I could. Most of my recovery friends said I should've dumped him because he would only bring me down. But I ignored their advice and decided to stick by him. And why not? I figured since we were both trying to recover, we could do it together. Unfortunately, I hadn't yet realized that recovery isn't for people who *need* it; it's for those who *want* it. And Brett didn't want it – at least not badly enough. He still had one reservation, or rather a misconception: he believed that, since he'd never been fired and was able to keep a job – a good job – he wasn't *really* an addict. So, although he was able to get clean, this one lil reservation prevented him from *staying* clean. He never got more than four or five months before relapsing.

I refused to allow Brett's troubles with staying clean to interfere with my commitment to the same. I followed the suggestions I'd previously refused: I changed the places where I hung out. I didn't go to any more nightclubs or bars. I changed the people I hung out with, including Rose. She didn't get angry about it, though. Instead, she said she understood and actually agreed with my decision.

'Girl, it's obvious you can bullshit me,' she replied when I explained that we wouldn't be hangin' anymore. 'I don't know nothin' 'bout them 12-step programs. Do what you need to do to get better. Because you was fucked up!'

We both cracked up because not only was it was funny, it was very true. I also cut Tommy loose. Surprisingly, he didn't put up much of a fight. He said he realized it was truly over the night I'd met Brett. He said he'd noticed the way I looked at Brett. When I asked him in what way was that, he replied, 'In a way that you haven't looked at me in years.' He was silent for a moment and then admitted that it was really more than Brett. He said I was changing – and he didn't like it. I asked him how had I changed, and he replied that he preferred the loaded Cup. She was more exciting and lively. He also said that he didn't agree with 12-step programs; he disliked them, and anyone who went to them. He refused to explain why.

Actually, I found his dislike for the new-and-sober Cup to be a relief. It meant that I wouldn't have to do any fussin' or fightin' to call it quits. We ended the conversation agreeing to part as friends, with Tommy taking responsibility for getting a divorce.

I had no emotion one way or the other about the end of my tumultuous relationship with Tommy. I just saw it as another chapter in my life coming to an end, while so many new ones were beginning.

Recovery was a continuum of lessons. First, I started working on my trust issues. V constantly reminded me that neither she nor anyone else could keep me clean and sober. She also reminded me that neither she nor anyone else could get me loaded or drunk. To stay clean and sober, I'd need a Higher Power, who I'd started to regularly call God. I don't know why. I just did.

V said I had to learn how to trust God with everything. Trusting Him to keep me sober came much easier than I thought, since my trust (in that area) grew with each passing day that I didn't drink or use. No, I had no problems trusting God to help me stay clean. The problem I *had* was trusting Him with every other area of my life. However, before I could trust God, V said that I'd have to stop being mad at him, and a good starting place would be forgiving Him for taking my mother. This one was especially hard for me. I had routinely blamed everything that ever happened to me on God – starting with my mother's death. Had she not died, Larry and I wouldn't have been given to the sperm donor.

Speaking of Larry, my mind interrupted itself, *I wonder how he's doing and where he's doing it?*

I didn't allow myself to linger on Larry too long. I hardly ever thought about him. It'd been years since we'd talked and even longer since we'd seen each other. 'Out of sight, out of mind' was still my motto. So my mind continued with why God was to blame for my life.

If Momma hadn't died, we wouldn't have gone to Lancaster. If I'd never gone to Lancaster, there would never have been a Pete or a Candy. If no Candy, there would have been no booze, drugs, 'business partners,' or anything else. Besides, not only did God take my mother, but he allowed me to be the one to find her. What kind of God lets an eleven-year-old child find her mother's dead body? And this is the same God I was expected to trust?

V reminded me that the God 'of my understanding' did not have to be the hell-and-brimstone God that I'd heard about and often had in mind when thinking about my mother. More important, she encouraged me not to focus on what I perceived to be negative about God but instead focus on the positive. She instructed me to write down some of the surprising outcomes of various events during my hellacious life.

When I first began writing, I didn't see anything 'positive' about God – that is, until I really began to take stock of my past. It didn't take long to acknowledge that there was no way that, as an eleven-, twelve-, or thirteen-year-old girl, I could have hitchhiked up and down the California highways, at all hours of the day and night, getting into anyone's car with nothing but a *butter knife* in my sock, and never have gotten raped, beaten, or even killed. Looking back on it, I realized that someone or something had to be watching over me. I thought about the numerous gang fights I'd been in; yet I'd never suffered any serious injuries. I thought about the many homies I'd lost to gang violence and drive-by shootings. I thought about the night I'd gotten shot. I should have been dead, or at least paralyzed; yet, I'd walked out of the hospital, despite the doctor's doubts.

Over the next several days, I thoroughly cataloged every

horrendous event of my life. When I finished, tears fell as I admitted to myself that *something* had to have been protecting me.

'But why?' I asked V when I went over to her place to tell her I'd finally finished writing. 'Why did God let me go through all that shit?' The anger I thought I had previously squashed began to rise up again.

For a few moments V said nothing. Finally, she did speak.

'I don't know why things happen. I don't know why some are taken, yet others live.'

She paused again, as if continuing to think. We were sitting in her living room. Her sixteen-year-old daughter was in her room doing homework. Soft jazz was playing on the stereo. I looked at V. She was so beautiful: her long black hair lay beautifully around her shoulders; her long manicured nails and light blue silk pajamas exemplified her femininity.

'But, how about this,' she said softly. 'Instead of asking *why* you had to do it, how about just thanking Him for safely bringing you *through* it.'

As usual, she floored me. Not only about what she'd said, but about how right she was. I promised her I would follow her suggestion. And I meant it.

Slowly, I did become grateful for the things I'd survived, though the gratitude didn't come overnight. My relationship with God was like everything else I'd encountered, learned, or experienced sober – I had to *work* at it. But slowly, my hatred for Him began to lessen.

I also had to learn that, in trusting God, I didn't have to fight and struggle against anything or anyone. Fighting and struggling was all I knew. As a child in the streets, I had to fight to keep my shoes, struggle to hustle food and shelter, struggle to keep out of foster homes, fight to keep someone from stealing my jacket. With the Gangstas, I'd had to fight to become one of them, fight for their respect, fight for rank, struggle to stay out of jail, struggle not to get killed. As a dope fiend and drunk, the fights and struggles were endless. Even in my marriage I'd had to fight. I was always fighting.

But no more. V reminded me that if God had something for me, no one could take it – it was mine. And she was right. I don't know the exact moment when my relationship with God

469

changed; when my hatred turned to love and I began to trust Him completely, with no animosity, malice, fear, doubt, or resentment. What I do know is that the more I worked on it, the better I got.

Next, according to V, I had to learn to be all right with me, starting with doing a probingly thorough moral inventory of myself.

'I ain't got no damn morals,' I snapped when she told me what we'd work on next. I was becoming agitated with the recovery process. It seemed like there was always something to do, some type of *work*. I just wanted to be sober, sit on my ass, and watch TV. I didn't want to have to work at anything anymore. But V reminded me that I hadn't become an addict overnight. In fact, none of my negative behaviors, conduct, or traits were learned overnight. I'd worked at them.

'Practice makes perfect,' she said. 'So be careful what you practice.'

Another profound, but true, statement. Through the years, I'd practiced trickin', drinking, using, stealing, cheating, robbing, and a host of other negative behaviors till I'd perfected them. In fact, I'd never practiced anything positive, except going to work, and even that was practiced while drunk or loaded.

'Damn, you're smart,' I said with awe as I realized how right she was. 'You're fuckin' amazing!'

'It's not me,' she immediately corrected me. 'Never put me on a pedestal, Cup. Remember, I'm a drunk just like you; I sit in meetings *next to you*. Most of the things I say come from divine direction: prior to every conversation we have, I pray and ask God to let me carry *His* message, not mine.'

She added that the other suggestions were given to her by other women in recovery, one of whom was an old-timer named Chaney. It was the first of many times that V would remind me that she was human and equal to, not better than, me or anyone else.

She went on to say that that once I'd completed the twelfth step, I would have a responsibility to pass it on.

'But, you can't give away something you haven't got.' She warned, 'So you'd better get busy.'

And I did. I began to 'practice' changing all of my negatives into positives. I practiced being honest. I practiced being kind. I practiced liking others. I practiced liking myself – which was the hardest of all, since it meant looking at my character defects and being okay with myself anyway. I had to learn to accept life just the way it was. Since I was a little girl, I'd justified everything with a bunch of *ifs*: *if* I were light-skinned, I'd be pretty; *if* I had long hair, someone would love me; *if* I had had a mother, I'd have been all right. I had to let go of the *ifs*.

I also had to learn to love and accept myself – just the way I was. I'd spent so many years beating myself up for the way I looked. I hated my skin color. I hated my crooked teeth. I hated the noticeably huge gap I had in the middle of my mouth. I hated my flat chest. I hated my two-toned big lips. I hated everything about myself. And I didn't want to be me; I always wanted to be someone else. When I was little, I wanted to be Marcia Brady. Then I wanted to be Jayne Kennedy, a beautiful black woman with light skin and long beautiful hair. She was the first black female sports commentator and all the men thought she was gorgeous. I wanted someone to think *I* was gorgeous.

I went from wanting to be Jayne to wanting to be V. V was pretty and sober and smart. She was everything I wanted to be: she had beautiful light brown skin and long, flowing black hair; she had over five years of being sober; she was attending community college; worked at a job she loved; had a great apartment with nice furniture and all of the amenities; and she had a beautiful teenage daughter and a younger sister who she'd raised as her own daughter, both of whom loved her dearly. Yup, V had it going on.

Then I went from wanting to be V to wanting to be Monique, V's only child. I envied Monique because she had something I never would have – a mother; a mother who loved her like only a mother could. I would have killed to be Monique.

When I revealed these things to V, she smiled, and reminded me that I could never be Marcia Brady, Jayne Kennedy, her, Monique, or anyone else. I was stuck with Cup.

'But,' she added quickly, 'you have to realize that Cup is enough.' She said that the next step of recovery would be learning and believing that I was good enough, period.

We were sitting in my small living room when we began my process of obtaining self-acceptance, self-love, and self-esteem.

V announced that we were going to write positive statements about me on Post-its. When I responded that I couldn't think of a single positive thing to say about myself, she asked me what I would want someone else to tell me.

'I'd want them to tell me I was pretty.'

She wrote, 'Cup, you are pretty' on a Post-it.

'And I'd want them to tell me they liked me just the way I am.'

She wrote that on another Post-it. We continued this process, always beginning the sentence with my name. V said this practice would make it clear to me who the message was for. When I couldn't think of anything else positive I'd want someone to say about me, or to me, she did. She wrote, 'Cup, you're perfect. Love, God.' And she wrote, 'Cup, you're beautiful. Love, V.' 'Cup, you have a beautiful smile.'

Now, she was writing feverishly. 'Cup, you're a great person.' 'Cup, you deserve happiness.' 'Cup, you have beautiful skin.' 'Cup, you have pretty feet.'

Seeing her acknowledging all of these wonderful things about me made me want to join in again. Tearing off one Post-it after another, we continued to write. Soon, I was racing to think of things and characteristics we liked about me (actually, V thought of things she liked; I thought of things I wished I liked).

When we could think of no more sayings, we'd gone through two pads of Post-its. We then began sticking them all over my apartment. No space was safe. They completely covered the kitchen cabinets, stove, and fridge. They stretched across every wall in every room. They were on the TV, dresser, doors, light fixtures, bathroom mirror, and medicine cabinet. V even stuck one on the back of the toilet. When I gasped, she replied:

'You can still sing a positive self-song when you're sitting on the throne!' We both cracked up laughing and continued sticking.

When we were finally done, the place was covered in Post-its. Not only did I think they made my tacky little apartment look even tackier, I thought it was a stupid idea. I couldn't see how reading those little yellow pieces of paper would change anything. When I shared my doubts with V, she explained.

'We've got to change the tapes,' she said.

'What tapes? I ain't got no tapes! Hell, I ain't even got no records!'

'Not those kinds of tapes, Cup. I'm talking about the tapes in your head. I'm talking about all of those negative messages about yourself that you and others have been telling you all of your life. These lil Post-its are going to begin the process of positive reinforcement. Now, don't get me wrong; it's not the cure-all. You're going to have to do a lot more work on yourself to love yourself. But it's a start. And, you'll never achieve anything if you never start.'

And a great start it was. Those damn things were everywhere I looked. I couldn't get a cup of coffee, take a shower, brush my teeth, take a piss without seeing something nice being said about me. No matter what I did or where I looked, I was constantly reminded that I was enough, that I was okay *just the way I was,* and that I was loved – *and* had pretty feet. Slowly, *very slowly,* I began to believe it.

Then, I began to go through black magazines and cut out pictures of black women with dark or brown skin: Oprah, Alfre Woodard, Cicely Tyson, Tina Turner. These women had been around for years, I always threw their images aside. It wasn't until I began to post them all over my house that I realized that black really was beautiful. I couldn't remember who had convinced me that brown or dark skin was ugly – or why. It was a lie. Black women come in all shades – and all shades were beautiful – including mine.

Another process in building my self-esteem was learning to be nice.

'If you want self-esteem,' V said, 'do esteemable acts.'

This was easier said than done because I'd always seen being nice as being a sucker, a mark, a punk; and I was nobody's punk. But again, V reminded me that my belief system was all fucked up. It was time to develop a new one. So, I practiced saying 'excuse me' when I stepped on someone's toe (I *used* to say, 'Bitch, you see my foot there!'). And I practiced not going off when someone stepped on my toe (before, if you stepped on my toe, I'd cut cha). I practiced saying 'thank you' and 'please.' When I complained to V that I felt dumb because these things seemed like stuff I should have learned when I was a child, she snapped that I hadn't been a 'child' since I was eleven years old.

On top of that, she reminded me that I'd learned how to live in a different kind of school: I had been learning in 'street'-rooms, while other children were learning in classrooms.

'Besides, whether you *used* to do it is irrelevant,' she said. 'What's important is that you're doing it *now*.' She gave me a big hug and sternly instructed me to never beat myself up for trying to better myself.

It was then that I realized why God had chosen V to be the one to mold me and teach me. She had the challenging task of changing someone who society would argue was unchangeable. Of loving someone who society would say was unlovable. And she was entrusted with the arduous task of teaching someone who society was convinced couldn't learn a damned thing.

V and I were sitting around having our weekly one-on-one chat in her living room when she told me that God puts people into our lives for a reason, but that everyone who came into our lives wasn't meant to stay. At the mention of this, I told V my greatest fear: that eventually, everyone I loved – Daddy, Jr., Ken, and even she – would either hurt me or leave me.

Upon hearing this, V looked up at me in surprise. I admitted other secret worries: I'd actually been waiting for Ken to announce he'd decided to fire me after all, and for *her* to announce she didn't want to be my sponsor anymore.

'Cup, why would you think that?' she asked. 'Ken has shown you nothing but love, encouragement, and support. Every time I talk to you, all you talk about is 'Ken this and Ken that.' Do you honestly think that now, after all he's gone through with you, he'd fire you?'

I nodded.

'And why would you think I wouldn't want to be your friend anymore?'

I explained to her that sooner or later (probably a lot sooner than later), I'd do something to piss her off and she'd leave. She sat silently for a moment with her head cupped in her hands, her shoulders hunched in deep thought.

'Have you ever grieved your mother?' she asked as she straightened up suddenly.

Her question caught me totally by surprise. Here we were

talking about me getting fired or losing a friend, and she was asking if I'd grieved my mother.

But once I thought about it, I realized it was actually a good question.

Grieve Momma? No one had ever asked me that before. *Had I?*

I told her that I honestly didn't know. So she made me tell her about the days and events surrounding Momma's death. For the first time since I was eleven years old, I told the truth. I took my time and told her all about those horrible days. By the time I'd finished talking, I was crying. At first, I tried to stifle the tears, trying to look hard. But V held me in her arms, stroked my hair, and let me cry; *encouraged* me to cry.

'You've been holding this pain and hurt inside for all these years. It's okay to cry, Cup. It's *healthy* to cry.'

And cry I did. I cried as I reflected back on Momma's body sprawled across the bed. Bawled as I remembered her body landing on top of mine as I tried to lift her head so I could see her face. I sobbed as I remembered sitting with her head in my lap singing our song. By the time my flashback got to the part where I was being snatched away from Daddy and Jr., I'd begun to wail. V never said a word and never tried to hush my tears. Instead, she continued to hold me and let me cry. For hours I cried as I relived the atrocities that I'd drunk and used to forget or pretend never happened: the abuse in Lancaster, the rapes by Pete, my first night out with Candy. Everything.

Finally exhausted from 'mourning,' I fell asleep. V was concerned that the grieving process may have been too much for me. She thought I might wake up and, still distraught, have a desire to drink or use. Determined to be there for me if that happened, she sat with me all night. I slept through the night.

The next day, V warned me that that was not the last time I would grieve or feel the pain of my past. But she told me to never again suppress my feelings – happy or sad. Whenever I felt the need to scream or cry or was experiencing any emotion about events, conduct, and experiences in my past, I was to let them out. Suppressing them, ignoring them, or pretending they didn't exist would cause me to get drunk. That day I learned that feelings – even negative ones – were good. You see, for so long I used and drank to escape negative feelings. I hated feeling sad, scared, or any negative feeling. But in recovery I learned that that's where the healing is – in allowing myself to *feel*.

And feel I did. Whenever a memory would come up, I'd just start bawling, regardless of where I was. The first time it happened at work Ken, as usual, was concerned. But once I explained to him what was going on, he told me that, from then on if I needed to cry, or just wanted to go someplace quiet, I could use his office.

The practice of 'feeling,' i.e., of being able to mourn my past and grieve my mother, allowed me to free my mind of a negative self-image, and instead, to start the process of building a positive self-regard. I realized that, although I'd been through some bad things, and had even done some bad things, I was not a bad person. Before long, I even began to like what I saw when I looked in the mirror – even my body, which had changed completely. As I stayed clean and began to eat regularly, I continued to put on weight. That weight, for some odd reason, distributed itself in the most perfect of places. What were once long, scrawny poles were developing into elongated, shapely legs. The bony body that, a short time ago, looked like a twig was turning in a voluptuously sexy physique. The cynical, withdrawn, irate person who had entered rehab was turning into an optimist, of all things.

Not only was I learning to like and accept myself, but I was also learning *about* myself. I learned that I was a loner. I didn't really like a lot of people around me. The more and more I got to know myself, and the more I practiced liking myself, I learned that I actually enjoyed my own company. I'm not sure why I became loud, obnoxious, and violent when I was drunk or loaded. But the real me was not any of those things. I wasn't a gangbanger or a fighter. I discovered that the real Cup was quiet, friendly, and often shy.

I also discovered that I loved being sexy. I don't know why. It had nothing to do with sex. I just loved my new, curvaceous body. I wore clothes that revealed my body so that others would be able to appreciate it too. The women in the meetings hated the way I dressed and regularly complained about it; often telling V that she should talk to me about my attire. V refused, telling them that that part of me would grow and change in time. The most important thing was that I remembered not to drink or use no matter what. She told them that she didn't care how I talked (I still frequently cussed) or how I dressed because she knew that if I stayed sober long enough, I would have the chance to work on everything else. Then she'd give them a sly grin and remind them that most of them hadn't walked through the doors of recovery looking or acting like 'ladies' either. And that since they'd had time and opportunity to learn and develop appropriateness in behavior, speech, and dress, they should allow me to do the same.

However, that's not what she'd say to me. Gently and lovingly, she'd tell me that I didn't have to be half-naked to be sexy because sexiness was a feeling – an *internal* feeling. She promised that if I continued to work on myself, better myself, and get to know and respect myself, I'd understand what she meant. When that happened, I'd change my attire because I'd want to – not because folks were hollerin' at me to put on some clothes.

She was right. About a year and a half later, I threw away all of my daisy dukes, tube tops, miniskirts, and 'short-shorts' (but I kept my stiletto high heels – I had a limit, you know). I'd realized I was sexy, not because of what I wore, but just because of who I was and how I carried myself. I called my new style 'sexy with attitude and a lil hood.' I still wore short dresses and skirts with my stilettos to allow appreciation of my thick, curvaceous legs, which I'd learned to love instead of loathe. I wore lip liner to accentuate my full lips, which I'd learned to appreciate. And I changed my hair to a curly style instead of the 'Buckwheat' look.

And you know what? V was right. The more I worked on fixing up my inside, the better I became at improving the outside. All of my hard work at loving myself, accepting myself, and loving others was slowly paying off. It wasn't until I had five years sober that I could look in the mirror and truly like – no, love – what I saw.

I had been sober about a year when Jr. called to say that Connie had called him, asking for my phone number. Jr. wouldn't give her my number, but told her he'd call me and give me hers. Although it had been over ten years since I'd left Lancaster, just the mention of her name brought back fear and intimidation; the frightened little girl I used to be immediately returned. I called Venita in a panic. She calmed me down and suggested that I call Connie. She reminded me that, now that I was clean and sober, I no longer had to fear anything or run from anyone. She also suggested that getting some things off my chest might help me release my resentments against Connie and her mom. V hadn't steered me wrong yet. So nervously I agreed. I said a prayer and dialed the number.

Right off the bat, Connie was pleasant, though at first she kept calling me La'Vette. I firmly instructed her that she was to call me Cupcake. She ignored me. After she'd said La'Vette for the fourth time, I warned her that if she said it once more, I'd hang up. She seemed surprised at my terseness, but didn't use La'Vette again. She casually began informing me of what she'd been doing since I left: her mother died several years before. Connie had then sold the house in Lancaster, gotten married, and moved to the East Coast.

I wasn't really paying attention to her chatter. One question kept running through my mind. *Why are you calling me?*

Then, without warning, she changed topics and began telling me that she was trying to track down some of the former foster kids, but no one seemed to want to talk to her and – get this – for the life of her, she couldn't figure out why. That was the opportunity I was waiting for.

'Because of the fucked-up things y'all did!'

There was a momentary silence, then she quietly asked what I was talking about. I gladly told her. I talked about the beatings at the hands of her mother.

'Well, *I* never got beat,' she indignantly retorted.

Ignoring her, I continued by talking about often having to go without food.

'*I* was never hungry,' she snapped.

I was losing my cool and decided it was time to cuss her out. Then it suddenly hit me: *she* didn't experience any of those things. Her memories were of *her* childhood, and hers was a damned good one. She never went hungry and was never beaten.

Having come to the realization that our memories were different, I figured I'd might get through to her better if I changed the subject to an event that involved her: the lock and chain around the fridge, to which she had one of the two keys.

'But you guys were stealing food,' she said defensively.

Bitch! I started to scream, but then again, it hit me. She was able to defend her mother's behavior because she truly believed her mother's sick rationale for it. Obviously, she continued to hold on to those beliefs. Still, I couldn't let her ignorance make the behavior acceptable.

'We were stealing food because we were hungry!' I snapped. No one said anything for a few moments.

As I sat fuming, I realized that no matter how I tried, I wasn't going to change Connie's memories nor her rationalizations. But that didn't mean I couldn't release the anger I'd been holding in for years. So, without raising my voice and using minimal cusswords, I told her how fucked up her mother had made my life; how I'd used drugs, alcohol, crime, and men to hide the pain; and how, through recovery, I'd finally learned to deal with my past. I told her that I forgave her and her mother.

'Forgive us for *what*?'

Ugghh! She truly didn't get it, and I didn't have the energy, desire, or interest to try to make her understand.

'You know what?' I replied nonchalantly. 'It's not even important anymore. What *is* important is that you know that I never want to speak to you again.'

I hung up and immediately dialed Venita. Through tears of joy and relief I told her what had happened. Then I called Daddy and Jr. and repeated the story to them. We all agreed that that chapter of my life could finally be closed.

My first couple of years of recovery were a whirlwind of feelings, lessons, learning to take direction and follow instructions, and revelations. It felt like I was on a never-ending roller coaster. And like any roller coaster, sometimes the ride was full of fun-filled glee and elation, other times it was frightening and scary. Regardless of the type of emotional or physical feeling the ride gave me, I refused to get off. I didn't drink or use.

Recovery wasn't easy. It meant changing everything about myself. It meant learning how to live life without a drink or a drug; learning to be responsible and accountable for my actions, my conduct – behavior *and* language. It also meant *changing* my actions, behavior, and vernacular. It meant getting rid of my pride and ego, admitting that I needed help, having the willingness to ask for help, and being willing to accept it. It required being honest about what was really going on with me, and being willing to trust someone else – especially God. It consisted of discovering my true self, as well as acknowledging my true feelings and allowing myself to *feel* them, not stuff them back inside or ignore them. It meant appreciating my limitations, accepting my inadequacies, understanding my shortcomings, *and* being able to do the same with others. It required working through, and then discarding, resentments and fears. The longer I stayed sober, the more I recovered. And the more I recovered, the more I grew mentally, spiritually, emotionally, and physically.

Now, don't get the wrong idea. Recovery wasn't all bad. Quite the contrary, it was (and is) all good. I was no longer running from emotions, people, or myself. Hell, I was no longer running from *life*. I was dealing with it. Each day sober, each obstacle overcome, only strengthened my relationship with God. As a result of recovery, working on myself and accepting life's lessons, I was getting healthier mentally, physically, emotionally, and spiritually; my thinking was changing; my behavior was changing; my *life* was changing.

Of course, all of this changing and growing didn't happen overnight, though it happened so fast that oftentimes it seems like it did. But the people in my corner would often remind me that it didn't make sense to rush because there's no finish line in the race to change (or improve) your life. So I moved slowly, but steadily. I purposefully took my time, realizing that the old cliché is right: it's the journey – not the destination – that's important.

During my first two years of recovery, I continued seeing Brett. We even got engaged. But it wasn't long before the relationship began to go downhill. He was never violent. Never raised his voice to me, and continued to treat me like a queen – when he was around. The disease of addiction began to take over his life again. He was getting high more and more often, and the repercussions were blatantly apparent. What started out as a beautifully perfect match was turning into ugly opposites. I was going to meetings; he was going to the crack house. I diligently worked the 12 steps; he kept getting loaded. I worked on staying out of fights; he worked on staying out of jail. I was persistent about bettering myself; he was seeking self-destruction.

Still, I tried to be there for him, tried to understand his disease while I worked diligently to keep mine under arrest. Holding on to him was difficult, especially since he was the only person in my life who was still using. The danger was that he posed a serious risk of relapse for me. I couldn't afford to be in a bad space one day, and then have him come over with a pipe and rock in his pocket. In a weakened state, I might get loaded. I was going to have to make a difficult choice: it was going to have to be my love for Brett or my love for myself.

Late one night, he showed up at my house beaten up, loaded, and broke. He was banging on the door, asking me to let him in. I looked through my peephole, saw him there: skinny as a pole, eyes so big they looked like they would pop out of his head at any moment, lips scabbed and ashy, clothes dirty and unkempt, hair uncombed, pipe still in his hand. I knew then and there that I'd have to make a decision.

As he stood outside my door, knocking, pounding, begging to be let in, I contemplated my options: loving him enough to stick by him or loving myself more by protecting my own sobriety. It was a difficult decision. First of all, I was afraid of being alone. I'd always been told that 'half a man was better than no man at all.' And I'd never been without a man. And Brett was a good man, the best man I'd ever had – at least he was when he was clean. Problem was, he was hardly ever clean. When loaded, he was just like any other nigga in the crack house: pitiful, distrustful, financially unstable, and emotionally, physically, and mentally, unavailable. Since I'd become sober, I'd experienced more and more moments of clarity. Standing there trying to decide what to do, I had another one.

What do you mean half a man is better than no man at all? Gurl, half a man IS no man at all.

To make matters worse, because he was regularly smoking up all his money, he no longer sent flowers and we never went anywhere or did anything that cost money, unless I paid. At first, I couldn't believe how something that was once so beautiful had turned into something so awful. But then I remembered the disease we had. Addiction is like a bull in a china factory – it destroys *everything* in its path. I would not allow this bull to destroy me.

Standing in front of my door, with tears streaming down my face, I made a choice. Sobbing as I talked through the door, I told Brett that I couldn't take his relapses anymore. More important, I couldn't, and wouldn't, take the chance of losing the clean time I'd worked so hard for. So I couldn't be with him unless he committed himself to treatment *that night* and got serious about getting himself together. He listened intently as I informed him that if he wanted to be with me, he'd have to not only get clean, but stay clean *cuz I wasn't fuckin' with no more dope fiends, drugs, criminals, or anyone else indulging in self-destructive, illegal, or unhealthy behavior*. And I meant it. The ball was now in his court. It was his turn to make a choice: get clean and keep me, or stay loaded and lose me.

Brett said nothing for a moment, as if contemplating his choice. Then, quietly, he sighed, 'Okay, Cup,' and walked away from my door.

I figured his 'okay,' meant that he'd chosen me. So I was surprised when days had passed and I hadn't heard from him. He wasn't at any of the meetings we normally attended, and none of his friends had seen him or heard from him. He just disappeared.

I sat around waiting, and expecting him to call and apologize; to tell me he'd been in treatment and wasn't able to make phone calls. I just knew he'd call to say he'd gotten himself together so we could get back together.

Two weeks later, I was still waiting for his call. It never came. At first, I didn't realize he was really gone. I refused to believe that he'd actually chosen dope over me – until I called the number for where he worked. His supervisor informed me that two weeks before (the day after I'd given him the ultimatum), Brett walked in and suddenly quit. He didn't say why and he didn't say where he was going. Still refusing to believe he'd chosen dope, I called his roommate who informed me that, two weeks before, Brett came home in the middle of the afternoon (the same day he'd quit), packed his stuff, and 'up and left.' I hung up the phone with tears in my eyes.

I'd forgotten how baffling and powerful the disease of addiction was.

The heartache hurt. This was the first time I had to experience a broken heart without anything to anesthetize the pain. I had to feel and deal with that pain sober, but not alone. My faith, which was growing more and more each day, sustained me and gave me hope. But God works through people, and the people in my support group helped me get through it.

V pointed out the positive. I didn't see anything positive coming out of the situation – until she told me how she saw it. There were several lessons to be learned. First, I was being forced to learn how to be alone. Also, losing Brett helped me trust God even more. Oh, I was learning to trust Him in other areas of my life; I just hadn't trusted Him when it came to my love life. Now, I'd have to trust and believe that, when the time was right, the right man would come along.

Finally, besides the lessons in losing Brett, there had been one in having him: he taught me to accept kindness, that I did deserve to be treated like a lady, and to set a new standard of how I should, and would, be treated. I was finally loving myself enough to protect me; to stand up for what I did and didn't want – in spite of the fear of being alone.

As usual, Daddy and Jr. rallied around me, giving me encouragement, support, and a shoulder to cry on. Despite my pain, they, too, were glad that Brett had decided to leave. They later told me that several times they'd sat and discussed their concern that my being with a man who got loaded would cause me to do the same. They regularly gave me pep talks by reminding me that the right man would come along when the time was right.

And of course there were my 'mommas.' Almost overnight, I'd gone from having no mother to having three. Shortly after getting sober, a new secretary, Gail, came to work at the firm. Standing about five foot four, in her early fifties, Gail was strikingly beautiful. (Daddy would see her and say, 'That Gail is one good-lookin' chick!') She wore extremely nice clothes; I mean the woman *stayed* sharp. But it wasn't her clothes that made me want to get to know her – it was her personality. Even though she worked for an attorney who was known to be difficult (he'd gone through four or five secretaries that year), Gail had the happiest disposition I'd ever seen. No matter how difficult things became for her at work, she still treated everyone as if they had signs on their chests that said 'Make me feel special.' And that's exactly how she made me feel. I later learned that, shortly after Gail began working at the firm, she'd befriended Maria – the lady who'd given me the dishes. Maria had shared with Gail my difficulties with drugs and alcohol.

Both women took to me immediately; though at first, the feelings weren't mutual. I was distrustful of them. I thought Maria was nuts, and Gail . . . well, she just seemed too 'together,' too sophisticated and prosperous to want to be friends with someone like me. But somehow (I don't know when or how), the two women had gotten it into their heads that they'd been placed in my life by God, so they wouldn't take no for an answer. Though they were never pushy, they were damned persistent. Finally, I relented and allowed them in. I've never regretted it.

Together, Maria and Gail sort of took me on as their daughter, though I felt closer to Gail because, although she had two boys, she didn't have a daughter; Maria did. I called them Mom #1 and Mom #2. These women regularly gave me words of advice as I dealt with the many crises and dilemmas I encountered sober, including the anguish and sorrow I felt about the breakup with Brett. They'd each been married twenty-plus years and so freely shared words of wisdom. No matter what I was going through, one of them always had a story from her own past that helped me see things in a different light. I grew to love our little chat sessions because they never fussed at me, judged me, or laughed at me. So I regularly sought out their advice and words of wisdom on how to deal with my crushed heart. Like the rest of my family, they encouraged me to stay sober, keep taking care of myself, and God would send the right man when it was time.

'Well, I hope He hurries up!' I snapped in irritation. I truly believed that I needed a man to be okay. What I didn't know was that this experience was the start of yet another lesson: like V said, the only time a woman is ready for a man is when she doesn't need one. Still I stayed sober and continued working on myself and loving myself, finally realizing that I was okay – with or without a man.

My third 'momma' was a black woman named Chaney Allen.

Chaney was the older black woman who'd sat next to me the second day I was at the Alano Club looking for V. She was the one who asked me if I was looking for a seat and then pulled me out of the way of approaching foot traffic. Chaney was the first black woman to write an autobiography on alcoholism. She was also one of the cofounders of the Southeast Alano Club, the place where I'd first seen V. From the day I met V there, I attended meetings at the club regularly and soon became a member.

At first, I was intimidated by Chaney because of her long-term sobriety. At the time, she had had twenty-plus years and was one of the most well-known and respected 'old-timers.' I figured someone with that much sobriety wouldn't want to be bothered with a struggling newcomer like me. But when I told this to Chaney, she said it was just the opposite. She said that the newcomers kept her sober because they reminded her that alcoholism was still destroying lives.

Almost immediately, Momma Chaney and I took to each other. I loved talking with her because she was a vessel of knowledge, wisdom, and insight. She would rip you apart with tough love, but she had the unique gift of being able to put you back together again before the conversation ended. She gave me her insight on my breakup with Brett. She assured me that God had something better if I just waited. She also promised it would be worth the wait. She called me almost daily and made me pick her up and take her to meetings. She was determined to make sure this setback didn't derail me.

With the addition of the three mothers, my 'family' had grown quite a bit since I first entered Mesa Vista. I was grateful for the mismatched group that had been placed in my life. Among Daddy, Jr., V, my three moms, and Ken, someone was always reminding me that nothing was worth drinking over, that things would get better, and that I had to deal with whatever emotion I was going through – not hide it, ignore it, or try to go around, over, or under it. I was surrounded by encouragement. So although I thought about drinking, I didn't. Hell, there were even times when I *wanted* to drink, but I didn't. Instead, I prayed, leaned on my support group, cried, cussed, and 'felt.' Oftentimes, I'd literally sit on my hands and wait for the urge or pain or fear to pass. I did everything *but*

drink or use. And my family was right. I did get through it –
clean and sober.

The more I analyzed the cluster that had become my family,
the more obvious it was that only God could have put this
divergent group together and make it work. We were of varying
ages and races. We had wildly different cultural, social, and
economic backgrounds. We had different life experiences. Hell,
we even had differing spiritual and religious beliefs. In short, we
were people who naturally would not mix, but somehow our
oddly shaped individual pieces fit into an unusual puzzle –
perfectly.

50

Okay, I've got two years clean and sober. I've ended my engagement to the best man I'd ever had. I'm twenty-seven years old and I don't drink, drug, fight, or party (though I was still prone to telling someone off). My life had changed drastically. I was staying clean and I was staying sober. And, I was learning that the qualities I sought to achieve and perfect – recovery, self-esteem, responsibility, love for others, etc. – would be a lifelong journey. When it came to me, there would always be something for me to work on, something to fix, something to improve on, something to change. So I continued the process of learning to love and accept my body just the way God made it. I continually tried to be respectful and most times played nice with others. I continued learning to be open and honest with my feelings, as well as learning to trust and depend on others. Most important, I continued to build, fortify, and strengthen my relationship with, and my trust in, my Higher Power, who I called 'God.'

Yeah, yeah, yeah. Blah, blah, blah.

Suddenly, all of the 'spirituality,' 'growing,' 'learning,' and 'feeling' became B-O-R-I-N-G. Angry, restless, and discontent, I gave V a piece of my mind about it.

She didn't snap back. Instead, she sat silently for a few moments. As usual, her response floored me.

'What is a dream you had that drugs, alcohol, and the streets stole from you?' she asked.

Dreams? I didn't have any – at least none that I could think of. She instructed me to think about it for a few days and get back to her.

A couple of days later, I sat contemplating her question. As I looked back over my life, I became more and more frustrated by the realization of *not having* any dreams. Still, I searched, though I had to go waaaaaay back to before Momma died. But, suddenly, an answer came to me. Once I mentally locked on to it, memories came flooding back.

I was about five or six years old when I began to question Daddy about Santa Claus. I was always an inquisitive child, always asking tons of questions – questions that wouldn't cease until I got what I perceived to be a satisfactory answer.

'Where does he live?' I'd asked Daddy innocently as my big brown eyes stared into his.

'At the North Pole,' he said, returning his attention to the television, believing that to be the end of the conversation. It wasn't.

'Have you ever been there?'

'No.'

'Do you *know* anyone that's ever been there?'

Daddy let out a big sigh and began fidgeting.

'Well?' I didn't wait for an answer. 'If *you* never been there and you don't know no one else dat's been there, how you know it's there?'

He tried to think of some response, but couldn't. I later learned that he didn't want to lie to me, but at the same time, didn't want to ruin the childhood experience of 'Santa.' He mumbled something about having to take care of something and quickly walked away, believing for sure that this time the conversation was over. It was, but for only a little while.

A couple of days later, I was back in front of him.

'Who else lives there?'

'Where?' he asked as he took a sip of his coffee. He'd forgotten about our previous conversation, so my question caught him completely off guard.

'At the North Pole.'

'Aw, shit,' he grumbled, realizing that I hadn't let it go. 'Umm, ummm, Santa's family,' he replied as he attempted to shoo me away. I wouldn't move. I had questions and was determined to get answers. So I took a deep breath and started firing.

'Who's in his family? How many kids he got? How old are the kids? What do *they* do there? Do they make toys too or just boss everybody else around? What his wife look like? Why he only come out at Christmas? How he know where we live at? How he get in when we don't have no chimney? How come, when he breaks in, he don't get shot?' This last question bothered me the most, especially since it was common knowledge that most people in the hood kept some type of 'protection' in their homes. Anyone caught coming through a window or down a chimney would've got a bullet in the ass. What made Santa so damn special?

Daddy was bewildered at the quickness with which I threw out questions. While he sat dumbfounded and dazed, I continued, though my posture had changed from innocent to feisty: I had my hand on my hip and a stern look on my face as I sassily brandished my forefinger in the air.

'And how you know it's Santa and not just some white man dressed in a red suit so he can rob folks at Christmastime? Is Santa white? All the pictures of him is white. They ain't got no black or Mexican Santas? Is there more than one? What's wrong with his belly? Why don't he shave?'

Daddy was quickly losing it. He was irritated and annoyed by my badgering. Still, he tried to hold out by mumbling half-audible responses. But I was throwing too many questions too fast; he didn't have time to make up answers. Realizing that I wasn't giving up and sticking to his belief in not lying to children, he finally relented.

'There IS no Santa Claus, okay?' he yelled, visibly frustrated. 'I'M Santa Claus! Your mother and me! We go get the presents, hide them, and when you go to sleep Christmas Eve, we wrap them and put them under the tree!' He slumped against the back of his chair, exasperated. He looked at me despairingly, hoping his answer not only would satisfy me, but would shut me up as well.

I paused for a moment, analyzing this new information.

'Then why didn't you just say so!' I shrieked as I walked away, satisfied with the truth.

From that moment forward, Daddy told me I should be a lawyer. He said only lawyers could ask questions without ceasing and only lawyers *cared* about the answers. And, I wanted to make my daddy proud. So I had dreamed of one day being a lawyer.

Then Momma died, I was dropped into hell, and forgot about the dream. Until now.

I rushed to the phone, called V, and shared the 'Santa' story with her.

'I dreamed of being a lawyer,' I said, excited to remember that I had once had a dream. 'That's the one that was stolen from me!'

'Steal it back,' she said firmly.

'Steal it back?'

'Yes. Steal it back,' she repeated, more firmly than before.

'How in the hell am I supposed – ' Before I could finish, she cut me off. Now she was irritated. 'How do people become lawyers, Cup? They go to school! Take *your* ass to school!'

She had to be kidding. I was a trash-can junkie, a pass-out drunk, a callous Gangsta, liar, thief, hustler, and a ho. People like me didn't become lawyers.

V refused to listen to my excuses. 'You can do anything you want to, Cup. You can be anything you want to be. If you're willing to do the foot work.'

I hated it when she came out with those profound statements. They were always right and usually what I needed to hear. But I hated them nonetheless.

Of course, I went to everyone in the family and asked their opinion, though I was apprehensive about telling Ken. My résumé, the one on which he based his decision to hire me, said I had a high-school diploma or G.E.D. (I'd lied so much and to so many people, I couldn't remember which lie I'd put on the résumé I'd given him.) Going to him now would require telling the truth.

'Unless, I don't tell him I don't have a G.E.D.,' I said quietly as I sat trying to figure out how to get around telling the truth.

The Voice piped up. *Cup, we're living honest lives now, remember? You're going to have to just trust that whatever happens, God will sustain you.*

Is God gon' give me another job? I thought irritably. But I only had to think about it a moment longer before I realized that I'd done enough lying in my life. Hell, I'd lied just about *all* my life: told lies, spread lies, lived lies. It was time for me to learn to tell the truth.

The next day, I said a little prayer and then walked into Ken's office.

As usual, my fears were for nothing. Ken was completely

supportive, although at first he was surprised that I didn't have a high-school diploma or G.E.D.

'Did *I* know that when I hired you?' he asked.

I paused for a moment to think about what my answer should be.

No more lies, Cup. It's time to tell the truth.

I quietly admitted that I'd lied on my résumé. For a moment he didn't say anything, though he chuckled softly. He said he was glad I was getting myself together so that we could turn the information on my résumé from lies to truth. He also said that if there was anything he could do to help me in this effort to fulfill my dream, to let him know.

Everyone else in the family also thought my becoming a lawyer was a great idea and immediately joined V in efforts to encourage me to go to school. Actually, their encouragement got on my nerves. Of course *they* loved the idea. It's always easy to tell someone else what to do. It didn't matter though, because regardless of what they said, I had my own doubts.

It wasn't just uncertainty that was holding me back from returning to school. Before my mom died, I regularly attended school, even loved it. But since then, I'd developed a general dislike for it. I didn't remember much about my sporadic attendance in junior high, and remembered even less about the short-lived high school. What I *did* remember was why I never went – I *hated* it. I hated everything about it: the teachers, the tests, the homework. I especially hated homework. I always believed that only nerds did homework. Shit, I was too old to be a nerd.

If truth be told, neither my feelings of self-doubt or hatred for school were really stopping me from going back. Oh, the emotions were genuine, but they were still excuses. The bottom line was that I was afraid. I was afraid I was too dumb to make it; too pathetic to take it; and too old to fake it. Although on paper I'd dropped out of school during my first semester of the eleventh grade, once you factored in my recurrent ditching, missed semesters, and the lengthy bouts of running away and living on the streets, I probably had enough actual school to take me to the ninth grade. *The ninth grade.*

Luckily for me, I'd learned various mottoes to help me deal with fear. Whenever I was afraid (an emotion I encountered regularly when newly sober), V would say:

491

'It's okay to be afraid. It's not okay to let the fear *stop* you.'

And Momma Chaney would put one hand on her hip and stick the forefinger of the other in my face and say sternly:

'Cup, always remember the acronym for 'fear' can mean one of two things: 'Fuck Everything And Run or Face Everything And Recover.' Now which one YOU gon' do?' Then she'd stand there glaring at me, waiting for a response. Of course, the first time she said this, she had to explain what an 'acronym' was. From then on, though, I always chose the latter version. Shoot, I was afraid she'd kick my ass if I didn't. Momma Chaney refused to let me wobble or weaken when it came to doing things that would change me for the better. She'd force me to march on in spite of whatever it was I was afraid of, or whatever it was she felt I was allowing to hold me back. And I appreciated her immensely for it.

So, it was those mottoes I used to sustain me when I made the decision to go to school regardless of the fear. And a part of me wanted to at least try. Not to be a lawyer; that dream seemed too far fetched, too unrealistic. I wasn't signing up for that joke. But there was nothing far fetched about getting a G.E.D. Hell, at least it would be a start.

Problem was, I didn't know where to go or what to do to get started. Did I have to get my school records? Where *were* my school records? I'd gone to at least three different junior highs and three different high schools. The realization that I didn't even have a starting point thwarted my plans – that is, until I shared my frustration with V.

V was attending school at San Diego City Community College, so she was able to tell me about the adult school located across the street that offered continuing-education classes – though she didn't know how to enroll or even the hours of operation, but, since it was right across the street from the community college, she suggested I go talk to a counselor there to get some guidance on how to get into the adult school.

I called the community college and made an appointment to see a counselor. I missed the first one. I was too scared, and I convinced myself that the whole thing was just a waste of time. When V found out what I'd done, she hit the roof.

'You're going to make another appointment, you hear me? And you're going to show up for it. I don't care if you have to close your eyes, clench your teeth, and force one foot in front of the other. You will walk into that next appointment! And when you get there, you're going to talk to the counselor and answer his questions!'

Damn, she was bossy – and I loved her for it. With V listening on the three-way, I made another appointment for the following week. She offered to go with me, but I refused. I had to learn to start doing things for myself and by myself. Before hanging up, she shared something with me that someone else had shared with her: 'If you put God in your plans, you can make them as big as you want.'

The day of the appointment, I was so anxious I could hardly work. I stood outside the door to the counseling office for a good twenty minutes. When it was finally time to go in, I closed my eyes, clenched my teeth, and forced myself to put one foot in front of the other.

The counselor was an older black man named Mr Johnson. He greeted me with a big smile and a warm, hearty handshake. Instead of starting to talk about me right off, he told me a little about himself: where he went to school, what his major was. Sharing about himself allowed me the ease to open up about myself so that when he asked why I was there, I was ready to tell him.

I told him I wanted information about the adult school across the street because I wanted to get my high-school diploma or G.E.D.

'Well, what do you want to do – eventually, I mean?' he asked. I hesitated for a moment.

I was afraid he'd laugh at me. But then it suddenly occurred to me that he didn't know my past, so why would he laugh?

'I think I want to go to law school,' I replied.

'Well, no law school is going to ask you where you went to high school. They'll only want to know if you have a bachelor's degree. Besides, how old are you?'

I replied that I was twenty-seven.

'Oh, you're too old to be going back to high school. So I wouldn't waste my time. If I were you, I'd start right here at the community college. You can get your associate's degree and transfer on to a four-year university.'

Most of what he said was foreign to me. I wasn't sure of what a 'four-year university' was and why it was so different from the community college. Hell, I thought college was college. What I did understand was that I was too old for high school and that it wasn't required for law school.

Mr Johnson said the first thing we had to do was test me.

I hated tests. 'Maybe this isn't such a good idea,' I said as I stood up to head for the door.

Mr Johnson stood up, gently took my arm, and almost begged me to sit back down. I started to say no, but the pleading in his eyes told me he really didn't want me to leave. So, I returned to my seat.

'Don't worry about it,' he said calmly as he began searching for something in a book. 'These tests are a good thing.'

'I always flunk tests,' I protested.

Mr Johnson assured me that these tests could not be flunked. He said the purpose of them was to help the school determine my learning level.

He went on and on about how the school would assist me every step of the way and about how community college was a great starting point for someone like me – someone who wasn't used to being a student. After a little more convincing, I agreed to take the test, but I left thinking, *What the fuck have I gotten myself into?*

I showed up for the test scared, insecure, and pissed that it took me twenty minutes to find a damn parking space. But I showed up nonetheless. There were about thirty or so other people in the testing room. I was too nervous to notice them or even care about them. I was too worried about whether I'd smoked, snorted, and drunk all my brain power away.

If I had some speed, at least I'd be more alert.

In response to my fear, old thinking kicked in. As I'd been doing since getting sober, I ignored it.

As the proctor passed out the tests, I said a small prayer – nothing big or fancy, but one of my favorites: *Help me!*

I loved the English portion. I was able to answer almost every question. I didn't know if the answers were *correct,* but I was able to put something down just the same.

The rest of the test was a disaster: math, social studies,

history, and some other shit I didn't know. I couldn't write down anything, I couldn't even guess most of the time. So I left most of the answer spaces blank. With each blank space, I began to feel dumber and dumber. I left feeling like an idiot and convinced that going back to school was a bad idea.

Who needs school anyway? I told myself. *You've been doing just fine without it.*

When V asked how it went, I responded with an inaudible grumble. I didn't want to talk about it. She let it rest, for the moment.

A week or so later, Mr Johnson called. He wanted me to make an appointment to come see him so we could discuss my test results. I wasn't going back there. I didn't need him to tell me I was an idiot. So I made up some excuse as to why I couldn't make any of the dates he suggested. He said he'd call back in a few days to see if my schedule had cleared up.

Every couple of days, V would ask about my test results. I told her that I 'hadn't gotten them yet.' It wasn't a lie, it just wasn't all of the truth. But I forgot that V was a dope fiend like me. You can't bullshit a bullshitter. After a week, she no longer accepted my excuses. She said she knew it didn't take that long to get results, and that I was just running scared. She 'strongly suggested' I show up for the results.

Mr Johnson called me almost daily for a week. Each time, I had a reason as to why I couldn't make the appointment. Finally, he, too, caught on.

'Cup, it's not as bad as you think. Please, come in and give me fifteen minutes,' he pleaded. 'I promise you it won't hurt.'

I tried to make up another excuse, but he wouldn't hear it. He scheduled an appointment for me the next evening. Of course, V was ecstatic that I was finally going in to get the results.

I slowly walked into Mr Johnson's office and sat down. He flipped through some papers until he found what he wanted: my test results. He then explained how the testing worked. In various areas of academia, I was rated between a 1 and a 5, with 1 being the lowest and 5 being the highest.

'Your English score is five,' he said calmly.

Five? Did he say five? I was stunned.

'Isn't five the highest?' I asked in disbelief.

'Yes – you did very well in English.'

English had always been my favorite subject, though it never occurred to me that I'd remembered any of the crap I'd learned during my sporadic stints in school. Apparently, I had.

'The rest of the test, however, was not as good,' he said quietly.

My joy immediately turned to anguish.

'Your math score is .24.'

'Is that good?' I asked. 'I mean, where is that between 'one' and 'five'?' I truly didn't know.

Mr Johnson looked at me as if trying to determine if I was kidding or not. But, after taking another glance at my score, he realized I *couldn't* be kidding. He gently explained that .24 was less than 1.

'Less than one?' I shrieked, jumping to my feet. 'You mean I ain't even on the scale? I flunked?'

Mr Johnson reminded me that the test could not be 'flunked.' It was simply a guide to tell us where I needed to be. He calmly stated that I would just have to start my math classes at a 'beginner's' level. He tried to change the subject by moving on to my other scores, which didn't help, since, although they were slightly higher, they were still bad. I didn't get anything above a 2. It was concluded that I could take an intermediate English class, but every other class would have to start at the beginner's level.

I left his office feeling like an idiot. I was discouraged and distraught. I knew my family was waiting to hear about my results, and I didn't want to tell them; I thought they'd laugh at me.

But, as it turns out, I was the only one who'd perceived the results negatively. Ken thought it was great that we now had a 'starting point.'

'Cup, one thing's for sure about starting at the beginning,' he said gaily. 'You can only go up!' He was just a little too damn cheerful about the whole situation.

V felt the same way as Ken. And Daddy and Jr. were just so glad I was returning to school, they didn't care where I started – so long as I started. My moms encouraged me to return, especially Momma Chaney, who herself returned to community college when she was forty-plus years old and got her associate's degree.

496

So I returned to Mr Johnson for an 'attack plan.' He reminded me that his ultimate goal was to get me into San Diego State University. I reminded him that *my* ultimate goal was to get into law school.

Assuming I make it that far. I could always count on a smart-ass thought of self-doubt.

He quickly pointed out that our goals were actually one and the same, since no particular type of bachelor's degree was required to get into law school. He gave me a San Diego State course book and suggested I pick a major that truly interested me so I would stay focused as well as dedicated. As I flipped through the San Diego State catalog, I didn't see anything that caught my fancy, and impatiently told that to Mr Johsnon. Ignoring my irritation, he instructed me to look through it again. I did, this time stopping at the criminal-justice degree, which I must have missed the first time. I was instantly interested. I'd always been fascinated by the criminal mind (probably because I used to have one). I excitedly told Mr Johnson that that was what I wanted to major in (again, assuming I got to San Diego State). He tried to convince me to take awhile and think about it because I might change my mind as I progressed through school. But I wouldn't hear of it; I knew what I wanted – criminal justice.

Seeing that I was dead set on that major, he got out an 'education plan' and began to map out the community-college classes I needed to take. He explained that the community college didn't have a criminal-justice program, but, their liberal arts degree was the closest parallel. Thus, if I acquired an associate's degree in liberal arts, I would be halfway to earning a bachelor's degree in criminal justice.

Once he mapped out all the courses I would need to get my associate's degree, Mr Johnson explained that I had to complete all beginner courses first. However, once I'd done that, I could take the rest in any order I wanted, depending upon the course availability and my financial situation. But since math was by far my worst subject, whatever classes I decided to take, he strongly recommended that beginning math be one of them.

That night, as I sat with my education plan and course book, I picked out four classes, creating for myself a full-time schedule. But V warned that going from no school time to

497

full-time was too much, too soon. It had been years since I'd been in school, and even when I had been enrolled I'd never attended, I would need to learn how to be a student – learn how to study, learn how to show up, be mentally present, and sit through three hours of class time. V told me to take only one class.

'When can I take more than one class?' I asked during a phone conversation.

'When you don't have to ask,' she replied, and hung up.

Damn, she worked my nerves. But she'd never steered me wrong. So, following her instructions, I decided to take one class: beginning mathematics.

You would think that, for me, at twenty-seven years old, signing up for school would be a simple process. It wasn't. Every step of the enrollment procedure was a challenge: figuring out how to complete the enrollment form (which I screwed up twice), standing in line to enroll, wandering the seemingly huge campus to locate the bookstore, figuring out which books I needed, finding the stupid books. None of it came easy. But I trudged on. By the time I got home, I was mentally and physically exhausted from the whole ordeal, but proud to be a student officially.

The first night of class, Ken let me leave work early; actually, he insisted. He said I'd need the extra time to find my class. Boy, was he right – the campus seemed much bigger and more complicated to navigate than before. After asking for directions five times, and going to the wrong class three times, I finally found mine. I walked in and went straight to the back row. I sat in the room, silent, scared, and unsure if I belonged there. I didn't talk to anyone and hoped no one talked to me. They didn't. I think my defensive posture and antisocial grimace kept them from doing so.

The teacher, an unassuming white man, walked in, took the roll, and immediately jumped into 'instruction' by telling us to open our books to the first chapter. Although I'd had my book for a week, I'd never opened it. I was afraid to. I didn't know why, or what I was afraid of. I just knew that I was scared. So the first night of class was the first time I'd opened the book. I was stunned at what I saw. The first chapter literally started with '1 + 1.'

One plus one? Twenty-seven years old and I'm starting *at one plus one?* My embarrassment hit an all-time high. I wanted to run; I wanted to scream; I wanted to cry. But I didn't. I couldn't because I kept hearing my damn family in my head:

This is a positive. Now we know where to start you.

You can only go up from there.

The best place to start is *the beginning!*

So I fought the urge to run and stayed put. Though, I'm not going to lie, it was very difficult to do so. As I looked around the room, I couldn't help but notice that I was surrounded by kids much younger than me – most were straight out of high school. And it seemed as though they had a lot more free time than I did; I had responsibilities they didn't have, like work, groceries, rent. I started to think that maybe I had too many responsibilities to go to school. Momma Chaney squashed that idea instantly by reminding me that it was only fear that created that notion and pointed out that many people work and go to school. So I continued. And so did the problems.

I had a problem with humility. Out of habit, I automatically sat at the back of the class (cool kids always sat in the back). The problem was that I didn't understand a lot of what was going on, so I always had questions. But I rarely asked them because of the derision I saw in the faces of the other students and the snickers I heard. Obviously, they thought my questions were stupid and the last thing I wanted to be was stupid. When I shared this dilemma with V, she suggested I sit in the very first row.

'That way, you won't hear the snickers in the back and you won't be able to see the faces.'

Me, 'Ms. Cool,' in the first row? I'd never, ever, sat in the front of the class, let alone the first row. I tried to think of alternatives, but it was apparent that I had no other choice. So the next class, I found myself sitting in the front, and feeling very, very out of place. Nevertheless, to my surprise, it worked. Since I was in the front, I was able to raise my hand as often as I wanted and ask as many questions as I wanted, all the while oblivious to whatever reaction was taking place behind me.

And, you still 'cool'! I teased myself.

From that day forward, I always sat in the first row.

I remember the first time I stayed after class to ask my teacher a question. It took a lot for me to ask for help – the idea of it still filled me with shame and embarrassment – and I was convinced he'd laugh at me. If he did, I gave myself permission to cuss him out. But he didn't laugh. Instead, he stayed behind for over an hour, answering my questions and helping me understand the concept of long division. So, I took what he taught me and I studied. Though at first, studying didn't come easy.

I had to learn how to study. The first problem was that I couldn't sit still. I'd study for a few moments and then all of a sudden have to get up and do something. For example, I hated cleaning. But whenever I was supposed to be studying, I'd get the compulsion to clean – anything – the bathroom, living room, even the sidewalk out in front of my apartment.

Next, even if I could sit still, I couldn't concentrate. My mind raced rapidly with a variety of thoughts, most of which were stupid, unimportant, or irrelevant. I mean, I thought of everything, like how many students were enrolled at the community college. I wondered what Ken, Daddy, Jr., and even the president were doing at the moment. I wondered how television worked. I thought about how an interior decorator decided on colors and styles. I wondered, when babies started learning how to walk, if they didn't know that they *couldn't* walk.

On top of that, I couldn't seem to remember anything. Something we'd learn in class that night would be forgotten by the next day. I found it funny that for years I'd heard that drugs fucked up the mind, that weed – supposedly the 'harmless drug' – destroyed brain cells that never grew back. I never paid any of those warnings any attention – until now – now that I needed brain cells. Ironically, I realized that I was living proof of what drugs and alcohol did to the mind. Mine seemed to be gone.

As usual, all hope was not gone. First, I prayed that God would help me concentrate and help me remember. He did. Then V gave me some suggestions. She told me to set aside a set time to study and then to do so in short intervals. I started out by studying for five minutes (that's about as long as I could go before my mind changed directions) and then taking a ten-minute break. Study for five, break for ten. Of course, this made doing homework take forever, but at least I was doing it. Slowly, I increased the study time and reduced the break time. Within a month, I'd advanced to studying for ten and breaking for five. After two months, I could study for almost a half hour without a break.

There's something to be said about baby steps.

Oprah Winfrey also helped me get to studying. I loved Oprah and was always watching her talk show when I was supposed to be doing my schoolwork. One day, V called to see how the studying was going. I admitted that I wasn't doing it, but was checking out Oprah instead. V's response would carry me through the rest of my educational career.

'Oprah got her money,' she snapped. 'You trying to get YOURS! Now, turn off that fuckin' TV and get to studying!'

After that, whenever I wanted to watch Oprah or any other TV show instead of study, I'd remind myself, *Oprah and them got their money. You tryin' to get yours!* Without hesitation, I'd turn off the TV and pick up a book.

Ken was also a big help. He would often let me take additional time at lunch so I could study. And on exam days, he'd let me leave work early to get in a little extra studying. But no amount of help from V, Oprah, or anyone else could have gotten me through school because the bottom line was that it was up to me. So I gave it everything I had. Sometimes, I would be so exhausted from work and studying, I'd fall asleep, face-first, in my food. Soon, I'd practiced studying enough so that I could do it for hours at a time without needing a break. And, although my memory never completely returned, it did slowly improve.

I found out that amazing things happen when one studies. All those years I thought I was stupid; I thought I hated math. But, as I began to study, I quickly realized I wasn't stupid after all. My hard work and persistence paid off. I aced that beginning math course. I couldn't believe it. An A! I stared disbelievingly at the report card for at least ten minutes. It was only one class and it was only one A. Still, I'd earned it, fair and square. Feeling good about myself, I immediately signed up for another class, though just one. I still didn't feel comfortable taking more.

My second class was intermediate math. Applying the study aids I'd learned, I aced that too. I'd completed my first year of community college with a straight-A average.

My first thought was, *Thank you, God.*

My second was, *Hot damn! I'm on a roll!*

From that point on, I attended classes regularly and faithfully. That first A instilled a sense of dedication in me I hadn't had before. I decided that I was going to stay on the road to education no matter what. Several 'no matter whats' came up. It cost me some friendships. Several sober girlfriends complained that I studied too much or didn't have time to hang with them. Without hesitation, I cut them loose. I missed numerous parties and barbecues. I was dead set in my determination that no one, and I meant no one, would ever again prevent me from being good to me, or doing good for me. So I stuck with it.

Although the community college was a two-year program, it took me five and a half years to graduate. Some semesters I took one or two classes; other terms I attended full-time. The number of classes I took depended on my available funds and, since I was still working full-time, on the availability of evening courses. I didn't realize it had taken that long because I wasn't keeping track of the time. I didn't care how long it took to finish, as long as I did. So my rule of thumb was to keep my eye on the long-term goal – law school – but *focus* on the present goal – completing community college.

When it did finally come time for me to get my degree, five and a half years after taking that '1+1' class, I *glided* across the stage. As I glided toward the dean whose arm was stretched out toward me, his hand holding a piece of white paper rolled up into a tube with a bright red string tied around it, I heard my family wildly cheering in the crowd. As I grabbed the tube and shook his hand, I realized it was worth every barbecue I'd ever missed, worth every party I'd missed, worth every friend I'd lost, and even worth every Oprah show I'd missed.

On top of that, the chick who'd started at '1+1' graduated with honors. I had no special gifts, skills, or talents – *whatsoever.* What I did, anyone could do. All it took was a little bit of faith and a whole lotta hard work, perseverance, and dedication – now if only I could keep it up.

51

Mr Johnson assisted me with my San Diego State application. While I awaited their decision, all I could do was pray.

Finally, the envelope came.

'Congratulations!' the paper read. 'You've been accepted to SDSU!'

I was ecstatic – until I remembered that I didn't have a high-school diploma or G.E.D. I wasn't sure if State required one, but if it did, that would probably ruin my admittance.

But who said I have to tell 'em? I asked myself. *I mean, it's not like they asked!* The more I thought about it the more I decided I didn't need to tell them – until I talked to V. She reminded that I was a changed person, living honestly and truthfully. She asked me what the old 'Cup' would do, and then told me to do the opposite. Doing the opposite was exactly what I was afraid of.

As usual, my fears were in vain. The nice lady who I talked to at San Diego State didn't care that I didn't have a high-school diploma or G.E.D. She informed me that since I had an associate's degree, I was coming in as a transfer student.

'What's that mean?' I asked.

She explained that, because of my associate's degree, I had been admitted as a junior.

'That means, you're "in." Period.' She said humorously.

I was excited about being 'in' – until I got on campus. At State's invitation, I attended an 'orientation' in which juniors and seniors gave incoming students a tour of the campus. At first it seemed like a good idea, since the campus appeared so overwhelmingly large. But once I showed up, I realized it wasn't a good idea after all. I was the oldest 'incoming' student at the orientation. The others were freshmen, fresh out of high school. And even our guide, an aggravatingly cheerful blond girl named Shelly, couldn't have been older than twenty-two or twenty-three. Hell, I was pushing thirty-three!

Damn, stuck with a bunch of kids again! I thought irritably.

Despite my lack of interest, I continued with the tour and tried to look happy for Shelly's sake, all the while trying to hold down the fear that was building up inside, especially as Shelly began to point out what she thought were great attributes of State, but only made it clear to me that I was entering a whole new world: City had three thousand students; State had over thirty thousand. City was on forty acres; State on over two hundred. State was larger and bigger in every way. And I was scared to death. But as I had been doing, I didn't let the fear stop me.

So I finished the orientation and enrolled. Unfortunately, there were several stumbling blocks in my way.

First, although I was gearing toward a criminal-justice degree, State's criminal-justice program was not geared toward evening students. There was no way I could graduate with the degree without taking day classes. But Ken and I worked it out so that I started work at 8:30 instead of 9:00. Twice a week I left at 10:30 for an 11:00 class. Once that class was over (at 12:30), I returned to work and stayed until 6:30, at which time I left again for a 7:00 class. It was a difficult schedule, but I did it – for three years straight. Just like that, one stumbling block was removed.

Next, was the problem of getting the courses I needed. Because the criminal-justice program was 'impacted,' there were always more students wanting to take a class than there were seats. So I had to 'crash' almost every class, which meant going to class on the first day and hoping the teacher would let me in. Most times, they did. Many times, however, they didn't. In those instances, I had to scramble to find other available classes. The problem with this was that because the classes only met once a week, each time I failed to crash one meant another week I'd be behind in a class I did get in.

One particular semester, I tried to crash three separate courses. Each teacher refused to let me in. Frustrated and at my wits' end, I had one class left to try: Prosecutorial Functions, which was taught by Assistant U.S. Attorney Larry Burns, a tall, slim, handsome white man with a serious disposition, but a warm personality.

I made sure to get to the class way before it started. Luckily, Mr Burns was also early. He listened intently as I explained my predicament of being in desperate need of his class. He responded that although he was sympathetic to my plight, he didn't think my crashing would be a good idea, since his course was a difficult one and required quite a bit of work. He was also concerned with the fact that if he let me in, I'd already be three weeks behind the rest of the class. He started walking away, believing that to be the end of the subject. It wasn't.

I jumped in front of him, blocking his way. Talking fast, I begged him to give me a chance. I told him that I wasn't looking for a handout, just a chance. I assured him I'd do all of the work he expected of his students, with no excuses or complaining. I promised him that if he let me in, he would not regret it. Seeing that I was desperate, and genuinely serious, he agreed to let me in.

Prosecutorial Functions became one of my favorite classes, and Mr Burns one of my favorite professors. As promised, I was there every week, on time, my homework completed, with an attitude of gratitude. I showed up ready, eager, and willing to participate in class discussion. Mr Burns could call on me at any given time and get a correct answer.

Not only did I finish Mr Burns's class after starting three weeks late, but I finished it with one of the highest grades. Besides teaching me a lot about a prosecutor's functions, the course jump-started in me an interest in becoming a prosecutor. Once the class ended, I asked Mr Burns if I could continue to seek him out for advice, and we quickly became friends. Although I saw him only on campus, whenever I could, I talked to him about the courses I should take, what law school would be like (if I ever got there), how I could get a job as a prosecutor, etc. He was a wealth of knowledge and never seemed to tire of my questions.

One day, he was telling me he believed I'd make a great prosecutor because I seemed to be able to talk to people easily and make them feel comfortable talking to me. He said that a good prosecutor needed to be able to talk and relate to a lot of different people: the jury, the defense attorney, the judge . . .

'Judge!' I blurted out in horror. 'Who said anything about talking to a judge? I don't talk to judges! I don't like judges.'

'What do you mean you don't like judges?' he asked perplexed.

I clarified that it wasn't so much that I didn't like them; I just hated them. I then gave him a quick history of my life, hoping it would explain my feelings. I started with the judge who gave me to the sperm donor. Then I briefly discussed the roles judges played in contributing to my time in and out of foster homes and shelters. I told him about the judge who didn't believe I'd been beaten although Jr. and Aunt Pam had both personally seen the welts. I quickly went over my gang involvement (without specifics); touched on how I'd seen many friends get railroaded by what I perceived to be crooked judges; and ended with a brief account of my trying to get my life together by returning to school and trying to stay away from the criminal justice system altogether – that is, until I'd decided on my major. I explained that his class made me want to be a prosecutor, but I wanted to do it without having to deal with judges.

He listened intently, making no facial expressions except every once in a while raising an eyebrow in surprise. When I was done, he sat silently for a moment.

'I've got someone I want you to meet,' he said.

He gave me his business card and instructed me to call him the following week. I did, and we scheduled a lunch date.

When Mr Burns picked me up and told me we were going to a nearby restaurant, I thought nothing of it, until he informed me that a friend of his would be meeting us for lunch – his friend the judge.

'A judge?' I shrieked. 'You're bringing a JUDGE?'

Was he setting me up? Had I robbed this judge and forgotten? Had they discovered some old stuff on me and were planning to lock me up right then and there? My mind raced frantically. Recovery had not diminished my paranoia and fear. I hated meeting new people because my memory was bad, and I'd robbed, burglarized or screwed over so many people, I was never sure if I'd done something to them in my past.

As we entered the restaurant, Mr Burns led me toward the back. There, sitting in a booth with a pretty young white woman, was a burly but well-built white man. He was very handsome and extremely friendly. As we walked up, I noticed he was laughing and talking with the waiter. The waiter!

'Cup,' Mr Burns said as we approached the table, 'this is Judge Frank Brown. Frank, this is Cupcake.'

I didn't know what to do, so I stood and waited for him to make the first move.

'Cupcake!' the judge exclaimed as he reached for my hand. 'Does that mean you're sweet?' He gave me a hearty handshake and the biggest smile I'd ever seen. I immediately became more at ease.

I don't know what I was afraid of. By the middle of the lunch, I was glad I'd come because Judge Brown was extremely respectful, very friendly, and quite helpful. He asked me questions about my education and the direction I wanted it to go. He told me that he agreed with Mr Burns about my being great prosecutorial material. And, like Mr Burns, he never seemed to tire of my questions. He also insisted that I stopped calling him 'Judge Brown.'

'Judge Brown is too formal,' he said. 'Call me Frank!'

I continued my education at State but began worrying that I was getting too 'old' to be in school. I'd been in school six years and still was nowhere near being done. So I attended full-time and around the clock: spring, fall, summer, and winter. Yup, I even took classes during the winter sessions – the three-week break during the Christmas season. If I wasn't at work, I was in class. I didn't have time to get to know anyone at State (except my professors), or participate in any extra curricular activities. All I did was go to work, school, and 12-step meetings – and in that order.

I was nearing graduation when I learned that the criminal justice major required a student to either volunteer for an internship or take the 'prison tour.' My choice was already made for me, since I couldn't do any volunteering while working full-time and going to school full-time.

The prison tour was run by a tall, slender white professor named Paul Sutton. Professor Sutton had been running the tours for years. The tour was a five-day bus trip to seven or eight California prisons, including some of the toughest: San Quentin, Folsom, Soledad (which used to be known as

'Gladiator School'), California State Prison–Sacramento, and the notorious Pelican Bay State Prison (home to some of the most famous criminals in California). The tour was a once-in-a-lifetime – we hoped – opportunity that allowed students to experience, first-hand, what prison – and inmates – are really like. This was especially important since all of the students were criminal justice majors.

The prison tour was an amazing experience. We had an in-depth tour of six men's and two women's prisons. Some of the tours were even led by prisoners. We saw places that are rarely, if ever, seen by the public. The tour of each prison included the mess hall, cellblocks, education rooms, industries area, and the yard. We were also able to walk the entire length of the fifth tier (the top one) of Folsom's famous #1 Building, where the movie *American Me* was filmed.

The weapons presentations were my favorites. Most of the prisons had a room where they displayed weapons that had either been confiscated by officers during a 'shake down' or removed from a dead or seriously injured body. These rooms were filled with everyday, usually harmless, items that had been turned into lethal weapons: a toothbrush had a metal shaft drilled into its end turning it into a deadly dagger; a small plastic comb had been melted and shaped into a knife. Even pens could be turned into a weapon. But by far, the most innovative weapon was a gun. Yes, a gun (called a 'zip' gun in prison). Using scraps of wood, metal, and rubber bands, a prisoner had made a gun that shot real metal bullets. These guns were created by inventive inmates, and my mind conjured up memories of various homies and street buddies over the years that had wasted similar talents.

Indeed, inmates had even made a cannon – .50 caliber – fashioned in the metal shop as part of an escape plot. It was to have been used to take out the tower officer. We were told it had been test fired at the state lab and was accurate to fifty yards! A prison snitch had turned in the conspirators, averting what would certainly have been a catastrophe.

We were also given a tour of the execution chamber at San Quentin and saw the women's death row in Chowchilla. During the entire week, I wasn't afraid of the prisoners or possible violence. But when I stood in front of those death chambers, the hair on the back of my neck stood straight up.

I ended that tour with a new awareness of the meanings of grace and mercy. I was saddened to see so many young men and women, mostly minorities, locked behind bars. On the other hand, I was grateful that it wasn't me, when it easily could have, and probably should have, been. I had done many things over the years to earn a place in a six-by-four-foot steel cell. I often questioned God as to why others ended up in jail and I didn't, but my questions were never answered. I soon quit asking. I'd learned not to put a question mark where God put a period.

Yet another good thing came out of that prison tour – I was able to get honest about my past.

Most of the students on the tour were much younger than me; we had little in common. So I spent most of the time in the front of the bus chatting with Professor Sutton. It was during these chats that a friendship began to develop. First, he told me that, although I'd passed the background check required for all students going on the tour, the prison official who had done my check mentioned to Professor Sutton that I had an 'interesting' past. Professor Sutton looked at me as if he expected an explanation. I didn't offer one.

Then I found out that Professor Sutton was sort of a gang expert. So our discussion turned to comparing his 'book' knowledge about gangs with my 'street' knowledge. He knew so much about street life that I was comfortable talking to him about things I swore I'd never tell anyone. He didn't seem surprised by any of it. As a result, he quickly earned my trust, so much so that when he began to question me about my past, I answered him honestly.

By the end of the tour, he knew everything – and was in awe that I'd survived.

'You've got to tell people,' he said, full of excitement.

'Tell them what?' I retorted.

'Tell them about you! Cup, you've got to tell people about you!'

I liked Professor Sutton. I really did. But I was now sure that he was a few sandwiches short of a picnic and obviously didn't understand the significance of what he was saying. I explained to him what Tommy had told me – that society was afraid of people like me. So I told him about my perfect lil Marcia Brady past and made it clear that no one needed to be the wiser.

Realizing I wasn't budging on the Marcia Brady story, he asked if he could tell some people.

'Go ahead,' I said, 'but don't come running back to me when you get your feelings hurt.'

I thought the subject was dropped.

Two weeks later, Professor Sutton summoned me to his office.

'NBC News wants to talk to you,' he announced proudly.

I was instantly alarmed. In the past, whenever I was told someone wanted to 'talk to me,' it usually meant they wanted to kick my ass for something I'd done. My mind raced with fear as I tried to remember if I'd ever robbed anyone at NBC.

Professor Sutton calmed me down and explained that he'd done what he'd said he'd do. He'd talked to some people about me. They'd started interviewing him about gangs. Halfway through the interview, he began talking about me. They decided to scrap that story and, instead, wanted to interview me.

I was speechless. When I could talk, I said no. 'Fuck no,' actually.

But Sutton was relentless. It took a while, but he finally convinced me to say yes.

A week later, for the first time in over twenty years, I publicly got real about my past for the local news interview. After it was over, I waited for the negative backlash I'd always been expecting. It never came. The phone rang, all right. But the calls were from people who wanted me to come and speak. They wanted *me* to speak. The speaking requests were many more than I could fill. But I did what I could. For the next ten years, I spoke as often as I could – and for free.

Professor Sutton was right. I was helping people with my past. Finally, something good was coming from having lived all those years in hell.

Although it took three long years of attending State full-time, graduation day was finally approaching. Several weeks beforehand, a woman who identified herself as representing San Diego State called me to inform me I was graduating 'magna cum laude.' I had no idea what that meant. (It's not like we sat around the crack house saying, 'You know so-and-so graduated

510

magna!') Over the years, I'd heard people mention student loans; I thought that, since I had a job, I wasn't eligible for a loan. (A price I paid for not asking questions.) So the entire time, I paid my own way through school – books, tuition, everything. To me, *magna* sounded like 'more.' I thought she was saying I owed the school more money before I could graduate. I began to go off.

'I'm not giving you people another damn dime!' I was hot! The nerve of them, asking me for more money!

'I've paid my own way the WHOLE time I've been here. And even through City College. I paid for my tuition, my books, my—'

'Whoa! Whoa! Whoa!' the woman exclaimed, interrupting my ranting. She then explained to me what it meant to graduate magna.

For a few moments I was speechless.

'You mean *I'm* graduating with high honors?' I asked, unsure if I truly understood what she'd said.

'Yes! That's quite an accomplishment! And I understand you've worked full-time the entire time?'

'Uh-huh,' I said softly.

'Well, you should be very proud of yourself.'

I was too stunned to be proud. I wasn't trying to graduate magna. Hell, I was just trying to *graduate.*

Eight and a half years after starting community college, I graced the stage at State. Again, I glided across. Again my family was in the audience screaming and cheering me on. Again, as I took the scroll I realized it was worth every social event I'd ever missed – I had achieved yet another goal I thought was impossible for someone like me.

I reminded myself that, with a lil bit of faith and a whole bunch of dedication, perseverance, hard work, and the support of loved ones, maybe anything *was* possible.

I just hope this crap works in law school!

52

Part of the law school–application process is taking the Law School Admission Test, or the LSAT. The conventional wisdom is that unless a student scores at least 165 on this test, they should hang it up – they're clearly not law-school material. If the score is less than 142, law schools won't even look at you.

I knew how important this test was, and I was determined to do well on it. I took an expensive study course that was specially designed to teach people how to do well on the LSAT. I attended every class and I studied diligently. But, try as I might, I could never get a practice score above 139. I believed the test was culturally biased, and I informed the teacher of my opinion. Of course, he didn't believe me and set out to prove me wrong. He announced to the class that we would attack the next question as a group. The part of the test we were working were 'assumption questions.' In doing these, a scenario would be laid out and then the student needed to make certain assumptions to be able to pick the correct answer.

The scenario of the next question just happened to involve a police officer pulling over a car full of kids.

'Now,' he asked the class, 'what's the first thing you'd want to know to be able to answer this question?'

The class was silent for a few moments. I didn't have to think long before speaking up.

'I'd want to know the color of the occupants.' I was trying to sound proper.

Everyone looked at me – stunned.

'What?' he asked, truly confused at my response.

'I'd want to know what color the folks in the car are! Because if they're black or Mexican, that's going to play into my answer about why they were pulled over!'

He paused for a moment before speaking.

'Who else would have wanted to know that?'

No one raised their hand.

'Okay,' he said slowly, 'did anyone else even think of that?' Again, not one person raised his or her hand. (Oh, did I mention that I was the only minority in the class?)

He instructed the class to return to individual study and turned to me.

'I see your point.'

Though he didn't go so far as to admit that the test was biased, he did agree that my thinking was definitely different. But he also warned that the test was what it was, and if I wanted to do well on it, I had to learn to think like 'they' did. He returned to his desk, indicating to me that the discussion was over. I returned to studying but knew I was fucked.

That night, I told Momma Chaney what had happened. I told her that there was no sense in my taking the test, since there was no way I could pass – *my thinking was different!* (It's funny how, if we're not careful, we'll allow one lil setback to make us throw in the towel.) But Momma Chaney wasn't trying to hear anything I was talking about.

'Cup, you're thinking's *been* different. Still, you've managed to excel all the way. So what's so different now?'

'But you don't understand!' I pleaded. 'Those other tests weren't based on my *thinking*! This one is, and my thinking is different!'

'Cup, that doesn't even make sense. All tests are based on thinking – and yours is fine!'

Ken also refused to listen to my excuses. Instead, he gave me an extra hour at lunch *every day* to study. So I kept trying. It paid off a little: my score jumped to 142. It was a slight improvement, but still not good enough. At the snail's pace at which my score was inching up, there was no way I'd get it to a decent number before the date of the actual test – if ever. I could take it and hope for the best or wait until I thought I was good enough to pass.

Fuck it, I thought, and signed up to take the LSAT.

* * *

I studied for the test right up until the moment I walked into the testing room. I said a prayer and picked up my pencil.

By the middle of the exam, it was very apparent that I didn't know what I was doing. So I slammed the testing booklet closed, jumped up, and walked out.

Don't ask me what my score was. I never found out because shortly thereafter, I contacted the LSAT people and told them I didn't want my score. (You see, within a specified time period after the test, you could choose not to receive your test score. Choosing this option, however, meant that not only would you never know your score, but no one else ever would either because it would never be released. It would be as though you didn't take it.)

I sank into a depression. I felt stupid and defeated. I began thinking that maybe I'd been right all along – law school was just a pipe dream. I mean, I'd always believed it was unlikely that I'd actually get into law school. But that unlikelihood had turned into a clear-cut certainty of failure.

'Oh, get off the cross!' V shouted when I shared my thoughts with her on the phone. 'We need the wood!'

Any other time, I probably would have realized she was telling me, in her oddly comical way, to quit feeling sorry for myself because there were people out there suffering from way worse things. But I was so deep into my pity party, all it did was hurt my feelings. And piss me off.

Oblivious to how her comment had hit below the belt, and refusing to join in my 'poor me' indulgence, she spent the next half hour making me remember where I'd started from ('1+1'), reminding me about my vow to go on 'no matter what,' and declaring that no one who quits can ever be successful at what they've quit.

'Huh?'

'If you quit practicing basketball, you'll never get good at basketball. You may perfect other stuff, but never *basketball*. To perfect *basketball* you have to keep at *it*.'

I hated it when V got all positive and philosophical. I hated it even more when she was right. She talked and talked until she wore me down. By the end of the conversation, I agreed to retake the test.

'And I don't care if you have to guess at every question.

DON'T YOU MOVE!' She commanded before slamming down the phone.

Again I signed up for the test. Again I studied, giving it my all. Again, I prayed before picking up my pencil. And again, before long, I wanted to run. The only thing stopping me was V's voice screaming *DON'T YOU MOVE!* So I didn't, although during the last half hour of the exam I *did* have to guess at every question.

In spite of everything, I left the exam feeling good about myself for at least finishing.

The good feeling didn't last long. My score was a 145. All that kept running through my mind was the fact that a score of less than 142 – the unofficial bottom – meant that schools wouldn't even look at you. Shit, I was only three points from the bottom! I was immediately depressed again. 'Apply anyway,' V said calmly when I told her the bad news.

'Apply anyway,' Daddy said when I told him my score. He was trippin'. I figured that he and V were ignorant of the reality of the situation. Hell, I'd flunked the damn test!

Wasn't no law school gon' let me in!

I didn't really think seriously about applying until Daddy, Jr., Ken, and all three moms insisted that I apply.

'Cup,' Momma Gail pleaded, 'you've come too far to quit. And, God didn't bring you this far to drop you.'

Well, somebody *dropped the ball!* I retorted in my mind. They all couldn't actually believe the crap they were laying on me.

'You'd better apply!' Judge Brown barked when I called to tell him how horribly I'd done. 'With all that you've been through, any law school should be kissing YOUR boots to get you to come there!'

I didn't take his comment to heart. I knew he was just being polite. He was way too nice a judge to say what we all knew: I was an idiot.

Larry Burns also jumped on the bandwagon. 'Look what you did in my class! You started out three weeks behind and came out first – all the while working full-time and taking a full class load! Put in those damn applications!'

I figured I'd put in a few applications to get everyone off my back.

So with three letters of recommendation – from Ken, Larry, and Frank – I completed five applications, sent them off, and waited. While I waited, I calmed my fears by reminding myself of one of my many rules: *you do the foot work, and leave the results up to God.*

The first four replies came within the same week. Every one of the schools had denied my application. It seemed that, because of my low LSAT score, they didn't believe I was law-school material. A week later, I received the fifth and final envelope. It was from the University of San Francisco School of Law.

'Lord, I just can't take one more no,' I whispered as I stared at the white envelope with the school's name printed in pretty green letters in the upper left-hand corner.

Open it, the Voice urged.

I did. The first word I saw was, 'Congratulations!'

I'd been accepted! And not only did USF accept me, they gave me money to come. I was ecstatic. Tears were flowing down my cheeks as I danced around singing and thanking God.

Yeah, but you got into only one school!

Over eight years sober and I was still fighting negative, self-depreciating thinking. Almost immediately my joy was gone.

'How many schools can you go to at once?' V asked when I shared this thought.

As I contemplated her question, I realized she was right. So what if I got into only one law school? I could attend only one! I'd gotten into one, and dammit, I was going to one.

Pack yo' shit, girl, I sassily told myself as I resumed celebrating by jumping and dancing around. *We's goin' to law school!*

53

Several weeks before I was to start law school, I had a panic attack. I'd begun to convince myself that San Francisco was too far away from my family and friends; that if something, anything, went wrong, I wouldn't have anyone around to help me; and that I couldn't hack law school. Hoping to get some solace, I decided to call Carol Wilson, the person whose signature was on my acceptance letter.

When Carol answered the phone, I began talking extremely fast – as I often did when I was nervous. In less than five minutes, she'd learned my name and the story behind it, my life history, and all the reasons why I could flunk out of law school. I spoke so fast, periodically interjecting slang, that she probably didn't understand most of what I said. When I finally stopped to take a breath, she began speaking very slowly as if trying to talk someone out of committing suicide. She comforted me as best she could and assured me that everything would be fine. I hung up feeling a little better. (I later learned that she was instantly convinced I was some nut and probably wouldn't make it through the first year of law school.)

Several weeks later, I got to meet Carol face-to-face. She was a tall, slender white woman with long sandy-brown hair. Although she never wore a stitch of makeup, she had a natural beauty enhanced by her cheery personality and welcoming smile. Carol ran USF law school's Academic Support Program (ASP), a sort of 'alternative' admittance program, since it didn't use 'traditional' screening methods to determine a student's eligibility. If a student's LSAT score or grades didn't 'meet the cut,' his or her file was forwarded to professors and other school administrators who volunteered to sit on the ASP panel. The panel considered the LSAT score and grades, but focused on other conditions that could have affected the student's school or LSAT performance – like age, learning disabilities, difficult or challenging childhoods, financial challenges, or personal troubles. Most of the minority students in my class, including me, were admitted through ASP.

As administrator of ASP, Carol's job was to mentor, tutor, and guide students through the hell called law school, from help with classes, to help with housing and finances, to armchair psychiatric assistance. Carol had also attended USF, so she had firsthand knowledge of the challenges and pressures of law school. As a result, she often went above and beyond the call of duty.

I wasted no time in utilizing Carol's services, knowledge, and experience. Thanks to years of recovery, which required humility and emphasized the necessity of asking for assistance, I had no problem saying 'HELP!' And I needed a lot of help.

I had a hard time learning to think and analyze in the way that law school required. I'd be given an issue. I was then supposed to research the law relevant to that issue, apply the law to the facts (called 'analyzing'), and then, based on my analysis, draw a conclusion. It sounds easy. It wasn't – at least not for me. So I was constantly in Carol's office, doing practice exams, asking questions, going over my notes and outlines, crying. I spent so much time with Carol that it wasn't long before we developed quite a bond. I appreciated the time and effort she spent on me. She appreciated and admired my persistence and determination.

Carol wasn't the only one I bugged. All my professors came to know me very well. I took advantage of each's office hours and regularly hemmed them up after class with questions.

Still, I was plagued with fear and self-doubt. It was during these times that I'd call on my support group (Daddy, Jr., Ken, Frank, Larry, or my moms Chaney or Gail), always in tears; sometimes I'd be hysterical. They never hurried me off the phone, but instead took as much time as required to calm me down and convince me that I had what it took to make it.

On one such occasion, I'd called Frank, crying and babbling about how the other students seemed so much younger than me;

how they seemed to be catching on much faster than me; and how terribly tough law school was.

'Oh, forget them!' he interrupted. 'They couldn't take *a fifth* of the shit you've been through!'

His reaction startled me. He'd gotten harsh with me before, but never to this degree and with such intensity.

I continued with my babbling, crying about how tough law school was.

'Law school ain't tough. You want to know what's tough? Girl, *you're* tough! Now you wipe your snotty nose and get back to studying!'

It was the kick in the butt I needed. He'd awakened the fight in me. I wiped my nose, grabbed my pen, picked up my books, and returned to studying.

Still, I knew that I couldn't just count on Carol, my professors, and my family for help. I had to help *myself*. I had to do like I'd been doing all my life, whether engaging in negative or positive conduct: I had to give it everything I had, go the extra mile, do whatever it took – which, by the way, was always a necessity for studying. The law text books were filled with words I didn't know. Of course, it would have been easier, and faster, to just say 'big word' and keep going. But I knew that 'pretending' to comprehend meant I was only cheating myself. So when I came across a word I didn't know, I did what V taught me to do years ago when I'd first started school: I'd underline the word and look up the definition. Once I found a meaning I could grasp, I wrote that new meaning above the word. Then, I'd reread the entire sentence (or paragraph) substituting my newly ascertained meaning. Of course, this meant it took twice as long to study. I didn't care. I'd come too far to start shortchanging myself.

Determined that lack of trying wouldn't be the reason I flunked out, I gave law school everything I had, studying day and night. My hard work and persistence paid off. At the end of the first semester, I was in the top 10 percent of the class.

I remained in the 10 percent the entire first year of law school. Although I'd started law school wanting to be a prosecutor, I couldn't seem to land a position in a district attorney's office. My grades were so good that Carol suggested I participate in on-campus interviewing with law firms who send represent-atives to campus to interview students for summer associate positions. These were highly sought-after positions because not only was the pay enough to live on throughout the year, but you also got a glimpse of what it was like to be a lawyer, and you spent the summer being 'wined and dined' at San Francisco's best restaurants. The best part about getting a position as a summer associate is that it almost guarantees the student a position with the firm upon graduation.

I was hesitant to interview because I'd never done one clean or sober.

I applied to ten firms but got only two interviews, both with prestigious firms. On the day of the first interview, I was having lunch with Candace, one of my tutors who was one year ahead of me in law school.

'I thought you had an interview this afternoon,' she said as we sat in a Japanese restaurant, enjoying the only kind of meal starving students could – cheap.

'I do,' I replied.

'Well, where's your suit?'

Since I didn't like being questioned, this question pissed me off.

'I got my suit on!' I snapped, sincerely insulted. And I did. I had on a yellow-and-off-white knit pants suit. The pants were a bright yellow, while the matching long sleeved top had off-white trim around the waist, cuffs, and neck. I had on large bright yellow earrings and off-white high heels. *I* thought I was cute in my suit.

Candace explained 'proper' interview attire. She said that you were supposed to wear a plain suit of black, dark blue, or gray. And, just in case the interviewer was an 'old-fashioned chauvinist,' women should wear suits with skirts, not pants. She said that any jewelry and shoes should be conservative.

I sat speechless. I'd never heard of these rules. I'd never worn a suit before when interviewing for a word-processor or legal-secretary position. In fact, I usually had on something like a miniskirt or short top. No one had ever complained before – at least not to my face. It never occurred to me that interviewing for a lawyer position would be any different.

Immediately I panicked. 'What am I going to do?' I asked

Candace. My interview was in a little more than an hour, but my apartment was at least an hour and a half away. Besides, going home wouldn't have made any difference, since there were no suits there. I didn't own any.

'Don't panic,' she said as she hurriedly paid the check. 'I'll think of something.'

Luckily, Candace lived one block from school. We scurried to her house where she tried to create a 'suit' for me. She was at least four inches shorter and two sizes smaller than I was. Still, she whizzed through her closet, trying to find something that would fit. We found a pair of black slacks that were too big for her. I made myself squeeze into them. They were skintight and too short. I looked like Urkel – the nerd from *Family Matters* whose pants were always 'floodin'.' We couldn't find a shirt to fit me, so I was stuck with my bright yellow sweater. She threw on a black jacket that, like the pants, was too tight. Since her shoes were three sizes smaller than mine, I'd have to wear the ones I had on.

'Now, you're ready,' she said as we looked at my makeshift 'suit' in the mirror.

Picture this: I had on black pants that were too tight and too short, making my off-white high heels really noticeable. A bright yellow sweater bulged from under a black jacket that was too short and so tight it looked like it would bust at the seams at any minute. There was no denying it. I looked like a clown. But at least the outfit was black and it was a 'suit.'

The interview was a disaster. I was already nervous, but my odd attire made me even more uncomfortable. I left knowing I didn't get the job and aware of the fact that, if I didn't get a suit soon, I wouldn't get the next one. And the next one was the one I really wanted. It was with McCutchen, Doyle, a large, well-known, and much-sought-after law firm. The rumor was that it was a 'good ol' boy' firm with few minorities. The rumor mill also said that most of my classmates were shocked I'd even gotten an interview with such a prestigious firm; and none of them believed I'd actually get an offer. One thing was for sure, I wouldn't get one if I didn't get a better suit – a real one. The problem was, I was a starving law student. I barely had money to live on, let alone to buy a suit.

The next day, still panic-stricken over the interview, I went to

521

Carol's office. Distraught, I told her about my recent discovery of 'interview' attire, the insane suit Candace had pieced together for me, and the catastrophe of the first interview. Frantic and distressed, I told Carol that I had no clue about what to do for my interview with McCutchen, which was scheduled for the following week. Carol calmed me down and said she had an old suit that was too big for her, but might fit me. She said she'd bring it in the next day and if I could fit into it, I could borrow it for the McCutchen interview. We agreed I would come to her office and try it on the next evening before I went to class.

The next night, when I arrived at Carol's office to try on her suit, she was beaming from ear to ear.

'You're not going to believe what happened today,' she chirped as she pulled me into her office, sat me down, and handed me an envelope.

'What's this?' I asked, puzzled.

'Open it,' she said, almost jumping out of her seat.

I did, and gasped at what I saw. Inside the envelope were bills of crisp, green money. As I stared at the money, Carol explained what had happened that day.

As promised, she'd brought the suit in. During the day, however, she got a little chilly and put the jacket on. Another professor passing by her office couldn't help but notice her unusual outfit: faded jeans, t-shirt, and a fancy jacket. He stopped and asked her why she was wearing such a nice jacket. She told him the story of my disastrous interview and my lack of proper interview clothes. He listened intently as she explained that the jacket was part of a suit she was going to let me borrow for an important upcoming interview with McCutchen.

When she was done telling the story, the professor stood silently in her doorway for a few moments, looking down at his feet. Finally, he spoke.

'No, that won't do,' he said softly as he reached into his wallet, pulled out a hundred-dollar bill and handed it to Carol.

'I'll be back,' he said as he disappeared down the hall.

Several hours later, he returned and handed Carol more money. He explained that he'd gone around to other professors, told them the story, and collected more donations for me. The envelope that Carol handed me held a total of $560 – contributions from several professors to help me buy a new suit.

Before she could finish the story, I was crying in shock, and gratitude.

'But who?' I asked through tears. 'Who did this for me?'

Carol responded that she couldn't tell me; the professors had asked to remain anonymous, even the one who initiated the donation campaign. That floored me even more, because to me it meant they didn't want any recognition or acknowledgment for what they had done. They'd simply heard of a person in need and acted from the goodness of their hearts.

Even if I couldn't know who they were, I had to at least thank them. So I asked Carol if she could at least tell me *how many* there were so I could write the appropriate number of thank-you cards. She agreed. The next day I returned with seven thank-you cards, each one simply addressed to 'God's Angel.'

Oh, the miracle wasn't over yet. The next day, I got two hundred dollars from Ken. The day of the botched interview, I'd called Ken at work, distressed and depressed. However, during the conversation, I never asked for money to buy a suit. Actually, the thought never occurred to me. Since getting sober, I'd never asked anyone for money. Help? Yes. Guidance? Yes. Advice? Yes. But money? Rarely. Once, I'd borrowed money from Daddy and Jr. to pay for books. When I tried to pay them back, they refused to take it. Still, I didn't ask for money because I believed I had a responsibility to make it on my own. Besides, no one owes anyone – especially me – anything. So when I called Ken all upset, I was just seeking some advice on how to handle the next interview. Feeling my pain, wanting me to land that job at McCutchen, and being the generous person he was, Ken had sent the money on his own.

Boy, let me tell you. When I walked into that interview with McCutchen, I was *sharp*! I'd taken the money and bought two new designer suits, as well as four blouses to mix and match with them, two pairs of shoes, and matching jewelry. I even had enough money to put some gas in my car to get to the interview. It's true that dress gives confidence. Now that I knew I looked good and was dressed appropriately, my self-esteem and self-assurance soared. I felt I was the right person for the job; I acted as though I were the right person. They agreed. I was offered, and accepted, a two-thousand-dollar-a-week summer associate position with McCutchen.

'Ain't God good?' my mom Gail asked when I told her the good news.

'No, Mom. He's not good. He's great!'

The next miracle also came from an unexpected source. I was nearing the end of my first year of law school and had run out of money. Of course, once I started my summer job at McCutchen I'd have more than enough to pay the six hundred dollars for my rent. But the job started almost a month *after* my rent was due. I wasn't worried about the gas and light or phone bills, since I knew I could double up on those the following month without their being shut off. I couldn't do that with the rent.

Unfortunately, it was also finals time, so I didn't have the time (or energy) to stress over rent or money. I had to focus on studying and passing those exams. I'd emotionally burdened my family so much during the year, I didn't want to burden them with the rent problem too. I decided to go to one source and one source only: I had a talk with God.

'Okay, you know I'm trying. You've got to see me down here giving this thing everything I've got. Now, I need some rent money and I need it fast. I'm not gonna worry about where it's gon' come from. I'm going to leave that up to you. But I'm trusting you to come through for me.'

I told absolutely no one of this conversation. Usually when I prayed, there was a small amount of doubt. But for some unexplained reason, this time I knew God would come through for me. I had no idea about where the money would come from; I didn't know how or when He'd do it. I just knew He would.

Three weeks later, Ken called to tell me he was sending me 'something.' When I asked what, he told me this story. He was in San Diego having a meeting with Bill Logue, a long-time client of his who'd created and developed an energy bar. I loved these bars because they were the perfect balance of protein, carbs, and sugar and helped me stabilize my hypoglycemia. When I had worked for Ken, I was always friendly with Bill, often talking with him for a while before putting Ken on the phone. In fact, after I'd left San Diego, Ken called to tell me that several clients had called and become alarmed when I hadn't answered the phone.

When Ken would tell them I'd quit, they were saddened, but then he'd quickly add that I'd done it to attend law school. Most told him to be sure to tell me that they would miss me and were rooting for me. Bill Logue was one of those clients. So when he asked about me during his meeting, Ken thought nothing of it.

Ken told him that I was doing well in school, but was still a starving student. He talked about how expensive law school and the Bay Area were. When I had worked for Ken, Bill often gave me several boxes of his nutrition bars because he knew I liked them. Ken said he'd figured Bill had asked about me because he wanted to send me some more free bars.

But as Ken continued talking, Bill had reached into his pocket and pulled out his checkbook. Ken, still talking about my struggles as a starving student, had taken no notice of Bill's actions – that is, until he'd handed Ken a check, made payable to me, for five hundred dollars. Then, he had reached into his bag and given Ken ten boxes of his bars to send me, along with the check.

As Ken relayed this story, I sat on the phone, dumbfounded. *Five hundred dollars*. It was almost what I needed for the rent, though I was still one hundred dollars short.

'Oh,' Ken continued, interrupting my thoughts, 'I'm sending a one-hundred-dollar check with it – as a belated birthday gift.'

I hung up after thanking and saying good-bye to Ken, and began dancing around the room thanking God. Neither Ken nor Bill Logue knew that I didn't have my next month's rent. Neither knew I needed exactly six hundred dollars. No one knew but God.

I sent Bill a thank-you card. I've never heard from him since. But I've never forgotten him and what he did for me.

I also had a scary experience in law school that reminded me that I needed to continue to work on, and be aware of, my speech. The lesson was that I couldn't risk complacency.

I was externing for the Honorable Justice Joyce Kennard of the California Supreme Court. Depending on the judge, extern responsibilities vary, but generally include researching various legal issues, drafting legal memoranda and opinions, and providing any other legal assistance the judge, and his or her chamber attorneys, require. I enjoyed working for the justice and recognized the once-in-a-lifetime opportunity it afforded me. Justice Kennard had two externs working for her. The other was a young, handsome Vietnamese man named Khoi (pronounced 'Coy'). Khoi and I had a lot in common. Although he wasn't from the streets, he too was an outsider, coming from Vietnam and having to start from scratch in America with no knowledge of the language or culture. So he was familiar with struggle and hardship. But what I liked about him most was his sense of humor. He found humor in everything and always made me laugh, regardless of the situation. So it wasn't surprising that we hit it off from the jump and became fast friends.

One day, one of the justice's chamber attorneys stopped me in the corridor and questioned me about a case. No longer nervous about working in the supreme court, and extremely confident that I could relay the facts, I began.

'Okay, I'm going to tell you what went down.'

When I said 'down,' she looked at the floor.

'No,' I said, waving my hands as I realized she hadn't understood me, 'I'm going to tell you what went down in the case.'

Again she looked down.

Aw, shit! I exclaimed to myself. *How do I translate 'what went down'?* I couldn't remember how to say it any other way. The part of my mind that did the 'proper' talking had gone on vacation.

I'm gon' give you the 411! I'm gon' hip you to the skip! All I could think of was slang.

She remained poised in front of me, growing impatient waiting for a response.

Okay, okay, I told myself. *Don't panic. Maybe if you say it slower, she'll get it.*

Speaking very slowly, I said it again.

'O-k-a-y. I'm . . . going . . . to . . . tell . . . you . . . what . . . went . . . down.'

Again she looked down, this time visibly puzzled that every time she did, there was nothing there to see.

My mind raced frantically. For the life of me, I couldn't think of any other way to say it. It was as though slang had taken my mind hostage, and wouldn't set it free.

Oh, Lord! I shouted in my mind. *What do I do? HELP!* I was at my wits' end.

Just then, Khoi came around the corner. As he walked toward us, the chamber attorney and I repeated our song and dance.

'No, no. I'm going to tell you what went *down*.' I figured putting emphasis on 'down,' would help with the translation.

It didn't. Again, she looked down.

Now *I* was becoming frustrated. Shouldn't it be that if 'we' have to learn proper English, 'they' should have to learn slang? Of course, my philosophical views weren't going to help at that moment.

We stood staring at each other, mutually perplexed. She, wondering why I wasn't answering her question; and I, wondering why she couldn't understand my answer.

Khoi was now upon us. As he passed, he spoke softly. 'She means she's going to tell you what *occurred*.'

He looked at me and winked, but kept walking.

'Yeah – yeah,' I stuttered, startled by his unexpected assistance, 'I'm going to tell you what occurred.'

'Oh,' she said, glad she could comprehend what I'd been trying to say. When I'd finished talking, she gave me a terse 'good job' and walked away. As soon as she was out of sight, I let out the anxiety and tension I'd been holding in.

'Whew!' I sighed as my body slumped against the wall. *That was a close one!*

I immediately went into the extern office and thanked Khoi for coming to my rescue.

'No big deal,' he said nonchalantly, then returned to his work.

No big deal? It *was* a big deal to me. You see, it wasn't just his rescue that I was grateful for; it was *the way* he'd done it. He didn't explain what I had said condescendingly or patronizingly, or like he was talking to the chamber attorney about an idiot. Most people would have. I honestly believe most people would have responded to my predicament with a 'You dumb shit, can't you talk?' attitude.

'Cup,' he said when I continued to express my gratitude, 'don't mention it.'

And he hasn't – ever again. To this day, Khoi never talks about that incident. If anyone tells the story, it's me.

Besides helping me to realize I had a true friend, the incident provided me with a rude awakening to the fact that I still had some things to work on.

I had never had a graduation party before. So I decided to throw myself one for my last and final stroll across the stage. I picked a nearby restaurant and reserved the banquet room for a sit-down dinner and party. The restaurant manager informed me that if I had at least thirty people for dinner, the room would be free. I *prayed* thirty people would come!

I went all out: purple and red decorations consisting of fancy streamers and balloon pillars, fresh roses on tables covered with purple and red linen tablecloths and napkins.

I sent out invitations and waited. Slowly, the RSVPs began to filter in. Still, the number was nowhere near thirty. I kept praying.

The night of the party, ninety-five people filled the room, eighty sat for dinner. I couldn't believe it. When I walked in, they gave me a standing ovation. A long table that had been set up for gifts was piled high with pretty, decorative boxes. There were so many, that some of them were sitting on the floor.

People traveled far and wide to share in my special celebration. Of course, my 'Diego peeps' were there: Daddy, Jr., my mom Gail and her husband, LeRoy, and Ken and his family. V flew in from Washington, D.C. (she'd moved there to go to law school and remained there to practice). One of Daddy's sisters and her husband came from Ohio. Carol and my legal writing professor were there. Even Mona and Rose came up. (I hadn't spoken to them since I'd had two years sober.) The room was filled with people who wanted to celebrate with *me*. I was flabbergasted.

Uncle Jr. led the blessing of the food. During dinner, I allowed a few people to say a lil something. It was a trip sitting there listening to the wonderful things people said about *me*. After the speeches, we danced and partied until two in the morning. Then everyone retired to their hotels to rest up for the graduation ceremony the next day. I went to bed that night, filled with love and appreciation. I didn't think the joy could get any greater. I had no idea of the surprise that awaited me the next day.

Although I'd gotten only three hours sleep, I was hyped, excited, and nervous at the graduation ceremony the next day. I'd donned the black robe and square black cap twice before, but the robe I wore that day was different because it was draped with beautifully colored layers of material across the back. I learned it was actually called a 'hood' and was part of the doctorate graduation attire. Since a law degree (a J.D.) is a doctorate, we donned the hoods.

'I'll be damned,' I said as the student next to me explained the purpose behind the hood. 'You learn something new every day!'

'Cup, you're so funny!' she exclaimed, obviously thinking I was playing when I said I didn't know about the hood's significance.

The familiar graduation march started as we walked, two by two, into the large church that was facilitating the ceremony. Just the sound of the music made me want to cry. I could see my people jumping up and down and screaming like crazy as we entered.

That's when reality hit me and the tears began to fall.

'I'm actually graduating law school!' I shouted to anyone and everyone I passed as I marched on. 'I'm actually *graduating*!'

The people I was shouting at probably couldn't hear a word I said. They were too busy shouting and cheering for their own loved ones. I didn't care. They didn't need to hear me. I just needed to say it.

Once all the graduates had been seated, the ceremony began. Jeff Brand, the dean of the law school, stood up and began talking about the various awards being handed out. First, he gave the award for the highest grade point average in the class. Then, he went on to the 'Judge Harold J. Haley Award for Exceptional Distinction in Scholarship, Character, and Activities.'

I never heard of that award, I said to myself, *but the name is sure long as hell!* I giggled at my own joke.

Unaware of the comedy taking place in my head, Dean Brand continued explaining that the award recipient was determined by a vote of the faculty. The winner would have his or her name engraved on a plaque that would forever hang in the school's foyer.

'And that student is . . .'

'Wow, someone's gon' be really blessed,' I whispered to my girlfriend Lourdes, who was sitting next to me.

'. . . Cupcake Brown!'

At first I didn't move. I wasn't sure I'd heard him right.

'It's you, Cup!' Lourdes yelled as she pulled me up out of my chair. 'It's YOU!'

I made my way toward the stage, but as I did so, I felt as though I were moving in slow motion. I looked out over the crowd and saw all my friends and family wildly jumping up and down, cheering, screaming, crying. It looked as though they were moving in slow motion too.

'Congratulations, Cup,' Dean Brand said as he shook my hand and gave me the award. 'It was one of the rare times we had an almost unanimous vote!'

I still couldn't believe it. As I slowly walked back to my chair, several questions kept running through my mind.

They think I'm *outstanding? They think* I *have character? Don't they know who I am?*

The quiet Voice responded.

Of course they do.

EPILOGUE

I thought you might want to know what happened to some of the main people who were a part of my story. Let's start with me. Even though I'd graduated law school, I still had to study for and pass the bar exam. Each state has one; California's is one of the hardest, with less than a 50 percent passage rate for first-time takers. The pressure was on to pass, especially since it felt like the whole world was watching – several newspapers and local news stations interviewed me at graduation and each had asked that I report whether I'd passed or not. On top of that, I couldn't be a lawyer unless I passed. Then, of course, all of my friends and family *expected* me to pass. The pressure was overwhelming.

For eight weeks I gave up my life and put everything I had into studying. In July 2001, I took the California bar exam. And then waited for four agonizing months.

Results are available at the bar's website on the third Friday of every November. I asked Carol to do it with me so she could type in the necessary information. I was afraid I'd be too nervous and would type in the wrong information. I still remember it like it was yesterday.

We held hands and said a prayer. Then she typed in my name and social security number. The screen blinked at us to 'wait – retrieving results.' It seemed to take forever. Finally, a message came up.

'Cupcake Brown has successfully completed the July bar exam.' Instantly, Carol began jumping up and down.

'I knew it! I knew it!' she shouted.

You knew what?! At first, I didn't understand what the

message was saying. Hell, I was looking for something that said, 'You passed, girl!'

Seeing the puzzled look on my face, Carol explained. 'Cup, you passed! You passed!'

'I passed?' I asked unbelievingly.

The tears began to fall.

'I passed?' I repeated, still unsure of what she'd said.

'Yes!' she shouted as she grabbed my hand and pulled me up off the chair, 'You passed!'

Like a bullet, it hit me.

'I PASSED!' I began screaming as I jumped and cried and danced. 'I PASSED!' I just kept saying it over and over as the tears continued to fall.

Several days later, I (with Daddy and Uncle Jr. present) and Khoi (with his parents present), had a private swearing-in ceremony by U.S. District Court Judge Martin Jenkins and California Supreme Court Justice Joyce Kennard. Justice Kennard administered the oath with me in tears the entire time.

Today, I'm still clean and sober; I practice law and do quite a bit of motivational speaking.

I haven't seen Larry since 1976. When I had about a year sober, he tracked me down (through Social Security) and we would talk every now and then by phone. Unfortunately, we still don't get along and have mutually agreed that it's best we don't talk. He does, however, stay in communication with Daddy and Uncle Jr., who regularly give each of us updates on the other.

My daddy and Uncle Jr. are both still very much a part of my life, and in fact, are the two most important men in my life. And although my mom's been dead over thirty years, they still refer to each other as brother-in-law and remain the best of friends.

Venita is still my sponsor and best friend. She lives in Texas with her daughter, Monique, and sister, Faith. She always told me that working with me was a blessing to *her*. Even now she says, 'In working with you, Cup, I always got more than I gave. Always.'

I'm still very close to my mom Gail (and her husband LeRoy). My mom is a constant source of encouragement, guidance, inspiration, and love. She's always been there for me and, knowing her, she probably always will be.

Momma Chaney died during my second year of law school. But I'll be forever grateful for the wisdom she gave me and the lessons she taught me. And I'll always cherish the memories she left me.

Maria moved to another state shortly after I graduated from San Diego State. We didn't keep in contact and I haven't spoken to her in years. But I will always appreciate the support, encouragement, and love she gave me during my early years of recovery.

Ken and I remain extremely close. He continues to encourage and support me in everything I do. He and his family have been at every major event in my life since I got sober.

Frank Brown is still a San Diego Superior Court judge and continues to be one of my best rooters. He regularly shares my story with defendants, juries, and spectators that come into his courtroom.

Larry Burns is now a U.S. District Court judge for the Southern District of California and also continues to be one of my best rooters. Larry and Frank also remain close friends.

After Brett left my doorstep that night, I didn't see or talk to him for the next eight years. He really did just disappear. During my second year of law school, I was invited to a church in San Jose. That same day, a friend of Brett's invited him to the same church. (The people who invited us did not know each other.) It was wonderful to see Brett after so long. However, to tell what happened would require the writing of another book. Let's just say that *this time* I was able to say good-bye.

Tommy is remarried and has several children. We don't talk, though he and his parents did attend my graduation from San Diego State. I was finally able to thank his mom for giving me such a beautiful wedding, and I was able to apologize for being too loaded to appreciate it.

Once I moved into my own apartment shortly after getting out of rehab, I spoke with Mona and James very infrequently. After my relapse, I spoke with Rose even less. By the time I'd celebrated two years sober, I'd completely ceased communication with all of them. I hadn't seen or spoken to any of them until Mona and Rose came to my law school graduation party. Even though we hadn't seen or talked to one another in eleven and a half years, their attendance was special for all of us.

Fly is married, has four children, and no longer bangs. When writing this book, I contacted him to verify some facts. Prior to that conversation, we hadn't spoken in many, many years, and we haven't spoken since that conversation. But he'll always be my favorite 'homie.'

Speaking of homies, several years ago I went to L.A. to try to catch up with Rabbit and Trish. I was able to locate Trish, who told me that Rabbit was the mother of a baby boy and had moved to Mississippi. Trish quit banging and was a single mom raising five children – one of which was fathered by Hoover Rick. Rick was in jail and would be there for a while. I wasn't upset that Trish and Rick had hooked up. In fact, I was happy about it. The cool thing was that, while I was at Trish's, Rick called from jail. We spoke briefly and he caught me up on what had been happening in his world: most of his brothers were dead. The saddest news was that his nephew, lil Timmy, was killed during his teenage years. I never learned if it was gang related or not.

Since getting sober I've seen one other homie: Yokey. We ran into each other in Los Angeles at a women's convention. We 'bout lost our minds when we saw each other. At first we just stared at each other, mouths wide open in shock, each of us wondering if the other was who we really thought she was. Then, in unison, we screamed, 'What's up, cuzzz?!' and embraced each other for a long time. We then spent hours talking and catching up. Of course, we reflected on good, and bad, times with the set. All in all it was a great visit. It felt good to see that someone else had made it out alive. She had been sober for a couple of years, was married, and had a couple of children.

Shortly after I graduated from law school, Dave Curnow read an article about me in a San Diego newspaper and tracked me down. We've remained in contact ever since. The accident rendered him a quadriplegic, but not helpless.

Carol still runs USF's Academic Support Program and is still one of my closest friends.

Kelly and I saw each other every so often (usually to get high) after she moved out of our dilapidated shack. Once I got sober, and continued to *stay* clean and sober, we grew apart. She said sobriety made me too 'uppidity.' I haven't seen or talked to her or Lori for over eleven years. Daddy hasn't talked to or seen either of them in over ten years.

Paul Sutton still teaches at San Diego State and still runs the prison tour program. He remains a close friend and confidant. Every time I see him I thank him for convincing me to slay 'Marcia Brady' and tell my *real* story.

I haven't seen the asshole/sperm donor since the day he gave me to Diane, and I haven't spoken to him since cussing him out when I turned eighteen.

I've never seen any of my foster parents (or their children) since moving to San Diego and getting emancipated, although I did talk to Connie once more. You'd've thought she would have gotten the hint when, at one year sober, I told her I never wanted to speak to her again. She didn't. Fourteen years later she tracked me down yet again. This time I wasn't so polite (though I never yelled). I asked her why she kept calling me. She said she didn't know. In an attempt to get through to her one last time, I brought up the painful memory of losing my baby as a result of her and the other girls jumping on me. She chuckled. *She chuckled!* That was the last straw. I firmly told her I didn't want to be her friend, I didn't give a damn about what she was up to, and to never, ever call me again – for *any* reason – then I slammed down the phone. I haven't heard from her since.

Through my faith in God, the process of recovery, and with the support of family and good friends, I can now close the door to this part of my life. I have completely forgiven everyone who's ever hurt, harmed, failed, or doubted me, starting with – *and especially* – me.

ACKNOWLEDGMENTS

There's an old saying: 'it takes a village to raise a child.' That is so true. Unfortunately, by the time I'd decided to try and turn my life around, I was no longer a child. I was an adult. It takes a community to change an adult. Luckily for me, my 'community' has been filled with wonderfully supportive and loving people. I always say that when God knows you're going to battle, He sends his best warriors. I'd like to thank *some* of my warriors:

God: The commanding officer of this army. Thank you for loving me enough to position such a crazy bunch of warriors on the battlefield.

My daddy, Tim Long (whom everybody calls 'Pops'): Daddy, first executive officer of the battalion, you led and fought for me with such force and determination, and I thank you immensely for it. I remember when I was at my worst, someone told you that I was hopeless, useless, and worthless, that you should quit wasting time and just give up on me. You turned on that person like fire and sternly replied, 'As long as there's breath in her body, there's hope for her.' Thank you, Daddy, for never giving up on me. You're the only daddy I've ever had, the only one I've ever known, the only one I've ever needed or wanted. Love, your baby girl, Punkin.

My uncle, Ray Stearns (Jr.): June, second executive officer of the battalion – actually, during my younger years, you *were* the battalion because you alone were the glue that God used to hold my crazy ass together when I was runnin' wild. You stood fast for me; you stood firm for me. Society labels us uncle and niece, we fight like brother and sister, but I love you like a father.

Thanks for always being there for me. And thanks for being my 'other' daddy. I love you.

To the remaining platoon leaders and dedicated soldiers who joined in the battle for my life:

To my brother: Simply I love you.

Venita Ray: V, where do I begin? You've believed in me every step of the way, even when you had to push, shove, and/or drag me to (and through) the next step, level, challenge, and/or lesson. Yet you've always refused to take any credit and instead insisted that you were simply the vessel God used. Well, thanks for allowing Him to use you. Thanks for never turning on me, judging me, or hating me. You are an example of a *real* friend. A true friend. I love you, girl.

My mom and dad, Gail and LeRoy Westwood: Thank you both for allowing me to be the daughter you never had. (Ron and Bill, thanks for sharing your parents with me.) Mom, thank you for stepping in for the mother I lost so long ago. You've stood by me through some of the most difficult times in recovery. And you were truly my rock during the writing of this book. (You always knew the right thing to say.) You've persistently been a remarkable friend and confidante. Dad, thanks for being my 'third' dad. I love you both.

Ken Rose: Thank you for your love, support, and friendship throughout the years. You allowed me into your family (thanks Nancy, Robert, and Jordy), and willingly joined mine. Most important, thank you for helping me demonstrate that genuine love transcends any and all differences. I love you.

Khoi Nguyen (my best male friend): Thanks for the 'translation' help during our externship (and a special thanks for never throwing it in my face). Your idea for the website intro was brilliant (as are you), and the picture you took for the book jacket is beautiful. Most of all, thanks for always accepting me *just as I am*. You da bomb, bay-bee!

Paul Sutton: You know you started all of this – convincing me to assassinate 'Marcia Brady' and get honest about my past – and I thank you tremendously for it. You always insisted that my story needed to be told. Here it is! Thanks for the continuous laughter, friendship, and guidance. And please keep up those prison tours. It is truly a tremendously enlightening experience.

Larry Burns and Frank Brown: My zany, but solid, rocks of steel. Thank you for your (sometimes) mind-blowing confidence in me. You guys have made me laugh and let me cry. But you've never let me quit. I love y'all.

The Honorable Martin Jenkins: Thank you for the wonderful experience of externing for you. But that was just the beginning. You have become a true friend and a regular source of inspiration. Most important, thank you for always reminding me *whose* I am and that He will carry me through anything.

The Honorable Joyce Kennard: Thank you for the incredible experience that you provided me when I was just a fresh-faced law student. It was an honor to extern for you. And a special thanks for swearing me into the California bar.

To all my past, future, and present 'gurls' and sista-friends: Thanks for the love, encouragement, laughter, and tears. Thanks for helping me learn to accept myself, know myself, and love myself – just the way I am.

University of San Francisco School of Law: I'm so grateful that the school had (and continues to have) the good sense to look at a person as a whole, and not just LSAT numbers or grades when determining eligibility. And thanks for outstanding faculty, namely: Carol Wilson – Although you initially thought I was a nut, once you saw my dedication and determination, you never wavered in your confidence in me and my ability to succeed. Thank you for being a friend. Brian Mikulak – Thanks for helping me love legal research and writing. (And a special thanks for refusing to allow me to quit your class.) Peter Honisberg and Richard Sakai – Thank you for being my 'bar' angels. I have no doubt that your wisdom, suggestions, and guidance helped me pass that hellacious exam. Thank you, thank you, thank you! The professors who donated money for the suit – I still don't know who you are (don't you think it's time I do?), but I'm no less grateful. Thank you, from the bottom of my heart.

Bill Logue – Thanks for reaching out to me when I was in need – without even being asked! God bless you.

Samuel Autman: Who knew that your writing a newspaper article about me would result in such a friendship? Thanks for the words of encouragement, the bomb book proposal, and your constant belief in me and this book.

To the lawyers I've had the honor of working with: David Balabanian – you could have easily demanded that I choose between being a lawyer or an author but encouraged me to be both. I am also grateful to the other lawyers who taught me how to practice law and who continually showed support for this book: Dale Barnes, Geoff Howard, Karen Kennard, and John Pernick.

To Momma Chaney: You were the backbone and foundation for countless women, and men, in recovery – for those who didn't have mothers of their own, and even those who did. Most of my recovery was rooted in something you taught me or something someone else shared with me that you'd taught them. As you always told me, we have a responsibility to pass it on: Someone taught it to you. You taught it to us. The circle continues.

To the 'old-timer' women in recovery who were extremely instrumental in my recovery (names are followed by years of sobriety as of the publication of this book): Chaney Allen, 32 years (at death); Carol K., 31 years; Carolyn S., 26 years; Ms. Francis, 26 years (at death); Venita R., 20 years.

To Chris Jackson, editor extraordinaire: I'm sure there were times when I worked yo' *last* nerve. But you always responded with kindness and patience. You made me comfortable and you made me laugh. It was truly a pleasure working with you because you didn't just read my story, you *felt* what I was saying, as well. It showed in your editing. You're not just a good editor, you're a g-r-e-a-t one! Boo-ya!

Thanks to the Crown family for all your dedication and hard work on this project.

To the countless names and faces that God sent to help me along this journey, the numerous people who have come and gone throughout the years but nevertheless contributed in some way to me turning my life around – some were present in 12-step meetings, many were not – those who might have extended a hand, offered me a smile, given me a hug, or just shared your experience, strength, and hope with me: although you remain nameless in this book, you are in no way insignificant in my life. I thank you all.

Finally, to everyone who ever said I'd never turn out to be shit, thank you for allowing me to prove you *wrong*. And to those who believed in me and knew I could turn my life around if only I had the willingness, thank you for allowing me to prove you *right*.

– Cup

Cupcake Brown was born in San Diego, in the heart of the ghetto. After years of hard work and dedicated study, she achieved her ambition, graduating from law school in the spring of 2001. She now practices law at one of America's largest law firms and is a motivational speaker. She lives in San Francisco. Please visit her website at www.cupcakebrown.com